AFRICAN IS

**Gender
& Genocide
in Burundi**

The Search
for Spaces of Peace
in the Great Lakes Region

Rosano

077 35 49 960

Storie dati, racconti
immaginazione
dialogo.

Portelli Alessandro

AFRICAN ISSUES

Published in the US & Canada by Indiana University Press

*forthcoming

AFRICAN ISSUES

Gender & Genocide in Burundi

PATRICIA O. DALEY

University Lecturer in Human
Geography, School of Geography
& Jesus College, University of Oxford

The Search for Spaces of Peace in the Great Lakes Region

JAMES CURREY
Oxford

INDIANA UNIVERSITY PRESS
Bloomington & Indianapolis

FOUNTAIN PUBLISHERS
Kampala

E.A.E.P.
Nairobi

JACANA MEDIA
Johannesburg

James Currey
73 Botley Road
Oxford OX2 0BS
www.jamescurrey.co.uk

Indiana University Press
601 North Morton Street
Bloomington
Indiana 47404 U.S.A.
iupress.indiana.edu
Telephone orders 800-842-6796
Fax orders 812-855-7931
Orders by e-mail iuporder@indiana.edu

Fountain Publishers
P. O. Box 488
Kampala
www.fountainpublishers.co.ug

East African Educational Publishers
P.O. Box 45314
Nairobi
www.eastafricanpublishers.com

Jacana Media (Pty) Ltd
10 Orange Street
Sunnyside
Auckland Park 2092 S.A.
www.jacana.co.za

© Patricia O. Daley

First published 2007
First paperback edition 2008

The paper used in this publication meets the minimum requirements of American National Standard
for Information Sciences–Permanence of Paper for Printed Library Materials, ANSI Z39.48-1984

British Library Cataloguing in Publication Data

ISBN 978-1-84701-306-4 (James Currey paper)
ISBN 978-1-84701-307-1 (James Currey cloth)

Daley, Patricia O.
Gender & genocide in Burundi : the search for spaces of
peace in the Great Lakes Region. - (African issues)
1. Political violence - Burundi - History 2. Masculinity -
Burundi 3. Feminist theory 4. Genocide - Burundi -
Sociological aspects 5. Burundi - Politics and government
I. Title
320.9'67572

ISBN 978-9970-02-725-5 (Fountain Publishers paper)
ISBN 978-1-77009-410-9 (Jacana Media paper)

Library of Congress Cataloguing-in-Publication Data
A catalog record for this book is available from the Library of Congress

ISBN 978-0-253-21925-1 (Indiana University Press paper)
ISBN 978-0-253-35171-5 (Indiana University Press cloth)

1 2 3 4 5 13 12 11 10 09 08

Typeset by
Saxon Graphics Ltd, Derby
in 9/11 Melior with Optima display

Printed and bound in Malaysia

CONTENTS

MAPS

PREFACE &
ACKNOWLEDGEMENTS

My engagement with East and Central African politics developed quite early and was accentuated by my doctoral research in Tanzania in the mid-1980s when I examined the political and economic incorporation of Burundi refugees in Tanzania. Trained as a geographer, influenced by David Harvey to consider the politics of space, my own anti-racist intellectual heritage brought together my identification with the struggles of oppressed peoples. As an African woman coming from the oppressed class and a student of geography grappling with the political economy of space, I have also developed intellectually within the traditions of black feminism. These traditions, which, in academia, are termed class analysis, spatial analysis and gender analysis, inform this book. I am a product of the Bob Marley concept of emancipation, which, in Africa, has been articulated as the concept of *Ubuntu*. Feminist scholars, such as Jill Steans (1998), have made the distinctions between liberal (equal rights) feminism and emancipatory feminism, bearing in mind that the World Bank seeks to turn liberal feminism into a vehicle for imperial control, by imposing it as conditionality. Our variant of feminism draws heavily from Jill Steans's view of feminism, and, in this context, I identify with the scholarship of Dorothy Roberts (1996), Ifi Amadiume (1997, 2000a & 2000b), and especially that of Kimberle Crenshaw (1991) and Patricia Hill Collins (2000) who have developed the concept of the 'intersectionality' of race, class and gender. The critical issue for these scholars is how to enable the emergence of emancipatory human beings. Genocidal politics force us to develop a conceptual framework that breaks with the scholarship that can be used to justify genocide. As a geographer, I am seeking to develop an epistemological framework that will lead to more emancipatory politics.

Thousands of Burundi refugees in Tanzania fled genocidal violence in Burundi in 1972 and a second generation was born in exile. I spent a year among them in Katumba settlement in Mpanda District, Western Tanzania. Although the older generations used every opportunity to recount the discrimination and de-humanizing violence they experienced at the hands of the Tutsi, memories documented by Malkki (1995), the younger generation were keen to assert their right to be treated not as refugees, not even as citizens of their host countries, but as people. Not only did the experience of violence rob the people of their humanity, their presence as refugees – at the time of writing they are still classified as refugees – marked them out as non-persons. Such refugees, Soguk (1999) argues, fall outside the nation/state/citizen hierarchy, and are depicted as 'aliens', 'criminals' and 'undesirable products', coming from, according to the then Tanzanian President, Benjamin Mpaka (2005), 'factories that manufacture refugees'.[1]

Yet, as ordinary human beings – peasants – they produced maize, beans and tobacco for the regional and national markets and worked as migrant labour on tea plantations, yet they suffered years of psychological blight as non-citizens, existing in a liminal state. It was when I was trying to understand the mechanisms by which states, whether home or host, can leave tens of thousands of people to live in such a way that I was led to focus on the dehumanizing capacities of the modern state, exemplified sharply in genocidal violence, and the less horrific, but still disquieting abandonment and near imprisonment of thousands of people under the label 'refugees' and under the umbrella of humanitarianism.

Since then I have followed internal Burundi politics and external reaction – mostly indifference – to the masses of dead and displaced. This book is an attempt by a black woman to take up her responsibility as an intellectual, to make sense of the seemingly senseless, and to say that the people of Central Africa matter. Burundi may be a small and apparently insignificant country, but tolerance of genocide within its boundaries demeans human life, exposes our collective vulnerability and guilt, and has the potential, as shown in the case of Bosnia, to envelope us all.

This book is a culmination of research conducted over two decades. Fieldwork was conducted in Tanzania, 1986, 1994, 1998, 2001 & 2005; in Burundi 1987 and 2006; Rwanda, 1995; Belgium, 1997, 1998 and 2000; France, 1999 and Switzerland, 1999. Primary data were gathered through numerous methods: interviews were conducted with politicians, donor and NGO representatives, refugees, scholars from Burundi and other countries in the region, and with members of the facilitation team of the Burundi peace process. Archival material was gathered from national, regional and international newspapers, magazines and websites, in particular the national newspaper library in Colindale, London, Queen Elizabeth House library at the University of Oxford and the library of the *Daily News*, Tanzania. Online sources included the *BBC News Africa*, *Africaonline*, *Irinnews.org*, *ARIB.News*, *Abarundi.org*, *Burundi-info.com*. and *Ochaonline2.un.org/Burundi*. A range of grey literature also provided valuable information, especially documents from the Burundi peace negotiations (housed at the Mwalimu Nyerere Foundation in Dar es Salaam), and from the Geneva and Dar es Salaam offices of the International Documentation Network on the Great African Lakes Region. Of considerable use were reports from human rights organizations, especially

[1] Benjamin Mpaka, President of Tanzania, 2005, quoted in Amnesty International (AI), *Refugee Rights are being eroded in Central Africa*, AI, The Wire, February 2005.

Human Rights Watch (HRW), International Crisis Group (ICG), Ligue Iteka, Burundi and Amnesty International (AI); various United Nations (UN) agencies and their committees; the World Bank and the International Monetary Fund (IMF) and western governments, and those produced by Burundi political parties such as SAHWANYA-FRODEBU, UPRONA and CNDD-FDD. The historical discussion of the pre-colonial and colonial period is largely dependent on the use of secondary literature produced by numerous scholars who have made valuable contributions, in particular to Burundi's historiography, and to whom I am heavily indebted.

As with any major piece of work, numerous people have contributed to the production of this book. Over the years, I have become indebted to so many who have who have given of their time, material support and consistent encouragement. First of all, I am extremely grateful to those Burundians who willingly gave up their time to be interviewed and to Jesus College, Oxford for the funding of the field visits. My special gratitude goes to Professor Colin Clarke and Professor Horace Campbell who made incisive comments on an earlier draft. They have, throughout, provided much needed advice and encouragement. Horace and Dr Fareda Banda shared my interest in the intersectionality of gender, race and peace, and their insights into the nature of violence in the region have helped to strengthen this study. Fareda, along with Raufu Mustapha, Kate Meagher, Nyi and Maria Anubi have provided the additional material support that is essential for a single mother to do research away from home.

In the field, the research process would have been much more arduous without the help of a number of people. In Belgium, I am most grateful to Professor Erik Swyngedouw for allowing me the use of his family home and for his assistance with visas. In Tanzania, my friends and colleagues, Elaine Wamba, Ika Bunting and Dr Ng'wanza Kamata, have housed, fed and provided stimulating discussions over many years. In Burundi, my 'sister' and fellow countrywoman, Beryl Mutambwira-Carby provided the necessary base and contacts to facilitate my research. There are many who, because of confidentiality, cannot be named, without whose input the text would be less rich. I am grateful for the research assistance provided by Lewis Zacharia in Katumba, Deus Kibamba in Dar es Salaam, and Halima Khan, Oyin Anubi and Marjorie Morgan in Oxford. And Napoleon Abdulai, whose introduction to a number of contacts in Rwanda and Tanzania, helped to smooth the research process. As always, Ailsa Allen, of the School of Geography at Oxford University, produced the maps with great efficiency, and Caroline Warman of Jesus College made sure the French translations were exact. Most of all, I have to thank my teenage son, Sule Daley, for his unwavering support for this project. Without his exceptional maturity, this book would not have reached completion.

I would also like to thank the publishers and editors of *Third World Quarterly*, *Political Geography* and the *Review of African Political Economy*, for allowing the use of materials that have appeared in articles in their journals.

ABBREVIATIONS

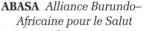

ABASA *Alliance Burundo–Africaine pour le Salut*

ACOTA African Contingency Operations Training and Assistance

ACRI African Crisis Response Initiative

ADF Allied Democratic Forces

AFDL *Alliance des Forces Démocratiques pour la Libération du Congo*

AI Amnesty International

ALIR *Armée de Libération Rwanda* (Rwanda Liberation Army)

AMIB African Union Mission to Burundi

ANNADE *Alliance National Pour le Droit et le Développement*

AU African Union

AV-Intwari *Alliance des Vaillants*

BFu Burundi Franc

CCM *Chama Cha Mapinduzi*

CEDAW UN Committee on the Elimination of Discrimination against Women

CNDD-FDD *Conseil National Pour le Défense de la Démocratie – Forces pour le Défense de la Démocratie* (National Council for Defence and Democracy – Forces for Defence and Democracy)

CNRS National Commission for the Rehabilitation of *Sinistrés*

DDR Disarmament, Demobilization and Reintegration

DRC Democratic Republic of Congo

ECA Economic Commission for Africa

ECOWAS Economic Community of West African States

FAO Food and Agricultural Organization

FAR *Forces Armée Rwandaise*

FDLR Democratic Forces for the Liberation of Rwanda

FEMNET African Women's Development and Communication Network

FLEC Front for Liberation of the State of Cabinda

FND *Forces National Défense* (National Defence Force)

FNL-Incanzo *Le Parti Front National de Libération –* ICANZO

FRELIMO Front for the Liberation of Mozambique

FRODEBU *Front Pour la Démocratie au Burundi*

Frolina *Front Pour la Libération Nationale*

HIPC Heavily Indebted Poor Countries

HRW Human Rights Watch

ICARA International Conference on

Assistance to African Refugees

ICCPR International Covenant on Civil and Political Rights

ICG International Crisis Group

ICIB International Commission of Inquiry for Burundi

ILO International Labor Organization

IMF International Monetary Fund

INGOs International Non-Governmental Organizations

INKINZO *Parti Socialiste et Pan-Africaniste*

ISCAM *Institut Supérior des Cadres Militaires*

JNR *Jeunesses Nationalistes Rwagasore*

JRR *Jeunnesses Révolutionnaires Rwagasore*

LRA Lord's Resistance Army

MDRP Multi-Country Demobilization and Re-integration Programme

MRC Movement for the Rehabilitation of Citizens

MUNOC United Nations Organization Mission in the Congo

NALU National Army for the Liberation of Uganda

NCDRR National Commission for Demobilization, Reinsertion and Reintegration

NGO Non-governmental Organization

OAU Organization of African Unity

OCIBU Coffee Board of Burundi

ONUB United Nations Operation in Burundi

Palipehutu-FNL *Parti Pour la Libération Du Peuple Hutu/ Forces National de* Libération

PARENA *Parti pour le Redressement National*

PDC *Parti Démocrate Chrétien*

PIT *Parti l'Indépendant des Travailleurs*

PL Liberal Party

PMCs Private Military Contractors

PP Parti du Peuple

PRA People's Redemption Army

PRGF Poverty Reduction and Growth Facility

PRGS Poverty Reduction and Growth Strategy

PRP *Parti pour la Réconciliation du Peuple*

PSD *Parti-Social Démocrate*

RADDES *Rassemblement Pour la Démocratie et le Développement Economique et Social*

RCD *Rassemblement Congolais pour la Démocratie* (Rally for Congolese Democracy)

RECAMP *Renforcement des Capacités Africaines de Maintien de la Paix* (Reinforcement of African Peace-Keeping Facilities)

RoB Republic of Burundi

RPA Rwandese Patriotic Army

RPF Rwandese Patriotic Front

SADC Southern Africa Development Co-operation

SAP Structural Adjustment Policies

SCF Save the Children Fund

SOJEDEM *Solidarité dé la Jeunesse Pour la Défense des Minoritées*

UNAMIR United Nations Assistance Mission for Rwanda

UNCTAD United Nations Conference on Trade and Development

UNDP United Nations Development Programme

UNESC United Nations Economic and Social Council

UNESCO United Nations Educational, Scientific and Cultural Organization

UNFPA United Nations Population Fund

UNHCR United Nations High Commissioner for Refugees

UNICEF United Nations Children's Fund

UNIFEM United Nations Development Fund for Women

UNITA *União Nacional para a Independência Total de Angola* (National Union for the Total Independence of Angola)

UNSC United Nations Security Council

UPDF Uganda People's Defense Force

UPRONA *Parti de l'Unité et du Progrès National*

USAID United States Agency for International Development

WNBF West Nile Bank Front

TABLES

GLOSSARY

Banyamabanga	Those responsible for political and religious cults, traditionally Hutus
Banyabururi	People from the province of Bururi – refers mainly to Tutsis
Banyaruguru	Tutsis from regions other than the southern province of Bururi
Action Contre le Génocide (AC Génocide)	A Tutsi militia in Burundi
Baganwa (Ganwa)	Aristocratic lineages
Batare	An aristocratic *Baganwa* lineage
Banyarwanda	People of Rwandan origin
Bezi	An aristocratic *Baganwa* lineage
Bashingantahe	Community-based tribunals, traditionally from Hutu lineages
Bashingo	A Burundi clan
Bayanzi	A Burundi clan
Colline	Hill and local administrative area
Coltan	Columbite – Tantalite
Gacaca	Community-based tribunals in Rwanda
Gardiéns de la Paix	Guardians of the Peace, a government-sponsored para-military group
Génocidaires	French term for those who commit genocide
Gutahira	Downward mobility from *Baganwa* to Tutsi
Interahamwe	'Those who stand together' or 'Those who fight together' (Rwandan militia of the 1994 genocide)
Intore	Most prestigious unit of royal army made up of children of the *Baganwa*
Mwami	King
Ubgenge	Intelligence, cunning
Ubugabire	A patron-client system in Burundi
Ubuntu	Humanity to others; humanism
Ukwihutura	Upward mobility from Hutu to Tutsi

Puissance d'autodéfense 'amasekanya'	Translated as power of self-defence – a Burundi militia
Sans Échec	Translated as the infallible – a Burundi militia
Sans Défaite	Translated as the undefeated – a Burundi militia

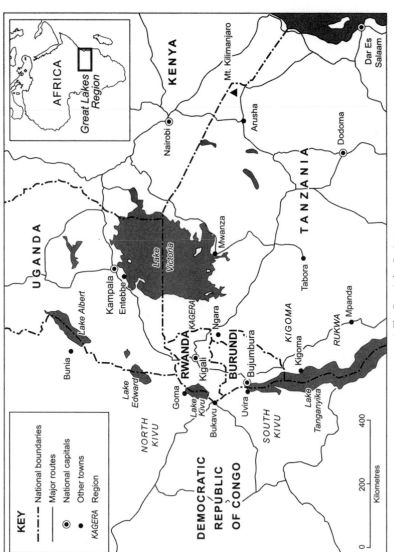

1: The Great Lakes Region

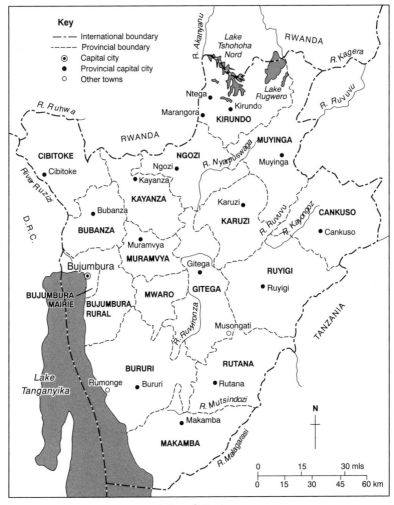

Key

- —·—·— International boundary
- ------- Provincial boundary
- ⊙ Capital city
- ● Provincial capital city
- ○ Other towns

R. Akanyanu

Lake
Tshohoha
Nord

RWANDA

R. Kagera

R. Ruvuvu

Lake
Rugwero

Ntega

Kirundo

Marangora

KIRUNDO

MUYINGA

Muyinga

R. Ruhwa

RWANDA

CIBITOKE

Cibitoke

NGOZI

Ngozi

R. Nyamuswaga

Kayanza

KAYANZA

Karuzi

River Ruzizi

D.R.C.

Bubanza

KARUZI

R. Ruvuvu

R. Kayongoz

CANKUSO

Cankuso

BUBANZA

Muramvya

MURAMVYA

Gitega

RUYIGI

Ruyigi

Bujumbura ⊙

**BUJUMBURA
MAIRIE**

**BUJUMBURA
RURAL**

MWARO

GITEGA

R. Ruwironza

Musongati

TANZANIA

Lake
Tanganyika

Rumonge

BURURI

Bururi

RUTANA

Rutana

R. Mutsindozi

Makamba

N

MAKAMBA

R. Malagarasi

0		15		30 mls
0	15	30	45	60 km

2: Burundi: Provinces

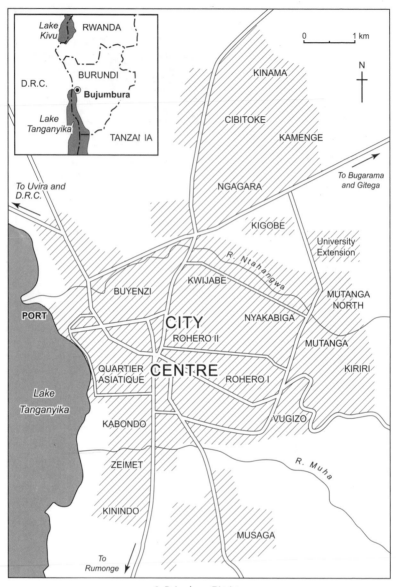

3: Bujumbura: Districts

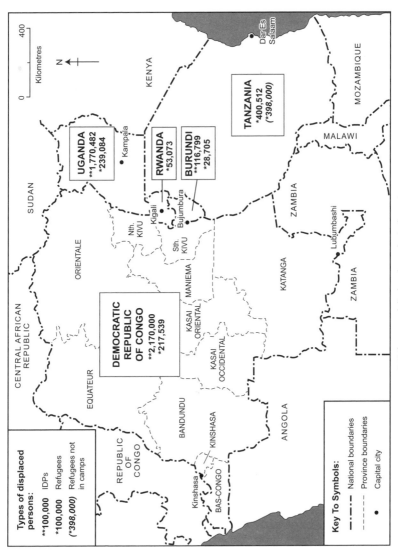

Types of displaced persons:

**100,000 IDPs
*100,000 Refugees
(*398,000) Refugees not in camps

Key To Symbols:

— · — · National boundaries
— — — Province boundaries
• Capital city

SUDAN

CENTRAL AFRICAN REPUBLIC

KENYA

**UGANDA
**1,770,482
*239,084**

• Kampala

**RWANDA
*53,073**

**BURUNDI
**116,799
*28,705**

• Kigali

Bujumbura •

**TANZANIA
*400,512
(*398,000)**

Dar Es Salaam •

MALAWI

MOZAMBIQUE

Nth. KIVU

Sth. KIVU

ORIENTALE

EQUATEUR

MANIEMA

**DEMOCRATIC REPUBLIC OF CONGO
**2,170,000
*217,539**

KASAI ORIENTAL

KASAI OCCIDENTAL

KATANGA

ZAMBIA

Lubumbashi •

ZAMBIA

REPUBLIC OF CONGO

BANDUNDU

KINSHASA

Kinshasa •

BAS-CONGO

ANGOLA

N ←

0   400
Kilometres

4: Refugees and displaced peoples in the region

5: Burundi refugee camps in Tanzania

1

Introduction: A Culture of Genocidal Violence

Burundi & the Great Lakes Region

Human beings are inviolable. Every human being shall be entitled to respect for his life and the integrity of his person. (Article 4, *African Charter on Human and Peoples' Rights, 1981*)

In 1972, according to one estimate, genocide in the Central African state of Burundi wiped out 3.5 per cent of the country's population in a few weeks (Lemarchand & Martin, 1974). Unfortunately, Burundi was not exceptional. In 1994, genocide in neighbouring Rwanda claimed some 700,000 lives in 100 days. Even after the recriminations over Rwanda, between 1994 and 2006, a further 300,000 people were estimated to have lost their lives in Burundi, while, across the border, in the Democratic Republic of Congo (DRC), fighting claimed over 3.8 million lives between 1998 and 2005.[1]

These extreme incidents of violence all took place in post-colonial Africa and have been explained away in popular discourse under media headlines of 'tribal bloodbath', 'age-old hatred' and 'an orgy of uncontrolled violence'. African warfare is represented as 'barbaric' precisely because of extreme acts of violence directed at non-combatants and the use of primitive technologies of war – machetes, small arms and AK47s rather than carpet bombing and stealth missiles signal a pre-modern turn in a post-modern age. Face to face killings are represented as non-sanitized and less humane than stealth missiles, yet what is left of the bodies of those killed by more sophisticated weaponry rarely appears in graphic form in our newspapers. Media images of violence in Africa seem to dehumanize both killer and victim, and appear increasingly banal to the audience.

At one level, the magnitude of the massacres appears to demand some sort of international reaction on the scale of the 'never again' following the Jewish Holocaust of Nazi Germany, yet, the history of western culpability in genocide on the continent forces us to treat with caution and demand an interrogation of any interventions that purport to address genocide (Jones, 2004). The persistent failure of the international community to seek out and prosecute the perpetrators of crimes against humanity points to a tacit acceptance of a 'culture of impunity' in African countries.

[1] IRC in Burundi, http:www.theirc.org/where/the_irc_in_burundi.html, [Accessed 12 July 2006]; International Crisis Group (ICG), 17 December 2004, *Back to the Brink in the Congo*, Africa Briefing N°21, Bruxelles, Belgium: ICG.

1

Presenting genocide as the irrational violence of an atavistic group has meant that rarely are Africans punished for crimes against humanity. Many violators of humanity are supported and feted by western governments and, through the vogue for post-conflict power-sharing come to form official political parties and take up seats in government. There is considerable evidence that in the Rwandan genocide of 1994, the perpetrators, who were dependent on international aid and lacked domestic legitimacy, were more concerned about international rather than local or regional opinion (HRW, 1999a; Organization of African Unity (OAU), 2000). The impact of the International Criminal Tribunal for Rwanda, which was set up in Arusha, Tanzania in November 1994, seems slight, considering the small number of people prosecuted, its distance from Rwanda (geographically and rhetorically) and from the glare of international attention, and the lack of commitment by some regional and international states to extradite those alleged to have committed genocide.

The outright failure of the region and the international community to show moral responsibility in cases of genocide in Africa has been interpreted by some political analysts and international lawyers as a question of the right to sovereignty over the right to life. A key principle in the Charter of the now defunct OAU was non-interference in the internal affairs of member states. Similarly, western governments tend to act only when their interests are threatened directly, then they seem to have no qualms in deposing dictators or even democratically elected leaders. It took protests from a plethora of international and regional advocacy groups, human rights and civil society organizations for the international community to consider seriously the possibility of taking preventative action against warfare and genocide. At the regional level, when African governments intervened to depose a tyrannical regime, as in the case of Tanzania against Amin's Uganda in 1979, it was considered ill-judged for financial reasons; then the ethics of the action were never brought to the fore. The more pro-active stance of the African Union, in the aftermath of the Rwandan genocide, signifies a greater recognition by regional states of their collective responsibility.

Conflict resolution has now become a major focus of international policy making, and, in recent years, peace agreements have been signed in several countries. The policy framework for peace and reconstruction in post-conflict societies are so prescribed that there is little room to discuss what constitutes security and peace for ordinary Africans. Peace agreements appear to provide the space for re-armament and, as the specificities of violence are insufficiently interrogated, direct violence persists even after the official war has ended. As concerned scholars, we need to interrogate the reasons behind such deficiencies in contexts that challenge our humanity.

Approaches to Violent Conflict in Africa

There exist three distinct approaches to our understanding of post-colonial, post-Cold War warfare in Africa. The first, referred to earlier, pervades much of the popular discourse and emerges in a somewhat different form in scholarly literature. Its premise is that African warfare is the consequence of innate dysfunctionalities within African societies. Warfare arises in states comprising intrinsically antagonist tribes, forced together in a political unit, arbitrarily designed, yet effectively policed by past colonial powers, whose unpropitious departure resulted in tribes regressing rapidly back to their primordial state of savagery. From the decolonization era of the 1950s to the 'war on terror' of the twenty-first century, the depth of 'tribal divisions' have been used as a barometer to measure a people's fitness for self-rule.

One variant of this thesis is that proposed by Chabal & Daloz (1999) that Africans 'prosper on disorder'. They contend that chaos and violence are resources, which are used instrumentally by political leaders and warlords, and that the 'barbarity' and 'savageness' of the warfare signify a re-traditionalization of society. Chabal and Daloz claim, rightly, that Africa is the only continent that has gone backwards as a result of modernity but we part company when they place the impetus purely on the shoulders of an 'obdurately traditional' culture that is Africanizing western modernity. Identity politics relating to 'an idealized nostalgic representation of the past' is, according to Kaldor (2001: 7), the goal of 'new' post-Cold War conflict in Africa. In her book, *New and Old Wars,* Kaldor professes that 'new wars' are quantitatively and qualitatively different; not only are they ideologically free, they signify a loss in state monopoly of organized violence, as numerous rebel groups, 'warlords' and diasporas challenge state sovereignty. Kaldor is quick to point out that she is not advocating 'the warring tribes' interpretation of African warfare, maybe, because her evidence for 'new wars' comes mainly from the European mainland itself, not from some distant periphery. But her discussion of Africa is influenced by what she describes as the 'compelling descriptions' of Robert Kaplan's social chaos or 'coming anarchy' (Kaldor, 2001: 145; Kaplan, 1994).

Another body of analysis uses the tribal narrative and the 'fear' of the 'other' to explain genocide (Lemarchand, 1995; Malkki, 1995). In this case genocide is a rational reaction to threats to one's person or group. These scholars, influenced by post-modernism and its focus on difference as the defining feature of relationships within society, relate an account of societies devoid of humanity, in which groups draw unquestioningly on a 'mythico-history' which dehumanizes others. The fieldwork for Malkki's (1995) highly original book was conducted at the same time that I was doing fieldwork in Mpanda district among the same group of Burundi refugees. We were asking different questions. Although people often mentioned the violence they suffered and their reluctance to return to Burundi while a Tutsi regime was in power, memories of violence did not dominate social life in the settlements. Many people were concerned more with their precarious existence as refugees; how their refugee status prevented them from improving their well being educationally and economically. Consequently, a focus on 'tribal narratives' and ethnicity drowns out alternative articulations of social and political life.

A second and long-standing explanation for conflict in Africa comes from the paradigm of environmental determinism underpinned by neo-

Malthusianism. According to this approach, warfare and genocide occur because of resource scarcity augmented by population pressure (Homer-Dixon, 1999; Kaplan, 1994). For those who subscribe to this viewpoint, the genocidal violence in the high-density countries of Rwanda and Burundi proves the resource scarcity argument. However, De Soysa (2000), among others, disputes the claim that land pressures alone can lead to outright warfare. The deterministic nature of the scarcity thesis means that politics is not considered a factor and the blame is placed onto some uncontrolled procreativity of the African.

Most scholarly research on the causes of post-Cold War rebellion in Africa tends to use the framework provided by the third approach known as the 'greed' or 'grievance' debate. Economists, particularly those influencing policy-makers at the Bretton Woods institutions, have argued that it is economic opportunity or 'greed' that causes rebellion not grievances related to inequality, political rights or even ethnic or religious difference (Berdal & Malone, 2000; Collier & Hoeffler, 2002 & 2004). Such a position is based on the mathematical modelling of several grievance and economic proxies from which they surmise that rebellion is more likely to take place where the ratio of primary commodity exports to Gross Domestic Product (GDP) is high, because of 'the opportunities such commodities provide for extortion, making rebellion feasible and perhaps even attractive,' (Collier and Hoeffler, 2004: 588). As part of the 'greed' causality, recent wars are branded 'resource wars', where the propensity for rebellion is dependent on the 'lootability' of resources such as oil, timber or strategic minerals (Le Billion, 2001). However, there are qualitative differences in understanding the causes of wars and what sustains them. Natural resources may not be the cause of war but can be used to sustain them, considering the increased accessibility to markets for the sale of raw materials and the purchase of weapons in a de-regulated globalized world.

Political scientists see greed and grievance as arising from 'failed or collapsed' states. To them, warfare occurs in states that have lost their capacity to provide security, representation and welfare services to their citizens. Many African states have been classified as either failed (Burundi, DRC), collapsed (Liberia, Somalia) and even collapsing (Nigeria) (Milliken & Krause, 2002; Reno, 2002). Proponents of the 'failed states' thesis argue that state capacity and effectiveness have been undermined by internecine violence – sometimes deliberate – and the exigencies of a neo-patrimonial and a rent-seeking political elite (Bayart, 1993; Bayart *et al.*, 1999; Reno, 2002). Neo-patrimonialism, or the distribution of state funds through patronage based on kin, religion or ethnic group, is applied almost universally to explain political struggles in Africa (Reno, 2000). It is argued that neo-patrimonialism has become acute in the late post-colonial period as declining resources have intensified competition and patronage. Richards (1996) interprets the 1990s war in Sierra Leone as the result of social exclusion – a 'product of the crisis of patrimonialism' in a post-colonial context. In contrast, Abdullah (2004: 28–30), critical of the use of neo-patrimonialism as an explanatory framework, challenges us to focus on a 'wider set of issues relating to the politics of war'. His analysis of the same Sierra Leonean war addresses the centralization of power, its concentration in the capital, the 'selective and indisciplined use of violence' by politicians and the military, and the position of the elite *vis à vis* the state in the context of changing economic relations. David Keen (2005), in turn, questions the dominance of the economistic explanation for violence in Africa, and calls for greater consideration of genuine or perceived grievance. He writes, 'the war in Sierra Leone was partly about the manipulation and perversion of ordinary human desires, including the desire for wealth, safety, justice and respect' (Keen, 2005: 297). Not surprising, many Sierra Leoneans just wanted to be treated as human beings.

What is striking about much of the 'conflict' literature is its focus on factors internal to the state; ethnic hatred, overpopulation, neo-patrimonialism, greed, barbarism, re-traditionalization – all contributing to a pervasive image of inherent dysfunctionality in African societies. No doubt, such perspectives may find resonance in some African states, but, empirically, they miss the complexities of African political life, and thus serve to obscure the multiple cleavages and points of contestation within the society, which may account for the high level of organized violence and institutional decay. Differences, be they ethnic, regional or religious, are not in themselves necessarily conflictual. Nnoli (1998) draws our attention to the positive contributions of ethnicity especially during the period of nationalist politics. The key issue is the degree of acceptance and inclusion of difference in the state.

The linkages between Africa and the rest of the world; colonialism, neo-colonialism, globalization, trade, economic liberalization and aid, are often either under-explored in these analyses of warfare or are seen as insignificant to the internal dynamics. When explanations stretch beyond the continent, they focus on the negative influences of North American Rambo films, hip-hop and gangster culture or the financial contributions of warmongering diaspora communities (Richards, 1996; Kaldor, 2001). Such studies fail to note the simultaneous rebellious yet positive influence of the emancipatory politics of Robert Nesta Marley, or, with the exception of Le Billion (2007), the interconnections between warfare in Africa, western cultural accoutrements and the new communications and trading networks that have emerged as a result of globalization. Misrepresenting Africa as being marginal to the global system not only stifles African agency, but prevents Africans full participation as equal partners in global humanity. African responsibility and complicity in exacting genocide is in no doubt, but such systemic violence is not uniquely African, nor are Africans acting alone; western culpability has tended to be overlooked or skirted around (Jones, 2004).

In general, the literature discussed above represents the outpourings of a hegemonic school on warfare in Africa. With one or two exceptions, it seems there is little space for African oppositional forces or rebel movements articulating alternative ideologies to be heard, without them being seen as a 'smokescreen' for opportunistic motives. The end of communism meant the end of proxy wars and the end of ideology, thus African warfare loses its intellectual direction and becomes just 'mindless violence'. To some, in a corrupt, dysfunctional Africa, there is no credible voice articulating a new type of politics. Yet in almost every war-torn African country such voices are present, in amongst the rebels or in civil society. Every text on the subject makes claim to scientific objectivity, with real empirical evidence or robust datasets, yet they continue to ignore Africa's diversity and fail to hear the multiple voices of scholars, politicians, women and peasants, especially those demanding genuine social justice and sustainable spaces of peace. The explanations provided by the majority of these texts have exhausted their potential for the clarification of the political process.

A prolific body of literature on warfare in Africa comes out of a range of non-governmental and human rights organizations (Human Rights Watch, African Rights, Justice Africa, International Crisis Group) promoting truth, peace, gender equality, reproductive rights, the right to health and intellectual property rights. Their rigorous documentation of almost every facet of warfare in Africa and their sustained critique of international organizations is to be applauded. They differ substantially in their approach, while claiming objectivity, some appear determined to reinstate an assumed pre-war stability; whilst others adopt a more humanitarian/ethical stance, exposing gross abuses, without developing an intellectual direction that will bring about real changes.

The challenge now is to shift the paradigm on warfare from that belonging to an ideation system which devalues African lives to one whose starting point is the reassertion of the humanity of African people. African communities live in a context of systemic insecurity. Even with western complicity, post-colonial violence in Africa is largely committed by Africans against other Africans. How have Africans reached such a state when the total destruction of a group is seen as a viable political option? How did the concept of *Ubuntu* (humanity to others) disappear from social intercourse and how, historically, did the culture of impunity evolve in Africa, and what factors led to the devaluation of African lives. The challenge at the theoretical level for scholars in Africa and beyond is to grasp the social and economic conditions that impelled war, racism and ethnicity so that the 'never again' principle becomes a reality in Africa. This challenge has been taken up by feminist scholars, human rights activists and non-state actors, who want to go to the heart of the motivation for genocide.

African scholars have long critiqued the short-sightedness and partisanship of mainstream scholarship (Amadiume & An-Na'im, 2000; Campbell, 2002; Campbell & Mealy (2005); Mustapha, 2002; Chachage, 2003; Depelchin, 2004). Wamba dia Wamba (1997: 3) writes 'the prevailing preoccupation with phenomenal manifestations or essentialist explanations ... has made it difficult to grasp political dynamics underlining the tragic histories of the regions.' Wamba, himself a former rebel leader, calls for conceptual work that recognizes the multiple sites of politics. He goes on, 'the hypothesis of an independent political capacity emanating from sites of politics – such as the factory, neighbourhood democratic associations, poor peasant associations, associations of students from different origins and so on – have been left in silence, if not forced into taking on an ethnic character.' African politics is reducible to the actions of the elite or to ethnic differences. Its multiplicity and diversity, solid bases for democratic transformations, are

turned into discriminations (Wamba dia Wamba 1997: 3). Campb .
(2002) calls for analytical frames that place emphasis on Africans as
human beings, with the capacity to make history and halt the trajectory of
repression, militarism and genocide. Such analytical frame requires an
epistemological and ontological shift in the way we study Africa. Today,
emancipatory feminist scholars are at the forefront of this intellectual
challenge. Feminists, in the course of understanding gender relations and
gendered forms of violence, have questioned prevailing conceptualizations of power, national security, citizenship, identity, militarism and
peace (Peterson, 1992; Young, 1990; McClintock, 1996; Steans, 1998;
Enloe, 2000; Amadiume, 2000a). Adopting a gendered perspective will
not just provide intellectual rigour but will give recognition to the critical
positions women have occupied historically at the forefront of peaceful
transformations of society. Norbert Elias (1982: 81), writing on the shift
from militarism to peace in medieval Europe, notes that 'it is about
women that the first circles of peaceful intellectual actively were established.' Elias's observation is not used here to essentialize women's experience, but to highlight that those who are not practitioners of war have
the time to conceptualize about the nature of peace. Contemporary
understandings of gender oppression embraced by black feminist
thought require a paradigmatic shift in our thinking of power relations
one that, Patricia Hill Collins (2000: 273) notes, 're-conceptualizes the
social relations of domination and resistance'.

This book adopts a black feminist geo-political methodology, drawing
on the methodological framework of 'intersectionality' as promoted by
Kimberle Crenshaw (1991) and Hill Collins (2000). For them an understanding of black women's oppression comes not from focusing on a
single 'difference' – race or gender – but from a consideration of these
differences as 'intersecting oppressions... that work together [to produce]
social injustice'. These intersecting oppressions, Hill Collins argues,
form a 'matrix of domination' that is constituted by 'domains of power',
which can be either 'structural, disciplinary, hegemonic' or 'interpersonal'. She writes, 'these domains constitute specific sites, where oppressions of race, class, gender, sexuality and nation mutually construct one
another' (2000: 203).

Investigating these 'domains of power' requires what in traditional
scholarship amounts to a multi-disciplinary and multi-scalar approach
that addresses the intersection between multiple sites of oppression and
their overlap across different spatial scales. More specifically, the domination and oppression that produces genocide is the outcome of the
intersection of race, ethnicity, the patriarchal state, masculinity, the geo-
political economy and militarism. Therefore, the book recognizes the
historical processes that are at the foundations of contemporary warfare
and the existence of, and interrelationship between, structures of
oppression at multiple spatial scales and sites in reproducing violence
and social injustice. This approach breaks down the divisions between
the global, national, local and domestic, and between the public and
private, and revealing how realist approaches that separate these sites
and scales can contribute to the protracted nature of warfare and the
persistence of endemic violence.

Defining the Contours of the Genocidal State

This text treats violence holistically. It refers to any act that causes bodily harm to the person or group. In the first instance, it prioritizes extreme forms of violence such as crimes against humanity and genocide. But, the argument here is that 'genocide', a legal term discussed extensively in Chapter 2, does not encompass the institutionalized and discriminatory forms of violence against the body, the person or the group that occur as part of everyday life or under conditions of war. For this reason, I have adopted the term 'genocidal violence' to include those forms of intentional violence with genocidal characteristics that have not been legally-defined as such. Therefore, genocidal violence encompasses all manifestations of direct and structural violence: wars, massacres, child abduction, sexual violence, forced displacement and disruption of livelihood activities – anything that impacts on the well-being of an individual or group that relates to their membership of a group.

In conventional political theory, the liberal state is perceived to have social contractual obligations towards its citizens; extending and protecting rights and providing security, especially in times of warfare. According to Cheikh Anta Diop typologies of state form, and a genocidal state occurs where, 'the conquering ethnic group refuses to mix with the indigenous conquered element and bases its domination on this absolute separation' (Diop, 1991: 132). Therefore, I posit that there exist certain conditions under which groups seek to accumulate power for themselves that lead generally to the development of a genocidal state.

An objective of this book is to map out how genocidal thinking that is based on the politics of exclusionism, produces histories, institutions, politics and economics that are genocidal, and how these are given meaning through the state.[2] I propose that the existence of the following conditions predisposes a society to genocide:

i. If it possesses a history of colonial genocide that turned social identities into racial and ethnic categories for purposes of social and political control;

ii. The presence of genocidal thinking induced by spaces and institutions of genocide. This is the kind of thinking that devalues the lives of other human beings on the basis of their ethnicity or race. For example, if a car knocks down a person on the street the driver will come out and say, it is only a Hutu or in the case of Nazi Germany, it is only a Jew, or in the case of colonial Algeria, it is only an Arab. These forms of thinking correspond to ideas of eugenics and of social Darwinism. Genocidal thinking gives coherence and legitimacy to the devaluation of human lives.

iii. The popularization of a genocidal history; this is when a specific reading of the society, 'mythical histories', is reproduced in order to justify genocide. This was manifest in the historical renditions of Belgium in Africa, of Germany and the history of the Jews in Europe

---

[2] These concepts came out of a discussion with Professor Horace Campbell in 2005 on the nature of violence in the Great Lakes region of Africa. I am grateful for his assistance in the clarification of my thoughts.

and in the case of Central Africa the so-called history of conquest of Tutsi invaders from Ethiopia. This history was reproduced in 1959 by the political party, Parmehutu, in Rwanda and became the history reproduced in schools and universities (Chapter 3).

iv. The presence of genocidal institutions: these include those institutions that are reorganized for incitement to genocide. In particular media institutions such as the press, especially hate radio. Church and religious institutions are also reorganized under these conditions for the promulgation of genocide.

v. The dominance of genocidal politics that occurs where the politics of exploitation, exclusivism, racism, eugenics, militarism, extremism and patriarchy intersect in a society. The politics of competition then results in acts of genocide, and, in turn, create the conditions for the reproduction of genocidal politics.

vi. The imposition and promotion of genocidal economics; these are the forms of economic engagement that require the physical elimination of competition. This type of economics comes from a form of competition for resources which is militarized, racialized and linked to the characterization of economic opponents as vermin. This form of economics is heightened by conditions of capitalist crisis. The elements of this kind of economics were best expressed in Germany of the 1940s.

vii. The presence of violence emanating from militarism, wars and the expansion of the spaces for genocide; this is exemplified by the training of militaries for the domestic control of citizens, the penetration of militarism into societal institutions, the continued supply of weapons and military training to genocidal African states and the regional expansion of warfare, through the transferral of genocidal ideas relating to the conduct of war.

Genocidal thinking then produces a particular mode of politics at multiple geographical scales, the analysis of which will form the basis of this book. In sum, the genocidal state occurs in a society where the nature of state power is reproduced for genocidal politics (hierarchical systems of domination) and the institutions of the state are developed for the reproduction of genocide.

Using evidence primarily from Burundi, but also from other countries in the Great Lakes region of Central Africa – an area covering the states of Rwanda, Burundi, Uganda, Democratic Republic of Congo (DRC)[3] and Tanzania – the book makes the case for the development of a new paradigm to help us understand the growing expendability of African lives. This book argues that genocidal violence in the Great Lakes region is neither a post-colonial nor post-Cold War, post-ideological phenomenon. Violence is rooted in the historical experience of the continent and the progressive dehumanization of the African people. Burundi and Rwanda are two states where the struggle for political power led to the refinement of a genocidal state; the socio-political and economic institutions of the colonial state and the drive towards

---

[3] The Democratic Republic of Congo (DRC) was previously known as Congo Free State (1885–1908), Belgian Congo (1908–1960), Congo (1960–1971) and Zaire (1971–1997).

modernity produced the conditions that laid the foundations for genocide. These were reproduced after independence and became enmeshed with global militarism during and after the Cold War. Ethnicity and patrimonialism are not privileged as critical factors but as the manifestations of myriad intersecting causalities.

The final goal of this book is to examine the search for spaces of peace through an analysis of the peacemaking and peace-building process under way in Burundi and its regional and international contexts. Here, the question is to what extent prevailing concepts of peace and security valorize Africans? Unpacking the peace problematic through feminist interpretations of national security and peace and their intersection with patriarchy and regional and global geo-politics allows for a greater understanding of contemporary peace initiatives and their failure to deal comprehensively with genocidal violence.

Burundi in the Regional Context

The small state of Burundi is situated in the intralacustrine zone of Central Africa (see Map 1). The area is rich in resources, and, historically, was able to support several small states based on hierarchies of class, which involved agricultural communities in tribute-paying relationships with pastoral Hima aristocracies, scattered across undulating hills (*collines*). Rwanda, to the north, was one of those states. Both Rwanda and Burundi are carved out of the same land as their much larger neighbour – the Democratic Republic of Congo (DRC). The DRC has a vast territory, 2.3 million sq. km. – the size of Western Europe – that is endowed with considerable natural resources – the water of the 3,700,000 km² Congo River basin, a rich tropical bio-diversity and considerable deposits of strategic minerals. On the basis of primary resources, the DRC should be the richest country in Africa and among the wealthiest in the world.

In contrast, Burundi and Rwanda are both geographically small, covering an area of 27,834 and 26,338 sq. km. respectively. Burundi's population of 6.6 million inhabit some of the most densely-settled areas in Africa; population densities range from 97 to 458 per sq. km. in the provinces of Cankuzo and Ngozi province respectively (Map 2), and possessing an overall average density of 215 per sq. km. – the second highest in mainland Africa. Burundi's population is predominantly rural and agricultural; only 8.2 per cent live in urban areas. Burundi's demographics are mirrored in Rwanda, with its 8.3 million people, average density of 300 per sq. km. and 16.6 per cent living in urban area. Neighbouring DRC, in contrast, has a population of 58 million and a density of 24 per sq. km. (UNDP, 2003).

Agriculture of a largely subsistence nature constitutes the primary economic activity for over 90 per cent of the population in the region. The demographic pressure means that land subdivision has reached unsustainable levels, with average farm size amounting to less than half a hectare in some regions. In Rwanda and Burundi export of traditional cash crops such as coffee, tea, sugar, rice and cotton provide the principal source of foreign exchange earnings, despite declining commodity prices on international markets. With underdeveloped industrial sectors (employing only about 2 per cent of the labour force) and small private sectors, the elites have relied heavily on public sector employment and the exploitation of their country's strategic location in Central Africa; the latter makes them important transit routes for gold, coltan and other strategic minerals from the turbulent eastern DRC (UNSC, 2001a & 2001b).

While Burundi's and Rwanda's minuscule size might suggest an irrelevance to the political and military strategy of the West, these countries have long acted as an *entrepôts* for informal resource extraction in the region and, since the 1960s, have been staging posts in the ideological and economic battle for the DRC. Burundi's proximity to the DRC places it on an axis that forms part of the historic centre of global economic extraction and geo-politics on the continent (Map 1). Due to the nature of its incorporation into the global economy, the resources of the mineral-rich DRC have not led to real material benefits for the mass of its citizens or those of its neighbours. All three countries rank low on any measure of social and economic indicator (Table 1.1). Burundi, for example, had a Gross Domestic Product (GDP) per capita of US \$83 in 2003 – a fall from \$210 in 1990, and well below the sub-Saharan African average of US \$633 (UNDP, 2005).

Between 1990 and 2003, over 50 per cent of the population lived below the income poverty line of US \$1 per day; this rose to some 70 per cent in conflict-affected areas, while 89 per cent were living on less than US \$2 a day (RoB, 2003; UNDP, 2005). Social indicators such as life expectancy (43.5 years), adult literacy (58.9 per cent) and school enrolment (33 per cent) were among the lowest in Africa (UNDP, 2005). HIV/Aids prevalence represents an aspect of the human welfare crisis that has beset these countries; adult prevalence rates are high: 13 per cent in Burundi, 6.4 per cent Rwanda and 4.9 per cent in DRC, although there are considerable geographical, gender and age variations (UNAIDS, 2005). Uganda, the scene of high prevalence rates in the 1990s, seemed to have bucked the upward trend in new infection rates.

Towards an Understanding of Genocidal Violence in the Region

It is the region's political history and image as an arena for genocide that have propelled these countries into the international limelight. Since the 1950s virtually all of them have experienced episodes of violent warfare and genocide. There have been 11 outright wars in the DRC and two in Rwanda. Uganda experienced genocidal violence during the regimes of President Idi Amin (1971–9) and Milton Obote (1980–85), and persistent warfare since 1979. The region has also been the scene of Africa's first continental war, drawing in seven nations to fight in the DRC war between 1996 and 2000. Only mainland Tanzania has remained unscathed, although it has borne the brunt of the refugee burden.

Table 1.1: Regional Demographic and Human Welfare Data, 2005

Country	Population Millions (2004)	Population Density per sq. km.	HPI % (2003)	HDI value (2003)	HDI Ranking (out of 177)	Population living under $2 per day	Adult Illiteracy rate (% age 15 and above, 2003)	HIV Prevalence (% pop 15–49) (2003)	Life Expectancy 1970–75	Life Expectancy 2000–05
Burundi	7.3	286	45.8	0.378	173	89.2	41.5	5.4*	44.0	40.8
Rwanda	8	331	44.7	0.450	159	83.7	33.2	5.1	44.6	38.6
DRC	54.8	24	42.9	0.385	168	–	34.7	4.2	45.8	41.8
Uganda	25.9	119	45.9	0.508	144	–	31.1	4.1	51.1	46.8
Tanzania	36.6	41	35.8	0.418	164	72.5	30.6	8.8	49.5	46.0

Source: UNDP, Human Development Report, 2005; World Development Report 2006.
Note: HPI: Human Poverty Index measures the percentage of population below a threshold level in the basic dimensions of development. HDI: Human Development Index measures three dimensions of human development: health, education and standard of living.
• 2005 data

The introduction of the modern state began with colonial rule towards the end of the nineteenth century. The conditions for genocidal violence were laid in the late nineteenth century. Although Rwanda and Burundi existed as separate pre-colonial states, they were conjoined as Ruanda-Urundi under European colonial rule for 65 years; firstly, as a German colony (1897–1916), and after the Germans were defeated in the First World War, they were placed under Belgian trusteeship (1916–62) and were incorporated into the same overarching colonial sphere as their neighbouring colony, the Belgian Congo. What was critical for these countries was the militarized and discriminatory nature of the state form which emerged under colonialism and western modernity.

Belgian colonialism laid the conditions for the traditions of genocide in the region, and what I claim to be its genocidal history. The construction of a genocidal state began in the DRC in the late nineteenth century. Acquired as the personal property of King Leopold II of Belgium, the Congo Free State, as it was known then, gave freedom to western capital, and death and enslavement to the indigenous population (Hochschild, 1998). The territory became the fiefdom of concessionary companies whose practice of forced labour for rubber, timber and mineral extraction was so odious that it provoked outcry in Europe. Over 10 million people were killed during Leopold's rule, and the acquisition of the Congo Free State by the Belgian government in 1908 did not alter radically the nature of governance in the new colony (Nzongola-Natalaja, 2002). Belgium was later implicated in the assassination in 1961 of the Congolese Prime Minister, Patrice Lumumba.[4] Congo's independence struggle and ensuing civil war were fuelled by a colonial state seeking to retain control over its prized colony amidst Cold War superpower rivalry and United Nations ineptitude (De Witte, 2001).

Unlike the majority of modern African states, Rwanda and Burundi were political and geographical entities in the pre-colonial period, and their people shared a common socio-cultural and linguistic heritage. Pre-colonial Burundi and Rwanda were monarchies with hierarchical social structures, of varying degrees of rigidity. Social groups, including those known as Tutsi, Hutu and Twa, were enmeshed in the complex familial and socio-economic relations characteristic of pre-capitalist societies.[5] Beginning with colonial rule, these social groups have been politicized to be called ethnic groups and once the concept of ethnicity was internalized, these groups became a political force for genocide and the conditions for genocidal politics were laid. The social groups in Rwanda and Burundi became classified as Hutu (85 per cent), Tutsi (14 per cent) and Twa (1 per cent), with the Tutsi represented as interlopers, foreigners from

---

[4] In February 2002, the Belgian parliament, after an investigation into its role in the country's assassination of Lumumba, publicly apologised (*BBC News Africa*, 'Lumumba's son hails Belgium apology), 6 February 2002.

[5] In Kirundi, the language of Burundi, the people are Barundi (pl.) and an individual is Murundi. The social groups are *Baganwa* (pl.), *Muganwa* (sg.); *Bahutu* (pl.), *Muhutu*(sg.) *Batutsi* (pl), *Mututsi* (sg.) and *Batwa* (pl.), *Mutwa* (sg.). The abbreviations *Ganwa*, Tutsi, Hutu and Twa were first used for convenience in the colonial period. In most cases, I have used these abbreviations because they continue to be widely used within and outside the region. In quotations, I have deferred to the terminology employed by the document being quoted.

North East Africa, who dominated the indigenous groups. The transformation of social groups into hierarchical ethnicities was aided by the racial ideology of social Darwinism that put the White colonizers at the top of the imposed hierarchy of human beings.

Genocide in Rwanda between the Hutus and Tutsi began in 1959. Known as the 'Hutu Revolution', it was a violent uprising against Tutsi colonial functionaries, which was spurred on by the Hutu elite, fearful of the prospect of the Tutsi gaining full control of state power with independence. The murder of Tutsis at the height of the Cold War, was sanctioned by the Belgian administration and ignored by the UN, despite its occurrence in its own trusteeship. The lack of western response to protect the lives of Africans signalled to many on the continent that such violence would be tolerated by the international community, if the interests of the perpetrators coincided with that of the west. For decades, external observers presented Rwanda's post-colonial history as relatively peaceful, despite the exclusion of the Tutsi from power, military coups and the capture of the state by a narrow elite from the northern provinces. Since independence in 1962, militarist solutions have been deployed to effect change in Rwanda. There were coups in 1965 and 1973 and outright war (1990–94) and genocide instead of democratic transition in 1994, when over 750,000 people, Tutsis and some moderate Hutus, were killed. The Rwandan genocide has generated numerous scholarly texts, articles, policy assessments and human rights reports (African Rights, 1994a & 1995; Dallaire, 2003; Human Rights Watch 1999a; Mamdani, 2001; Melvern, 2000; Prunier, 1995; Uvin, 1998). It is not my intention to review them here, except to point out their focus on the prevarications of the UN and western governments during the genocide and to note how the genocide fitted into a regional and global framework that so dehumanized African lives that over three-quarters of a million people could be killed while the world watched. An understanding of the politics of geographical scale was central to the operational plans of the genocidal state.

Post-colonial genocide represented the political elites' attempts to use an extreme militaristic solution to the problems of representation and diversity. For genocide to succeed, the institutions of the modern state had to be mobilized to provide weaponry and to plant ideas of militarism into the minds of ordinary people. In Rwanda, this was done effectively through the patriarchal harnessing of the energies of the young into violent action. The concept of the *interahamwe* (those who work together), a paramilitary organization of young Hutu men, mirrored the role of the infamous *Force Publique*, in King Leopold's Congo Free State – the latter charged with bringing back the severed hands of recalcitrant Africans. In Rwanda, as in Burundi, the modern media, particularly radio broadcasts, exercised considerable authority, being throughout the period of military rule the arm of the state. It was on this basis that the infamous *Radio Télévision Libre des Mille Collines* (RTLMC) could play such a significant role in inciting people to genocide.

The post-colonial Burundi state has also been highly unstable, with six governments between 1962 and 1966, the abolition of the monarchy (1966), four successful *coup d'états* (1965, 1976, 1987 & 1996), the assassination of its first democratically-elected president, Melchoir Ndadaye, in October 1993, and a civil war which ran from 1993 to 2006. Violence of a genocidal nature has produced one of the most intractable refugee problems on the continent and the death of more than 400,000 people.

The war, which involved the national army, three armed guerrilla groups and various militias, intensified after October 1993. Criticisms of international negligence in the case of Rwanda led regional and western governments to adopt a more determined effort to finding a solution to the Burundi crisis, not necessarily due to respect for the sanctity of African lives, but for fear of the whole region being engulfed by violence (Dallaire, 2003; Melvern, 2000; OAU, 2000). In 1996, neighbouring countries, having played host to refugees, opposition political parties and guerrilla groups, forced the warring parties to start peace negotiations under the leadership of Julius Nyerere of Tanzania, who was succeeded, after his death in October 1999, by Nelson Mandela, former President of South Africa.

The negotiations culminated in the signing of the Arusha Peace and Reconciliation Agreement for Burundi in August 2000, in the presence of the then President of the USA, Bill Clinton, even though a ceasefire had not been agreed. Since then, the civil war has continued amidst efforts to implement the peace agreement with the formation of a transitional government (2001–05) followed by the installation of a democratically-elected government in August 2005. The United Nations has lent its support to the regional initiatives. The Secretary General appointing special envoys to the Great Lakes and to Burundi and, through the use of special rapporteurs, has tried to investigate some of the more extreme incidents of violence. Between 1995 and 2006, some seven Security Council resolutions were made on the situation in Burundi, and despite the presence of a UN peace-keeping force, the United Nations Operation in Burundi (ONUB), insecurity and human rights violations by state and non-state actors have persisted.

Do small states such as Burundi, Rwanda or even the Great Lakes region matter globally? Only insofar as the market imperatives of the west necessitate the direct or indirect colonization of any space that might have the potential for the accumulation of wealth, however small. Despite providing the bulk of the funding for the peace negotiations, western governments did not fully support the regional peace initiative. The sometimes counterproductive role of their special envoys, along with the involvement of numerous international and regional non-governmental organizations (NGOs) in the peace process, demands critical attention.

Tribal narratives attribute the interrelatedness of the violence in the region to the prevalence of a common ethnicity across colonially-imposed national boundaries which divided communities of Tutsi, Hima, Hutu, Ha and Lendu and complicated by historical and more recent migratory movements and the presence of long-term refugee communities and armed political groups. Similarities in the polarized ethnicities of Rwanda and Burundi, for example, have encouraged commentators to suggest that what happens in one country is likely to reverberate in the other and that violence in one cannot 'be understood independently' of the other (Lemarchand, 1994b: 585; Prunier, 1995). Despite this, the two had significantly different pre-colonial and, to some extent, colonial experiences. Burundi had a less centralized state in which Hutus occupied important positions at court and, in spite of replica colonial policies, the Burundian Hutu was able to make some social advancement in the modern state, however limited. This had implications for the cross-ethnic alliances evident among Burundi's political class. In contrast, the 1959 genocide in Rwanda played a major role in shaping the 'systematized ethnic antagonism' which emerged in the post-colonial period.

Outline of the Book

The principal aim of this book is to initiate a paradigmatic shift in the epistemological and conceptual framework that we use to understand genocidal violence in Africa. To this end, in Chapter 2, I introduce and define the dominant concepts being used in the text – genocide, militarism, modernity, masculinity, geo-politics, ethnicity, humanitarianism and peace, and trace their intersectionality and applicability towards our understanding of violence in African societies. The chapter begins with a discussion of the concept of genocide and its relationship with modernity and the state, and theorizes about the specific conditions that predisposes a state to genocide. It shows how the introduction of the modernizing practices of science and philosophy, especially the human evolutionary ideas of social Darwinism, contributed to produce intersecting hierarchies of race, ethnicity and gender in the context of colonial domination and capitalist penetration. The argument here is that genocidal violence results from the further intersection of these hierarchical relations with militarism, violent masculinity and liberal and neo-liberal paradigms of development, including the international humanitarian regime. The chapter ends with an examination of the hegemonic neo-liberal approach to peace and reconstruction, as utilized by the international community in ethnically divided societies, questions its applicability to African contexts and outlines alternative feminist approaches to peace.

Chapter 3 examines the historical foundations of the genocidal Burundi state; it briefly considers the structures of power and social hierarchies in the pre-colonial period and the later superimposition of the modern state form under colonialism. The chapter shows how the workings of the ideas of Social Darwinism, through the popular constructions of Hutu, Tutsi and Twa and the promotion of racial and gendered hierarchies, led to the reproduction of genocidal histories and the embeddedness of discriminatory social and political practices in the institutions of the modern Burundi state. The chapter ends with a discussion of the relationship between ethnicity, militarism and global geo-politics in the late colonial era and the emergence of militaristic violence as part of the political order.

Chapter 4 focuses on Burundi's turbulent transition to independence on 1 July 1962. My contention here is that it was at this juncture, when global geo-politics intersected with political competition between regional and ethnic elites, that the genocidal state consolidated itself nationally and gained political acceptability internationally. The chapter details the entrenchment of genocidal politics through an analysis of events surrounding the assassination of the first democratically-elected leader, Prince Louis Rwagasore, on 13 October 1961, the influence of anti-communist forces, the overthrow of the monarchy and the capture of the state by the military. Of emphasis are the further masculinization and ethnicization of politics linked to the rise of a militarized political culture during the presidential rule of the coup-makers: Captain Michel Micombero (1966–76), Lt Col. Jean-Baptiste Bagaza (1976–87) and Major Pierre Buyoya (1987–93) and spurred on by the bitter intra-elite and inter-ethnic competition as manifested in the 1972 genocide.

Chapter 5 examines Burundi's transition to democracy in the early 1990s under the conditions of genocide. The discussion focuses on external and internal pressures for representation and the struggles among the political elite, the 1993 elections and the overthrow of the democratically-elected government later that year with the assassination of the president in October. The discussion includes an analysis of the role played by the political elite, the military, the media, the militias and civil society actors in the political violence that accompanied the democratization process. Particular attention is paid to the then President of Burundi, Pierre Buyoya (1996–2003), in his multiple roles as military leader, 'strong man' as political leader, head of an NGO, and later peacemaker and transitional president. As political conditionality was linked to donor-sponsored neo-liberal economic reform, the chapter also comments on the genocidal economics, underpinning Burundi's economy and the effects on the society of international aid and the economic liberalization programmes sponsored by the International Monetary Fund (IMF) and the World Bank.

Chapter 6 turns to the specificities and spatialities of violence in Burundi, especially the occurrence of violence across the binary conceptualizations that see state and non-state, private and public, and urban and rural as distinct spheres of activities. Here, the key question is what are the ethnic, geographical and gendered characteristics of the violence associated with state power and rebellion? Feminist conceptualizations of militarism and its relationship with modern state power help us to unpack the gender specific nature of much of the violence. The discussion explores the ways in which the state exercises its power, through the perpetration of various acts of genocidal violence, the targeting of civilians through massacres, their forced displacement and the sanctioning of gendered and sexual violence, and promotes a culture of impunity by perpetuating the discriminatory practices associated with the ideologies of ethnic and gender hierarchies. The chapter concludes by examining how the state absolves itself from blame in the international arena by distancing itself from the military, ratifying various international conventions and in effect performing a scalar form of politics, which emphasizes the immutability of sovereignty at the expense of the rights and humanity of its citizens.

Chapter 7 addresses the regional and international context of warfare, particularly the support for genocidal and militaristic regimes, and for rebel forces. The interrelatedness of the regional conflicts are examined, especially the impact in Burundi of genocides in Rwanda and Uganda and the recent wars in the Democratic Republic of the Congo (DRC). Burundi's pivotal geographical position and its regional integration are illustrated with reference to the cross border movement of illegal goods, rebel armies, refugees and peasants. Of particular importance are the material assistance given to the rebel armies by neighbouring territories and international complicity in the deepening militarization of the region. The significance of illegal arms transfer and refugeeism for the processes of militarization and the protractedness of warfare are discussed. These issues are illustrated by an analysis of the political situation of Burundi refugees in Tanzania, and the growing hostility of the Tanzanian state to their plight. The chapter ends with a consideration of the emerging concept of regional citizenship, as a means of overcoming the marginalization, prejudice and violence experienced by refugees and migrants.

In Chapter 8, the regional and international dimensions are further explored as the concepts of forced migration and humanitarianism are interrogated in the context of Cold War and post-Cold War geo-politics. The experience of Burundi refugees in camps in Tanzania is used to argue that the extension of the international refugee conventions to Africa and the accompanied relief/humanitarian regime have undermined notions of asylum and integration of alien communities into African societies. While this is not revelatory in terms of contemporary critique of humanitarian organizations, it does, however, link humanitarianism with militarization and places it firmly within global geo-politics.

Chapter 9 unpacks ideas about peace and reconstruction in the context of the genocidal state through a focus on the Arusha peace negotiations (1996–2000) and its aftermath. The questions posed are: What concepts of peace inform contemporary peace negotiations in Africa and how can they be engendered and Africanized? In fact, how useful is neo-liberal post-Cold War peace-making in resolving contemporary warfare in Africa? And, what lessons can be learnt from ten years of peace and ceasefire negotiations? Central to the discussion is the emergence of the regional thrust for peace through the interventions of regional leaders. This regional initiative marked a significant and progressive step to the ending of genocidal violence and the revalorization of African humanity. But, do the conceptualizations of peace and reconstruction by the multiplicity of actors allow for such thinking? These issues are explored through a discussion of the role played by heads of state, the mediators (Julius Nyerere and Nelson Mandela), the Burundi political elite, civil society and women peace activists, and western governments and international multilateral and non-governmental organizations.

Chapter 10 explores further the will for peace as espoused by the parties to the negotiations. This is done through an examination of the modalities of the peace negotiations and the tenets of the Arusha Peace and Reconciliation Agreement, the key debates, and the negotiating positions of the political parties at the various rounds of the negotiations. The prospect for a sustainable and, potentially, emancipatory peace is considered through an analysis of the implementation of the peace agreement, in particular, power-sharing and the establishment of a transitional government, the ceasefire negotiations, and the reconstruction packages that address neo-liberal economic reforms, demilitarization and truth and reconciliation. The role of violence in legitimizing claims, at critical stage in the peace process, is also examined. In conclusion, the chapter highlights the limitations of the 'liberal peace', with its masculinist and militaristic approach, to provide a transformative framework that can transcend the genocidal state.

Chapter 11 concludes the book with a summary of its key contributions and suggests ways in which a paradigmatic shift, which involves a focus on a black feminist methodology, can help in the creation of spaces of peace in Africa. To better understand the reasons for the persistence of genocidal violence in Burundi and in Africa in general, the book posits a shift from our myopic pre-occupation with ethnicity as the principal analytical framework for studying African societies and, instead of seeing the dehumanizing tendencies of violence as being peculiarly tribal or non-African, unveils the thoroughly modern nature of contemporary violence and its embeddedness in the security apparatus and the extractive practices of the modern state, and its scalarity, in terms of its representation and production at different spatial scales.

The book reinforces the considerable possibilities and scope for autonomous regional African initiatives for peace that formulate solutions, which reaffirm the sanctity of African lives. Unfortunately, prevailing concepts of national security, peace and reconstruction that inform peace negotiations remain Eurocentric in their formulations and are thus unable to transcend ethnicity, militarism and territorial sovereignty and open up the possibility for social transformations that embrace African humanity and African people as part of an inclusive political community.

2

Constructing A Feminist
a Paradigm Perspective on
of Violence Genocidal Politics

Introduction

> Only a shallow empiricism can fail to see that such monstrous societies are
> not the product of a national peculiarity or a system of government but are
> part and parcel of our [modern bourgeois] civilization. (CLR James quoted
> from Grimshaw, 1992: 153)

This conceptual chapter aims to assert and validate the ordinary
humanity of the victims of genocidal violence as well as that of the perpetrators, with the intention of not to further banalizing the horrific crimes
perpetrated in Africa, but of illuminating the normative circumstances
under which such extreme violence occurs. The key question throughout
is what the conditions are under which genocide has been produced on
the continent. In other words, what predisposes a society to genocide? To
this end, the chapter examines the conceptual frameworks currently
deployed to understand the intersection between genocide, national
security and peace. It begins with an interrogation of the concept of
genocide; unveiling its legality and its use with respect to crimes against
humanity. The relationship of genocide to the modern state is explored,
particularly the structural, representational, gendered and personal insecurities that arise as a consequence of the 'civilizing process'.
Conceptually, genocide is positioned as the consequence of intersecting
oppressions, and as a violent manifestation of how difference is constituted in the modern state according to hierarchies of domination based
on social class, race, ethnic identity and gender. A concomitant argument
is that extreme violence not only creates and reflects hierarchies of dominance, but is also reinforced by and practised according to hierarchies of
space, within and across sovereign space. The chapter then proceeds to
identify the historical and structural conditions that have led to the emergence of the modern genocidal state in Africa, beginning with the 'civilizing' practices of the colonial period, leading to the growth of
militarism and its association with modernity, violent masculinity, genocidal economics and humanitarianism. Finally, the chapter explores the
contradictions in the hegemonic liberal concept of peace and its variance
with African and feminist perspectives on peace.

Genocide, Modernity and the State

Tragically, as the Jewish Holocaust and the Bosnian war have shown, genocidal violence is not peculiar to the African continent. Violence aimed at the eradication of one group of people based on nationality, race, religion and ethnicity constitutes the most heinous crime against humanity. The existence of genocide in modern society poses considerable challenges to our understanding of human development and our moral responsibility as human beings.

Genocide, a word describing the intentional destruction of a group of people, is a twentieth-century term (Hinton, 2002). Yet violence that befits the term is not a purely twentieth-century phenomenon. Evidence of genocidal violence abounds in history and antiquity. Genocide occurs because of the existence of differential power relationships between groups, perceived as being arranged in a hierarchical manner, whereby the powerful group by denying the humanity of the other, can justify their abuse and ultimately their elimination. Genocide is a contested term and scholars, human rights lawyers and policy-makers have attempted to be highly prescriptive in the application of the term to incidences of mass killing; and, in spite of its gravity, it is not beyond manipulation. Hinton (2002: 2) stresses that 'terminological rigor is crucial ... both for analytical clarity and to avoid diluting the term'. Yet, such an assumption assumes moral objectivity in how the term is understood and applied.

If academics are quibbling over the use of the term, then surely the existence of a legal definition must provide operational clarity. In 1948, after the Jewish Holocaust of the Second World War, the victorious nations, under the umbrella of the United Nations, passed the Convention on Genocide, which provides the basic principles by which violence is defined as genocide in international law. The convention defines genocide as:

any of the following acts committed with intent to destroy, in whole or in part, a national, ethnical, racial or religious group, as such:

(a) Killing members of the group;
(b) Causing serious bodily or mental harm to members of the group;
(c) Deliberately inflicting on the group conditions of life calculated to bring its physical destruction in whole or in part;
(d) Imposing measures intended to prevent births within the group;
(e) Forcibly transferring children from one group to another. (Article II, United Nations Convention on Genocide, 1948)

Legal scholars, however, address the specificities of the convention, but not the political and economic conditions that produce genocide.

The Convention on Genocide was passed at a time when many African territories were colonies of European powers. Arriving at a definition that recognised the severity of the crimes committed by Nazi Germany and which, at the same time, excludes the actions of the allied states, generated highly controversial debates (Hinton, 2002). Imperial powers and those professing alternative ideologies to capitalism argued for a definition that would exclude their suppression of political dissidents and cultural groups. The enforcement of the convention was also contentious. Hinton (2002: 5) notes, 'while few countries have a problem indicting a genocidal regime that has fallen from power, most become very resistant to passing legislation that could compromise their sovereignty' or economic interests.

Recent literature has drawn our attention to the historical complicity of western governments in either sponsoring or through their 'silence' sanctioning genocidal regimes in the non-western world (Gewald, 2004; Hinton, 2002; Jones, 2004). Jones (2004), for example, wants western audiences to challenge the body of opinion that presents western democratic countries as the pivot of civilization, and therefore above genocide. This view is echoed by the Caribbean writer, George Lamming (2004), who remarked that 'people in western culture perceived themselves to be not a branch of the human family but guardians and custodians of humanity'. Such a viewpoint leaves westerners little room for questioning the domestic and foreign policies of their governments. As Jones (2004: 11) remarks, 'the atrocities committed by Western states and their allies are systematically ignored, explained away, defined out of existence, or openly celebrated' creating 'an effective culture of impunity'. Understanding the role of the west in genocide in the non-western world is of critical importance in ending such extreme violations of humanity.

Even a casual reading of the Convention on Genocide suggests scope for its application historically and more contemporarily to violent events in Africa. Although at the international level there is an agreement about 'never again', it has not been applied with respect to Africa. Despite the well-documented and publicized episodes of violence that appear to fit the definition, for example the 1985 UN commissioned report describing the 1965 and 1972 slaughter of Burundian Hutus by the Tutsis as genocide,[1] only thrice have members of the international community (UN Security Council) used the convention definition with reference to violent conflicts in Africa: in German Namibia retrospectively, in Rwanda 1994 and in Darfur 2004. Independent observers have documented numerous acts in Africa, notably in Burundi, that constituted crimes against humanity and could have been legally defined as genocide (Bowen *et al.*, 1972; Lemarchand & Martin, 1974). Even when genocide is acknowledged, the response might be problematic; for example, the term has been open to manipulation to serve political interests, not the cause of justice.

The continued presence of genocide in Africa and elsewhere is an indictment of 'modern' society. When genocidal episodes are given analytical scrutiny they seem to have characteristics more akin to modernity than primitivity. Modernity refers to the transformations in western intellectual thought beginning with the enlightenment period, when developments in science led to the emergence of rationality and evolutionary explanations for human behaviour. The possibilities of human progress, unrestrained by metaphysics, stimulated theorizations about state–society relationships. This occurred at the time of the development of capitalist forces and the commodification of the body as

---

[1] See UNESC (1985) The Whitaker Report, Part 1, note 15.

labour. During modernity the freedom of the human became entwined with capitalism's emphasis on individualized human endeavour.

Bauman, in his study of the Jewish Holocaust, has made important contributions to our understanding of genocide in modern society. According to him, 'modern civilization was not the Holocaust's *sufficient* condition; it was, however, most certainly its *necessary* condition. Without it, the Holocaust would be unthinkable' (1989: 13) [his emphasis]. Bauman shows how the planning and operationalization of the Holocaust required the direction of a scientifically managed organization, using the factory system of an advanced capitalist society and modern bureaucratic institutions. Genocide necessitated the dehumanization of the victims, such that the killings posed no moral dilemmas to the perpetrators. The scientific method of objectivity and the bureaucratic operation of reducing objects to a set of quantifiable measures served this purpose.

Genocide appears fundamental to the concept of the modern Westphalian state, with its assumption that cultural and political homogeneity are desirable goals of the state. Forging the nation requires the elimination of cultural difference; religious and ethnic. The nation state, often captured by the hegemonic group and perceived as acting in the common good, could enforce conformity through the legal system and the bureaucracy. As modernity was associated with 'the civilizing process', Bauman is critical of Norbert Elias's (1987) thesis that the formation of the modern nation state was accompanied by increased security as the state came to monopolize organized or legitimate violence. He states that, 'modern genocide is an element of social engineering, meant to bring about a social order conforming to the design of the perfect society' (Bauman, ibid.: 91). Genocide could be perceived as legitimate violence at the core of the civilizing process.

Feminist scholars have questioned the assumed universality implicit in the concept of national security (Blanchard, 2003; Peterson, 1992; Steans, 1998). Peterson, for example, maintains that the concept of state-sponsored security for all is a contradiction in terms, especially when considered in terms of military expansionism, the injustices of uneven development and the structural violence of gender, class and racial hierarchy. She calls for a recognition and critical examination of the systemic 'structural insecurities internal to [liberal] states – constituted by gendered (and other) divisions of labour, resources and identities – as well as androcratic politics' (Peterson, 1992: 2). Adopting such an approach necessitates a radical rethinking of security, especially that of realists and neo-realists who see security purely in terms of the nation-state. Steans asks us to see the state as a process which involves including and excluding people on the basis of race, gender or class. She (1998: 109) writes: 'in the "making" of the state the construction of the hostile "other", which is threatening and dangerous is central to the making of identities and the securing of boundaries.' Physical space is central to our understanding of these systemic insecurities generated by the 'civilizing process' or modern state-making. Gendered, racial and structural insecurities are more pronounced in peripheral and marginal spaces, as in colonial outposts and the private sphere of the home (Peterson, ibid.). Intersecting insecurities as manifested in the use of extreme violence, livelihood disruption, the displacement of communities and the introduction of uneven capitalist development constitute a matrix of domination that has at its core ideas about the body and ideologies of race purity.

Genocide, Hierarchical Relations and the Civilizing Process

Bodies are not just physical and biological entities; they are constituted through dynamic socio-political practices. Economic imperatives necessitated the control over the productive and reproductive capacity of the human body, though the nature of control and the processes change over time and space (Harvey, 1996). In the colonial periphery the use of force in production, wars, mutilation, and the organization of the corporeal body for labour could be carried to its extreme. Harvey refers to Elias's 1982 proposal of an evolutionary and developmental view of the body. Elias conceptualized the civilized body as one that is highly individualized and rational, divorced from its social and natural environments and in control of its emotions, unlike the uncivilized, which 'sought to satisfy bodily desires without restraint or regard for the welfare of others' (Elias in Harvey, 1996: 275).

Feminist scholars have made considerable progress in rethinking how control of the body is expressed in gender relations, though institutions of patriarchy and ideologies of race, masculinity and femininity. Young (1990) introduces the concept of cultural imperialism to explain the oppression experienced by non-whites that cannot be understood through the lens of capitalism. She shows how European society separates mind/reason from the body, and, in turn, how scientific and philosophical reason became associated with men and whiteness, and affectivity and the body with women and non-white men. This dichotomy 'persists in the context of a society structured by hierarchical relations of class, race, gender and nationality' (Young, 1990: 127). Besides, the identification of reason with a particular group gives that group a privileged authoritative position as the subject of knowledge, meanwhile 'groups they defined as different thereby slid into the position of objects correlated with the subject's distancing and mastering gaze' (Young, *ibid.*). What Young terms the 'scaling of bodies' led to the positioning of white male bodies as the norm and all other bodies as degenerate. However, the exact position that these other bodies occupied were determined by the intersection of class, gender and race. Those bodies considered aesthetically unpleasing and debased could, at times, be subjected to extreme forms of violence.

In much of western thought African bodies came to represent that of the 'uncivilized'; they could be shipped as slaves, mutilated, and displayed for public spectacle.[2] The 'civilizing process' or modernity was

---

[2] For example, for two months in 1897, King Leopold of Belgium recreated Congolese villages as a spectacle in the grounds of Tervuren Palace, near Brussels. See Maurits Wynants (1997) *Des Ducs de Brabant aux Villages Congolese: Tervuren et L'Éxposition Coloniale 1897.* Belgium: Musée Royal d'Afrique Centrale, Tervuren.

associated with social Darwinian ideas of human evolution that positioned the African body close to the base of the evolutionary ladder. Europeans, spurred on by the science and philosophy, including Christian theology, claimed moral superiority and used the 'civilizing mission' to justify land expropriation and the destruction of indigenous socio-cultural practices. Africans, according to Fanon (1961), were painted in zoological terms, representing their position on the evolutionary ladder, and were embodied as evil and destructive of nature and of others. Fanon declares:

> The native is declared insensible to ethics; he represents not only the absence of values, but also the negation of values. He is, let us dare to admit it, the enemy of values, and in this sense he is absolute evil. He is the corrosive element, destroying all who comes near him; he is the deforming element, disfiguring all that has to do with beauty and morality; he is the depository of maleficent powers, the unconscious and irretrievable instrument of blind forces. (Fanon, 1961: 32)

The 'uncivilized' native was constructed as a naturalized being, ruled by child-like emotions and thus capable of senseless, irrational destruction.

The 'civilizing mission' necessitated the production of a knowledge system that would enable the regulation and control of the African body. Michel Foucault (1997) terms this strategy 'bio-power', or the exercise of power through being able to control the human body – a process that he locates as starting in late eighteenth and early nineteenth-century Europe. In effect, the essence of life was captured by the modern state in its monopolization of the means of violence, and reached its extreme in the ideology of eugenics. With the use of modern scientific knowledge harnessed by the bureaucracy of the modern state, the African body became an object of measurement; racially and ethnically defined and classified, sometimes drawing on pre-existing knowledge, sometimes creating completely new ones. The 'civilizing process' required the delineation of physical and cultural boundaries that took the form of binaries: white/black, colonial/native; citizens/subjects; educated/uneducated; urban/rural (Fanon, 1961; Mamdani, 1996). These binaries denoted hierarchical relations based on notions of superiority and inferiority that became internalised both by wider European audiences and Africans. For some time, representations of Africans in the institutional structures; the state, the church, education, in the economy, on the plantations, in the media, and through a variety cultural outputs: scholarly texts, travel writing, photography and film served to reinforce the characteristics that marked them out as inferior human beings (Pieterse, 1992).

A vast body of literature now exists on the social construction of ethnic identities in Africa, particularly the role played by colonial administrators and missionaries acting with the assistance of African functionaries as they 'invented tradition' (Ranger, 1983; Vail, 1989). Arising from this is the debunking of popular discourses that see all African communities as existing in primordial 'tribal groups', but also an understanding of the malleability of identities and their propensity to become 'fixed' under particular conditions. The role of the state in identity formation is given prominence in the work of Mahmood Mamdani (2001: 20–22) who introduces the concept of political identities or 'legally inscribed identities' that are constructed on the basis of group access to state power. He writes:

> If the law recognizes you as a member of an ethnicity, and state institutions treat you as a member of that ethnicity, then you become an ethnic being legally and institutionally. In contrast, if the law recognises you as a racial group, then your relationship to the state, and to other legally defined groups is mediated through law and the state. (Mamdani, 2001: 22)

In general, racial and ethnic identity formation was very much a state-determined process, linked to modernity. As identities or affectivity became the basis for understanding corporeal differences, social organization, group affiliations and political participation – they reinforced assumptions of 'primordialism' and of African inferiority. A methodological problem with the preoccupation with identity is that it fails to take account of in group differences, a point Crenshaw makes with respect to African-American. She notes, 'ignoring difference within groups contributes to tension among groups' (Crenshaw, 1991: 1242). Gender differences and patriarchal practices intersect with racial hierarchy to produce distinct features of genocidal violence.

Recent studies on gender-based violence have exposed the differential violence perpetrated against men and women in the context of war and genocide (Baines, 2003; Cockburn & Zarkov, 2002; Jones, 2000 & 2002; Turshen & Twagiramariya, 1998). Jones (2000: 185) labels this 'gender-selective mass-killing' as 'gendercide'. Men, he argues, especially 'non-combatant men … not covered by the bonds of kinship or culture … have been the most frequent targets of mass killing and genocidal slaughter, as well a host of atrocities and abuses' (Jones, ibid.: 186–7). In contrast, women are targeted because their bodies are perceived as being symbolic of the nation or racial/ethnic group. The close association of women with nationalism meant that their sexuality was constrained by men as part of the process of nation-building – a situation McClintock (1996: 264) explores in the space of the colonial world. Linking nationalism with evolutionary race theory, she showed how the state became constitutive of racialized bodies and how the national narrative became gendered.

The colonial context provided the domain in which total domination could occur. Colonial spaces were extra-judicial spaces, existing outside the realms of metropolitan laws. People power – majority power – was put down with, as Arendt (2004: 241) describes, 'men's artefacts [weapons], whose inhumanity and destructiveness increase in proportion to the distance separating the opponents.' A situation Beinart (1992: 462) affirms, when he notes that colonial wars of pacification could 'be particularly brutal, partly because of the imbalance of technology and partly because of the dehumanization of the victims'. State power was a vehicle for the mobilization and extraction of resources – a process Harvey (2003) terms 'accumulation by dispossession'. Harvey's characterization of the conditions of imperial plunder did not address the conditions that were established in Central Africa, but Hochschild

(1998), using empirical evidence, brought out the facts of genocide. Genocidal violence was facilitated by forced production, taxation, absence of working-class might and the role of the militias – *le Force Publique* – for carrying out violations (Chapter 7).

Militarism and Masculinity in the Patriarchal State

Realist conceptualizations of the state see militarism as a fundamental component of statecraft and as essential for national security. A state, permanently organized for war, inevitably reproduces itself in warlike fashion – in its institutions, in gender relations, and in the everyday activities of its citizens. Militarism has profound effects on the nature of society, such that feminists have sought to broaden our understanding of the concept. Cynthia Enloe (2002: 23), for example, defines militarism as 'a compilation of assumptions, values and belief ... about how the world works, [and] about what makes human nature tick'. Core beliefs of militaristic ideology, she continues, assume 'that humans are prone to conflict ... that tensions can be resolved ultimately through the use force, and that 'hierarchical relations are essential for effective action' (Enloe, ibid.: 23/24). Conceptually, militarism prioritizes domination on the basis of hierarchical difference between human beings. As Steans (1998: 105) notes, 'militarism is both rooted in and fosters a refusal to recognize the humanity of others'. These values can permeate 'all state and non-state institutions within a society ... even and especially under conditions of peace' (Enloe, ibid.: 24).

Feminist scholars have articulated the relationship between militarism and the patriarchal social order (Cockburn & Zarkov, 2002; Enloe, 1983 & 2000; Steans, 1998). Militarism emphasizes a mode of masculinity that is dependent on male power and dominance over society (patriarchy). Under militarism the state is the representation of manhood and becomes the terrain for the reproduction of masculinities. Theoreticians, such as von Clausewitz (1918), have argued that war was a natural function of man. War and the ability to win war was a manifestation of power, and the qualities that were to be nurtured in a society were the aggressive behaviour that taught men the importance of conquest and domination. To get men to fight, concepts of manhood, masculinity and valour have to become closely associated with militarism. Enloe (2002: 24) points out that in the ideology of militarism, a gendered hierarchy positions women as needing armed protection in times of crisis and 'any man who refuses to engage in armed violent action is jeopardizing his own status as manly man'. In fact, Jones (2002) has already alerted us to the mass slaughter of non-combatant men or those deemed inferior or deviant from the norm.

Connell's theorization of the concept of masculinity is instructive. While recognizing the existence of multiple definitions of masculinity, he defines it as 'simultaneously a place in gender relations, the practices through which men and women engage that place in gender, and the effects of these practices in bodily experience, personality and culture' (Connell, 1995: 71). Masculinity is oppositional to femininity; it is also an historical product. Connell (ibid.: 67/68) suggests that while all societies have 'cultural accounts of gender, not all have the concept of masculinity'. The concept, he points out, 'presupposes a belief in individual difference and personal agency. In that sense it is built on the conception of individuality that developed in early modern Europe with the growth of colonial empires and capitalist economic relations'. It seems, therefore, that masculinity is linked to the emergence of Elias's 'civilized' body. As it is conditioned by the way in which modern society is gendered, it is, therefore, culturally specific.

The origin of patriarchy in Africa is much debated by feminist scholars. Amadiume (1997), writing with reference to West Africa, shows the conditions under which militarism was constrained in the precolonial period and argues that a militarized patriarchy was brought gradually into West Africa through Islam and that the constraints on extreme masculinity were removed by the subjugation of the society under colonialism. In her view, the colonial state undermined the matricentric production unit and destroyed or reconfigured pre-existing mechanisms for social control. She drew on Chiekh Anta Diop's (1989) theorization of the origins of patriarchy in European social systems to argue that 'the ideology of violence was monolithic masculinist patriarchy' (Amadiume, ibid.: 95). Colonialism, she argues:

> introduce[d] a new gender politics, favouring men and undermining the traditional system of balance of power politics between men and women. This European patriarchal system constructs power as solely male and subordinates the female to male rule. (Amadiume, ibid.: 105)

A Euro-American conception of masculinity has spread globally with colonialism, imperialism and Christianity. Colonialism was not only built on a hierarchy of race but within that a hierarchy of masculinities. Historians, feminists and psychologists have shown how the institutions of the imperialist British state promoted the link between the aggressive masculinity of the superior white male and empire-building (Enloe, 2000; Fanon, 1967; Mackenzie, 1984; Ranger, 1983 & 1993). White masculinity was what Connell (1995) terms 'hegemonic' masculinity and African masculinity as 'marginalized' masculinity. Hierarchies of femininities and masculinities were inscripted into the concept of nationhood. McClintock (1996: 264) declares that within the colonial world, 'White middle-class men were seen to embody the forward-thrusting agency of national progress.' Non-white masculinity was not a singular concept, different kinds of masculinities and femininities were constructed for the different peoples. Racialized and ethnic hierarchies intercepted with masculinity and femininity, as women and men from certain ethnic groups were favoured more than others.

Ranger (1983) refers to the construction of a feudal-patriarchal ethics by European settlers based on invented neo-traditional values of the nineteenth century; these they used to modernize Africa. Ranger writes:

> The neo-traditional gentlemen of empire ... with their simultaneous emphasis on toughness and chivalry, on monarchy and on rural hierarchy, were incomplete without the neo-traditional lady ... of course, required to

be emphasised by contrast to the 'other' – the immoral or helpless figures of native womanhood. There could be no question of transforming such creatures into ladies. But they might nevertheless be transformed into 'respectable' women, fitting subordinates of and objects of charity for white ladies in a hierarchy of maternalism which was erected side by side with the male administrative hierarchies of paternalism. (Ranger 1993: 66–7)

For McClintock (1996: 268) instituting a new system of patriarchy was central to the capture of female labour by the colonial power and to 'disrupt the patriarchal power of the colonised men'. McClintock (ibid.: 265), drawing on Fanon's *Black Skins, White Masks*, notes how military violence and the authority of a centralized state strengthen and enlarge the domestication of gender power within the family. She quotes Fanon to show how 'militarization and the centralization of authority in a country automatically entail a resurgence of the authority of the father' (Fanon 1967: 141–2). State promotion of 'legitimate' violence in the public sphere enables violence to permeate into the private and the personal. As militarism progresses, domestic violence, including the rape of women, intensifies, on a scale dependent on the ability of state institutions to intervene.

And what happens to gender relations in military regimes? As Luckham (1998: 23) notes 'they embody ideological relations between male protectors and female protected.'

Until the latter part of the twentieth century, the military regime was a predominantly male institution and even though women were able to enlist, very few, if any, reached the senior ranks. Although women have participated in wars of liberation and in rebel movements as fighters, most women were co-opted as wives, prostitutes and slaves, and it were to those positions that fighting women were expected to return post-conflict. In military regimes, women's roles are more circumscribed by the state. As Mama (1997) found in Nigeria, the military can be contradictory in its approach to gender equality. This can be partly explained by the military's perception of its modern international status, on the one hand, acceding to the requirements of progressive international conventions, while on the other reinforcing its masculinist tendencies within the national space (Luckham, 1998). Military men, in particular, appear adept at manipulating the politics of scale, supported by the fact that the state is constitutive of militarized entangled gender relations at the local, regional and international levels.

As Fanon (1961) contends, violence was a fundamental component of the colonial project and a prerequisite for national liberation. Independence struggles necessitated the adoption of militaristic values, while advocating a vision of society different from the dehumanization of the colonial era. However, in the era of decolonization, this struggle for a new dispensation was complicated by the imperialists' search for African agents of modernization who would secure the mode of extraction. To this end, the departing colonial powers employed strategies that emphasised ethnicity and factionalism rather than national unity. Military support became part of the international aid budget, even though military equipment and knowledge were often directed at internal repression or genocide. As military regimes became the dominant form of government, coup leaders or 'strong men' were legitimized by the international community who saw the military as the most modernised and, therefore, progressive element in African societies (Hutchful & Bathily, 1998; Pye, 1959). In Cold War ideology, western trained military men were seen as potential allies against communism and internal social and political unrest. That the Cold War occurred at the precise historical moment that Africans seemed to be on the brink of an emancipatory future was disastrous for Africans, as the assertion of African humanity was subsumed in the quest for global security. The so-called stability of the Cold War years was not experienced in many southern and north-east African countries, subjected to proxy wars that destroyed the little material benefits of modernization that existed and deepened the processes of militarization.

Militarism, Modernity and Development

Militarism informed the dominant post-colonial, Cold War development paradigms, whether capitalist or socialist. Development, according to such thinking, occurs when societies undergo changes modelled fundamentally on the historical experience of western societies. The modernity of the West was juxtaposed with its opposition – the traditionalism of non-western others. According to Rist (1997: 9), conventional development thinking presupposes the rise of 'individualism (developing the personality of human beings)' in line with the neo-classical concept of rational economic man. Socially cohesive collectivities of African societies – extended families, clans, ethnic, religious, linguistic and economic groupings, were seen as anathema to development and had to be broken down for development to succeed. Various states, at least in the early years of independence, attempted to transform the inequity of the inherited system, but ended up reproducing inequalities and further militarization to protect the political class; ordinary Africans were envisaged as expendable.

The economic spaces that produce genocidal economics in Africa are revealed in Peter Uvin's analysis of the intersection between development aid and the genocidal state in Rwanda. Since the 1960s, African people have been at the receiving end of modernizing development projects that involve the greater penetration of state and capital into their everyday lives. Externally-funded development projects often involve the continuation of the economics of forced production which pertained during the colonial period, aided and abetted by the local elite. Uvin (1998: 226) writes that in pre-genocide Rwanda foreign aid was so important that it was 'nearly impossible or meaningless, to separate it from the socio-economic and political processes that take place domestically'. The development enterprise, with its hierarchies of power and wealth, produces and reinforces 'structures of oppression' and 'strengthens the processes of exclusion'. Its [dehumanizing and infantilizing] power ... 'directly and actively contributes to inequality and humiliation' ... and leads to violence (Uvin, ibid.: 143).

The global economic crises of the late 1970s and early 1980s, which crippled African countries, gave room to the IMF and the World Bank to impose, as part of their loan conditionalities, neo-liberal economic practices (known locally as Structural Adjustment Policies (SAPs). After being discredited in the 1990s, they were renamed Poverty Reduction and Growth Strategies (PRGS)) and claimed African ownership. Africa is the only continent that has not benefited from globalization. There is nowhere to hide the glaring statistics that illustrate the regression that has taken place in many African countries over the last 20 years of supervision by the IMF and World Bank. According to UNCTAD (2005: 26) 'The period since 1980 has been one of slower and more volatile growth, not only in comparison to dynamic developing regions but also compared to the region's own previous economic record.' Average life expectancy, as a development indicator, has fallen from 50 years in 1983 to 46 in 2003, and the adult literacy rate likewise.

From the weight of grounded evidence, it seems improbable that human well-being will be advanced through the liberation of 'individual entrepreneurial freedoms and skills' within the context of the free-market (Harvey, 2005). Moreover, Harvey (ibid.: 3) contends that 'the process of liberalization' has entailed much 'creative destruction', substituting all 'ethical beliefs' for the ethics of the market. Liberalization reinvigorated the process of 'accumulation by dispossession', as land and resource grabbing, under the policy of privatization, resulted in the displacement and subsequent impoverishment of communities. State retreat from service-provisioning created a 'protection gap' that has been filled by non-governmental organizations (NGOs) (international and local) – a situation intensified by the increasing incidence of wars. With budgets greater than most post-conflict governments, the proliferation of NGOs has led to numerous questions of accountability and, in the context of genocidal violence in Central Africa, whether humanitarian action has transcended the hierarchies of race and has slowed the pace of militarization.

The strong anti-statism of neo-liberal policies simultaneously undermined and strengthened violence. Whilst being encouraged to ensure security for capital and markets, the systemic violence, which, in some states, had been kept under control, largely though the integrity of communities, came to the fore with growing social breakdown caused by impoverishment and disease. Communities became disempowered and lost their abilities to mediate or to call on the judiciary – mob justice became popularized, wherein youths frequently lost their lives for the attempted or suspected theft of foodstuffs, a mobile phone or a shirt. Decentralization of state functions and the disintegration of state responsibilities allow for the emergence of alternative purveyors of violence whether localized as in the formation of militias and paramilitary groups or globalized as in the privatized security of mercenaries or private military companies (Leander, 2003; Musah, 2002). This trend has been reinforced with the promotion of 'military humanitarianism' – 'soldiers taking on humanitarian work' (Slim, 2003). Militarism and humanitarianism have become, essentially, two sides of the same coin, as militarism inevitably produces humanitarian crises. In such contexts, a state of peace that retains the characteristics of militarism is the inevitable outcome.

Conceptualizing Peace in the Context of Militarism

Peace is on the agenda of a multiplicity of regional, local and international, multilateral, governmental and non-governmental organizations. Since 1990 peace negotiations have taken place in Mozambique, South Africa, Angola, Sudan, DRC and Eritrea. A veritable industry of experts in conflict resolution has emerged. Much like development, the benefits and modalities of peace seem to be so well understood, that it need not be debated. Yet, even after peace agreements have been signed and new governments have been elected, most societies still seem to exist in a state popularly described as 'no peace no war', so much so that the phrase 'peace is a process' has become a mantra for policy-makers. Questions about what type of peace is being built and who should be the architects are absent from the discourse of conflict resolution experts. Such silences demand an examination of prevailing conceptualizations of 'peace' and security?

Peace is a multifaceted term possessing multiple meanings. Emmanuel Hansen, in his seminal edited volume on *African Perspectives on Peace and Development* (1987), argues that there is more than one perspective on peace, even though there is a general agreement that it is a universal *desideratam*. Realist paradigms of peace dominate. What Hansen terms the 'establishment perspective' interprets the concept of peace as the absence of war. It promotes the minimal conditions for peace; the removal, resolution or management of conflict, without addressing the social and material conditions which caused tensions and lead to conflict. This perspective is often imposed on Africa, sometimes in the form of conflict management.

The evidence from recent conflict resolution in Africa indicates that peace is formulaic and procedural. Peace negotiations take place among those who make war, between the state, leaders of political parties and rebel movements, mediated by a regional or international team. Issues of sovereignty and identity politics dominate, despite the factionalism of ethnic elites. Differences are expected to be resolved eventually through power-sharing. Agreements are signed, fighting is supposed to stop, but rarely does, a power-sharing transitional government is put in place, followed by elections and an elected government, which is somewhat tweaked in its composition in order to incorporate potential trouble-makers or spoilers. Peace, it appears, is concerned with securing the integrity of the national space, which may not necessarily result in the ending of direct violence – and certainly not gender-based violence which continues to be perpetuated even by peace-keepers (*The Times*, 2004; HRW, 2005a).

Hansen (1987: 4) advocates the adoption of an 'African perspective' on peace that links the ending of conflict with broader issues of human well-being and development to prevent further conflict. Hansen's thesis draws from Johan Galtung's theorization of peace. Galtung (1969), looking at the articulation of conflict with unequal distribution of resources, argues that there are two types of violence; 'direct violence' (fighting) and 'structural violence'; the latter explains how poverty and powerlessness constitute an indirect form of violence, which can lead to outright violence as in civil wars. 'Negative' and 'positive peace' results from the ending of direct and structural violence respectively. However, Galtung, like many peace scholars, view social justice as utopian; nevertheless, he argues for an extended concept of peace that includes not only a reduction in direct violence, but also action to fight against social injustice.

Recent experience of peace making indicate an abhorrent distaste for the kind of redistributive justice needed to sustain long-term peace. According to Duffield liberal peace involves 'reconstructing social networks, strengthening civil and representative institutions, promoting the rule of law, and security sector reform in the context of a functioning market economy.' The goal of 'liberal peace', therefore, is to enforce rapid modernization of African societies by 'transform[ing] the dysfunctional and war-affected societies that it encounters on its borders into cooperative, representative and, especially, stable entities' (Duffield, 2001: 11). This neo-liberal trajectory, with its attendant impoverishment, is applied as the natural order of things in the absence of alternative political ideologies. Hanlon (1996: xv), with reference to the neo-liberal conversion of Mozambique, contends that 'peace had not brought prosperity' to the country, which 'seems to be reverting back to its colonial past'.

Liberal peace depends on the entrenchment of neo-liberal political economic practices, which undermine state sovereignty, focusing as they do on non-state actors: the market for economic development and personal liberation, civil society and/or external ('non-territorial') actors for humanitarian and welfare intervention and multi-partyism for diffusing political tensions and mediating competition. Theoretically, multi-partyism and democratic elections should lead to greater representation and accountability but evidence suggests that, in the context of neo-liberalism, they are easily manipulated by the elite, and can lead to xenophobia and sectarian violence. Rather than, as Duffield (ibid.: 11) claims, 'liberal peace reflect[ing] a radical development agenda of social transformation', it constitutes, instead, a form of 'negative peace' that normalizes direct violence, as it does not necessarily result in the end of direct fighting and crimes against humanity. 'Liberal peace' ends up reproducing the economics and politics of the genocidal state.

Richards also questions the promotion of a 'liberal peace' in contemporary Africa, which, he argues, takes wars out of their social contexts and sees peace as being achievable through humanitarian intervention and post-conflict reconstruction. His project is to re-socialize war by 're-directing the social energies deployed in war to problem-solving ventures on a co-operative basis' (Richards, 2005: 18). I share his concern that approaches that denigrate traditional culture undermine 'respect for those hybrid aspects of the West African cultural heritage that might be of the greatest potential value in making peace' (Richards, 1996: xviii). The importance of community participation for long-term peace is indisputable. Peace must rest with the return of agency to the people affected. But the shortcomings of Richards' analysis lie with his focus, in Sierra Leone, on those aspects of traditional society – creolization, patron-client relationships and witchcraft – that can be harnessed to reproduce genocidal thinking.

Feminists argue that prevailing conceptualizations of peace essentially see it as a return to the status quo. Enloe (1993) claims that so long as security continues to be constructed in military terms, then peace will not change the nature of violence in the society. This is well illustrated by the current approach to de-militarization in the region. Demilitarization is viewed as a component of the peace process. International agencies have coined the acronym DDR (Disarmament, Demobilization and Reintegration) to describe the aid programmes dealing specifically with 'security sector reform'. Such programmes focus on the disarmament of combatants, the destruction of arms, the formation of an integrated national army, the payment and retraining of surplus military personnel and their reintegration into society. DDR appears to reward militarism and has had limited success because the financial inducements have been small. Rather than the state re-establishing its monopoly on violence, DDR under neo-liberalism seems to spawn more privatized and atomized forms of militarism, evidenced by the movement of ex-combatants into private security firms, vigilante groups and armed violence (Cock, 2004).

This experience reflects Enloe's (2002) claim that militarization can still proceed well after the ceasefire agreement has been reached, creating a militarized political culture, in which security is viewed only in terms of militarized security. And, as Peterson notes, in a state system:

> in which direct violence is the ultimate arbiter of social conflict(s), peace can only be 'negative peace' as violence can only be regulated but not transcended; justice, and associated constructions of peace and security, can only be established by direct violence, as domination, or by indirect violence, through enforcing abstract, universalist contractual claims. (Peterson, 1992: 48)

Agencies involved in post-conflict reconstruction present demilitarization as a developmental as opposed to a political problem. Western governments, such as France and the USA, are now determining the form of militarized security that is appropriate for Africa though the creation of regional peace-keeping forces and military deployments in the 'war on terror'.[3] These programmes provide regional states with opportunities for strengthening their military capacity to deal with internal opposition (Keenan, 2004; Omach, 2000). Enloe (1993) rightly states that it takes years to de-militarize a society. For emancipatory feminists, true demilitarization necessitates more far-reaching social transformation. Many societies, particularly in Africa, have been socialized to accept structural insecurities as part of everyday life. Often what Cock (2004) terms 'consumerist' or 'banal' militarism have become so entrenched in the society that change is near impossible under conditions of globalization.[4]

---

[3] I am referring to the French-led *Renforcement des Capacités Africaines de Maintien de la Paix* (RECAMP) and the American-initiated African Crisis Response Initiative (ACRI, 1997–2001) and African Contingency Operations Training and Assistance (ACOTA, 2002–) and the Pan-Sahelian Initiative (PSI) now renamed the Trans-Saharan Counter-Terrorism Initiative (TSCTI).

[4] Cock (2004) refers to cultural goods that reflect militarization: clothing, films, etc.

Effective de-militarization requires a national debate that addresses questions such as what national security, what role for the security apparatus, and what social order? Without such fundamental debates preceding or occurring concurrently with the formulation of development goals, militarism will remain entrenched in the socio-political life of a society.

Engendering the Peace Problematic

The issues of gender, humanity and peace are complex. While there is an urgent need for peace negotiations to address gender-based violence and to allow the greater participation of women at the negotiating table, there is concern among emancipatory feminist about the essentialist association of women with peace and its deployment to further entrench neo-liberal values. Women, they argue, have no intrinsic capacity for peace and have been active fighters or *génocidaires* (African Rights, 1995). Furthermore, not all women are disadvantaged by war, some gain considerable freedom and independence, which evidence show, they lose once patriarchal tendencies are reasserted under conditions of militarized peace. The deployment of a language which equates women universally with peace could rebound on campaigners, if it involves the incorporation of elite women whose allegiance and class interests rest with the patriarchal state (Amadiume, 2000a). The Rwandan genocide of 1994 exposed the essentialist argument that women are naturally non-violent with the uncovering of women as perpetrators of genocide (African Rights, 1995). For Jones (2002), the important consequence of this is the need to unearth the range of policy and cultural mechanisms that allow or inhibit women's genocidal tendencies. Claims of women's affinity with peace should be viewed with caution, especially if unaccompanied by a conceptualizing framework that questions the interconnections of women's wider role in society.

Until very recently there was a silence surrounding sexual violence, which was not even considered a war crime in international law. Feminists have challenged the representation of mass rape of women as part of the spoils of war or a 'natural' act for testosterone-powered men. As a consequence of the horrors of the sexual violence that took place during the Rwandan genocide, pressure on international organizations to recognize such violence in international law and to establish protection for women led the UN Security Council to pass Resolution 1325 in 2000, which calls on member states to take:

> Measures to ensure women's equal participation and full involvement in all efforts for the maintenance and promotion of peace and security [and] to incorporate a gender perspective in peacekeeping operations and greater representation of women in national, regional and international institutions. (Para. 5 & 8)[5]

---

[5] UNSC Resolution 1325 (2000) was adopted by the Security Council at its 4213th meeting on 31 October 2000.

Despite the transformatory potential of such a focus, we should not be afraid of interrogating women's organizations and well as recent efforts of global institutions to implement Resolution 1325. Kandiyoti (2004), for example, asks international women's movements to be cautious about expecting successful outcomes of donor, UN and NGO competition in the 'gender market' in post-conflict Afghanistan. The political settlement, she argues, while conceding to international instruments on equality, may take a different form on the ground, where strong patriarchal and Islamic laws oppose gender equality. A non-contextual technocratic approach, she writes, can 'inadvertently disempowers the constituencies that it seeks to support' (Kandiyoti, 2004: 136).

In Africa, regional and international organizations such as OAU/AU, UNESCO and UNIFEM have spearheaded the move to implement UN Resolution 1325. African women's peace activism was given institutional support when in 1998 the OAU and the ECA launched jointly the African Women's Committee on Peace and Development. The Pan-African Women's Conference on a Culture of Peace held in Zanzibar in May 1999 produced the 'Zanzibar Declaration on Women and a Culture of Peace' and launched the 'Pan-African Women's Movement for Peace'. African women's organizations appear to have structured their campaign, whether strategically or not, around women-centred international and regional legislations and have articulated a normative viewpoint that 'naturalizes' women's concerns with peace.

There is no doubt that because political power is essentially masculine and political violence is normally planned and instigated by men with little thought of the impacts on civilian life, women suffer disproportionately from the violence; many are brutally raped and exposed to diseases, and/or forcibly co-opted into the war-machine as soldiers, 'bush' wives and porters. This picture concurs with Elias's description of women in a militarised society:

> Women were generally regarded by these men as inferior beings. There are enough of them available. They serve to gratify desires to their simplest form. Women are given to men 'for his necessity and delectation' ... What they sought from women is physical pleasure; apart from this; 'there is scarcely a man with the patience to endure a wife'. (Elias, 1982: 82)

A feminist methodology enables us to problematize the concept of peace and ask questions that are contextual: What concepts of war and peace are being deployed in peace negotiations and post-conflict peace-building? What do 'peace' and 'democracy' mean in the context of a genocidal state and under conditions of genocidal economics with their structural insecurities? Marshall (2000: 9) rightly claims that a feminist conceptualization of peace requires a 'redefinition of what constitute politics and identification of alternative arenas and methods of conducting politics'.

Interrogating peace will lead to a problematization of hegemonic understandings of concepts such as security, identity, ethnicity and nationality and regional citizenship. According to Peterson (1999) definitions of citizenship are closely linked to political identity and to who counts. Women's struggle for political participation indicates the degree to which political identity is linked to masculinity. But in Africa, as historically in the West, political identity was associated with the modern state blocking avenues for women's participation, as the physical and ideological separation of the public and private spheres led to the redefinition of 'women's work' as that which is confined to the domestic space – caring, reproductive activities and so on. The redefinition of the concept of African 'women' with modernity and imperialism has been explored by Amadiume (1997) and Oyewumi (c. 1997) amongst others. To them the domestication of African women was ideologically link to the strengthening of patriarchy and resulted in their confinement to the private sphere and their exclusion from the very public politics of the state. Any approach which argues for a mode of politics and a wider political community should tackle women's subordination in these inter- secting domains of power.

These are issues being debated by women in the region, especially those campaigning for member state ratification of the African Union's Protocol to the African Charter on Human and Peoples' Rights on the Rights of Women.[6] Peace and security are among the bundle of rights that the protocol seeks to protect and promote. Article 10 (1) states, 'all women have the right to a peaceful existence and the right to participate in the promotion and maintenance of peace'. Supporters, such as Mary Wandia of the UN agency, FEMNET, argue that international and regional legislation on human rights deal only with the realm of the public, leaving the private to be dealt with by customary law and practices. In this way, cultural relativism is being used to prevent action against discrimination and violence towards women that predominantly occur in the private realm. As Wandia (2004: 2) asserts 'this distinction between the private and the public sphere is detrimental to women'.

Conclusion

Conceptualizing warfare in Africa narrowly as either 'natural' to uncivi- lized identity-riddled societies or as the consequence of 'greed' limits our capacity to institute the sorts of transformations needed to assert African humanity and its right to a peaceful existence. Genocidal violence in Africa is shown to be linked to the de-humanizing tendencies inherent in the African experience of modernity and capitalism. Militarism or the culture of state-centred and state-sponsored violence has become embedded within many societies, where, historically, the modern state has institutionalized discrimination through racial, ethnic and gendered hierarchies.

The challenge for concerned people is how to end genocide; to move beyond the categorizations of racialized and ethnicized bodies; to

---

[6] The Protocol to the African Charter on Human and Peoples' Rights on the Rights of Women was adopted by the second summit of the African Union on 11 July 2003 in Maputo, Mozambique, but it was not until October 2005 that it was ratified by the 15th member which allowed it to come into force on 25 November 2005.

recognize our common humanity and validate African lives. The conventional militarist approach to peace is inherently disempowering and promotes masculinized cultures of violence rather than cultures of peace. Liberal institutions attempt to grapple with this issue by framing their actions within the generalized and essentially de-politicized concepts of human security and human rights. In seeking to reconstruct a just society without politics, liberal organisations have been forced to go back to the pre-colonial past to revive mechanisms for peace such as the *Bashingantahe* and the *Gacaca,* traditional collective organisations that recognised the humanity of the people, and circumscribed the rights of the individual within the society. While we should applaud the recognition of value in African traditional society, one should be cautious of not reifying pre-modern injustices that may be embedded in these institutions (Nindorera, c. 2000).

Engendering the peace problematic will challenge the epistemological and ontological basis by which violence and peace are analysed in Africa and is likely to open up hopeful possibilities in the search for spaces of peace. Feminists have to be at the forefront of efforts to mainstreaming gender-based violence in peace negotiations in order for the prevailing practices of masculinity and femininity to be interrogated. This analysis must be spearheaded by local women and men, especially those with knowledge of local historical and cultural dynamics.

Peace, as conceptualized in current conflict resolution models, equates to violence by other means. Failing to take account of the historical and contemporary manifestations of violence and its relationship with the state has enabled a perpetuation of the very factors that lead to genocidal violence. Geo-politics and economic globalization are central to how the peace-makers, predominantly international institutions and western and some regional governments define peace in Africa; the outcome of which is not necessarily beneficial for Africans. This means a thorough examination of the motives behind extra-continental regional peace-building and peace-keeping initiatives. Hansen (1987: 6) and his co-contributors warned against succumbing to imposed European and American concept of peace that sees peace during the Cold War as 'a balance of terror' and, after September 11, 2001, as maintaining 'a war on terror'. In both cases, the 'peace of the world is based on fear and mutual suspicion instead of mutual trust and cooperation'. Their argument, almost two decades ago, that Africans should articulate and make 'practical a peace problematic' other than the one defined by western states and trans-national corporations is still relevant today.

3

The Colonial State   & the Ethnicization
    & Masculinization
    of Political Space

Introduction

This chapter examines the processes that led to the emergence of a genocidal state in Burundi through the introduction of genocidal thinking,
institutions, politics and economics. The birth of the modern state was
not contingent on the internal struggles of the Barundi people, but was
primarily the consequence of European colonial domination, the ideological foundation of which was unrestrained militarism, racism and
violent masculinity. This chapter examines the nature of the reproduction of the Burundi state during the pre-colonial and, especially the
colonial period (1886–1962). Here I focus on the hierarchies of domination, the characterization and politicization of Hutu and Tutsi as oppositional identities; the education system and its use in the reproduction
of these identities; the reconfiguration of gender and masculinity in a
racialized and ethnicized society; the restructuring of political and
economic power and the legitimization of violence against the people,
through the use of the military and a racist ideation system.

A Brief Note on the Politics of History

In popular reports, the modern Burundi state is almost synonymous with
genocidal violence. As with Rwanda, warfare is described simply as the
outcome of age-old 'ethnic hatred' between the Hutus and Tutsis. A pre-
colonial history of discrimination and a colonial history of manipulation
are normally invoked to give credence to the violence. As any explanation of contemporary violence must explore the significance of
ethnicity in Burundi's history, caution must be exercised when considering the historical records, especially in its written form, for two
reasons. First, its conflation with that of Rwanda; even though both countries shared similarities in ethnic composition and experience of colonial
rule, their different pre-colonial history and social hierarchies have
affected the specific character and scale of the violence. Second, the
sometimes racial and cultural biases in the historical accounts of
European and indigenous ethnographers have led to challenges to their
claim to authority. Post-colonial texts by Burundian scholars often

received mixed international reception in the academy; those by Emile Mworoha, Joseph Gahama and Raphael Ntibazonkiza among others, are viewed by some western scholars as less authoritative because of the authors' ethnic or political association, while those produced by outsiders are given greater recognition. It is in this vein that Depelchin exhorts the researcher of African history to be conscious of the enduring silences of analyses of situations dominated by colonial rule:

> that generated by sheer terror, repression, oppression, exploitation, in short by state power (and its various combination resting on gender, class, race, religion), and ... the silences which are later reproduced by the social scientists and, among them, historians. (Depelchin, 2004: 9–10)

The contested nature of popular history led signatories to the Burundi peace agreement to call for a clarification of:

> the entire history of Burundi, going as far back as possible in order to inform Burundi about their past. The purpose of this clarification shall be to rewrite Burundi's history, so that all Burundians can interpret it in the same way. (Protocol 1, Article 8 (c), Arusha Peace and Reconciliation Agreement for Burundi, 2000: 22)

For the Burundians, an agreed history, derived from sifting through the smokescreen of colonial and post-colonial ethnic reductionism, could give them back their humanity and thus be emancipatory. As Depelchin claims, 'knowledge which might make people more reflective ... is silenced' as 'knowing a history that should be known is emancipatory' (2004: 9). Historical memory of plurality and conviviality in societal organization has been lost; principles of *Ibanga* (discretion and sense of responsibility), *Ubupfasoni* (respect for others and oneself) and *Ubuntu* (humanism) have been replaced by dehumanization and othering through the propagation of mythico-history and iterations of genocide.[1]

In recent years, scholarly interpretations of genocidal violence in Burundi have become more nuanced, but the focus on ethnicity remains paramount (Chretien, 1996; Greenland, 1976 & 1980; Lemarchand, 1970, 1977 & 1994a; Lemarchand and Martin, 1974; Prunier, 1994; Weinstein, 1972 & 1974; Weinstein & Schrire, 1976). Any study of Burundi's history has to give recognition to the pioneering and thoroughness of Rene Lemarchand's historical work on the modern Burundi state. Studies of the Rwandan genocide by Mamdani (2001), Newbury (1998) and Prunier (1995) have helped to provide a starting point from which to consider the evolution of genocidal violence in Burundi.

Lemarchand (1998) interprets the conflicts of the 1990s as arising from the history of and the spectre of genocide in both Rwanda and Burundi. Ethnic similarities with Rwanda have led many commentators to focus on the adverse influence of the Rwandan conflicts and genocide on inter-

---

[1] Principles referred to in Protocol 1 (Article 7, 26) of the Arusha Peace and Reconciliation Agreement for Burundi.

ethnic relationships in Burundi. Lemarchand (1977: 5) blames the 'demonstration effect' of the 1959 Rwandan revolution on certain Hutu elites, and elaborates this idea further when he later argues that 'genocide is the central issue that underlies civil strife in Burundi and Rwanda.' For him, memories of genocide with impunity fuels iterations of genocide. I partly agree with him, but he limits his contextualization of genocide to the internal dynamics of the region. Lemarchand (1998) refers to the fear generated by the 1972 and 1994 genocides and failure of either group to accept blame. The picture painted by him is one of a people bound to act out a role prescribed by their ethnic identity. In relation to Burundi, he states:

> What is being remembered by many Hutu is an apocalypse that has forever altered their perceptions of the Tutsi, now seen as the historic incarnation of evil; what many Tutsi have forgotten, or refuse to acknowledge, is that they, and not the Hutu, were the first to use genocide in order to consolidate their hold on the state. (Lemarchand 1998: 7)

This is to accept that Hutus and Tutsis constitute undifferentiated masses, ruled by tribal hatred of the primordial type. Imagining the people purely as ethnic beings submitting to some kind of irrational logic not only absolves the perpetrators, but also prevents the viewer from noticing people's capacity for forgiveness and to exercise respect and responsibility even after being exposed to extreme violence and dehumanization. Newbury (1998) makes reference to how, in April 1994, the collective will of the Hutu and Tutsi residents of Butare combined to thwart genocide and prevented killings for the first two weeks of the genocide. I have also been told of cases where DRC-based Hutu rebels used their Tutsi contacts to send money to their families. Furthermore, if communities and ethnic groups were so polarized, how would one account for the high degree, almost 25 per cent in Rwanda, of the population having both heritages! (Newbury, ibid.).

Evidence on the ground suggests the need for a more nuanced understanding of ethnicity. Constructions of the violence as 'civil' or 'ethnic' conflict divorce it from its political and economic context. As in the Rwandan genocide of 1994, Burundi politicians have articulated internationally the language of genocide as a consequence of African primitivism in order to deflect scrutiny of government repression. Concentration on the problem of ethnicity has helped to deflect serious analysis of the specific character of the modern Burundi state both in the colonial and post-colonial era, and the extent to which the reproduction of the political class has been progressively identified with ethnic identity. Successive Tutsi-dominated Burundi regimes have attempted to avoid culpability by blaming the colonial state for ethnicizing communities.

Mamdani (2001: 23), in trying to uncover the cause of the Rwandan genocide, focuses on the construction of Hutu and Tutsi as racial categories and political identities under the tutelage of Belgian colonialism. He argues that what is important is to consider the dynamics by which political identities become polarized. To do so, 'we need to look at polarized identities at the end point of a historical dynamic; rather than positing them at its starting point.' Mamdani's historical approach is useful in helping to construct a genealogy of Burundian and Rwandan ethnic identities. What he does not do is to interrogate the gendered relations, militarism and masculinity embedded in these identities.

The Pre-Colonial Period

The hierarchical states of Rwanda and Burundi evolved a particular form of politics that was peculiar to the intralacustrine region. Cheikh Anta Diop (1991: 132) named his typology of the minority-dominated genocidal state, the 'Tutsi type of state'. Such state forms had the potential for genocide; domination was not always contingent on the deployment of military power but on the absolute separation of the rulers from the ruled through carefully constructed social hierarchies.

Burundi's pre-colonial history is highly contested with respect to peopling of the territory and the relationship between the different social groups and the nature of governance. As this history was written by Europeans and Tutsis, it is difficult to obtain an objective picture of the relationship to power of the different groups. Both European and indigenous historians refashioned the past to fit the cultural precepts of the dominant European culture, even if unintentionally. One of the key texts focusing on ethnic discrimination in pre-colonial Rwandan society, Jacques Maquet's *The Premise of Inequality* (1961), was produced while the two countries were in the throes of a bitter national liberation struggle, suffused with ethnic conflict.

Similarly, successful Tutsi-dominated post-colonial regimes' rejection of the reality of ethnicity in Burundi society meant that those who advocated a non-ethnicized pre-colonial culture were often accused of supporting Tutsi hegemony. At the same time, Hutus preferred to reinforce the mythical history of the groups as constructed by the colonials, as it gave international legitimacy to their claim of Tutsi oppression and their struggle for self-determination. The limitations of oral history of over several centuries make reconstructing the past problematic and a truly political project. In the light of iterations of genocide, historians of Rwanda have sought to rewrite that country's pre-colonial history in an attempt to find parallels in the pre-colonial past (Vansina, 2004). This may be a noble effort to provide clarity, but it remains a history re-examined through the lens of the victors. Even if political instability and genocidal tendencies existed in states of the distant past, they have been overlaid or subsumed by the political, ideological and material conditions of European imperialism and colonial rule. Accounts that paint a less conflictual picture of the African past, disparagingly labelled 'merrie Africa', are often dismissed as romanticized. Could Africans not have developed a form of governance that promoted peace and *ubuntu* even in the midst of having to defend their territory?

Hierarchy and Governance
The kingdom of Burundi was a hierarchical society, with a complex web of social relationships. The monarch (*mwami*) did not have absolute

political power; it was shared with the noble families of royal descent (*Baganwa*), who as deputies administered the provinces. The *banyama-banga* (keepers of state secrets) organized the rituals and festivals to ensure communal peace and prosperity. Lower down the administrative hierarchy were three groups of administrators charged with mediation and ensuring social stability within the communities; the deputies (*Vyariho*), arbitrators (*Bashingantahe*) and administrative assistants (*Bakozi d'abakuru*). At the bottom were the peasants (*Banyagihugu*) (Mworoha, 1977).

Burundi society was further divided into some 220 clans (*umuryango*). Clans or extended lineages operated at two levels; linked firstly through the paternal grand-father (*abavindimwe*) and secondly through the maternal grand-father or paternal aunt (*incuti*) (ibid.). The first, according to Mworoha (ibid.: 38), formed 'a fundamental social unity. It is represented by a sort of spokesperson who is chosen according to his age and abilities and who stands in for him with the political authority.' The second set of clan links is associated with maintaining group solidarity by providing gifts and participating in family reunions. Clans did not occupy a specific geographical area, but they could be distinguished by the common name of an ancestor – often derived from ancient myths, known ancestors or regions of origin. For Rutake and Gahama (1998: 82) clans remain the 'basic elements of social organisation in Burundi', and on 'various occasions Barundi identify themselves not in terms of their "ethnic" belonging but indeed on the basis of their clans'. Clans remain understudied in Burundi's history, yet, as shown in Chapter 4, they have played a major role in politics and political violence.

The elite *Baganwa* families were divided into competing clans, originating from earlier kings; of the dominant clans, the *Batare* stem from *Mwami* Ntare II Rugaamba (1795–1852) and the *Bezi* from *Mwami* Mwezi II Gisabo (c.1852–1908). Regional distinctions were also made between the *Tutsi-Banyabururi* (southerners) and the *Tutsi-Banyaruguru* (countrywide), who were, in turn, associated with the *Bezi* and the *Batare* respectively. Other forms of geographically-based collective identity were and remain significant; attachment to locality (*colline*), for example.

The use of the terms Tutsi and Hutu seems to have been associated with occupational specialization and particularly wealth, measured partly by the ownership of cattle. Those with large herds (Tutsi) occupied a higher social status than the cultivators (Hutu), and the hunters and gatherers (Twa). Not all cattle owners were Tutsi; the Hima (later classified among the *petit*-Tutsi), for example, were of lower status to the Tutsi, and some Hutus owned cattle. The Twas were differentiated between the sedentarized and the hunters and gatherers and were largely ostracised by the other groups. With the exception of the *Baganwa*, clan membership traversed these occupational categories. Occupational hierarchies were common to other societies in the intralacustrine zone of the Great Lakes, although the rigidity of the social hierarchy and degree to which the state was centralized varied from one kingdom to another.

It was the existence of a clientelist system (*ubugabire*), based on the unequal distribution of cattle and wealth between the patrons (Tutsis) and the clients (Hutus), which seems to have partly provided the basis for later ethnic classification.[2] However, *ubugabire* clientage was not confined to Hutus, as Himas also entered patron-client relationships, and in some areas, particularly those with small Tutsi populations, wealthy Hutus joined the elite group and had clients of their own (Trouwborst, 1965). Though emphasis is often given to *ubugabire* as the example of inequality in pre-colonial Burundi society, the Arusha Peace and Reconciliation Agreement (2000) identified a number of other pre-colonial practices that, 'depending on the circumstances, constitute sources of injustice and frustration both among Bahutu and the Batutsi and among the Batwa' (Article 1, 4: 15). They included *ubugeregewa* (bonded serf), *ukunena* (discrimination in the sharing of food and drinks) and *gutanga ikimazi-muntu* (punishment by human sacrifice). The existence of these practices suggests that no group was necessarily singled out for injustices, which were common to all levels in the hierarchical system. Patron-client relationships acted as glue cementing different social strata of the society together and ensuring that elite rule was rarely threatened from below.

What is contested among scholars is the origin of these social categories and the degree of oppression and social mobility between them. Newbury (1998: 83) interpreted Hutu and Tutsi as socially produced categories, that were dynamic and that changed over time and with locale. He asserts, 'there is not a single coherent "Tutsi history" or "Tutsi culture, just as there is no single "Hutu history" or "Hutu culture"...'. Mamdani (2001) also recognized the lack of common cultural community within the respective ethnic groups. While Lemarchand maintains that Burundi's past was 'relatively free of racial tensions [because] the degrees of social distance within the Tutsi stratum were at times far more perceptible than between Tutsi and Hutu' (1970: 24). He quotes one prominent *Ganwa*, as saying, in 1957, 'in Burundi social rank was determined by individual merit, regardless of race, except for the Twa' (ibid.: 44).

There is also no evidence to support the portrayal by Hutu intellectuals and political parties of conditions of slavery-like oppression during the pre-colonial period. Concepts of superiority and seniority (*ubukuru*) were powerful forms of social control and pervaded all relationships, not unlike the divine right of European kings or the mythical 'blue blood' of the British aristocracy. *Ubgenge* (intelligence, cunning), a criterion for success, was normally attributed to superiors and inferiors alike. The stereotype of the Tutsis as being skilled in matters of statecraft became more prevalent during the colonial period.

Lemarchand (1994a) and Mamdani (2001) acknowledge the possibilities of status change by referring to the phenomenon of *ukwihutura* - upward mobility from Hutu to Tutsi, and *gutahira,* downward mobility from *Baganwa* to Tutsi, but argue that there was no 'social demotion' from Tutsi to Hutu. On the other hand, Newbury (1998: 84) refers to

---

[2] The client (*garagu*) would seek the patronage of the lord (*shebuga*), who would bestow him cattle, over which the client had usufruct rights, and was then expected to repay the lord in the form of tribute labour and agricultural dues. Cattle were the main form of wealth used in marriage transactions. The clientelist system is described for Rwanda in Maquet (1961) and for Burundi in Lemarchand (1970).

downward mobility of Tutsi who had 'endured hard over several generations and could be considered "Hutu".' Similarly Berger (1981) mentions the gradual absorption of poor pastoralists into the agricultural group. Other scholars, such as Mworoha (1977) and Chrétien (1993), argue that Hutu and Tutsi were widely incorporated into the administrative structure of the state. Chrétien (1993: 319) notes, 'at the end of the nineteenth century, a rise in Tutsi influence is perceptible, but the Hutus are not "serfs". All subjects are in debt to influential people both Hutu and Tutsi, there are rich and poor people in both camps.'

The nature of governance was critical to stability; the monarch was a symbol of national unity, with the Crown acting as a nexus for the various collectives.[3] Evidence of internal hostilities refers only to political rivalry between the *Baganwa* clans, from among whom the monarch was chosen. The monarch mediated between the rival clans and both Tutsi and Hutu functionaries were active at court and had administrative positions. The *Bashingantahe* (local judiciary) in their role as community mediators cemented social contracts and ensured stability. The *Bashingantahe* were also an institution to constrain the excesses of masculinity and violence. The elites controlled the state, but were not exclusively of one ethnic group or clan. Burundi scholars, Rutake & Gahama (1998: 83), write, 'The pre-colonial state in Burundi was based on the characteristics of a nation. It was composed of a human grouping in which individuals were united with one another through material and spiritual relations and saw themselves as different from individuals of other national grouping.' Evidence from other parts of the continent suggests the use of strategies of social cohesion by the ruling elite, even in highly differentiated and militaristic societies (Mustapha, 1999; Nnoli, 1998). There seems to be some plausibility in Nnoli's assertion that states in the pre-colonial period exhibited 'strong tendencies towards the integration and inclusion of ethnic groups with the goal of enhancing production and commerce' (1998: 23).

Social cohesion, however, did not deter the state from using violence both in respect to expansionist projects and in retaining loyalty among its subjects; practices such as *ukunyaga* (dispossession), *ukwangaza* (banishment) and *uguhonya* (wiping out of a whole family) were common. From the late 1860s to the early colonial period, violent conflicts took place between rival royal dynasties in their struggle for territorial gain. As the *mwami* was far from despotic, the *Baganwa* had sufficient latitude to establish relatively autonomous chiefdoms. The fact that the *Baganwa* and the *mwami* could obtain support from both Hutu and Tutsi suggests less unity among the ruling elite and the diffusion of political power (Lemarchand, 1970). The stability of the state appears then to have been predicated on rivalry among factions of the elite and the absence of state monopoly of power and organized violence. Certainly, the military was sufficiently weak for the *mwami* to look continually to his subjects for the manpower to deal with rebellious *Baganwa*.

In summary, to use current ethnic categories to explain social relations in pre-colonial Burundi society would be to simplify a very rich and

---

[3] For further details of the social structure of pre-colonial Burundi see Lemarchand (1977 & 1970), Chapters 1 & 10 and Gahama (1983).

complex social-political situation. An important question is why one particular form of social identification in pre-colonial society has become such a central component of social organization in colonial and post-colonial Burundi polity, and another is the question of what has happened to other forms of identity.

Colonial Domination (1897–1962)

Colonial conquest ushered in the modern state in Burundi. Until its independence in 1962, Burundi was part of the German colony of Ruanda-Urundi (1897–1916) and then under the trusteeship of Belgium (1916–1962). The impact of colonialism on the society was more far-reaching and disruptive than is suggested by historical interpretations that emphasize continuity. Colonial conquest of the region was bloody. In their effort to gain control of the territory, the Germans found ready allies among the *Batare* who were estranged from the *Bezi* king – *Mwezi* Gisabo. The king's initial resistance to German rule earned the Crown great popularity with the masses, which it was able to manipulate towards the end of the colonial period. The Germans later recognized the legitimacy of the Crown and switched their support to the *Bezi*, thus enabling Gisabo to consolidate his rule over the territory.

Pacification of rebellious chiefs was carried out with the use of extreme violence. Lemarchand (1970: 52/23) notes that 'in October 1905 von Grawert penetrated [chief] Kilima's fiefdom [in the north-west] and destroyed every village in his path.' Lemarchand presents German military intervention as unavoidable, if only to prevent the territory deteriorating into complete chaos. Belgian rule began with the military defeat of the Germans in the First World War and was modelled on the Congo; a place where the natives were exposed to violence of genocidal proportions (Hochschild, 1998). In *The Wretched of the Earth*, Fanon (1961: 29) discusses the pervasiveness of violence in the colonial world. The colonizer, he proposes, claims to be 'an upholder of peace, yet he is a bringer of violence into the home and the mind of the native'. Indeed, security in the colonial space, 'lay only in the accumulation of power' (Ake, 1996: 3). Furthermore, the destruction foreign rule had on the structures that regulated society and ensured peace and stability in the territories is not often acknowledged. Ranger (1996: 275) notes that 'physical violence was accompanied by cultural violence'. He comments:

> Many historians have described how under colonialism bounded ethnicities replaced previously much more fluid, multicultural and multilinguistic networks of interaction and identity. But we have perhaps stressed too much the intellectual processes which underlay the production of ethnic units – the dialectic between colonial inventors and African imaginers – and not enough the great disruption involved in drastically narrowing down the African religious, social and economic world while at the same time enlarging the administrative and political. (Ranger, 1996: 274)

In Burundi, the destruction and insecurity that colonialism brought by reorganizing society for the purposes of administration and production is often reduced, in a singular way, to its greatest accomplishment, the social construction of ethnicity.

The Social Construction of Ethnicity

Ethnic consciousness derived from assumptions of racial and moral differences can be traced back to the colonial period. Mafege (1971: 253) argues, 'if tribalism is thought of as peculiarly African, then the ideology itself is particularly European in origin'. Europeans imagined and thought it administratively advantageous for 'uncivilized' people to live in small bounded communities called 'tribes'. Tribal people shared a common culture and adhered to pre-modern practices that had to be transformed through the civilizing and modernizing process. African collaborators played a critical role in the construction of tribes. As Ranger (1993) points out, Europeans may have constructed the shell of ethnic groups, but they were filled by Africans reimagining traditions in the cultural image of the conquering power.

The Germans and later the Belgians entered Burundi with entrenched ideological preconceptions of racial and class superiority which they used to interpret the sophisticated hierarchical political and economic structures of the society. A considerable body of anthropological and historical literature became preoccupied with the exotic – the ethnic dimensions of the social hierarchy and with patron-client relationships (d'Hertefelt, 1971; Lemarchand, 1970; Trouwborst, 1965).

Burundi society came to be seen through the lens of a 'naturalized' ethnicity. Its complex pre-colonial social groupings were ascribed genetic interpretation. The Tutsi, whose physical appearance resembled North-East Africans, were considered to belong to a different racial group, one that migrated southward and conquered the indigenous peoples. Their perceived Caucasian heritage marked them out as genetically superior to the Bantu-looking Hutu cultivators, and the pygmoid Twa hunters and gatherers.

What was termed the 'hamitic hypothesis' was used to justify European support for the Tutsi as natural leaders under the policy of indirect rule.[4] As with the Europeans, the governing race had to come from outside (Fanon, 1961). Therefore, 'the Belgian government is convinced that it must continue to maintain and consolidate the traditional position of the Tutsi governing class because of its great qualities, its undeniable intellectual superiority, and its potential to lead' (Official proclamation of 1938, quoted in De Heusch 1964: 98).

Mamdani's conceptualization of Hutu, Tutsi and Twa as political identities in Rwanda is also relevant in the context of Burundi. These identities were not based on cultural communities or kinship and were given meaning only in relation to the state; its discriminatory institutions

---

[4] The 'Hamitic hypothesis' is racist in content. Early Europeans in Africa, believed that most of the rulers in Bantu Africa, originated from North Africa, were Hamites, not negroid, and therefore superior. See Sanders (1969) for a more thorough discussion of the role of the 'hypothesis' in African history.

helped to determine who was a Tutsi and who a Hutu. 'Legal enforcement', Mamdani (2001: 22) notes, 'makes these identities the basis of participation in state-organised institutional and political life'. Economic criterion – wealth and cattle – were used to further identify and enlarge the social category Tutsi. These ethnic identities were crystallised in the 1931 census and the possession of identity cards legally marked out those whose identity was not physically apparent.

For Mamdani (2001), though political identities may be devoid of a common cultural community, they testify to a common project for the future. Such identities become problematic when they become polarised; differences are binary and hybrids cannot be tolerated; you are either one or the other. Colonial society with its policy of indirect rule was divided first by race and then by ethnicity. The non-indigenous had a different set of rights from the indigenous who were fractured into a plurality of ethnic groupings, each governed by a separate set of customary laws.

Re-categorized as non-natives, Tutsis had privileges that were denied the native Hutus. As the subject race, Tutsis had access to the resources of the state: tracts of land, political office and education. Though elevated above the native, they were still lower down the racial hierarchy from the master, and identified with the master as well as agitated against him. Demarcated as local elites in the context of a modern state founded on the principles of 'accumulation by dispossession', the Tutsi asserted their ethnic differences as a tool to ensure access to the resources of the new dispensation. According to Linden, ethnicity became the dominant ideology of the colonial period, 'in reality what had once been a fluid ethnic boundary between two socio-economic groups hardened under Belgian rule into an unchangeable barrier between Hutu and Tutsi defining access to the political class' (Linden, 1977: 4). Colonial policies – political, education and religious – combined to produce rigid ethnic boundaries, and enabled the consolidation of Tutsi power over other groups.

Christianity, Education and the Reproduction of Genocidal Institutions
Christianity, the cultural arm of western imperialism, played a critical role in the modernizing process. Culturally, the introduction of Christianity had two main impacts. First, it attempted to replace the prevailing socio-political order that regulated economy and society with biblical teachings and foreign domination. Missionaries, along with the colonial administrators, zealously suppressed traditional belief systems. According to Albert (1971, footnote 5: 215), 'the cult of Kiranga, the ancestor cult and every other aspect of traditional religion and belief [were] legally suppressed.' Mworoha (1977) dates the disappearance of the *Banyamabanga* (men of secrets) in the 1920s to the time when their ritualistic role in the national fete of the blessing of the sorghum (*muganuro*) was taken over by the missionaries. The *banyamabanga* held responsibilities for state secrets, for performing the rites and rituals at the funeral of royals and, through the cult of *kiranga,* ensured the society was protected in times of natural catastrophes such as famine or drought. A major metaphysical element in Burundi society disappeared, as their role was incompatible with that of the colonial state and Christianity (Mworoha, 1977). Missionaries saw African religious beliefs as mumbo-

jumbo, and proceeded to destroy them, leaving a gap that was only partially filled by Christianity. Lemarchand (1970: 70) also notes that Christianity meant the 'desacralization of the *Mwami*-ship, and the relegation of the office-holder to a subordinate position'. The adoption of Christianity by young chiefs was important in the struggle for power between rival *Baganwa* clans, as the new religion undermined the power of the *Mwami* and enhanced the chiefs' position with the colonials.

Second, the Church instilled modern values and European ideas about African society through the western education system. Greenland (1980) recalls the affirmation of one colonial official:

> Only the Catholic Christian religion, based on authority, can be capable of changing native mentality, of giving our blacks a clear and intimate awareness of their duty of inspiring in them respect for authority and a spirit of loyalty towards Belgium. (Louis Franck, 1930, *Le Congo Belge*, Bruxelles: *La Renaissance du Livre*, 1: 311)

The role of the church mission in augmenting 'ethnic' differentiation has been well documented for Rwanda by Ian Linden (1977), and Greenland (1976 & 1980) and Verme (1994) for Burundi. The first christian mission in Burundi was established among the pastoral Hima, in the southern region, away from the *mwami*'s capital at Gitega in the centre of the country. After the 1930s the Catholic Church, in compliance with the state, actively encouraged the conversion of Tutsi nobles to the Christian faith, which had previously been restricted to the poorer Hutu and Hima communities.[5] This was followed by the enrolment of the sons of the aristocracy in Mission schools, which increasingly preferred to educate the children of the elite. Linden (1977: 164) refers to the segregation and streaming in schools that 'guaranteed the Tutsi were given a superior education, and [were] the means by which the Belgians were able to impose an ethnic definition of eligibility on the new political class'. The distribution of pupils in the prestigious *Groupe Scolaire d' Astrida* (Butare) confirmed the ethnic basis for selection (Table 3.1).

Table 3.1: Distribution of Pupils at Astrida (Butare) *Groupe Scolaire*

	1935	1946	1947	1948	1949	1950	1953	1954
Hutu	11	9	12	13	14	9	19	19
Tutsi	41	44	42	85	85	95	68	63
Twa	0	0	0	0	0	0	0	0

Note: The data include Hutus and Tutsis from Rwanda and Burundi.
Source: Adapted from Lemarchand (1974: 9) and Gahama (1983: 258).

[5] Gahama (1983: Chapter 1, Part 3) discusses the Christianization of Burundi society, and the dominance of Catholic and Protestant Missions in the educational sphere. Although he excludes data on the ethnic composition of converts during the colonial period, Table 31, still shows a dramatic increase in the number of converts from 45,111 in 1930 to 365,000 in 1940 (p. 219).

The principal aim of the school was to create a new social class and to provide trained manpower for the new administration, thus priority was given to the education of sons of chiefs. As Newbury (1988) argues, Hutu life chances were restricted by the discrimination in the Catholic education system, which after 1926, admitted very few. *Groupe Scolaire*, founded in 1932, had a minimum height requirement, restricting entry largely to Tutsis whose average height stereotypically was greater than that of Hutus. Hutus were also limited in their choice of courses and were not taught French – the language of administration.

The church colluded with the colonial administration in its effort to gain greater control over local leaders. In the 1930s, Mgr. Classe, who at one time was head of the local Catholic Church, warned the Belgian administration to retain the traditional hegemony of the Tutsi. He remarked, 'we have no chiefs who are better qualified, more intelligent, more capable of appreciating progress and more fully accepted by the people than the Tutsi (P.M.C. 19th session 1930, quoted in Lemarchand, 1970: 43). Newbury (1988: 116) concludes 'the state and the Catholic Church encouraged the creation of a new Christian "ruling class" to be composed exclusively of *Tuutsi* (sic).'

Missionaries and local catechists were also instrumental in writing a history of Burundi that perpetuated the myth of the Tutsi as divine rulers, producing what were essentially genocidal histories (Linden, 1977). The school curriculum incorporated the ethnic message. A 1950s school booklet, '*Essai d'histoire Burundaise*', promoted the hamitic hypothesis and the first *Français – Kirundi* dictionary, written by a priest, contained descriptions of the ethnic categories (Verme, 1994). In 2000, a delegate to the Arusha peace negotiations remarked: 'A teacher told me I was a Tutsi and I came from Misri (Egypt). I did not know where Misri was. I did not know where I came from.'[6] After World War Two, the new Belgian Catholic priests, coming themselves from a divided society, contributed to the growing ethnic tensions by stoking Hutus' awareness of their oppression as a collectivity and a majority.

Masculinity and Femininity in an Ethnicized Burundi Society
In the racialized and ethnicized hierarchy of colonial Burundi, there were rigid forms of masculinities and femininities. The colonial state was a gendered state and Belgium was the archetype of a colonial state that produced genocidal conditions. As discussed in Chapter 2, European men embodied a militarized form of masculinity that was hegemonic. European women, on the other hand, embodied an idealized form of femininity. African masculinity was determined by ethnicity; Tutsi men and women were elevated above the Hutu, and Hutu above Twa. African masculinities typified Connell's (1995) concept of marginalized masculinity. Ganwa and Tutsi men who accrued power through chief-tainships and bureaucratic positions were subordinate to the European administrator but retained considerable power over the labour and product of Hutus.

---

[6] PRP delegate, speaking at the general debate on Democracy and Good Governance, Arusha III, First Plenary Session, Tuesday, 13 October 1998.

The colonial championing of the superior intellect of the Tutsi and their right to govern through indirect rule reinforced the feelings of superiority and inferiority which pervaded the relationships between patrons and clients under *ubugabire*, and extended it to the wider group relationship between Hutu and Tutsi. Such emotions were tied up with concepts of masculinity and continue to pervade interactions between Hutus and Tutsis. Even at the Arusha peace negotiation, some Tutsi expressed the view that the Hutus present could not have come up with ideas of their own accord, preferring to believe that they were being manipulated by the Tanzanians or other regional leaders.

Despite the abundance of praise heaped on Tutsi men, they were still regarded by the colonials as having most of the negative qualities of man: depravity, unscrupulousness and 'cruel instincts'. Towards the late colonial period when Tutsi men started to agitate for independence, they came under considerable criticism from the Europeans, who commented on their idleness, cunning, licentiousness, opportunism and dissimulation (Lemarchand, 1970).

In his discussion of political identities, Mamdani (2001) failed to comment on the colonial impact on gendered identities and the implications that had for violence. In the stereotypical description characteristic of social Darwinian racism, Tutsi women were said to be tall, slender, light-skinned and the epitome of beauty. Basically their pre-colonial social status (as superior femininity) was enhanced even further under colonial rule and they were therefore coveted by Hutu men; not unlike Fanon's (1967) description of black men's desire to be initiated into 'authentic' manhood by going with white women.

The degree of intermarriage is used to determine the prevalence of ethnic ideology. The colonial myth is that Hutu men could marry Tutsi women, but Tutsi men would not marry Hutu women. Yet, Lemarchand (1970: 44) quotes a prominent *Ganwa* who said in 1957 that 'many *Baganwa* gave their daughters to Hutu and Tutsi alike'. During the Rwandan genocide, Tutsi women's supposed standoffishness was used to denigrate them and explain the brutal and degrading sexual abuse they encountered (Jones, 2002: 78). According to Jones (ibid.), 'Hutu women's "subordination" to Tutsi women was doubtless a powerful motivation for the atrocities those women would inflict on other women.'

Civilizing Africans required their adoption of the values and norms of western culture, which if acquired successfully, could lead to their evolution into higher human beings. This idea was embodied in the Belgian colonial concept of the *évolué* – an African, normally male, who had abandoned his traditional cultural practices and sought to be European through missionary education, urban residential location and employment largely in the colonial service. Through the concept of the *évolué*, the colonial state could reshape gender relations and transform prevailing concepts of masculinity and femininity.

Nancy Hunt's (1990) study of the domestic training programme set up by the Belgians for the wives of *évolués* in Bujumbura, showed how missionaries and colonial administrators, through the *foyers sociaux,* attempted to instil European values into African society by promoting the nuclear family and a gender division of labour that confined women to the private sphere. African women left to their own devices were in European conceptualization 'loose', dirty and incapable of rearing good citizens. Women were taught housekeeping, child rearing and sewing and had their homes inspected. The furthest 'evolved' could participate in the 'most-beautiful-house contest'!

> House visits, contests and ceremonies, sewing, housekeeping, motherhood classes, and meetings to solicit the cooperation of husbands in disciplining wives were interlocking elements in the Belgian colonial project to refashion gender roles and instill a western family ideology into urban life. (Hunt, 1990: 469)

European women, Catholic nuns especially, assisted in the mission to subordinate and domesticate the African woman to European patriarchal ideology. African women could only participate in the *foyers sociaux* with the permission of their husbands, who were encouraged to monitor their attendance. Yet, in the racial hierarchy of the colonial world, Africans could only mimic European domesticity, as civilization was reserved exclusively for whites.

> The word *évolué* was always a misnomer in Belgian colonial discourse, for civilization could never be reached by nonwhites. ... Complete duplication of the trappings of European life was not only structurally impossible, but also strategically not permitted by the curriculum and activities of the *foyer.* (Hunt, 1990: 469–70)

Despite this, Hunt notes that African and European women moved beyond these proscriptions and shared a wider knowledge. Many African women resisted the rigid demarcation of the private and public spheres and continued to pursue activities such as trading and beer-brewing. Nevertheless, the colonial inscription of gender roles was such that the public sphere of the colonial state was closed to African women. Men could become petty civil servants and soldiers in contrast to the prescribed ideal role for African women: that of housewives.

The literature on femininity in Burundi is sparse, even in the post-colonial period. What exists refers to men's feminine ideals, as well as attesting to the independence of women. In the patriarchal society of pre-colonial Burundi, the status of a woman was very much dependent on the status of her husband. Albert (1971: 180) was surprised that there were women in what she considered a patriarchal and patrilineal society 'who enjoyed considerable authority and who own or control cows, lands and other forms of wealth'. This she attributed to the nature of the hierar-chical social system; women were considered to be beneath men of their own social level but superior to all of lower social status. A woman was revered for using feminine guile to advance herself. This enabled Burundi women to accrue wealth independent of their husbands. Intelligent and wealthy women were made *Bashingantahe*. According to Albert (1971: 212), 'women who have this honoured position received cows, clothing, jewellery and serfs. On occasion, a woman of this kind may be wealthier than her husband, but he has every reason to be pleased that he has such a wife.'

Household gender roles and responsibilities were not as clearly defined. A household survey conducted by Adelski and Rosen (1991) found that men and women's economic role overlapped; women were predominantly in charge of agriculture, especially in areas such as Bututsi where men served in the military or carried out animal husbandry. Berger (1981) also notes the existence of a belief that women's greater strength made them better suited for manual labour than men. Adelski and Rosen (ibid.: 20) had difficulty unpacking gender roles as both men and women seem to 'report the social ideal, men as primary social and economic agents, rather than the reality of rural life'. This is exemplified in Mworoha's discussion of the role of women in Burundi society. Women, he claims, 'were taught to respect men and obey them in all circumstances ... chastity was the first virtue' (Mworoha, 1977: 133). This idealized representation of women's role at the time is supported by Mianda's analysis of the gender discourse found in the magazine of the *évolué* men in the Belgian Congo. She points out that they:

> ... produced a discourse, as well as behaviour and opinions about women, which conformed to the totality of understanding produced and circulated by the colonizers (the administration and the church) ... Thus the educational system in the Congo introduced a Western type of patriarchy and reinforced male domination with a new form of women's alienation encoded in a new model of gender relations. (Mianda, 2002: 158)

Attempts to emulate white people and be civilized resulted in the creation of a new social hierarchy between the sexes and 'a new concept of gender relations; women were not only economically dependent on men; they were completely under a husband's jurisdiction in legal matters' (Mianda, ibid.: 158). The construction of customary law led to the domestication and subordination of women; once flexible avenues for social advancement and accumulation became fixed, as men used customary marital and inheritance laws to extend their authority over women. Berger notes:

> Women of all social classes were expected to act subservient and obedient and to follow the dictates of their fathers and husbands. Local beliefs justified this situation by attributing to women such unflattering traits as clumsiness, lack of agility, inability to control their emotions and proneness to jealousy. (Berger 1981: 7)

Colonialism transformed the nature of patriarchy in Burundi society, creating a patriarchal alliance between European and African men. Mworoha's (1971) reference to the traditional obedient women does not fit with the history of the Queen-mothers and other matriarchs who wielded considerable power, and warriors such as the Hutu, *Inamujandi*, who led a revolt against the Tutsi king, before it was put down by the Belgians in 1931 (Ntibantunganya, 1999). Furthermore Burundi, one of very few African states, was able to appoint a female Prime Minister, Sylvie Kinigi, in the mid-1990s. Mworoha's interpretation of gender roles was very much influenced by his background in Catholic seminaries and the teaching of the Catholic Church that sought to make African women subservient. The church played a critical role in reshaping patriarchy to further the subordination of women and to undermine the collectivism of African societies, destroying the protection women gained within such a society.

Political Power and the Emergence of Genocidal Economics

The introduction of a single administrative power narrowed the opportunities for political power and economic independence by rival elite groups. The modern state was superimposed on a pre-colonial state that was riven with political rivalry. As ethnicity was a recent phenomenon and regional and clan identities quite significant, power struggles within the *Baganwa* and Tutsi elite continued throughout the colonial period. Lemarchand (1970) also notes the prevalence, after 1940, of inter-dynastic competition between the older generation of royalists and the younger mission-educated, westernized elite. This new factor in *Baganwa* politics was to heighten instability during the 1960s and in the struggle for self-rule.

In its integration of traditional power structures into the colonial administration, the Belgians selected and imposed their own chiefs from among the *Baganwa* and Tutsi. According to Reyntjens (1994), the 1930s was the period of the Tutsification, or more precisely, as Prunier (1994: 2) terms the '*Baganwaization*' of political power, as most of the chiefs were '*Baganwa* rather than 'ordinary' Tutsi'. By 1945 no Hutu chief remained. Chiefs, being directly responsible to the colonial authorities, were highly-bureaucratic and it was their duty to introduce to those in their territory a host of new legislation and economic obligations.

As in neighbouring Congo, the economic exploitation of the colony was viewed by the colonial administrators and the missionaries as an essential element in the transition to modernity. Unfortunately, this was done through the use of force in production; peasants became subjected to forced labour (*ubeletwa)*, compulsory cropping and marketing. Hatungimana's (2005) account of coffee in twentieth-century Burundi reveals the role played by the church and chiefs in the expansion of coffee in Burundi after 1930. These chiefs or *évolués* bore direct responsibility for the propagation of coffee cultivation. Chiefs and sub-chiefs were instructed to have their own plantations as well as forcing peasants to grow coffee. Chiefs were notorious as they took to their tasks assiduously. Peasants were fined or whipped with the '*chicotte*' (switch), if they failed to follow orders. Hatungimana (2005: 441/442) notes that in 1939 at Gitega, some 623 natives were whipped for not maintaining their coffee plants. The introduction of coffee throughout the territory, even in areas generally unsuitable for its production, affected adversely the ability of peasants to ensure household food security. Famine, a regular feature of Burundi society during the pre-colonial period, became intensified and remained a problem right up to the twenty-first century. Coffee is labour intensive and occupies land that could be used for more drought resistant and nutritious crops (Oxfam, 2002b; Oketch & Polzer, 2002).

As salaried employees of the colonial state, the chiefs lacked the benevolence of the former chiefs who had to rely on maintaining patronage relationships with their subjects for their livelihood. Colonial chiefs prospered in the new cash crop economy, being able to gain control of large tracts of land and labour via *ubugabire*: many, such as Chiefs Baranyanka and Mboneko were became 'coffee-kings'. Celebrated for the rapid expansion of coffee in their chieftaincy, they were decorated by the colonial state, exempt from taxation, lived in 'castles' and adopted western tastes (Lemarchand, 1970; Hatungimana, 2005).

The replacement of the *Bashingantahe* by the colonial 'native courts' (*tribunaux indigènes*) in 1943 intensified the burden on the Hutus. Administered by the new chiefs and guided by Europeans, native courts redefined and codified customary laws to the disadvantage of women and Hutus. The courts were Tutsi controlled, and required the payment of fees which were beyond the reach of Hutus, who subsequently could not compete successfully in such courts. This was compounded by the loss of past forms of appeal to one of the various chiefs.

Although wealthy Hutus maintained some economic independence, access to political power was reserved exclusively for the Tutsis. David Newbury, with reference to Rwanda, comments on the Hutus' growing ethnic awareness:

> Hutus came increasingly to recognize their common status, and to extend a common identity to those groups who formerly saw themselves as distinct from each other in regional terms or descent criteria. Greater oppression by the state, greater mobility of the workers, and greater visibility of class differentiation, all combined to intensify ethnic consciousness. (Newbury, 1998: 87)

By giving access to political power only to the Tutsis, the Belgians created a situation wherein the Tutsis could legally dominate all Hutus. In this new politico-economic system, prosperity and social status became dependent on one's relationship with the colonial authorities. When the Belgian state attempted to introduce democracy in the 1950s, through the setting up of territorial councils, individual eligibility for elections was restricted to chiefs and sub-chiefs or those with a Civic Merit certificate or Registered Natives award. The certificate and the awards were related to how westernized one had become. According to Webster (1966: 24), 'to be "registered", a native had to be of age and justify by his upbringing and manner of living a degree of civilization demonstrating an ability to enjoy the rights and fulfil the obligations provided for by written legislation.'[7] The Order of Merit was given to 'blacks who deserve the name civilised because they have rejected all the barbarous parts of the customs but who nevertheless do not wish to Europeanize and denationalize themselves completely.'[8] Clearly, from its introduction in Burundi, democracy referred to the political participation of the traditional and westernized elite (*évolués*), not the masses.

---

[7] Guy Malengrau (1952) 'Chronique de politique indigéne', *Zaire*, 6: 960, quoted in Webster 1966, p. 24.

[8] Sophier Antoine (1951) 'La Politique d'Intégration', *Zaire*, 5: 907, quoted in Webster, 1966, p. 24.

In the context of majoritarian democracy, this situation proved rife for the mobilization of kin and ethnic solidarities. By the mid-1960s, the breakdown of traditional socio-cultural structures and the integration of Burundi society into the capitalist system, gradually led to the replacement of the traditional elite by the new westernized elite – the *évolués*, whose role was to supervise the process of wealth extraction for international capital. The colonial state laid the conditions whereby the *évolués* – a minority differentiated by race and class and with access to the military, became the architects of genocide.

The Centralization of Violence:
Constructing the Modern Military

The security forces, especially the military, are seen as key players in post-colonial Burundi politics, primarily because of their partisanship and their use as forces of repression. The type of military imposed by the modern state was fundamentally different from that of the pre-colonial period. The colonial state used its superior military technology to concentrate and centralise violence. Its monopoly of the only legitimate form of violence removed the right of every household to participate in the security of the polity and the state. The so-called professionalization of the army had the effect of distancing the military from the people making it a more reliable arm of the state in terms of maintaining internal security.

In pre-colonial Burundi two armies existed; that of the *Intore* (royal guards) and that of the peasants who were mobilized by the *Baganwa*. The *Intore* were a permanent army based at Court and were made up of sons of the princes and families close to the Court. They fought in wars, put down rebellions and acted as Court policemen in times of peace. In warfare, peasant armies were mobilized by notables and sub-chiefs and organised by the chiefs before going on expeditions. All families were expected to provide men for military service (Mworoha, 1977). Military activities were directed at external forces or internal rebellions; those loyal to the *mwami* were protected.

During German colonialism and for the first six years of Belgian rule, Burundi was run by the military, which was 'entrusted with a wide range of administrative functions' (Lemarchand, 1970). The foreign military aided the *mwami* by helping to put down rebellious regional chiefs. Scorched earth policies were adopted as a means of preventing further uprising or challenge to the *mwami*'s (colonial) rule.

The creation of a centralized military force was vital for the security of the colonial establishment. Ordinary citizens would be protected if they complied with the demands of the colonials and their Tutsi bureaucrats. As in other parts of colonial Africa, the nature of military recruitment was dependent on how communities were perceived by the colonial administration. Recruitment of Africans into the new national army was often based on stereotypes of their brutality (Enloe, 1980; Luckham, 1998). Men from certain ethnic groups or regions were considered either to belong to a 'martial race' or were the right sort of outsiders needed to dispense justice. From 1916 to 1923 Burundi was run by the Belgian military. The Belgian colonial military (*la Force Publique*) which operated in the territory consisted of Congolese soldiers under Belgian Command. According to Ntibazonkiza (1993), the *Garde Nationale Burundaise* (in 1962 renamed *Armée Nationale Burundaise*) was formed in 1960 with 650 men, recruited equally from among Hutu and Tutsi – the latter mainly from among the low-status Hima. He claims that when the Belgians realized that the army was being politicized in favour of UPRONA, the political party of the nationalist leader, Prince Louis Rwagasore, they weeded out all party members. Subsequently, when the administration was establishing the gendarmerie just months before independence in 1962, its allegiance had shifted so much from the Tutsi that they recruited Hutus from Rwanda (Lemarchand, 1970).

Military rule led to the creation of a militarized culture. Terence Ranger reminds us that military men were used as the first colonial administrators and that attempts were made to instil military values in the children of African soldiers. The introduction of European military traditions was essential for colonial rule; they acted as a form of socialization into the hierarchical elements of European culture. Ranger (1981: 224) quotes Professor George Shepperson who noted 'the narrowness of the line between military and civilians ... It was through its forces as much as its missions that European culture was brought to the indigenous inhabitants of British Central Africa.'

The sort of professional and non-partisan military that Europeans sought to establish could not survive within the context of an ethnicized political culture. The African military was created in such a way that certain groups could capture the right and the mechanisms to perpetrate violence, ostensibly to maintain the security of the state. Consequently, the Burundi military, acting as a corporate group, could hide behind the professionalism of the modern army while acting in the interest of the small elite. And like the political elite, the military, could fracture along regional and party lines. Ntibazonika recognizes their singular status.

> The members of the 'Burundian national Army' considered that they belonged to the country's elite; they were well-educated, well paid and enjoying a real social prestige as protectors of the Crown. The soldiers of Burundi and their officers enjoyed very good job security. (Ntibazonkiza, 1993: 91)

As products of modernity, the Burundi military's alignment with the *évolués* was not surprising. Together, they formed the basis of the genocidal state, and the military – the machinery for the perpetration genocide.

Conclusion

I have dwelt on the political structure of the pre-colonial and colonial period in order to illustrate that the imposition of the modern state form was not merely superimposed onto pre-existing hierarchies. Rather it transformed socio-political relationships through the destruction of the previous polity and its religious and cultural components. Furthermore, the introduction of force in commodity production led to the emergence of class competition, which became the basis for genocidal violence.

What emerges from the historical accounts is that the variety of social identities that existed in pre-colonial Burundi was virtually silenced in the retelling of the country's history. Even though the people had a common culture, spoke the same language and shared the same rituals and festivities, there were clear forms of social identity, whether by occupational specialization, region, or kinship (clan) but there was no pan-territorial ethnic identity.[9] Instead the *Barundi* identified with the Crown and the state – an incipient form of national identity perhaps. The imposition of external rule was extremely disruptive of pre-colonial contractual arrangements that had provided the social cohesiveness of Burundi society.

Burundi's history reveals how the classification of African peoples, using the racist ideology of social Darwinism, produced hierarchies of human beings that were made meaningful through the institutions of the modern state. The divisive and discriminatory policies of the colonial state were justified by the ranking of people according to their physical characteristics and their perceived position on the evolutionary ladder. New authority structures and power relations necessitated new forms of gendered constructions, new masculinities and femininities. Ethnicity as a conflictual and violent phenomenon emerged relatively recently in Burundi's history, as group polarization with respect to the state became greater. Class allegiances and political power became bound up with race and ethnicity.

Although militarism existed in the pre-colonial state, the form it took as a result of colonialism was quite different, in that the modern state monopolized violence through the creation of a professional military and gendarmerie charged with the security of the colonial state, and not of the citizenry. Order was ensured not through consensus but by military violence. The frontier between the colonial world and that of the native was, as Fanon describes, delineated by barracks and police stations.

> In the colonial countries ... the policeman and the soldier, by their immediate presence and their frequent and direct action, maintain contact with the native and advise him by means of rifle-butts and napalm not to budge. (Fanon, 1961, reprinted 1990: 29)

Not only were the means of security removed from the people, so were the safeguards that prevented people from being abused.

---

[9] Lemarchand (1970) refers to strong regional consciousness among the inhabitants of the Mosso, Imbo and Mugamba regions.

4

The Masculinized State | & the History
of Genocide

Introduction

Apart from signifying the prevalence of ethnicity and genocidal violence
in Africa, the post-colonial Burundi state is also used to provide a classic
example of a 'failed state', defined as one which has lost its capacity to
provide security because of the loss of its monopoly on violence, its
inability to deliver welfare services to its citizens and its lack of political
legitimacy (Milliken & Krause, 2002; Pax Christi Netherlands, 2005). The
argument throughout this chapter is that the Burundi state has only ever
been legitimate for a matter of months; that from the period of decolonization forces were at large firstly to dislodge one set of elites and replace
them with another and, secondly, to destabilize the state to prevent a shift
to communism that would disrupt the processes of accumulation within
the region. Ethnicity and militarism were used instrumentally by the
departing colonial power as well as the competing elites. This chapter and
the next documents, historically, the processes by which political
violence became central to the reproduction of the Burundi state, which
became an arena for genocide. This chapter focuses on two historical
periods: 1961 to 1972 and 1973 to 1993. The periodization reflects the
differing struggles among the elite for control of the state.

The Post-Colonial State: 1961–1972

This period covers the difficult transition from colonial domination to
self-rule and military dictatorship. It began with emerging competition
for control of the independent state and ended with genocide. Burundi's
population had a small middle class; 93 per cent of its population were
peasants, six per cent workers, and the rest comprised members of the
ruling elite who prospered under colonialism. This small middle class,
promoted during the colonial period, was internally divided according to
pre-colonial social hierarchies and by colonial racial politics and social
engineering. Political competition occurred among the factionalized
elite; firstly, between the *Baganwa* clans, splitting the nationalist
movement which, unable to form a united front, was open to manipulation by the departing colonial power. Second, rivalry broke out

between the Hutu and Tutsi elite, as the former saw democratization as opening up the political space for majoritarian (Hutu) governance. And finally between high and low status Tutsis, the latter in danger of losing the advanced social status and access to power that they derived from colonial racial classification.

Due to these machinations and Cold War geo-politics, Burundi's elite had no possibility of developing democratic politics; instead the militarization of politics took on its violent form, where the state and oppositional groups opted for genocidal violence to resolve political differences. By and large, the gestating post-colonial Burundi state reflected the character of its colonial precursor. Of relevance is Ake's (1996: 3) point that the modern African state 'presented itself as an apparatus of violence, had a narrow social base and relied for compliance on coercion rather than authority'. Fanon (1961: 60) also recognized the 'aggressive anxiety' among the national bourgeoisie to occupy the spaces vacated by the colonials, retaining 'the atmosphere of violence, [which] after having coloured all the colonial phase, continues to dominate national life'.

The nationalist movement in the late colonial period rallied around pre-existing sources of social and political power. Factionalism among the elite had not been rooted out by indirect rule, which – on the contrary – concentrated power in the hands of the *mwami* and the favoured *Baganwa* faction. Throughout the period 1957–1966, tension existed between the leading *Baganwa* dynasties (the *Bezi* and the *Batare*) and the monarchy. The former dominated the two leading political parties: UPRONA (*Parti de l'Unité et du Progrès National*) formed by members of the *Bezi* aristocracy, and unofficially headed by the *mwami*'s son, Prince Louis Rwagasore, and the *Batare*-controlled PDC (*Parti Démocrate Chrétien*). Due to the charismatic leadership of Rwagasore and his marriage to a Hutu, UPRONA was able to unite Hutu and Tutsi anti-colonialists under the slogan 'unity and progress.'

Fifteen political parties contested the 1961 elections, appealing, largely to different ideological factions. Five parties (Hutu and Tutsi) established a common front opposing UPRONA, some because of clan differences.[1] Such cross-ethnic political alliances against the winning party will become a feature of post-colonial politics. Despite the political advantages gained by the Hutus through the introduction of universal suffrage in 1956, Hutu-dominated parties, like *Parti du Peuple*, lacked a traditional power base which they could mobilize, and could not compete with the *Baganwa*-backed parties. UPRONA won the legislative elections of 1961, primarily because of its opposition to colonial rule, Rwagasore's charismatic leadership and the party's alignment with the Crown.

Cold War Politics and the Emerging Post-Colonial State

Cold War politics and events in neighbouring Congo affected the positions adopted by Belgium and other western governments with regards to

---

[1] PDR (*Parti Démocrate Rural*), PDC (*Parti Démocrate Chretien*), UNB (*Union Nationale du Burundi*), PP (*Parti du Peuple*) & RPB (*Rassemblement Populaire du Burundi*).

Burundi's political future (Chapter 7). Nationalist African leaders, who sought to break unequal colonial relationships in order to pursue the social advancement of their citizens, looked for support from non-western countries. The West was concerned with Rwagasore's association with Patrice Lumumba and Julius Nyerere, and, later, at the size of the Chinese embassy in Bujumbura (Lemarchand, 1970; Webster, 1966).[2] It was suggested that the Chinese used their Burundi embassy to supply weapons to Lumumba. Belgium delayed the democratic elections in 1961, despite protestations from the UN, in order to influence the outcome and because it was channelling weapons through Bujumbura to the anti-Lumumba forces in Kivu Province, Congo.

Belgium's strategy, to prevent a shift to communism in Burundi, was threefold: first, it branded Rwagasore a communist and lent its support to the less radical PDC, which, though considered a republican party, was not in favour of immediate self-rule.[3]

> There was a certain connivance and even a direct complicity between our Authority and the PDC ... The main point of their program we caught upon was their refusal of immediate independence ... The PDC quickly became the bulwark we hoped to use in order to stop the cancerous metastasis of UPRONA's progress. (Jean-Paul Harroy (last Resident of Burundi, 1955–1962), 1987, quoted in Prunier, 1994: 3)

Rwagasore's assassination on the 13 October 1961, supposedly planned by the PDC leadership and the Belgians, led to the dissolution of the party and the *Batare* as a competing political force (*Observer*, 1.7.1962; Chomé, 1962). Belgium's alleged complicity in Rwagasore's murder is still contentious.[4] Chomé (1962: 347) refers to an interview with M. Regnier, the past Resident de Burundi, who was said to have remarked:

> At the end of the meeting, which lasted for four hours and was noisy and difficult, I summed-up; "there are many solutions", was the gist of what I said: that Rwagasore should disappear is obviously one of them. Or that your party becomes a resistance one like the Parmehutu in Rwanda: expeditions in the hills, destruction, terror operations. However, there is no structure in place for this action. And finally that your members adapt, work, stay in their posts in administration of elsewhere, and think about the future. (Reported in *Le Soir* du 28 Novembre 1962)

---

[2] Information obtained from discussions with Abdul Rahman Babu, 1991.

[3] Rwagasore was close friends with Julius Nyerere and Patrice Lumumba. The Belgians were opposed to this and according to Webster (1966) saw him as a second Lumumba. They were especially opposed to his idea of a federation with Tanzania.

[4] For a detailed discussion of the events relating to the murder of Rwagasore, the trial of the assassins and the role of the Belgians, see Chomé, J. (1962) 'L'Affaire Rwagasore', *Remarques Congolaises*, 14 December 1962, Bruxelles. All participants to the Arusha Peace Accord were in agreement that the Belgians were behind the death of Rwagasore. This point was made in earlier drafts of the Accord, but was removed after protest by the Belgians and Mandela's concern that Burundi would not receive support form Belgium once it was made public (see Chapter 10).

Second, the Belgian and other western governments sided with the neo-conservatives within a factionalized UPRONA, as old royalists and young radicals vied for power, and the different aspirations of the Hutu and Tutsi party leaders came to the fore. *Mwami* Mwambutsa, a neo-conservative and westernized 'playboy', acted in support of the status quo by appointing a Tutsi, Andrea Muhirwa, as prime minister after Rwagasore's death, even though eminent Hutus, such as Paul Mirerekano, the executive secretary of UPRONA, and Pierre Ngendandumwe, the deputy prime minister, were logical successors. The *mwami*'s support for the old regime and the Tutsi elite destroyed the cross-ethnic consensus that Rwagasore had forged in UPRONA. This later culminated in the expulsion and alienation of a significant proportion of the Hutu elite from the party.

The period between 1963 and 1965 is said to be one of the most tumultuous in Burundi's post-colonial political history. Lemarchand (1977) has argued that due to the threat of political instability, and the absence of a credible leader, the Crown was forced to take control, leading to a period of absolute monarchy (1962–5), as the powers of the government, the army, and provincial governors were steadily eroded by the *mwami*. Mwambutsa appointed six successive governments with alternating Hutu and Tutsi prime ministers whilst strengthening the position of the older *Baganwa* elements by allocating them key posts in the expanding Tutsi-dominated bureaucracy, reflecting at one level his inability to come to terms with constitutional democracy and the demands of competing social forces. At another level, the rapid reshuffling of government posts could be attributed partly to the ideological contestation in Burundi society between the left and right wingers.

In 1963, left-wingers had pushed for the establishment of diplomatic relations with China, supported civil rights movements in the USA and the anti-apartheid movement in South Africa, much to the chagrin of the *mwami* and the West. Later on, these actions fuelled speculation that certain western governments were involved in the assassination of the left-leaning Hutu Prime Minister, Pierre Ngendandumwe on 16 January 1965 (Ntibazonkiza, 1993; Evanzz, 1992). Ngendandumwe was shot by a Rwandan Tutsi employee of the American Embassy and soon after his death the *mwami* closed the Chinese embassy (*The Times*, 1.2.1965). Evanzz (1992: 312) reports that, 'in a statement on behalf of Mao Zedong, Peking, accused the CIA and Belgium of complicity in Ngendandumwe's murder.'

The third strategy of the departing colonial power, as referred to by Regnier above, was to destabilize Tutsi hegemony by supporting the Hutus as rightful rulers under a newly imposed majoritarian democratic structure. Independence saw colonial domination giving way to constitutional democracy – the hallmark of a modern state. However, the ethnic discriminatory policies of the colonial state disadvantaged the Hutu majority in terms of their ability to participate in the bureaucracy of the democratic state. For the *évolué* African, the state provided the main arena for wealth accumulation, yet social mobility continued to depend firstly on race and then political patronage. As Burundians moved in to fill the posts created by the new state bureaucracy, the discriminatory repercussions of colonial education policies were apparent as the plethora of new government posts were filled mainly by the better-educated Tutsi, excluding the lower status Tutsi-Hima and Hutu.

The tumultuous transition to independence and democracy in Burundi was typical of neighbouring Belgian colonies. A state founded on political and genocidal violence emerged in Rwanda as a result of the competition for political power between the 'communist-leaning' nationalist Tutsi monarchy and Parmehutu – the party seeking to establish Hutu power (*Sunday Times*, 29.9.1961; Mamdani, 2001). The colonial power's desire to leave compliant Africans in control of the independent state saw Belgium support shifted to the Hutus, who they helped to capture the reigns of power from the Tutsis. According to Mamdani (2001: 124), the Belgians used 'an embryonic Hutu-dominated armed force to support their position'.

The 1959 Hutu 'revolution' was the result of the massacre of thousands of Tutsis and their displacement from power, while the country was still under the UN trusteeship, administered by the Belgians. A UN mission to Burundi, that year, criticized the Belgian authorities for the 'lack of impartiality' (*The Times*, 7.12.1959). And, the socialist opposition in Belgium called for the Christian Democrat government to act to prevent further loss of life (*The Times*, 13. 11.1959). To compound the situation, on the eve of the democratic elections of September 1961, the Belgians stood by and watched as villages were torched, people massacred and forcedly displaced (*The Times,* 24.9.1961; *Sunday Times*, 29.9.1961). For Prunier (1994), the Hutu 'revolution' played a terrible role in shaping the repressive armed system in Burundi. He claims (ibid.: 11), 'at the back of every Burundi Tutsi's mind there was always the fear of "What would happen if they would all decide to rise and kill us to the last one".'

The establishment of a Hutu republic in Rwanda sharpened the small Burundian Hutu elite awareness of the potentialities of their ethnic base as a vehicle for accessing political power. And, the genocidal violence, associated with the birth of the Rwandan republic, was used by Burundian Tutsi lobbyists to campaign against Hutu power. As early as 1962, a youth movement, *Jeunesses Nationalistes Rwagasore* (JNR), became associated with ethnic violence, when its Tutsi members attacked Hutu trade-union leaders in Bujumbura, sparking the first flow of refugees into Zaire, Rwanda and Tanzania.

The May 1965 democratic election was the first in which the Hutu political class sought election by appealing to Hutu ethnicity. Whereas 50 seats were won by Hutus, compared to 14 for the Tutsis, the *Mwami,* faced with the threat of a Hutu takeover, once again appointed a Tutsi, Leopold Bihagumugani, as prime minister. This meant that the legitimacy of the Crown was open to challenge by two forces, by the Hutus as well as by the alienated left-wing elite of the *Bezi* faction, each group, in turn, mobilizing already irreversible ethnic sentiments to support their claims on the state.

The monarch's rebuff to the Hutu leadership forced the already disenchanted Hutu army officers and civilian elite to turn against him and to stage an abortive coup on the 18 October 1965, which caused the *Mwami* to flee the country. For a period of nine months, while the *Mwami* convalesced in Switzerland, the country was controlled by the army, the *Bezi* and the *Jeunesse*. Even though Mwambutsa was ousted by his son Charles Ndizeye (Ntare V) in July 1966, it was by then clear that the Crown was no longer indispensable. Ntare V had the support of the younger *Baganwa* elements and the army. Four months later, on 28 November 1966, he also was overthrown by his prime minister and former soldier, Lieutenant-Général Michel Micombero (a Tutsi-Hima from Bururi region), in a coup supported by sections of the military and the *Bezi* elite. Micombero declared Burundi a republic and justified his displacement of the democratic forces with the need to bring stability to the country.

Micombero's coup signified the arrival of the military and the Tutsi-Hima as a force within Burundi politics. For the first two years of the republic, the country was run by a military autocracy, the National Revolutionary Council, consisting of 12 army officers (Lemarchand, 1970). In his post-coup speech, Micombero banned all political parties with the exception of the increasingly 'Tutsified' UPRONA, and appointed himself its President. Hence, he forged a lasting alliance between the party, the military and Tutsi hegemony.

Micombero's regime speeded up the process of militarization. It attempted to instil military values into all social groups; into the young by creating a new youth movement, *Jeunesses Révolutionnaires Rwagasore* (JRR); military values in the workplace through the creation of a new trade union, *Union des Travailleurs du Burundi* (UTB), and into women's organizations via the newly-formed *Union des Femmes du Burundi* (UFB) (Lemarchand, 1970). The impression given to the outside world was that of a progressive military leader constructing modern transformative institutions. However, by imposing these institutions and their leadership, the military deprived the people they were supposed to represent of their own organic institutions.

The regime went into battle against the population on several fronts. First, with its senior ranks comprising mainly lower-status Tutsi-Hima from the southern province of Bururi, it challenged and overthrew the monarchy and the *Baganwa* elite. Second, it sought to rid itself of the competition from Tutsis from the central provinces and other parts of the territory; thirdly it sought to deal violently with the majoritarian pressures from the Hutu. In effect Micombero's regime committed genocide against all these forces.

Clearly, by the 1960s, the monarchy had become anachronistic, stripped of its symbols by the colonial power and, having lost mass support, it became susceptible to the more powerful of the new social forces – a military, dominated by the low-status Tutsi-Hima, many of whom were discriminated against by the pre-colonial state and seen as inferior by the *Baganwa* elite. While *Mwami* Mwambutsa had alienated sections of the Hutu elite, the institution of the monarchy itself could still muster some support among the Hutu populace.

Regionalism became the defining political feature of Micombero's regime. He restructured the political and security institutions by removing any semblance of a national character and promoting regional and factional interests. In time, the bulk of the political class came to originate from a narrow triangular area formed by the towns of Rutana, Matana and Vyanda in southern Burundi and centring on the province of Bururi (see Map 2). Virulent nepotism led to members of Micombero's clan – the *Bashingo,* dominating the army and the bureaucracy. Those military leaders aligned to Micombero were intolerant of opposition even within the Tutsi group, ousting left-wing elements from the party and the Cabinet. Micombero's military republic set the violent framework for dealing with future ethnic and regional grievances. Lemarchand (1970: 442) likens the role played by the army in post-colonial Burundi as similar to that of the *Baganwa* in traditional society, 'containing a variety of factions, clans, and ethnic interests'; many saw themselves as belonging to a privileged group which placed them above the ethnic fray. However, the military was forced to rely on civilian structures to govern, and therefore needed to form alliances with politicians; this is where regional and clan affiliations came to the fore.

Micombero relied on *Banyabururi,* essentially Tutsi-Hima support. An attempted coup against him in 1970 was the pretext for an attack on *Banyaruguru* leaders. The plotters, included Albert Shebura (Army commandant and Minister for Internal Affairs), Yanda Andrea (Minister of Justice), Gisimare Francois (Minister for National Education) and Artemon Simbananiye (Minister in the President's office & Chief Protocol). As with the attack against the Hutus, Micombero's reponse was to eliminate all *Banyaruguru* elements of any standing in the army and government (Lemarchand & Martin, 1974). Although the plotters were first given the death sentence with much publicity, it was later commuted because of international pressure.

Genocidal Violence and the Post-Colonial State

In post-colonial Burundi, violence played a pivotal role in blocking the process of democratization and in protecting minority access to state institutions. Political violence is directed at the opposition, whether Hutu or Tutsi and at the ethnic group. The spectre of the modern democratic African state made the prospect of Hutu rule clearly imminent, either via parliamentary democracy or social revolution. As a minority, the Tutsi elite could only ensure their control over the state through greater repressive measures and undemocratic practices. To many Tutsis this meant control of the army and the systematic exclusion of Hutus from political office, accompanied by recurrent violence aimed at keeping them in check and any uprising at bay. The JRR militia was given considerable freedom to use violent tactics with little or no sanction from army officers. In response, a significant proportion of Hutu opposition turned to violence and rebel movements emerged among the refugee communities in neighbouring countries.

Hutu resentment at being politically sidelined led to an attempted coup in October 1965, a year before Micombero's Tutsi-Hima coup. In retaliation Micombero, who was then principal secretary in the Ministry of Defence, ordered the killing of 86 highly-placed Hutus in UPRONA and the army, including Paul Mirerekano (Member of Parliament), Joseph

Bamina (Senator and Chairman of UPRONA), Emile Buchumi (Speaker of Parliament), and S. Miburo (Regional Commissioner). Thus began the process, which Prunier (1994) calls the 'tutsification' of UPRONA, and it becoming a party that upheld Tutsi interest. Lemarchand (1994a: 87) refers to the massacre of Hutu troops by their Tutsi commanding officers as the Tutsi elite's attempt to transform 'the army into a reliable instrument of coercion'. In September 1969, the alleged discovery of another Hutu-planned coup justified further purges of the armed forces and civilian leaders. Twenty-six prominent Hutus were arrested, twenty-three of whom were killed including Barabe Kanyaruguru (former planning minister), Gregorie Nicimbikye (former first secretary of the Barundi embassy in Washington) and Captain Bitariho Ferdinando (military officer) (*The Times*, 18.12.1969).

After this Micombero's regime began a period of organized discrimination against Hutus, to the extent that only three were left in his Cabinet of 1969, holding the less important ministries of Sports and Culture, Broadcasting and Information, and Works and Labour. By 1972 the military was purged of Hutu and only a few held government posts. For over three decades the unwritten policy was to limit the number of Hutus in the rank and file and block them from the command structure. With the army now the preserve of one ethnic group, Lemarchand (1994: 87) argues that, for the Hutu, 'armed rebellion was the only meaningful alternative to Tutsi hegemony'.

Micombero's anti-democratic stance has to be placed in a wider regional context, where Cold War politics had resulted in the capture of the state by military leaders, notably Idi Amin in Uganda and Joseph-Desirée Mobutu in Zaire. Genocidal violence in Burundi was developing as a component of the genocidal space. Mobutu and Amin were allies of Micombero, and were *génocidaires* themselves, and supported genocide in Burundi (Chapter 7).

1972: A 'Veritable' and 'Selective' Genocide
According to Lemarchand and Martin (1974) some commentators contend that the 1972 genocide of Hutu by government forces was planned by Micombero's regime as a "final solution" to the Hutu problem'. Another view is that the state used the pretext of a peasant uprising to carry out acts of revenge and subjugation. There is a general consensus that the violence began when 400 Hutus and Mulelists (Congolese rebels) and Tutsi monarchists, with bases in Tanzania and in Burundi, raided, initially, military targets, police stations, Gitega (home of the Mwami Ntare V, who was under house arrest) and the radio station in Bujumbura (Weinstein, 1972). Later, the rebels focused their attacks mainly in the southern provinces of Bururi, Nyanza-Lac and Rumonge, killing an estimated 2,000 people (Map 2). However, all reports of the conflicts noted that the counter-attacks carried out by government forces were excessive.

In a co-ordinated effort, the army and the JNR attempted to eliminate systematically Hutu leaders and intelligentsia, especially those in the university, secondary schools, hospitals and the church. The *école normale* at Ngaragara near Bujumbura lost 100 of their 314 students. One-third of the students at the University of Bujumbura were reported missing. Four Hutu ministers in the last government were immediately executed (*Le Monde,* 1.6.1972). Missionaries, journalists and visitors, describe situations where Hutu children were taken out of classrooms, loaded on to trucks and clubbed to death. At night, trucks loaded with corpses left Bujumbura (*Le Monde,* 1.6.1972; *The Times,* 9.6.1972). Twelve Hutu Protestant pastors and 14 Roman Catholic priests were reported killed; ostensibly, the plan was to destroy all present and future members of the Hutu elite (*The Guardian,* 4.6.1972 & 27.5.1972). Ordinary peasants and workers were also under threat as villages were burnt and crops destroyed, and about 500,000 people were made homeless (*Daily Telegraph,* 9.6.1972; *The Financial Times,* 20.7.1972). Overall, an estimated 200,000 Hutus were killed in the violence lasting from April to August. Because the reprisals were directed largely at the educated Hutu, peasants were better able to flee the country and thus constituted the bulk of the refugee population.

The extent to which the uprising was supported by local Hutus remains unclear. There are grounds to suggest that the uprising could have been the outcome of the increasing economic exactions on the Hutu peasants by the government and UPRONA. Weinstein (1972) reports the use of witchcraft symbolism by the rebels. This was consistent with earlier peasant protests and uprisings that were linked to religious sects; some breakaway Protestant groups and some indigenous (Weinstein, 1974). It seems, however, that the key strategists were the small Hutu petty bourgeoisie of the southern provinces who were frustrated by the discriminatory practices of the local Tutsi elite and the national state. Weinstein (1972) contends that regional differences in the political outlook of northern and southern Hutus militated against any pan-ethnic support for the rebels.

On the other hand, there is some conjecture that the government may have orchestrated the uprising in order to eliminate, once and for all, the Hutu and Tutsi opposition. Micombero may well have had knowledge of the attack, since he dismissed his Cabinet on the same day, 29 April 1972, and for the first two months of the conflict, was probably ruling by presidential decree (Lemarchand and Martin, 1974; Aupens, 1973). Characteristically, the government accused a former Minister of Communication, Pascal Bubiriza, of organizing the uprising in league with ultra-left wing groups (*Sunday Times,* 4.6.1972; *Daily Telegraph,* 23.6.1972). On the night of the attack, ex-king Ntare V, lured back to Burundi under the assurances of Micombero and Idi Amin, was arrested allegedly while trying to lead a coup with the help of white mercenaries (*The Times,* 30.4.1972).

The state played a duplicitous role in the genocide, using the radio to broadcast the perpetration of genocidal acts against Tutsis, which must certainly have intensified anti-Hutu sentiments and provoked retribution, whilst using the cover of 'genocide' to sponsor the execution of 100 members of the Tutsi opposition at Gitega (Kay, 1987). Furthermore, discrimination in the distribution of relief aid forced the International Red Cross to cease its operations in Burundi (Bowen, Freeman & Miller, 1972).

An estimated 200,000 Burundians, mainly Hutu, fled the country between 1972 and 1973, and sought refuge in the neighbouring territories of Tanzania, Rwanda and Zaire. Their presence close to the Burundi border posed a significant threat to successive Burundi governments, who have tried through direct military or diplomatic means to neutralize them. The hostility of the Barundi state towards their exiles resulted in the killing of repatriated refugees in Nyanza-Lac in 1975 – one year after their return. The continued violation of human rights in Burundi forced most of the 1972 refugees to opt for a life in exile; a population of about 160,000 have remained in western Tanzania for some 34 years.

Intra-Tutsi disputes persisted with *Banyabururi* ministers, such as Artemon Simbananiye and André Yanda, putting pressure on Micombero to rid the government of *Banyaruguru*. He, subsequently, dismissed his *Banyaruguru* prime minister, Albain Nyamoga, in June 1973, and took personal control of the most important ministries. From 1972 to 1976, while Micombero consolidated the hegemony of the Tutsi-Hima through violence and discriminatory practices, in Rwanda, a Hutu military leader, Juvenal Habyarimana, from northern Rwanda, overthrew the Hutu President, Gregorie Kayibanda, in a coup which saw the transfer of power from one regional political-military elite to another.

The International Response to the 1972 Genocide

> "It was clear that the government had a hand in it", admitted an American policymaker, "because the repression was systematic. They tried to skim off the cream of the Hutu". (An unknown source quoted in Bowen *et al*. 1974: 5)

The failure of the international community to act in the face of genocide has been recorded (Bowen *et al.*, 1972; Lemarchand and Martin, 1974). Was this because the Burundi regime was pro-West and attempted to eradicate not just Hutus, but left-wingers? Bowen *et al.* (1972) report that in May 1972 the US State Department already knew it was 'selective genocide', based on communications from its embassy in Bujumbura. Yet no action was taken against the Burundi government. Bowen *et al.* (1972) thought that the US, purchasing over 80 per cent of Burundi's coffee (its main cash crop), could have imposed sanctions. They also note the US government's hesitancy to criticize the regime, because it was already accused of meddling in Burundi politics – that is in the murder of Ngendandumwe. A US State Department memorandum (10 October 1972) shows that Burundi's strategic geo-political position as 'an important piece of real-estate at the vulnerable eastern door to Zaire' determined how the Americans reacted to the genocide. They were more concerned with not upsetting the Burundi government in order to retain a presence in the country so that they could 'monitor potential anti-Zaire activity', particularly the supply of weapons from China to the dissidents fighting the Mobutu regime.[5]

---

[5] National Security Council, 10 October 1972, Memorandum for Henry Kissinger, re: Burundi Policy. Foreign Relations, 1969–1976, Volume E-5, Documents on Africa, 1969–1972. http://www.state.gov/r/pa/ho/frus/nixon/e5/54745.htm.

Although Belgium described the conflict as 'veritable genocide', its leverage was insignificant, particularly since the Burundi regime had attributed ethnic divisions to the policies of the Belgian colonial power. In addition, Belgian leverage in Burundi had been usurped by the French, in their quest to expand France's sphere of influence in the region. France had, in October 1969, signed a military accord with the Burundi government for the 'organization, training and management of Burundi military personnel' (Bizimana, 1999: footnote 153). In fact, France, Zaire, Uganda and Libya supplied military advisers and equipment to quell the uprising. There were also unsubstantiated reports of French military personnel flying the helicopters that carried out the massacres (Lemarchand & Martin, 1974). Geo-political and other vested interests were major factors in the reluctance of the West to criticize genocidal regimes.

The UN also appeared impotent to prevent genocide, despite declaring retrospectively that genocide had taken place in 1965 and 1972, no action has been taken against the perpetrators.[6] According to Lemarchand & Martin:

> To put the matter crudely: as long as the killings involved only Hutu and Tutsi the crisis could be regarded as lying essentially within the domestic jurisdiction of the state of Burundi; only inasmuch as Hutu and Tutsi could be identified as being respectively pro-western and pro-Communist (which was no longer the case in 1972), could the matter conceivably be viewed as a 'threat to peace' by western powers. Only then could a rationale be established for intervention, and a criterion made available for discriminating between 'friend' and 'foe'. (1974: 21)

The OAU was also heavily criticized for its inaction. A resolution passed at its summit in Rabat in late June 1972, declared support for Micombero. It read, 'the Council of Ministers is convinced that, thanks to your saving action, peace will be rapidly re-established, national unity will be consolidated, and territorial integrity will be preserved' (quoted in Bowen *et al.*, 1972: 9). The political authoritarianism that came to envelope the post-colonial era in Africa meant that many African leaders would not openly criticize Burundi in case it later rebounded on them. For the West, the humanity of the African was further devalued in the quest for alliances during the Cold War. Burundi's regimes, seemingly adept at international politicking, appeared to have manipulated the representational politics of Africa and the country's strategic location in Central Africa, in the context of global geo-politics, to evade, sanctioning of its behaviour.

The Burundi government appeared quite skilful in manipulating the international media, claiming as it would do after future episodes of state-sanctioned violence, that the conflict was one of genocide against the Tutsi committed 'in the name of democracy', and supported by a

---

[6] See Whitaker Report (1985) of the United Nations Economic and Social Council Commission on Human Rights, *Revised and updated Report on the Question of the Prevention and Punishment of the Crime of Genocide*, (E/CN.4/ub.2/1985/6 – 2 July 1985).

'foreign element contributing moral, financial, and material support'.[7] A White Paper released by the Burundi Embassy in Washington (26 June 1972), castigated the international community and media for accusing the government of genocide against the Hutu. 'We do not believe that repression is tantamount to genocide, there is an abyss between the two. We do not speak of repression, but of a LEGITIMATE DEFENSE BECAUSE OUR COUNTRY WAS AT WAR' (Their emphasis).[8] Whether through disregard for African lives or ignorance, the failure of the international community to intervene gave successive Burundi regimes the green light to commit genocidal violence with impunity.

The Post-Colonial State: 1976–1993

This period covers the second and third military republics. It was characterized by the entrenchment of the military as political actors as *coup d'états* became the mechanism for political change; the consolidation of Tutsi control of the state, the homogenization of the military as a Tutsi force, and further factionalism within the military elite based on regional and personal allegiances.

External observers, in particular development agencies, view most of this period as a relatively peaceful one in Burundi's post-colonial history, interrupted by minor episodes of violence, notably in 1988 and 1991. This apparent calm belies the militarization of society and the socialization of violence into everyday life. Each Tutsi president ruled with the assistance of an exclusively Tutsi military council.[9] And the state pursued a developmental policy that was highly discriminatory and with the assistance of donors. As noted by Greenland:

> Foreign aid is being channelled into projects that favour Tutsi rather than Hutu development. Embassies have been discouraged from financing rural development projects in mainly Hutu areas ... Belgian ... teachers are back [technical assistance programs] in front of nearly 100% Tutsi classes. (Greenland, 1974, quoted in Weinstein 1976: 20)

The Second Military Republic
Throughout the 1970s and 1980s, with strict controls over the media and a general suspicion of foreigners, the Burundi state tried to generate propaganda showing a united nation which had solved its ethnic problems.

---

[7] Official statement on the events of 29–30 April 1972, issued by Government of Burundi on 17 May 1972.

[8] See The Embassy of the Republic of Burundi, Washington, DC, 26 June 1972, *The Truth on the Recent Events that occurred in Burundi*, reprinted in Weinstein (1972) Appendix 1.

[9] Under Micombero, it was known as the National Committee for the Revolution (10 members) and later the Supreme Council of the Republic (22 members), under Bagaza, the Supreme Revolutionary Council (30 members), and during the Buyoya regime, the Military Committee for National Salvation with 31 members – all members were Tutsi (Ntibazonkiza, 1993; Niyonzima, 2004).

However, as a Tutsi-dominated state, it was still unable to rid itself of the spectre of the 1972 massacre and the threat of a Hutu uprising. Its next strategy, then, was to speed up the process of militarization, by devoting a major part of the country's budget on equipping and enlarging the army.

A minor uprising in June 1973 also provoked attacks by the army (*Daily Telegraph*, 15 May 1973). The latter became a pretext for the tightening-up of security and the imprisonment and murder of hundreds of Hutus. The fact that Micombero's government was tainted with blood was one reason given for his overthrow by his cousin, Colonel Jean-Baptiste Bagaza (another Tutsi-Hima), on 21 November 1976. In turn, Bagaza also found it necessary to suppress Hutu dissent while affirming:

> The histories of the Hutu and the Tutsi are quite simply fictitious. In Burundi there is so Tutsi or Hutu territory. Neither Hutu nor Tutsi have their own separate language, culture or religion. There is therefore only one tribe – that of the Barundi. (Quoted in *Information sur Burundi*, April 1985: 5)

In spite of the denial by the Bagaza regime of the existence of regional, ethnic or clan affiliations, a survey of the ethnic composition of the army or government revealed a remarkable predominance of Tutsi. Bagaza privileged members of his *Bayanzi* clan and the *Banyabururi* as a group. In 1985 the army was 96 per cent Tutsi; two-thirds of the University of Bujumbura students were Tutsi; Hutu held four ministries out of the twenty-two in government and comprised seven out of 65 deputies in the National Assembly; no Hutu were among the 15 provincial governors and only one in the 45-member national committee of UPRONA (BIIB, 1985; Kay, 1987). Bagaza played a key role in consolidating the political dominance of Bururi's Tutsi-Hima by extending their access to education and to the military. The first military school was established in Bururi in 1960 (Cervenska & Legum, 1994). This accounts for the predominance of Bururi Tutsi-Himas in the higher echelons of the military. As a secondary education was vital for entry into the officer cadet training school, it is alleged that the military class used state education as a means of reproducing itself, giving preferential treatment to their children. A survey by Ndirima (1995) shows the disproportionate investment in primary and secondary schools in the province during the Bagaza regime. For the years 1975–1984, Bururi, despite being sixth in terms of population size, had more pupils in secondary school (24 to 26 per cent) than other provinces with greater population (Ndirima, 1995). Jackson (2000: 28) reports claims that in the late 1980s 'as much as 60 per cent of donor funds for education were allocated to Bururi'. The rise of a Bururi educated elite through the army was seen as necessary to counter the bureaucratic *évolués*, being produced by Mission secondary schools, particularly the one at Ijenda in Mwaro province.

Narrowing the educational base to a select few allowed the Tutsi elite to remain hegemonic and dominant in politics and the public sector. Gender discrimination also pervaded the educational policy with most women being excluded from formal academic courses, and having much lower literacy rates than men. Data for 2002 show an adult literacy rate of just 50.4 per cent (age 15 and above), 43.6 per cent for females. Though female youth have a relatively high literacy rate, 65.1 per cent, compared to males of a similar age (aged 15–24), the female primary net enrolment ratio was 48 per cent in 2000/1, dropping to 7 per cent for secondary net enrolment and, at the tertiary level, just one per cent of women in the relevant age group were enrolled (UNDP, 2003). Enrolment rates for men were only marginally higher and indicate the low priority given to education by the state.

Instead, state development projects were concentrated on ways of acquiring greater control over the rural population. For example, villagization (*Ibigwati*) was adopted as a development strategy by parliament in 1979. By 1983, 102 villages of between 50 and 200 families had been formed in the south of the country – in the location of the 1972 uprising. A pass-law, governing population mobility, was introduced, supposedly as a conservation measure to prevent unofficial relocation of people. Its abolition in 1988 was due to pressure from the World Bank/IMF for a social climate suitable to a free market economy (*Africa Business,* 1988).

A constant flow of educated Hutus seeking refuge in neighbouring territories indicated the persistence of violent episodes, arbitrary detentions, and obstacles to legitimate demands for political and civil rights. In 1979 and 1984, during the UPRONA national conference, hundreds of Hutus were murdered. UPRONA, as the only legal political party, had in 1984 up to 65 per cent of Burundi voters as members, and had successfully integrated women, workers and youth movements, the latter through the transformation of the JNR into the *Union de la Jeunesse Révolutionnaire Burundaise* (URJB). The high level of party membership suggests that the vast majority of Burundians preferred to comply with the requirements of the state (Kay, 1987).

The Catholic Church, which, in the post-colonial era, provided a mouthpiece, a meeting place and an organizational structure for the Hutus, was placed under severe pressure through restrictions on church activities to Sundays, imprisonment of church leaders, expulsion of foreign missionaries and a ban on church literature (*Le Monde,* 2.4.1985; Amnesty International 1984).[10] In March 1984, despite 70 per cent of Burundians being Christians, the government banned all church meetings except on Saturday afternoons and Sundays. President Bagaza gave his reasons:

> Firstly, there is a day reserved for worship: it's Sunday for the Catholics. Saturday and Saturday alone is kept for community and party meetings. (Bagaza, Press Conference, 1979)

Also of serious consequence for the masses was the closure of Catholic literacy groups, which taught over 300,000 people (*Daily News,* 6.10.1986). Too many church activities were said to obstruct development. Not only were the demands of development and nation-building associated with coercive state polices but they were also used to obscure discriminatory policies.

---

[10] Religious affiliation of the Burundi population is said to be 72 per cent Catholic, 16 per cent Protestant, 8 per cent Animist and 4 per cent Muslim.

Bazaga's suppression of dissent left active opposition to those in exile. Between 1972 and 1992 over 10 political parties were formed abroad: six in Tanzania, three in Rwanda and one in Belgium. Of these, *Parti Pour la Libération Du Peuple Hutu* (Palipehutu) and *Front Pour la Libération Nationale* (Frolina) were committed to using violence to overthrow Tutsi hegemony. Because of OAU legislation and bilateral agreements between the Burundi state and its neighbours, throughout the Cold War these political movements were largely ineffective as they had to operate covertly in neighbouring territories.[11]

The Third Republic and the 1988 and 1991 Genocidal Violence
Bagaza was overthrown in a *coup d'état* on 3 September 1987, while he was attending a summit of French-speaking African leaders in Canada. He was replaced by another Tutsi-Hima from Bururi – his cousin, Major Pierre Buyoya, a member of Micombero's *bashingo* clan. Both Buyoya and Bagaza originated from the same *colline* – Rutovu in Bururi. Bagaza's downfall was attributed to several factors. One was the heavy international criticism his regime faced after his attack on the Catholic Church and its European leaders. Some western governments boycotted national events and threatened to suspend development aid. Reyntjens (1994) argues that similar to the situation with Micombero in 1976, the Tutsi-Hima group from Bururi became so embarrassed by their leader that they instigated the coup. Ntibazonkiza (1993) suggests much more localized grievances, specifically the disaffection among 800 soldiers who were given early retirement from the army before the end of their eight-year tenure. He argued that it was they who instigated the coup and sought out Buyoya to head the new regime.

The coup leader, Buyoya, reportedly accused Bagaza of 'constant violation of the constitution' (*The Guardian*, 7.8.1987). To remedy the situation, he lifted some of the more restrictive measures relating to the Church, thus placating foreign-aid donors, while maintaining discriminatory practices when he appointed 30 Tutsi soldiers to the newly formed National Council of Redemption. Like Bagaza, he used his presidency and genocidal violence, to maintain Tutsi hegemony. In August 1988, a minor skirmish between local Hutus and Tutsis in the Ntega commune of Kirundo province resulted in a full-scale military operation against the Hutu (*Independent*, 22.8.1988; Reyntjens, 1994). About 1,000 Tutsis and an estimated 20,000 Hutus were killed in the villages of Gashikanwa and Kiremba and the towns of Ntega and Ngarangara in Kirundo province (*Observer*, 28.8.1988). The area which had a population of 150,000, among whom 98 per cent were Hutu, was deserted in a matter of weeks as people fled to neighbouring Rwanda or to other parts of the country.

As in previous episodes of genocidal violence, the Burundi government carefully controlled the information disseminating from the province. However, refugees who fled to Rwanda testified to the

---

[11] The policy of non-interference in the affairs of member states is embodied in the 1963 OAU Charter, and the 1969 OAU Refugee Convention strictly prohibited member states from promoting political movements other than those fighting white-minority rule.

atrocities directed at the Hutu population. Calls for an independent investigation by UN officials were rejected by the government, which was also hostile to foreign aid agencies working in the area (*Le Monde*, 20.10.1988). Several Hutu intellectuals, who called for an inquiry, were arrested.

The massacres occurred at the same time that the Burundi government sought US $1.03 billion to fund its 1988–1992 Five-Year Development Plan from the international financial institutions and western governments (*Africa Business*, October 1998; 37). It appears that donor reluctance, amidst widespread criticisms of state terrorism, may have influenced President Buyoya's decision to alter radically the ethnic composition of his government. On 19 October 1988, Buyoya nominated Hutus to eleven of the 22 ministerial posts, with Tutsis maintaining control of the key defence, foreign affairs and interior ministries (*Le Monde*, 21.10.1988). Increased representation did not signal any radical change in the decision-making apparatus in favour of Hutus. As one Hutu refugee comments, 'it is the army which controls the country, not parliament' (*Le Monde*, 21.10.1988).

External observers contend that the events surrounding the 1988 massacre marked a sea-change in the state's approach to ethnicity. Faced with external criticisms of its repressive actions and demands for democracy, Buyoya set up the National Commission to Study the Question of National Unity and investigate the 1988 massacres. Its report was heavily criticized for placing the blame for ethnicity solely on the colonial administration (Ndikumana, 1998; Lemarchand, 1989). Others refer to its usefulness in acknowledging for the first time the existence of an ethnic problem and in establishing a national debate on ethnicity (Reyntjens, 1994). Despite exonerating the Tutsi government, it led to the approval by referendum of a Charter of National Unity in February 1991, and the setting up of a Government of National Unity with 12 Hutus and 12 Tutsis – though, as in the past, the key ministerial posts were reserved for Tutsis. Further changes, such as the ending of discrimination against the Hutus in the education system, were made – the exception being the armed forces which resisted change (Reyntjens, 1994).

The incorporation of Hutus into the regime did not prevent further incidences of state-sponsored genocide, as in November 1991 when the security forces retaliated against the Hutu population following an insurgency by Palipehutu, in two northern provinces. There was no independent evidence supporting the government's claim that some 551 Tutsi were killed by the insurgents. There were, however, independent reports of the 'arbitrary killing of about 1,000 people, most of them Hutus … in the detention centres and military barracks of Bubanza, Cibitoke and in the capital, Bujumbura' (Amnesty International, 1992: 2). Throughout the period of military autocracies, violence became the hallmark of politics. Successive massacres of Hutus and of Tutsis on the ideological left, suggest a bureaucracy confident in its ability to act with impunity – certainly, without international sanctions.

Conclusion

This chapter illustrates the emergence of the genocidal state in the context of African competition for state power in the post-colonial period. The key factors here were the shift in colonial support from one section of the elite to another and the displacement of the traditional elite by the genocidal military elite that drew its inspiration from state/society relationship of the colonial period. The intrigue that characterized intra-elite interactions in the pre-colonial era resurfaced in a more violent form in the post-colonial period as accumulative strategies became closely linked to state power and the social controls once exercised by the *Mwami* and the wider political community had been severely undermined by modernity and colonial rule.

The chapter demonstrates the limitations inherent in the use of ethnicity as the basis for understanding political violence in Africa. It is shown that although the violence has taken on an ethnic character, it is rooted in a struggle for power within the political class; a struggle for which the underlying determinants are as much regional, clan and interpersonal allegiances as ethnic difference. The political significance and the saliency of ethnic groups increased during the post-colonial period with intra-elite competition for power. Since access to the state ensured greater control of the means of production, the exclusion or inclusion of groups in the political sphere resulted in the activation of group solidarity. The case for Burundi is succinctly put by Martin Ndayahoze, a Hutu cabinet minister and army officer, killed by the military in 1972:

> We can affirm that it is in the leisured class that the virus of tribalism is to be found. What happens is that evil comes down from the top. It is the un-deserving administrative staff who, in order to maintain their rank or rise to a post they covet, need 'connections', craftiness, and guile. It is the insatiable people in responsible positions who make a political strategy out of ethnic division in order to further their shameful ambitions. Thus if they are Tutsi they denounce a Hutu peril which must be countered. If they are Hutu they unveil a Tutsi apartheid which must be combatted. (Ndayahoze, quoted in Greenland, 1976: 119)

Importantly, however, the language of genocide is used instrumentally by each ethnic group and by different political parties. Genocidal violence became further institutionalized with the realization by military officers and politicians that it could be used to gain political advantage without international sanctions. The chapter also shows how global geo-politics, particularly the Cold War and the West's fear of the spread of communism shaped their reaction to genocide in Africa. This indifference to genocide could be interpreted as complicity and illustrates the lack of value attached to African lives by the West.

5

Genocidal Politics | in the Context
of Democracy
1992–2005 | & Development

Introduction

The 1990s in Africa were marked by widespread democratization across the continent. Authoritarian one-party and military regimes were under pressure from internal opposition and from donor-imposed political conditionalities to open up the political space and introduce multi-party democracy. There has been much criticism of the type of democracy being pushed by the West in Africa. Ake (1996) abhors the hurry to foist 'a crude version of democracy' on African countries where elections take place but repression continues and dictators can declare themselves democratic. He surmises:

> Even at its best, liberal democracy is inimical to the idea of the people having effective decision-making power. The essence of liberal democracy is precisely the abolition of political power and the replacement of popular sovereignty with the rule of law. (Ake, 1996: 130)

Ake also argues against the type of democracy, now popular in the West, where the state is captured by interest groups. For Africa, he seeks, instead, to introduce a 'protective theory of democracy', in which 'the citizen is protected against the state, especially by virtue of a vibrant civil society' (Ake, 1996: 130). In sum, a democracy, that will liberate the populace from the brutalities of the genocidal state, must give full recognition of the inhumanity of their lived experience and seek to put in place the necessary transformative and protective measures. It must be remembered, however, that a 'vibrant civil society' can exist within society that is discriminatory, in that only certain groups are represented by that society, while others are silenced; for example, the USA could be said to have had a 'vibrant civil society' during slavery.

The Democratization Process, 1992–1996

The traditions of genocidal politics in Rwanda and Burundi have been closely associated with the introduction of multi-party democracy and the perpetuation of genocidal economic practices. In both countries, demands for political expression and improvements in human well-being have been linked to an intensification of violence, seen at its extreme in Rwanda of 1994. It is in this context that the western institutions and governments imposed their reforming political conditionalities, demanding democratic elections and multi-party politics, without addressing the desperate need for the social transformation of the state. Burundi's president, Major Pierre Buyoya, was subjected to external pressure to introduce multi-party democracy. As the head of a francophone state, he came under pressure from President Mitterand of France, who pronounced on the need for multi-party democracy at the Franco-African summit at Baule in 1990.

Burundi's experience of democratization in the 1990s has to be understood in relation to the constraints on the militaristic accumulation strategies and their intersection with the changing global political economy (neo-liberalism) and the privileging of violent masculinity. Violence, which was abated during the run-up to the 1993 elections, resumed and, waged by an even greater multiplicity of actors, was able to overturn the democratic experiment through the assassination of the democratically-elected president, Melchior Ndadaye, after less than four months in office.

President Major Pierre Buyoya was the archetype of the militarist who promoted genocidal politics, but who, in order to get support from the West, used the language of democratization. Buyoya embarked on a carefully engineered democratization process, on the assumption that once his democratic credentials were proven, the people would elect him to the presidency (Buyoya, 1998). On 13 March 1992 a new constitution that allowed multi-party politics and elections was passed by referendum. Article 55 of the constitution encouraged 'political parties to subscribe to the Charter of National Unity: ... to prohibit intolerance, ethnicism, regionalism, xenophobia, and recourse to violence in any form', while Article 57 stipulated that 'political parties should be forbidden to identify themselves in form, action or any other manner, notably with a particular group, region, religion, sect or gender.' Opposition parties only required 32 members to be registered as a political party and, in practice, rarely conformed to the legal requirements laid down in the constitution.

Three candidates fought the presidential elections of 1 June 1993 and six political parties took part in the parliamentary elections of 29 June: UPRONA, *Front Pour la Démocratie au Burundi* (FRODEBU), *Parti Pour le Reconciliation du Peuple* (PRP), *Rassemblement du Peuple Burundais* (RPB), *Parti du Peuple* (PP) and *Rassemblement Pour la Démocratie et le Développement Economique et Social* (RADDES). The parties were clearly aligned with specific ethnic groups, even though the main ones (UPRONA and FRODEBU) had both Hutu and Tutsi members. Reyntjens (1993: 572) estimated that 25 per cent of UPRONA's members were Hutu and 12 per cent of FRODEBU's Tutsi. Nonetheless, there were grounds for associating FRODEBU with Hutu and UPRONA with Tutsi interests. This was aggravated by UPRONA's election campaign that labelled FRODEBU a Hutu extremist party. FRODEBU sought an alliance with Buyoya, offering to support his independent candidature for president, if he was to leave UPRONA. Buyoya refused, believing that his position was unassailable.[1]

In the presidential elections, FRODEBU's leader, Melchoir Ndadaye, a Hutu from the central province of Muramvya, won 64.75 per cent of the vote; the incumbent Buyoya received 33.39 per cent and the third candidate, Pierre Claver Sendegeya, a mere 1.44 per cent. FRODEBU was also declared the winner of the parliamentary elections, gaining 71.40 per cent of the vote to UPRONA's 21.43 per cent, and none of the four other parties managed two per cent (Reyntjens, 1993). The elections, which were declared fair and transparent by international monitors, did not deliver the result that many observers expected. Buyoya and his supporters, both internally and externally, expected his victory. Despite presenting himself as a moderate and the architect of national reconciliation and multi-party democracy, Buyoya received only 20 per cent of the Hutu vote.

Ndadaye was installed as President of the Republic on 10 July 1993. His Government of National Unity had Tutsis occupying 9 (40 per cent) of the 23 ministerial posts, with Sylvie Kinigi (a Tutsi from UPRONA) as prime minister. A political amnesty allowed the return of Hutu rebel leaders and former president Bagaza. Just over 3 months later, President Ndadaye, as well as his constitutional successor the president of the National Assembly, Pontien Karibwami, his deputy, Gilles Bimazubute, the minister of homes affairs, Juvénal Ndayikeza, the head of the intelligence service, Richard Ndikumwami and several provincial governors were assassinated in a military coup on 21 October 1993. The coup-makers quickly established a National Committee for Public Salvation headed by François Nzege (a Hutu deputy head of UPRONA, and former minister of the interior under Buyoya) and Lt. Colonel Jean Bikomagu (army chief of staff, who allegedly masterminded the massacre of Hutus in 1972), but eventually handed power back to the civilians. The coup failed primarily because of international condemnation: Rwanda, Mali, France, Germany and Belgium denounced the coup, and several western countries suspended co-operation with Burundi. On 11 November 1993, the president of the National Assembly, Sylvestre Ntibantunganya (FRODEBU) was appointed interim president until February 1994, when changes to the constitution allowed Cyprien Ntayrimana, vice-president of FRODEBU, to be elected president with Anatole Kanyenkiko (UPRONA) as vice-president.

Why was the democratic experiment curtailed so shortly and so violently? Analysis differs as to the attribution of blame, focusing on the erosion of the political influence of the Tutsis, economic crises, changes to the security services and the spectre of genocide. Gahama (1995) and Prunier (1994) put the blame on the exclusionary nature of FRODEBU's political and economic policies. Their analysis support UPRONA's criticism of FRODEBU's policy of replacing Tutsi bureaucrats with FRODEBU members. Gahama, noting that all the governors of the 15 provinces and the mayor of Bujumbura were from FRODEBU, states:

---

[1] Confidential interview with FRODEBU official 1998.

> Tutsi and Hutu UPRONA *functionaires* (civil servants) were replaced by militant Frodebistes (often incompetent) right through to the levels as low as the communal secretaries or the market security guards. (1995: 23)

Some commentators, Tutsis, in particular, derided the new Hutu appointees, even claiming that they did not have the skills to run the bureaucracy – a notion repeated by Prunier (1994). If, as Ngaruko & Nkurunziza (2000) contend, the bureaucracy was the basis for accumulation through predation, many Tutsis saw their opportunities for political patronage closed or threatened. Moreover, the implications of democratic politics and elections were not understood by all; Hutus interpreted 'winner-takes-all' democracy as an attempt to rectify many years of discrimination, while the Tutsis refused to accept the re-organization of the state that their loss of power entailed.

A third explanation for the coup concerns the reform of the security forces. The military, through the National Security Council, was quite influential in the political life of the country. It remained Tutsi-dominated; of the 20,000 soldiers only 1,024 were Hutus and only three Hutus were among the 700 senior officers (*Daily News*, 25.7.1997). It was apparent to all that Ndadaye, in order to guarantee the security of his government, would have to reform the state security services. The military was not open to reform and was supported in its resistance to change by the Tutsi parties, who saw control of the security forces as their guarantor against genocide. Even before Ndadaye took up office, there was an attempted coup on 2 July 1993. Ndadaye's intention to set up a presidential guard of 500 to include 150 Hutus and to start the recruitment of Hutus into the army may well have triggered the coup (*Africa Confidential*, 12 August 1994; Cervenska & Legum, 1994).

Evidence suggests that the minister of communication, Jean-Marie Ngendahayo, and the minister of defence, Lt. Col. Charles Ntakije, had prior knowledge of the October coup, even though senior officers, who were later implicated, claimed that it was mutiny. The International Commission of Inquiry for Burundi (ICIB), set up by the UN Security Council (UNSC), was charged with establishing 'the facts relating to the assassination of the President of Burundi and the massacres and other related serious acts of violence which followed' (Resolution 1012, 1995: Para. 1a). The UNSC found its work obstructed by the Burundi military. After pointing out considerable inconsistencies in the statements of the Tutsi officers interviewed, the report concluded that:

> The assassination of the President, as well as that of the person constitutionally entitled to succeed him, was planned beforehand as an integral part of the coup that overthrew him, and that the planning and execution of the coup was carried out by officers highly placed in the line of command of the Burundian army. (UNSC, 1996: Para. 213)

Following the coup, genocidal violence erupted in Burundi initiated by Hutus and FRODEBU militants, followed by retaliatory violence against Hutu civilians in several provinces, notably in Karuzi, Gitega and Ruyigi, killing an estimated 80,000 people (*Reporters sans Frontières*, 1995).

The violence which followed the assassination of Ndadaye and the over-throw of his democratic government was perceived differently by the inter-national community. The UNSC (1996) report labelled the killing of Tutsis and some Hutu members of UPRONA in the immediate aftermath of Ndadaye's murder, genocide, but not the military reprisals against the Hutus civilians, despite admitting that it had limited access to Hutu inter-viewees.[2] The commission, which was requested by the Burundians in late 1993, was set up two years later due to the UN's concern about the sensi-tivity of the investigation. The commission was underfunded and encoun-tered considerable obstruction in conducting the inquiry (Amnesty International, 1995b). Most of its sources and witnesses of massacres came from the Tutsi population. Nevertheless, the commission asserts that:

> Evidence is sufficient to establish that acts of genocide against the Tutsi minority took place in Burundi on 21 October 1993, and the days following, at the instigation and with the participation of certain FRODEBU func-tionaries and leaders up to commune level. (UNSC, 1996: Para. 483)

Later in Paragraph 485, it admitted that 'the evidence is insufficient to determine whether or not these acts of genocide were planned or ordered by leaders at a higher level'. Furthermore, it goes on to state:

> The evidence shows that indiscriminate killing of Hutu men, women and children was carried out by members of the Burundian army and Gendarmerie, and by Tutsi civilians. Although no evidence was obtained to indicate that the repression was centrally planned or ordered, it is an established fact that no effort was made by the military authorities at any level of command to prevent, stop, investigate or punish acts. (UNSC, 1996: Para. 486)

Not surprisingly, the UNSC has been perceived as biased by FRODEBU and as having succumbed to the campaign by the Tutsi political parties, church leaders and media to get the massacres of their ethnic group labelled 'genocide' (CAAB, 1999).[3]

The Burundi government failed to prosecute those responsible for Ndadaye's death.[4] A UNESC Report (1995a) listed several cases of violence with impunity, and mentioned specifically the reluctance of the regime to seek extradition from Zaire and Uganda of nine officers alleged to have been involved in the murder of the president.[5] The report notes:

---

[2] The Commission was established by UN Security Council Resolution 1012 of 28 August 1995, and was mandated 'to establish the facts relating to the assassination of the President of Burundi on 21 October 1993, the massacres and other related acts of violence which followed' (Para. 1a).

[3] Various Tutsi political parties and militia groups, including PARENA and SOJEDEM, produced statements in 1996 accusing FRODEBU of genocide. The Tutsi extremist group AC Genocide-Crimoso constructed monuments in memory of those Tutsi killed in 1993 and 1996.

[4] A list of senior officers, headed by Pierre Buyoya, who allegedly devised, organized and recruited the assassins, was in circulation.

[5] They were Major Busokoza and Lieutenant Jean-Paul Kamana. Another alleged plotter, Commandant Hilarie Ntakiyica, was also in Uganda.

In accordance with the extradition agreement between Great Lakes countries, of 21 June 1975, the Government with which the request is lodged may order the accused person to be remanded in custody, while the requesting Government makes a formal application for extradition. The Government of Burundi requested the extradition of the officers and they remained in custody in April 1994, but the formal application for extradition was never completed. Investigations were paralysed by lack of political and diplomatic will. (UNESC, 1995a: 8)

In August 1996, Buyoya appointed Lt. Col. Vincent Niyungeko as army chief of staff and George Mukarako as *gendarmerie* chief of staff (both were alleged to be involved with the October 1993 attempted coup). Apparently, the UN Special Rapporteur was also informed of Buyoya's involvement in the coup by low ranking Tutsi soldiers held in Bujumbura's prison. Later reports suggest that these soldiers were killed during a prison rebellion (UNESC, 1995a).

Hutu alleged *génocidaires* were not given impunity. Following the UNSC report, on 9 September 1997, the Government of Burundi enacted a law to prosecute those accused of genocide and crimes against humanity.[6] Later that year, there were trials of several hundred people responsible for the 1993 massacres of Tutsis. Some 44 people were sentenced to death. A report by Amnesty International (1998: 13) argues that 'the government used the term genocide to gain the moral high ground and to distract from the crimes against humanity committed by its own forces and the treatment, particularly the death penalty, meted out to the accused.'

The Post-Colonial State 1994–2005

The period 1994 to 2000 marked a distinct period in the militarization of Burundi society when numerous actors (the military, militias, political parties, rebels, youth groups) incited or perpetrated violence of a genocidal nature with impunity. A culture of systemic insecurity emerged, linked to the increase in military expenditure, the rapid recruitment of military personnel, the setting up of paramilitary groups by the military and political parties, the acute factionalism within the political elite and the rebel groups, and the forced displacement of civilians into protected villages under the government strategy of *regroupement*.[7]

The eighteen month period after Ndadaye's assassination was labelled by some as a 'creeping coup' (*Africa Confidential*, 4 August 1995). With the military prevented from taking over because of 'the threat of a hostile regional reaction and international disapproval', the parties embarked on fomenting chaos to gain political advantage (*Africa Confidential*,

---

[6] See Republic of Burundi: *Projet de Loi portant sur les procédures de poursuites et de mise enjugement des personnes coupables des crimes de génocide ou des crimes contre l'humanité*. 1997.

[7] *Regroupement* camps were set up by the Burundi government in 1996, supposedly in an attempt to isolate the rebels from their support base among the Hutu people in rural areas.

4 August 1995: 3). The death of the president and prime minister created a successional and constitutional crisis that was exploited by UPRONA and their allied Tutsi-dominated parties, which included PARENA (*Parti Pour le Redressement National*), the party formed by ex-president Bagaza after the 1993 elections. The goal of the Tutsi-dominated parties was to reverse the results of the democratic elections. This was done in three ways.

First, the Tutsi elite sought international sympathy by labelling the attack on Tutsi after Ndadaye's assassination as genocide. Second, they sought to mobilize domestic opinion against FRODEBU by accusing leading members of FRODEBU, such as Jean Minani and Leonard Nyamgoma, of inciting genocide, and forcing many of them to flee the country. In December 1994, violent Tutsi opposition to the political appointment of Minani as president of the National Assembly led to his removal after less than a month in office, and the explusion of the Tutsi prime minister, Anatole Kanyenkiko, from UPRONA. There is no real evidence that Minani had incited Hutus to commit genocide. He was in Kigali at the time of Ndadaye's death and was reported to have actually said:

> In the name of the government I represent, we appeal for the following: that every Burundian, whoever he is, stands up and disowns these criminals. I appeal to every Burundian, wherever you are, whether you are a Tutsi, a Hutu or a Twa, whichever party you are in, to realise that the infamy they have perpetrated is directed against you ... it is your loss because they have slain the leaders you chose for yourselves. (*BBC Summary of World Broadcast*, 23.10.1993)

Failing to capture the state through the October coup, UPRONA and other opposition groups set about the political destabilization of the country through the use of genocidal violence, which gained justification in April 1994 after the death of President Cyprian Ntaryimana in the plane crash that also killed the Rwandan president and the 1994 genocide of Tutsi in Rwanda (Chapter 7).

With most of FRODEBU's key politicians dead or in exile, a power-sharing arrangement brokered by the UN special representative, Ambassador Ahmedou Ould Abdallah, resulted in the signing of an agreement, the Convention of Government, on 10 September 1994, by the remaining members of FRODEBU and its coalition allies (PP, PL & RPB) and nine opposition parties (UPRONA, PIT, ANADDE, INKINZO, PRP, PARENA, RADDES, PSD and ABASA). A new power-sharing Government of National Unity was constituted on 5 October, comprising one *Ganwa*, 16 Hutus (three from UPRONA) and seven Tutsis. Sylvestre Ntibantunganya (FRODEBU) was re-elected as president, with the Tutsi, Antoine Nduwayo, as prime minister. The nine opposition parties gained 45 per cent of the ministerial posts, representing a substantial reversal of the democratic process.

The Convention of Government, which should have run through to June 1998, stipulated that the president of the republic should not have been involved in the overthrow of Ndadaye or any acts of genocide or shown support for militias. It also restructured the National Security

Council, removing the dominance of military officers (Article 17) and included a facility for a national dialogue (Article 52). The latter was impossible in the context of the extreme violence and destabilization being fomented by opposition groups. Ntibantunganya had to postpone a national debate scheduled for March 1995 to discuss the role of the army, the disarming of armed groups and the neutrality and independence of the judicial system. On 29 June 1995, the eventual collapse of Ntibantunganya's government was caused by the failure of the Tutsi-dominated National Assembly to approve his proposals for the introduction of emergency measures to deal with the widespread violence.

This move strengthened those members of the political elite who sought to create chaos in the country by fomenting violence, without sanctions. It allowed numerous political actors, especially extremist Tutsi political parties, to support openly the assassination of elected parliamentary representatives and to mobilize militia groups. With army sponsorship, Tutsi youth paramilitary groups, *Solidarité de la Jeunesse Pour la Défense des Minoritées* (SOJEDEM), *Jeunesses Révolutionnaires Rwagasore* (JRR), *Puissance d'autodéfense 'amasekanya'* (power of self-defence), *Sans Échec* (the infallible) and *Sans Défaite* (the undefeated), were formed during the 1990s and closed down urban areas in their *ville morte* (dead city) campaign, which involved the forced displacement of Hutus from certain districts of Bujumbura city and other major towns. Another group, *Action Contre le Génocide (AC Génocide)*, organized meetings on the 21st of each month in memory of the Tutsis massacred in October 1993.

These militias focus their recruitment on school pupils and students. *SOJEDEM*, led by a Dominican priest, was composed of youths who were often placed in the firing line (Human Rights Watch, 2001; UNESC, 1995b). In effect, as Amnesty International (1995a: 2) notes, 'a culture of violence and the use of lethal military weapons have thus entered school'. Such was the scale of violence that on a visit to Belgium in March 1995, President Ntibantunganya announced that genocide was taking place in his country. The President sought regional support for a foreign intervention force amidst violent opposition from UPRONA hard-liners, the military and Tutsi militias (Chapter 9).

Militarism, Masculinity and Genocide: Lessons from Buyoya
After almost three years of violence, the military coup of 25 July 1996 that brought Pierre Buyoya back to power was seen as inevitable by many observers. The impression given externally was that Buyoya, who was out of the country at the time of the coup, was offered the presidency by the coup-leaders.[8] There were considerable differences in international and regional reception of Buyoya's second coup. The OAU declared the military junta illegal, and, in line with the new mood in the region that coups constituted unacceptable changes of government, regional leaders openly condemned the coup. Many in the region held the view that Buyoya was the mastermind behind the assassination of Ndadaye and the overthrow of a democratically elected government. This was not helped

---

[8] Buyoya spent May and June of 1996 in the USA.

by the fact that the UN's inquiry report failed to mention Buyoya (UNSC, 1995). In protest, the Tanzanian government refused to recognise the new Burundi government, and it was two years before the credentials of Buyoya's new *chargé d'affaires* was accepted by Dar es Salaam. At a meeting on 31 July 1996, regional heads of state imposed economic sanctions on Burundi (Chapter 9).

In contrast, the international community – western governments – thought Buyoya's coup would bring security and stability to Burundi. While the Belgium government 'deeply regretted the coup', its foreign minister, Erik Derycke, stated that 'Major Buyoya's personality was not the worst, perhaps the most acceptable', and that 'Buyoya is the least of all evils.'[9] The US secretary of state for Africa, Warren Christopher, condemned the coup, yet, like the Europeans, many in his government saw Buyoya as the saviour of Burundi. Buyoya was able to garner a considerable amount of international support, from among others, the European Union and American representatives to the Great Lakes, and from international NGOs; the Catholic and Rome-based *Sant'Egidio* and International Alert of London.[10] Ironically, the American ambassador to Burundi was reported to have earlier said the USA would not tolerate a coup in Burundi, 'We shall do everything possible to isolate such a government and those responsible for it.'[11] Although the EU suspended development aid, the regime retained the full support of the French government, which was the first to give de facto recognition (*Africa Confidential*, 2 August 1996 & 6/8 March 1998).

Buyoya had won considerable international support for facilitating the democratic transition and 'national reconciliation' of the early 1990s. Praised by western academics and NGOs alike, he was seen as 'a victim of his own success' when he failed to win the 1993 presidential elections. One of the more challenging question would be why someone who promoted genocide would be given US $145,000 from USAID and money from the EU and UN to set up a private foundation for democratization studies (*Foundation for Peace and Unity*), a seat on the Council of African advisors for the World Bank, and a scholarship to attend a language course at Yale University (*Africa Confidential*, 6 September 1996). Buyoya also knew the significance of having the international community on his side. At the Arusha Peace talks, he was reported to have said, 'There are four ethnic groups in Burundi: Tutsi, Hutu, Twa and the international community' (Niyonzima, 2004: 304).

The West's support of Buyoya was also in line with the old military solution of Lucien Pye (1959), who propagated the 'strong man' approach to political stability in developing counties. Buyoya, schooled in Belgium and in Europe's military establishment and with the personal attributes of an *évolués*, represented the archetypical 'strong man' of Africa. After the coup, the French government stressed that 'a new strong man has been appointed as the interim president in a bid to give a new boost to national debate and democracy.'[12] The concept of the 'strong man' as ruler reflects

[9] *Belgian RTBF Radio, quoted in BBC Summary of World Broadcast*, 26 July 1996.
[10] Aldo Ajello (EU) and Howard Wolpe (USA).
[11] From *Radio Burundi, quoted in BBC Summary of World Broadcast*, 2 July 1996.
[12] *Belgian RTBF Radio, quoted in BBC Summary of World Broadcast*, 26 July 1996.

the military masculinism that pervades western ideas about governance in Africa, and sanctioned the use of authoritarian and violent measures to ensure political stability. Whether western governments had prior knowledge of the 26 July 1996 coup demands some consideration. It is alleged that, the day before the coup, Belgian nationals were advised to stay indoors, and the American special envoy visited Burundi several times in the days preceding the coup and spoke of 'gradual genocide'.[13]

Buyoya appealed for 'international understanding', claiming that 'the change in government had not been prompted by love of power or material benefits but by a desire to save the country, which was falling into an abyss while the elders looked on' (*Radio Burundi*, 26 July 1996). Later, he remarked that 'in the near future, we shall form a broad-based transitional government which will include personalities chosen individually, but who may belong to various sensitivities.'[14] Buyoya introduced a decree on 13 September 1996 which replaced his 1992 Constitution and increased his powers by taking over the FRODEBU-dominated National Assembly. A marked dissonance existed between Buyoya the international statesman and his image within the national territory. Buyoya's international image was of a democrat and 'moderate man of peace confronted with intransigent rebels on one side and narrow-minded extremists on the other' (ICG, 2001a: 5). The representation of Buyoya as a peacekeeper was challenged by members of FRODEBU, who posed the question, 'Why did he not stop the massacres?'[15] Regional states also questioned Buyoya's democratic credentials, and many perceived him to be the mastermind behind Ndadaye's assassination and the July 1996 coup. The led to the imposition of a regional trade embargo from 31 July 1996 to January 1999.

In 1997, amid criticism of his regime's reluctance to participate in the regionally-mediated Arusha peace talks (Chapter 9), Buyoya started his own internal peace talks with those FRODEBU members still in the country. On 25 January 1997, he reopened the National Assembly, lifted the ban on political parties and began a three-year transitional period, supposedly before returning the country to democracy. He made himself official head of the regime on 10 June and formed a government that appeared ethnically balanced. Two vice-presidents were appointed; a Hutu (Frédéric Bamvuginyumira) and a Tutsi (Matthias Sinamenye), and Pascal Firmin Ndimira, a Hutu and a former governor of the Bank of Burundi and World Bank consultant, as Prime Minister (ICG, 1998b). On 11 June 1998, he signed a Constitutional Act of Transition and a Platform of Agreement governing the transition regime (*Accord sur la Plate-Forme Politique du Régime de Transition, 6 June 1998*), without them being voted on in the National Assembly. The Act gave the President exceptional powers to make all senior appointments in the government, the civil service and in the military. In the platform Buyoya stated that he would be working towards peace, stability and a relaunching of the democratization process, and called for decisive actions against genocide, including an international commission of inquiry. A month

[13] *Radio France International, quoted in BBC Summary of World Broadcast*, 21 & 24 July 1996.
[14] *Radio Burundi*, 29 July 1996.
[15] Interview with FRODEBU activist, Brussels, 1998.

later, he enlarged the National Assembly to include representatives of more Tutsi parties: *Parti Socialiste et Pan-Africaniste* (INKINZO), *Parti-Social Démocrate* (PSD), *Parti L'indépendant des Travailleurs* (PIT) and *Alliance des Vaillants* (AV-Intwari). Some of them were created after the 1993 elections and, allegedly, had been involved in the violence that had engulfed the country.[16]

Buyoya was faced also with political competition arising from intra-ethnic and inter- and intra-clan politics within the Tutsi group. The regionalism that had dominated Burundi politics persisted in the 1990s with Bururi's Tutsi-Hima retaining their dominance in the army and the government; this led to intense competition with *Banyaruguru* Tutsi, some of whom were assassinated and the continuation of inter-clan rivalry. It is argued that he released the 1993 putschists and was behind the February 1998 helicopter crash, which killed Colonel Firmin Sinzoyiheba, a Tutsi and Minister of Defence, who, apparently, held anti-genocide views and was opposed to the killing of Ndadaye (Niyonzima, 2004).[17]

A major divide among the Tutsi-Hima military and political elite was the rivalry between Buyoya and former President Bagaza; the latter was supposed to have a strong following in the military. Buyoya, fearing a counter-coup, continually represented Bagaza, especially to the international community, as an extremist. Hutus, however, did not necessarily share this view of Bagaza as 'evil'. 'He is consistent – not an extremist', remarked one Hutu FRODEBU politician.[18] And another claimed, 'Bagaza is not a problem, he is not powerful.'[19] And spokesman for a rebel group was reported to have said, 'for us, the PARENA people are all the more acceptable because Bagaza's party was not guilty of genocide. We think it is far cleaner than UPRONA, which has blood on its hands.'[20]

[16] *Burundi Bureau, Press Release no.173*, 17/07/98.
[17] Interview with CNDD official, Brussels, 1998.
[18] Interview with FRODEBU activist, Brussels, 1998.
[19] Interview with FRODEBU activist, Brussels, 1998.
[20] *Africa Confidential*, 9 May 1997, 38 (10): 7.

Table 5.1: Burundi: Political Parties, Rebel Movements and Militias in 2000

Acronym	Full name	Background and Leadership
Pro-Tutsi Parties		
UPRONA	*Parti de l'Unité et du Progrès National*	Established in 1961 and was the party of Prince Rwagasore. From 1965 to 1992, it was the only political party allowed by the military regimes and had both Hutu and Tutsi members, although the latter were perceived by all to be the most influential. There were numerous splits over the party's position with respect to the Arusha negotiations; Charles Mukasi, Hutu leader was vehemently anti-negotiations and Luc Rukingama, Hutu, (information minister) pro-negotiations.

Acronym	Full name	Background and Leadership
Pro-Tutsi Parties (contd)		
ABASA	*Alliance Burundo-Africaine Pour le Salut*	Founded in 1993 and led by Ambassador Terence Nsanze who lives in Europe. The internal wing was led by Serge Mukaramarakiza.
ANNADE	*Alliance National Pour le Droit et le Développement*	Formed in 1992 and led by Patrice Nsababaganwa.
AV-Intwari	*Alliance des Vaillants*	Formed in 1993 and led by André Nkundikije.
INKINZO	*Parti Socialiste et Pan-Africaniste*	Formed in 1993 and led by Alphonse Rugambarara.
PARENA	*Parti pour le Redressement National*	Founded in 1995 led by Jean-Baptiste Bagaza.
PIT	*Parti L'indépendant des Travailleurs*	Formed in 1993 and led by Etienne Nyahoza.
PSD	*Parti-Social Démocrate*	Formed in 1993 and led by Godefroid Hakimana.
RADDES	*Rassemblement Pour la Démocratie et le Développement Economique et Social*	Formed in 1993 and led by Joseph Nzeyimana.
PRP	*Parti Pour la Réconciliation du Peuple*	Formed in 1992, led by Brussels-based Mathias Hitimana until 2004.
AC Genocide	*Action Contre le Génocide*	Organized meetings on the 21 of each month in memory of Tutsi massacred after Ndadaye's assassination.
Amase Kanya	*Puissance d'autodéfense 'amasekanya'*	Tutsi group, created in 1994 and headed by Diomède Rutamucero.
SOJEDEM	*Solidarité de la Jeunesse Pour la Défense des Minoritées* [Youth Solidarity for the Defence of the Minorities]	Formed in 1993 and led by Deo Niyonzima, a former Dominican monk.
JRR	*Jeunesses Révolutionnaires Rwagasore*	Formed during 1993 elections.

Acronym	Full name	Background and Leadership
Pro-Hutu Groups		
FRODEBU	*Front Pour la Démocratie au Burundi*	Founded in Rwanda in 1986 – operated underground until registered 23 July 1992. Won the first multiparty elections in June 1993; leader assassinated in October 1993; Led by Jean Minani in exile from 1993–2001; Internal wing led by Secretary General, Augustin Nzojibwami.
Palipehutu	*Parti Pour la Libération du Peuple Hutu*	Led by Etienne Karatasi – created in the late 1970s by Hutu refugees in Rwanda.
CNDD	*Conseil National Pour la Défense de la Democratie*	Founded in 1994 and led by Leonard Nyamgoma, former FRODEBU Minister of the Interior.
FROLINA	*Front Pour la Libération Nationale*	Formed in mid-1989, as a breakaway group from Palipehutu and headed by Joseph Karumba.
PL	*Parti Liberal*	Formed in 1992 and led by Gaetan Nikobamye.
PP	*Parti du Peuple*	Formed in 1992 and led by Shadrack Niyonkuru.
RPB	*Rassemblement du Peuple Burundais*	Formed in 1992 and is led by Balthazar Bigirimana.
CNDD-FDD	*Conseil National Pour la Défense de la Démocratie – Forces pour la Défense de la Démocratie FDD-CNP (National Circle of Patriots)*	Formed in November 1993; FDD broke away from CNDD in 1998, and in 2001, divided into two factions headed by Pierre Nkurunziza and Jean-Bosco Ndayikengurukye. Both reached ceasefire agreements with the transitional government in 2002/2003. Nkurunziza's faction (FDD-CNP) formed the political party which won the 2005 elections.
Palipehutu-FNL	*Parti Pour la Libération du Peuple Hutu/Forces Nationals pour la Libération*	Formed as the military wing of party, Palipehutu, which was established in 1980 in Tanzania, and headed by Rémy Gahutu until his death in 1990; the movement split into two factions in February 2001 (FNL-Cossan Kabura & FNL-Etienne Karatasi). These leaders were sidelined in August 2002 when the two main factions became headed by Alain Mugabarabona & Agathon Rwasa. Mugabarabona signed a ceasefire agreement in 2002; in 2004, Jean-Bosco Sindayigaya broke away from Rwasa and formed a separate wing. Rwasa signed a peace agreement with the government in 2006.

Source: Some information adapted from ICG (2000a)

The Politics of Genocide: Militarization, Factionalism and Rebellion
The failure of the democratic experiment and Buyoya's usurpation of
power reinforced the politics of genocide among some of those who were
elected in 1993. Hutu power was given renewed meaning as a militarized
force. Militarized Hutu opposition, namely *Parti Pour la Libération du
Peuple Hutu/Forces National de Libération* (Palipehutu-FNL), *Conseil
National Pour la Défense de la Démocratie/Forces pour la Défense de la
Démocratie* (CNDD/FDD) and Frolina, became a force to be reckoned
with after 1996 when factionalism engulfed FRODEBU and better-
equipped Hutu rebel movements were formed; the latter aided by
political changes in the DRC, which allowed the rebels to gain access to
refuge, sources of finance and weapons (Chapter 7). Palipehutu, which
was against the democratic elections, had already launched attacks
against the regime. Between 1993 and 1995, it had a strong presence the
Kamenge and Kinama suburbs of Bujumbura and supported Hutu militia
attacks against Tutsis after Ndadaye's assassination (Ntibantunganya,
1999; Amnesty International, 1996a).
   The Hutu political elite were never united in their opposition to
the military regimes. A significant minority sought co-operation with the
Tutsis by joining UPRONA – the majority of whom came from
the southern provinces. For example, Charles Mukasi (Hutu and a former
President of UPRONA) was considered by many Hutus as an opportunist
and extremist in terms of his views towards the Hutu rebels; others, such
as Firmin Ndirima, were bureaucrats who were drawn into government
by Buyoya.[21]
   Although many in the opposition campaigned for the election victory
of FRODEBU, they were divided as to the degree of co-operation with the
Tutsis, on the use of violence to effect change, and also on the basis of
personality and regional differences. On the rebels' side, the former
FRODEBU Minister of the Interior, Leonard Nyamgoma (from Bururi and
Buyoya's former classmate), was feared the most. He was well-known for
his activism, especially in the recruitment of people to register for
FRODEBU in the run-up to the 1993 elections, when many people
crossed from UPRONA to FRODEBU. Nyamgoma's style was qualitatively different from Ndadaye and, according to reports, they had quar-
relled well before the former's death.[22]
   The assassination of Ndadaye in October 1993 created a split in
FRODEBU between those advocating violence and those seeking a
peaceful resolution. After Ndadaye's assassination, Nyamgoma formed
Conseil National Pour la Défense de la Démocratie (CNDD) – the military
wing of FRODEBU. The leadership contest that ensued in FRODEBU,
between Nyamgoma and Sylvestre Ntibantunganya, led to a split in the
party and Nyamgoma's flight from the country in March 1999, taking
with him CNDD. In 1997, he held 'secret' meetings with Buyoya to
discuss possible power-sharing arrangements, justifying the assumption
by some Hutus of the struggle being primarily between people from
Bururi province and those from other regions. Initially, CNDD had Tutsi

---

[21] Interview with FRODEBU Activist, Brussels 1998.
[22] Interview with FRODEBU activist, Brussels 1998.

(northerners) as members, but as a party, it weakened when it moved from being multi-ethnic to ethnic and regional.

Nyamgoma dissolved CNDD's Executive Committee in March 1998 after disagreements with his Hutu party members, especially the youth, who accused him of regionalism and tribalism. The youth who were disaffected with Nyamgoma's style (reportedly dictatorial) broke away to form an armed wing, *Forces pour la Défense de la Démocratie* or CNDD-FDD. FRODEBU was also divided between its internal wing (those who remained in the country after Ndadaye's death, led by Augustin Nzojibwani – a supporter of Buyoya) and its external wing (those who fled into exile). Jean Minani, exiled in Tanzania, described those FRODEBU cadres residing in Bujumbura as prisoners and the Constitutional Act of June 1998 as an agreement between 'prisoner and gaoler'.[23]

The fracturing of the rebel groups became extreme in the early 2000s, with both Palipehutu-FNL and CNDD-FDD split into two separate wings (Table 5.1). CNDD-FDD's factions were headed by Pierre Nkurunziza and Jean-Bosco Ndayikengurukiye and Palipehutu-FNL's were headed by Alain Mugarabona and Agathon Rwasa. Numerous factions existed within these wings loyal to individual battalion leaders. Personal ambition seemed to have been the driving force rather than the degree of militancy. There were even suggestions that Buyoya's regime profited from the fracturing of these movements, and claims were made by Hutus that Jean-Bosco Ndayikengurukye, the leader of one faction of CNDD-FDD, was Buyoya's cousin.[24] Ndayikengurukye was alleged to have amassed great wealth during the rebels sojourn in the DRC (Chapter 7).

The relative size of the Hutu rebel movements was difficult to determine; before factionalism, CNDD-FDD forces were estimated to have been between 6,000 and 10,000 combatants based in DRC and Tanzania, FNL between 2000 and 3500 based in Uvira, DRC and *Front Pour la Libération National* (FROLINA) between 200 and 500.[25] According to HRW (2000a) Palipehutu-FNL operated around Bujumbura, with the two wings of CNDD-FDD in the East and South, and FROLINA in the East. Rebel movements recruited either volunteers from Burundi or from the refugee camps in Tanzania and the DRC, or through the kidnapping of young men in Burundi.

In 1998, attempts were made to unite the three Hutu rebel movements, but disputes broke out about the degree of Tutsi or *Baganwa* representation in the leadership. Later, after its ceasefire agreement with the government in 2002, the FDD joined forces with the military to launch assaults against the FNL in Bujumbura rural province (HRW, 2004a). Hutu militias, *Intagohekas* (those who do not sleep) – a break-away group from CNDD, also carried out attacks against Tutsis (*Africa Confidential*, 17 February 1995).[26]

---

[23] Burundi-Bureau, *Press Release no.169*, 16/06/98, Bujumbura-Bonn.
[24] Ndayikengurukye was also the cousin of Augustin Nzojibwani, the leader of FRODEBU's internal wing.
[25] Interview with member of Arusha Facilitation Team, Dar es Salaam 2005; Agence-France-Presse, Reliefweb, 16 June 2001.
[26] In January 1995, in Muyinga Province.

The Genocidal Media

One outcome of the democratization process of the early 1990s was the liberalization of the media, with the establishment of privately-operated newspapers and radio stations. The role played by a highly partisan media in inciting genocide has been well documented for Rwanda (HRW, 1999a). Not only could Barundi access the infamous Rwandan *Radio Télévision Libre des Mille Collines* (RTLMC), but Burundi had a flourishing hate media of its own supported by political parties and extremist individuals.

A survey conducted by Ndarishikanye and Dupaquier (1995) found that of the 26 print media established in the 1990s, ten were pro-Tutsi (*Le Carrefour des Idées, Le Citoyen, La Semaine, Pan Afrika, Le Patriote, L'Étoile, La Balance, Le Républicain, La Nation* and *Ijwi ry'abakera Kivi*), five were pro-Hutu (*Le Témoin, L'Éclaireur, L'Aube de la Démocratie, Le Miroir Nanakana* and *Kanura Burakeye*): and of the others, only one was truly neutral (*Le Phare*). The long-established papers such as the state owned (*Le Renouveau*) and party papers such as UPRONA's *L'Independant* and *Intake* stuck to the party line. Newspaper readership is predominantly urban-based and rarely extends to rural communities. Radios, on the other hand, have an extensive audience. Most notorious of the radio stations were the FM pirate ones, established by Hutus in the DRC town of Uvira after the death of Ndadaye. CNDD-FDD's *Radio Rutomora-ngingo*, in particular, was renouned for its extremism, inciting Burundians to fight the military. Changing its name to *Radio Démocratie – La Voix du Peuple*, did not diminish its propaganda and hate messages, which were broadcated twice daily (UNESC, 1995b). The rise of NGO funded 'peace radios' – *Studio Ijambo* and *Radio Umwizero* – has helped to counter the genocidal airwaves.

The goal of the Tutsi papers was to reverse the results of the democratic elections; initially, by declaring the elections illegal, then after October 1993, branding FRODEBU officials *génocidaires,* campaigning against external military intervention and refusing any form of compromise, even the Arusha peace negotiations. The newspapers drew on the racial stereotyping of the colonial period, accentuating the supposed phenotypical differences of Hutus and Tutsis and depicting Hutus as cannibals: 'those whom we have qualified as the most barbaric of the planet earth',[27] and incited people to violence. Using incendiary language and images, they called for the outright murder of FRODEBU politicians. *Le Carrefour des Idées*, for example, was 'offering a prize of one million Burundi Francs to the person who brings in the head of Léonard Nyamgoma or Festus Ntanyungu on the end of a spear'.[28] Hutu newspapers also drew on the racist stereotypes to depict Tutsi oppression in the military and the judiciary, and reinforced gender stereotyping by representing Tutsi women as beguiling, and those married to Hutu men as spies.

---

[27] *Le Carrefour des Idées* quoted in *Reporters sans Frontières*, 1995: 33.
[28] *Le Carrefour des Idées*, 47, 28 October 1994, quoted in UN 1995: 10.

Recruiting Génocidaires

If the military was under threat from Ndadaye's regime and the power-sharing Convention of Government, it was given free reign under Buyoya, after July 1996. The *Forces Armées Burundaises* (FAB) carried out day-to-day law and order functions and the *gendarmerie* became increasingly militarized. There were also a number of small security forces; the Public Security Police *(Police de Securité Publique)*, the Intelligence Service, *(Documentation Nationale)*, and the border and judicial police. To many Hutus 'the army has become a state within a state', acting not as a national institution but in the interests of its cliques (*Ijambo*, 9 November 1995).

The process of militarization speeded up after Buyoya's second coup, as the government called on citizens to provide financing for additional arms to equip military forces, and introduced compulsory 12-month military service (*Service Militarie Obligatoire*) for secondary-school pupils and first-and second-year university students as part of its new civil defence programme. Between 1995 and 2002, the army had more than doubled in size, from 22,400 to 40,000 (Table 5.2a). In 1996, to boost numbers, the period of training was reduced from one year to three months. The forces even admitted that all the new recruits were Tutsi, and included women and boys as young as ten (HRW, 1998).

Table 5.2a: Military Expenditure, Size of the Burundi Security Forces

Year	Burundi Francs	US Dollars (constant 2003 prices & exchange rates)	As a Percentage of Gross Domestic Product (GDP)	Forces Armées Burundaises (estimated)	Gendarmerie
1972				15,000	
1988	4,809	24.3	3.1		
1989	6,014	27.2	3.3		
1990	6,782	28.6	3.4	10,500	
1991	7,760	30	3.8		
1992	8,121	30.9	3.6		
1993	8,805	30.5	3.7	13,000	
1994	10,589	32	3.9	17,000	
1995	19,517	26.6	4.2	22,400	3,500
1996	15,408	30.8	5.8	30,000	
1997	21,800	33.3	6.4	35,000	
1998	26,300	35.7	6.6	35,000	
1999	28,500	37.4	6.3	40,000	
2000	30,500	32.2	6.0	40,000	
2001	44,200	42.7	8.0	45,500	
2002	44,200	45.6	7.6	45,500	2,000
2003	47,000	43.4	7.3		
2004	47,300	38.6	6.3		

Source: Stockholm International Peace Research Institute, available at http://www.sipri.org/contents/milap/milex/mex_database1.html [last accessed April 2007]; World Bank (2004b)

Table 5.2b: Regional Military Expenditure as percentage of GDP

Country	1990	2004
Burundi	3.4	6.3
Rwanda	3.7	2.2
DRC	–	2.1
Uganda	3.0	2.3
Tanzania	1.2*	1.1

Source: Human Development Report 2005; Stockholm International Peace Research Institute, available at http://www.sipri.org/contents/milap/milex/mex_database1.html [last accessed April 2007]

In 2002, military expenditure in Burundi amounted to US$42.13 million and constituted 5.5 per cent of Gross Domestic Product (GDP) (Tables 5.2a & b; SIPRI, 2007). Comparisons of social welfare data and military expenditure show that in 1999 the government spent 6.1 per cent of its GDP on the military compared to only 0.6 per cent on health (UNDP, 2001). Throughout the 1990s, government forces and the rebels were able to acquire weapons despite the regional and international arms embargo.[29] Military assistance, which included weapons and training, were supplied through official and private channels from China, USA, France, Germany, Belgium, South Africa, Mozambique, North Korea and, because of the arms embargo, were smuggled from regional ports into the country or to rebels in the DRC and Tanzania. According to HRW (1997):

> The French government has provided military technical assistance to Burundi under a May 1974 aid agreement. This has included the supply of military equipment (at a value of11.41 million French Francs, or about US $2 million, in 1995), the provision of additional equipment to the *gendarmerie* (... at a value [of] about US $3 million, in 1995), the training of Burundian officers in France (seventy-nine military officers and fourteen *gendarmerie* officers in 1995), and the use of French military advisors to train Burundian forces (24 advisors assigned to the military and seven advisors assigned to the gendarmerie in 1995). (HRW, 1997a: 55)

Shamed by its involvement with a genocidal army, France announced in May 1996 that it was suspending all military assistance and training to Burundi, and withdrawing its army instructors – ostensibly because of the army's massacre of Hutu civilians.

The rebels also found it relatively easy to acquire weapons from a variety of sources. Arms traders supplied and financed them with money gained from the illegal mining and trading of Congolese gold, coltan and cassiterite (UNSC, 2001a & 2001b, 2003). Also regional states and regional and international religious organizations provided financial aid and were involved in the transhipment of weapons to the groups (HRW, 1997a: Chapter 7).

---

[29] Not all western and regional countries instituted an arms embargo.

Financing Genocidal Violence

Burundian economists, working within the neo-liberal paradigm, have focused on institutional failure and state predation as explanations for the iterations of genocidal violence and state's impotence in the face of such violence (Ndikumana, 1998; Ngaruko & Nkurunziza, 2000). Ndikumana (1998: 40) contends that 'the Burundian state had degenerated into a private institution, which makes it unsuited for fulfilling its role of third-party enforcement agent in social exchange'. For him, the struggle to capture and monopolise state resources is underscored by 'three critical factors, ethnicity, regionalism and a politicized military that cause and perpetuate violence' (Ndikumana, 1998: 36). In their 'predation, rebellion, repression' model of the Burundi state, Ngaruko & Nkurunziza (2000: 384–385) claim that 'predation by power holders who share its rents has led to rebellions by those excluded, triggering, in turn, repression by the army, whose primary role has appeared to be the defence of the system of predation'. 'Repression ... in peace time', they continue, 'acts as a deterrent force against any potential rebellion'. Their 'index of predation' reflects closely the capture of power by the military and the rise of military expenditure.

For these authors, the solutions for ending the violence lie in globalized free-market economic reforms that reduce state control over the economy. The possibility that such reforms may, themselves, intensify impoverishment and, subsequently, warfare is not explored. Arguably, militarism in the region is closely bound up with capitalist economic practices that negate the humanity of the people; such practices intensify whenever there are crises within the system. Ngaruko & Nkrurunziza's (2000) thesis is plausible for the post-colonial period, but their limited historical perspective prevents them from seeing the situation of Burundi as part of a broader global phenomenon that links racism, globalization, resource extraction and institutionalized violence.

At the start of the twenty-first century, Burundi ranked relatively low on any social and economic indicator. Classified among the 39 low-income economies of the world, Burundi has experienced long-term decline in the general standard of living (Table 5.3). Over 89.2 per cent of its population live on less than $2 per day. Life expectancy, an indicator of human well-being, has fallen and morbidity is high, due to an HIV/AIDS prevalence rate of over 13 per cent in the population and adult malnutrition. While GDP per capita declined annually from 1989, between 1992 and 2002 it fell by almost 30 per cent in real terms (IMF, 2002). The genocidal economics of successive military regimes have entrenched regional disparities in the social landscape, with the wealthier areas being the southern and central provinces of Bururi, Muramvya and Mwaro. Due to their higher levels of impoverishment, the northern provinces of Ngozi, Kayanza and Kirundo have been nicknamed the 'Third World' by the Bujumbura-based elite. This erosion of social welfare could be attributed to a range of factors: declining terms of trade for primary commodities, the rise in international debt, introduction of austere neo-liberal economic policies, the destruction of productive capacity by the protracted warfare, and the sanctions imposed by region-al states (Chapter 9).

Burundi's modern economy was founded and continues to be dependent on revenue from the limited export of agricultural produce: coffee, tea, sugar, rice, cotton and hides and from locally mined minerals such as nickel, copper, cobalt, columbian – tantalum ore, tin and tungsten ore and gold. More importantly, the economy derived a consid-erable amount of legal and illegal income from its geographical proximity to mineral-rich Congo. After the First World War, Burundians were drawn into the ambit of the Belgian Congo with its brutal labour prac-tices. Hutus, in particular, were recruited as plantation labourers and many settled in the Congo. In the post-independence period, Burundi regimes retained close ties with President Joseph Mobutu, while allowing Congolese rebels to use its territory for the illegal exportation of goods, continuing a practice developed by the Belgians in the Second World War, when the country was used as a transit point for the export of manganese and coltan. Burundi was also a major exporter of ivory in the 1980s, despite having no elephants of its own. Throughout the turbulent 1990s, Congolese minerals such as cassiterite, gold, diamonds and coltan were illegally exported via Bujumbura, a city, which was linked to inter-national markets by hosting traders from Senegal, Pakistan and Greece, and mining companies from Canada and Australia (UNSC, 2001a & b).[30]

With its formal economy dependent on the export of cash crops, mainly coffee, Burundi suffered from the worldwide economic crisis of the 1970s and 1980s, experiencing a decline in the world price for its commodities and concomitantly a decline in agricultural and industrial output. In fact, by the early 1960s the price of coffee had already started to slide, falling by 40 per cent between 1957 and 1963 (Blakey, 1964). Then, coffee comprised 60 to 80 per cent of export earnings. The collapse of the inter-national coffee agreement in 1989 reduced state revenue dramatically. This caused the price of coffee to drop by 75 per cent and 'Burundi's average growth in export revenues correspondingly dropped from 3.3 per cent for the period 1965–1980, to -1.9 per cent for the period 1980–1990' (Oketch & Polzer, 2002: 145). In mid-2002, the Governor of the Bank of Burundi reported that the country was suffering from a deficit in the coffee sector, whereby the cost of production of coffee was higher than the sales price (Irinnews.org., 2002a). Between 1999 and 2001, losses in the coffee sector amounted to US $13 million and had to be underwritten by the Bank of Burundi (Oxfam GB, 2002b). To offset the deficit, the Burundi Franc was devalued by 20 per cent at the end of August 2002, pushing up the price of basic commodities by a similar margin.

As in the colonial period, coffee is grown mainly in the north of the country by about three-quarters of the population. Production is compulsory and the state carries out a five-yearly survey of coffee trees

---

[30] This point was made in the UNSC report (2001a & b, 2003) on the illegal exploitation of natural resources and other forms of wealth from the DRC. It was denied by the Burundi government, which supplied data that did not support its case, and the IMF 'lost' its own document which supported the UN Panel of Experts findings. Numerous interviews conducted by the author in the region from the 1980s onwards indicate that Burundi has been exporting a range of goods which it did not produce.

(Oxfam GB ibid.). Before 1993, the state used UPRONA party officials to mobilize coffee producers to meet targets; 'ensuring that projected government budgetary outlays for the proceeding financial year from projected coffee exports foreign exchange receipts, were met' (Oketch & Polzer, 2002: 138). Overall, the peasantry gained little from coffee and in the mid-1990s they were being encouraged by rebels to withhold their coffee crop and uproot trees, in order to deprive the regime of revenue (Oketch & Polzer, 2002). Such actions constitute criminal offences. Farmers were prevented from seeking more lucrative, and sometimes more vital alternatives under conditions of diminishing returns. Oxfam GB (2002b), after conducting a survey of coffee farmers in Kirimiro region, Gitega province, claims that profits and nutrition would increase if peasants were to grow more lucrative and nutritious crops. Those peasants who neglected their coffee trees had their land forcibly confiscated by the local authorities. The state coffee board (OCIBU) was a major source of accumulation for the elite and reflected the ethnicized politics of the state. Oketch & Polzer write:

> Coffee production, processing and marketing, including the crop's export, reflect and reinforce the country's ethnic divisions. The Tutsi play an almost exclusive part in the role of 'minority middleman' and the state, effectively controlled by a cabal within this group, expropriates the earnings, leaving little trickling down the peasants' way. (Oketch & Polzer, 2002: 133)

State reliance on the coffee sector was such that in 1999, at the height of the war, it was reported that 'the government had mortgaged future coffee production as payment for arms and ammunition' (ibid.: 142). With the decline in export prices, domestic sources of revenue became critical for the reproduction of the elite. Between 1993 and 2000, a substantial part of state revenue came from the brewery sector; the state had 40 per cent ownership in Brarudi, a subsidiary of Heineken, which sold Primus and Amstel beer mainly to the military.

The intersection between free market economic practices and political violence to produce genocidal economics can be illustrated by the 'gold wars', which were claimed to be a factor in the murder of Ndadaye. Roberto Cavalieri, in a book entitled '*Bujumbura, City of Death*', tells the story of the alleged 'coup of gold'. Burundi acts as an entrepôt for the processing and distribution of Congolese gold. It is estimated that 97 per cent of commercial minerals produced in the Congolese provinces of North and South Kivu passes through Burundi. And about 25 tonnes of gold produced annually goes through Bujumbura (Cavalieri, 1995). In line with the SAP conditionalities, a Free Trade Zone (FTZ), supported by the World Bank, was established in Bujumbura (Decree-law No.1/30 of 31 August 1992). To make it sustainable for investors, Burundi's FTZ had no financial or labour limitations. Investors paid no taxes and had exemptions from import duties for the first ten years. The only stipulation was that they should deal in activities in a non-traditional sector. One of the industries attracted to the zone was gold processing. The state aimed to make Burundi the epicentre of gold distribution in the region by increasing the annual amount processed to 50 tonnes, despite the fact that virtually all the gold is smuggled into the country (Cavalieri, ibid.). The bids for the gold processing licence in the FTZ attracted local and international competition. On 3 February 1993, the licence was given to AFFIMET SA, a company registered in Burundi six weeks earlier, on 22 December 1992, dealing with the mining, refining and exporting of precious metals. AFFIMET was established by *Tony Goetz et Fils*, a Belgian company, which had been involved in the exportation of gold from Burundi to Belgium since 1987 (*Sénat de Belgique*, 2002). Its shares were owned by six Belgians (999 shares) and a Rwandan (1 share) (Crawford and Lee, 2004). AFFIMET's competitors, French and Pakistani owned, IMAG and Ashons gemstones protested.[31]

AFFIMET's operations were not transparent. It made huge profits; between April and July 1993 AFFIMET exported gold worth 12 million dollars (Cavalieri, 1995). So successful were its ventures that it established an offshore bank, Africa Bank of Commerce, and ran an airline, City Connection Airlines, in order to transship gold from different places in the Congo and to secure its financial transactions (*Sénat de Belgique*, 2002). The company sought to establish a monopoly, with plans to process gold from other francophone African countries.

On accession to power on 10 July 1993, the FRODEBU government sought to levy taxes on companies operating in the FTZ. Prior to the FRODEBU regime, there were already internal struggles between the prime minister, Adrien Sibomana (a Hutu), and the minister of industry and commerce as to whether AFFIMET activities could be considered non-traditional and therefore benefit from the FTZ regime. The FRODEBU prime minister, Sylvie Kinigi (a Tutsi married to a Hutu), also questioned the terms of AFFIMET's contract. In August 1993 Ndadaye, following advice from the Council of Ministers, revoked AFFIMET's licence to operate in the FTZ.

It is claimed that the controversy that followed this act, led in part, to Ndadaye's assassination (Cavalieri, 1995; Prunier, 1994). In January 1994, the minister reactivated AFFIMET's licence, but it was revoked again in May 1995, following a study by the Washington-based, international consultants, AMEX International. The company was ordered to pay US $2 million in tax and custom duties to the government (Crawford & Lee, 2004). Reportedly, the acrimony over this decision led to the assassination of two leading politicians; on 11 March 1995, the Hutu Minister of Land and Mines and Head of RPB, Ernest Kabushemeye, was murdered by Tutsi hardliners; and Colonel Lucien Sabuku was kidnapped and murdered in retaliation (Prunier, 1995). AFFIMET's Belgian owners sought arbitration via the International Centre for the Settlement of Investment Disputes with respect to the Belgium-Burundi Bilateral Investment Treaty and, on 23 December 1998, they were awarded close to US $3 million in compensation to be paid by the Burundi government. The Burundi state reacted by expelling AFFIMET's owners in February 2000 and the company was sold to a South African.

---

[31] Interview conducted in Dar es Salaam, 2001 & Prunier, 1995. The partner of a World Bank representative in Burundi was said to have been a key player in one of the companies.

The AFFIMET affair illustrates the formal and informal connections between international capital and local elites and how the democratizing process can be problematic for wealth accumulation. When sanctions were imposed in 1996, *Tony Goetz et Fils* shifted its operations to Goma where it continued to buy and export gold (*Sénat de Belgique*, 2002). In 2002, one of the partners of *Tony Goetz et Fils* was questioned by the Belgian Senate about the company's association with individuals mentioned in the UN report on the illegal exploitation of minerals from the DRC (*Sénat de Belgique*, 2002; UNSC, 2001a).

Genocidal economics involves the merger of formal and informal networks of accumulation – a process that has been speeded up through the introduction of market liberalism. Other aspects of the informal economy flourished under conditions of war; drugs, cannabis grown in Rwanda, along with heroin and mandrax worth millions annually, were transited through Burundi.[32]

Donors and the Model African Country
The Burundi government, while hostile to criticisms from foreign powers, relied heavily on external aid to buttress its economy. According to Ndikumana (1998), successive military regimes were major recipients of loans from the international community, acquiring over one billion dollars between 1966 and 1983. He writes:

> The Bagaza regime (1976–1987) benefited the most from international aid. The regime obtained a total of $831 million, which represent an average of $75.6 million per year, compared to a total of $21.2 million ($2.1 million per year) for the Micombero regime (1966–1976) and $166 million ($27.7 million per year) for Buyoya's first regime. (Ndikumana 1998: 43)

Unlike many African countries, and, despite state-sponsored genocidal violence, since the 1970s, Burundi has been able to maintain a good working relationship with the donors. This could be attributed to Burundi being seen as a model African country, 'where things work' (*International Herald Tribune*, 6.9.1988). In the 1980s, Burundi was the highest per capita recipient of the World Bank's low-interest loans, and received over $153 million dollars of the Bank's International Development Agency (IDA) credits in the 1988 fiscal year (*African Business,* 1988). In 1986, Colonel Bagaza submitted to pressure from the World Bank and the IMF to introduce austere debt management and structural adjustment programmes (SAPs). However, it was Buyoya who sought to make Burundi a 'fiscal paradise', based on free market principles. According to *African Business* (1988), Burundi received a Structural Adjustment Loan (SAL) and has followed IMF conditionalities since mid-1988; these were followed through until the assassination of Ndadaye in October 1993. During that time, Burundi was considered a model reforming state and, eager to display the success of their market reforms, donors ignored state repression.

---

[32] Interview with a member of the facilitation team, Dar es Salaam, 2000.

Although some pressure was put on Buyoya to democratise after the 1988 massacres, external aid flows increased and peaked at US $312 million in 1992, the year before the second democratic elections, and virtually ceased in the mid-1990s (IMF, 1999). By 1998, Burundi's debt service burden was unsustainable at 123 per cent of GDP and 58 per cent of export good and service (IMF, Burundi, 28 January 1999). In 2003, Burundi's debt burden reached US $ 1.3 billion and debt servicing accounted for 63.6 per cent of export goods and service (Table 5.3). To meet its debt-service payments, the state had to borrow from the IMF, the World Bank, the Africa Development Bank, the EU and bilateral creditors (IMF, 2005a). In 2004, Burundi received some rescheduling of its debt to the Paris Club, although debt repayments still amounted to some 60 per cent of export goods and services (IMF, 2005b). Debt relief under the enhanced Heavily Indebted Poor Countries (HIPC) Initiative remained conditional on the successful implementation of Poverty Reduction and Growth Facility (PRGF)-supported programme (IMF, 2005b). Burundi's poverty reduction programme has not been able to deal with the levels of chronic unemployment experienced by young men. Consequently, the country has seen an increase in criminal activities by armed gangs. In a continuation of policy, official aid has not been affected by the state's repressive actions against political opponents.

Table 5.3: Regional Economic Data, 2005

Country	GDP US $bn (2003)	ODA % of GDP (2003)	External Debt in US $ billion (2003)	Debt service % exports of goods & Services 7 net income from abroad (2003)	Debt service % GDP (2003)
Burundi	0.6	37.6	1.3	63.6	3.02
Rwanda	1.8	20.3	1.5	10.0	1.3
DRC	5.7	94.9	12.9	11.1	16.2
Uganda	6.8	15.2	4.5	7.8	1.3
Tanzania	10.8	16.2	7.5	5.8	0.9

Source: UNDP, Human Development Report, 2005; World Development Report 2006.

Many donors suspended aid after Ndadaye's assassination and after Buyoya's second coup. According to ICG (2003a: 5), 'international aid was reduced by two-thirds, from an average of US $247 million between 1981 and 1995 to US $76 million between 1996 and 2000'. The signing of the peace agreement in August 2000 led to the unblocking of aid flows. In 1999, donors pledged US $410 million for post-conflict reconstruction and a further $832 million in 2001.[33]

---

[33] These pledges were made at donor conferences in Paris and Geneva respectively.

Actual aid transfers remain well below that figure. Grants from the IMF (US $54 million) and the European Union (US $191.25 million) were given from their respective post-conflict programmes to kick-start the economy on the understanding that Burundi would carry out further structural reform.

SAP was reintroduced in January 2004 under the new name of Poverty Reduction and Growth Strategy (PRGS) but with the same neo-liberal ·reforms: 'monetary and exchange rate policies … liberalizing external trade, privatizing public enterprises [and] reforming the civil services' (IMF, 2002). These had negative implications for the provision of social welfare policies in the post-conflict situation – a time of acute demand of health and other social services. Amnesty International notes:

> During a period when the Burundian population has been most in need of adequate and affordable healthcare, in 2002 the government of Burundi instituted policies of cost-recovery in the health centres. As a result, very few Burundians are now able to afford services provided by state health centres. (Amnesty International 2004b: 15)

Consequently, people have been detained in hospitals because of non-payment of hospital fees. HRW (2006) reports that 1076 people were detained in 2005, of whom 621 were held in the principal hospital. In Muramvya Province, 26 were freed when benefactors paid their fines as Easter and Christmas gifts (Ligue Iteka, 2006b). One of the first duties of ONUB's Gender Unit was to pay the fines of mothers held hostage in the maternity wards of the hospitals.[34] In 2005, it cost about US $30 to have a baby. The state was later forced to make a partial retreat on user fees and introduced free health care for mothers and under-fives. Since 2000, public sector workers, such as medical staff, teachers and the judiciary, have taken strike action for increased wage rates and the payment of overdue salaries (Irinnews.org, 7 March 2005).

The key structural reform in the PRGS is to liberalize the agricultural commodities sector: coffee and sugar sector in order to attract investors. The restructuring of the sugar wholesaling markets in February 2006 resulted in the ruling party (CNDD/FDD) members capturing the trade when the number of wholesalers was reduced from 156 to seven (Beaumont, 2007; ICG, 2006). Privatization of the coffee sector started with the rehabilitation of the washing stations in preparation for sale and the abolition of the government crop guarantee credit. According to the IMF, in the financial year 2004/5, the coffee sector had 'an operating surplus of FBU15.6 billion in 2004/5, for the first time since 1998/99 due to world market recovery in coffee prices (IMF, 2005b: 37). While these reforms may go some way in reducing the budget deficit, it is not clear how and when the very poor farmers might benefit. As far as the IMF and World Bank are concerned, Burundi is once again a good adjusting state, though its performance has been mixed (IMF, 2005b). In the meantime, the Burundi government is performing a difficult balancing act as they

---

[34] Interview, ONUB Representative, Bujumbura 2006.

try to please the donors without implementing fully the conditionalities that are likely to lead to social unrest.

Genocidal Politics as an Accumulative Strategy

The persistence of genocidal economics – funded by aid organizations and supported by a cadre of *évolués* helped to sustain the genocidal state. The dependence of the elite on state resources has been seen as a critical factor in the internecine character of the violence. The limited private sector, controlled largely by foreign firms, has left the state as the main avenue of accumulation. Historically, the *baganwa* and Tutsi elite, especially the chiefs, were given land by the colonial state and made enormous wealth. Accumulation in the post-colonial period was still dependent on state contacts. Ngaruko & Nkrurunziza (2000), claim that political power was closely linked to ones' ability to be successful in commercial ventures.

> Almost all large private firms belong to high-ranking civil servants. It has also been noted that in general, every change in the country's leadership at the highest level provokes changes in firms' profitability: a whole fringe of businessmen go bankrupt with the departure of former leaders, while at the same time, a new class of 'businessmen' emerge with the arrival of new leaders. (Ngaruko & Nkrurunziza, 2000: 387)

Ethnicity is closely linked to this; the Tutsi who have dominated Burundi politics for 35 years captured high-ranking positions in parastatals and developed close links to western businessmen; only a few Hutus were able to use their access to power to acquire wealth. The threat of losing income and lucrative opportunities was a factor in the violent protest by the Tutsi in 1994/95.

Another significant economic factor relates to land availability. Land grabbing by the elite has placed them in direct conflict with the peasantry. Burundi's population of 6.6 million is estimated to be growing at 3.1 per cent per annum; this places considerable pressure on a country whose population density is one of the highest in Africa, and where about 93 per cent are employed in agriculture. As a result, competition for land is intense and episodes of violence have been linked to struggles over land. Hutus displaced in the 1972 genocide have had their land reallocated to Tutsis, squatted or stolen. Repossession, following repatriation, has not been helped by the complexity of state legislation, with land policy falling under several bodies (Oketch & Polzer, 2002). Many of those repatriated were unable to repossess their land, without going through lengthy, costly and sometimes haphazard legal procedures that may not result in success.

The implementation of neo-liberal reforms has done little to transform the dependency of the elite on state resources. Rather than by-passing corrupt state actors, it has enabled them to capture revenue from external aid directed at NGO service provisioning, humanitarian interventions and privatization. This dependence on western aid has aggravated rather than facilitated improvements in the human rights record of the state, as capital is used to consolidate the hegemony of the elite economically and militarily. One can also surmise that the hegemony of the Tutsi provided the sort of political stability favoured by western donors. Consequently, in the post-colonial economy, militarism has continued to pay a vital role in the processes of extraction, both for the Burundi elite and those in neighbouring countries.

Conclusion

Burundi's experience with liberal democracy is instructive, but not uncommon for Africa. In the 1980s and 1990s, many dictatorial states began a transition towards multi-party democracy; some pressured by donors, others by popular revolt. Most regimes were able to manipulate the transition to ensure a continuation of the hegemonic class. In Burundi's case, democracy was always tied to changes in the relative power of the ethnic elites and intertwined with genocidal violence. The militarism of Presidents Micombero, Bagaza and Buyoya was associated with the repression of the human rights of the citizens, in order to secure the narrow self-interest of regional elites.

Buyoya's 'conversion' to democracy was done primarily because he was convinced that he had sufficient political mileage among the Hutu elite to ensure his election victory. His defeat was quite a shock and led to his reversion to undemocratic politics. What is interesting is how Buyoya convinced the international community that he was a moderate battling against all sides, even after overturning the democratic process and sanctioning violence against his citizens. One explanation could be that Buyoya's presidency and the masculine hierarchy that it entails was successful for international capital and donors. Nevertheless, these very forces combined to reproduce the genocidal economics of earlier periods. Burundi's economic history and development failure are the consequence of the practice of genocidal economics, a policy framework in which accumulation is dependent on the exercise of genocidal violence.

The long association of the Tutsi elite with the international bourgeoisie, and their intermediary relationship with international capital, has enabled them to garner continued support from external powers. Furthermore, Tutsis' experience of genocide in the Great Lakes region, coupled to international guilt, have allowed them to label their own acts of genocide perpetrated against the Hutus as self-defence and, thus, avoid international recriminations. It is in such a context that President Buyoya could curtail democracy, preside over a security apparatus that perpetrates genocidal violence and still continue to be welcomed in the international arena.

National security has meant the protection of the Tutsis at the expense of the Hutus. State prioritization of security, at the expense of social projects, encouraged the militarization of society through direct or indirect support for militias. The patriarchal harnessing of young, unemployed men into militias instilled a violent political culture. Though much of the violence had an ethnic character, it was not exclusively ethnic. Coup plotting, whether real or imagined, was used to carry out extreme acts of violence aimed at wiping out the opposition, irrespective of their ethnic background. The rebellion by opposition forces may have begun out of general grievances due to political exclusion, and found articulation in terms of ethnic inequalities, yet amongst the rebels, numerous alignments and differences militated against an ethnic explanation for the violence that accompanies political competition. Although hatred and genocide were promoted by sectors of the media, there is no clear evidence that the Burundi peasantry interpret the problems purely in ethnic terms, nor even the political parties, who are quick to form cross-party and cross-ethnic alliances to pursue their interests.

6

Spaces of Violence ▎ Exploring the Contours
of 'Civilian' &
Gendered Violence

Introduction

Much has been written on the specific character of genocidal violence in
the region, especially that of Rwanda in 1994. The wealth of material
testifies to the immense concern the genocide in that country generated
among fellow human beings; the depth of intellectual responsibility that
some scholars felt; and the sheer opportunism indulged in by others.
Nevertheless, the volume of material has meant that the Rwanda
genocide has been one of the most documented on the continent. Like the
Jewish Holocaust, the Rwandan genocide was so brutal and dehumanizing and such a media fest that it is often treated, in itself, as exceptional,
a unique event the world records with the hope that it will never happen
again. While it is imperative that genocides such as Rwanda's are well
documented, there is an enduring lack of interest in the persistent pattern
of genocidal violence in neighbouring Burundi and elsewhere in Africa.

Writing about violence in the past tense suggests that once peace and
elections have been held, political violence ceases. What is interesting,
both in Rwanda and Burundi, and elsewhere in Africa, is the persistence,
not just of structural violence but direct violence in quite overt forms. I
have already charted the historical forces that produced the genocidal
state, using the Burundian example. Now, by exploring the specificities
of violence in the country, its social character, spatiality and sequentiality, I intend to show how genocidal thinking produces and reproduces
particular forms of violence. Genocidal violence signifies the erosion of
respect for the sanctity of life and of the human being. Genocidal violence
in the Great Lakes region, though lacking the industrial scale of the
Jewish Holocaust, drew on the modern apparatus of state, the military,
the judiciary, the media, and the complicity or deliberate myopia of the
international community.

As previously argued, state power in a militarized society is predicated
on the use of violence for domination. Hannah Arendt (2004: 241), in her
treatise, 'on violence, contends that 'the equation of violence with power
rests on government being understood as domination of man over man by
means of violence.' Repeated acts of genocide in the region illustrate the
continued role played by violence as a legitimizing force in the modern
state. In Chapter 2, we challenged some of the assumptions of the social
contractual obligations between state and society inherent in the liberal

state model. The links between modernity and genocide and militarism and patriarchy were articulated and the concept of a national security that excludes gendered violence was questioned. The concept of the genocidal state was introduced to help us understand the dynamics of a state that has knowingly relinquished its social responsibility to sections of society, and where the institutions of the state are used for the reproduction of extreme violence.

Theoretically, state monopoly of violence relates to not just state ownership and control of the primary machinery of violence, but also to its ability to enact and uphold the rule of law. In a genocidal state, built on the assumption of hierarchies of human beings, the rule of law is not necessarily applied with respect to certain sections of the population considered racially, ethnically or socially inferior and perceived not to be worthy of protection. Arendt (ibid.) argues that the state is only powerful insofar as it is able to control the military, the police and other branches of the security apparatus. Military dictatorships represent the combination of political power with the coercive arm of the state. A state ruled by a military 'strong man' is *prima facie* a violent state – in which both direct (human rights violation, gender-based violence) and structural violence are commonplace. Within such a militarized culture, the state and members of the political elite commit or sponsor acts of violence with impunity, while representing such violence as legitimate violence committed in self-defence. Genocide is thus perceived as the only leverage to maintain domination – as a means of dealing with differences, settling disputes, and as recompense for rejection and retribution. In spite of Arendt's (ibid.) claim that rebellions occur where 'the means of violence are of no use ... [where] commands are no longer obeyed' and 'arms themselves change hands', it must be stressed that while state's monopoly on violence can no longer be effectively deployed to retain power, violence is still functional, as it is perceived as the primary mechanism for attaining and retaining power.

This chapter gives emphasis to the violence associated with state power, particularly its impact on civilians, its spatial and gendered dimensions. It explores, first, the ways in which the state exercises its power through the perpetration of various acts of genocide, as evident in the failure to distinguish between civilians and combatants, the militarization of children, the targeting of civilians through massacres and forced displacement, and the sanctioning of gendered and sexual violence. Second, it explores the way in which non-state actors, militias, paramilitaries, armed gangs and individual criminals contribute to and replicate genocidal violence. By focusing on the perpetrators, victims and spatial patterning of specific forms of violence, I am able to interrogate the interrelationships of power (political, patriarchal and masculine), space and violence. The chapter concludes with a discussion of the way violence is legitimated at different spatial scales, particularly at the national and international. How the political elite absolve themselves from blame by distancing themselves in international arenas from state institutions that perpetrate violence, ratifying various international conventions and in effect performing a scalar form of politics, whereby the language of sovereignty is used to protect the state, the elite and its geo-political international partners, while citizens are left defenceless and, in the context of neo-liberalism, dependent on the charity of humanitarian organizations.

The 'newness' of, and recent policy focus on contemporary civilian and gender-based violence are due partly to such forms of violence being relatively undocumented until quite recently. The silencing of these acts in the discourse of war and in post-conflict societies was a consequence of our perception of what constitutes historical knowledge, of our understanding of the public and private in the context of patriarchal societies, and of the intersection between prevailing forms of masculinity and femininity.

International NGOs, such as Human Rights Watch and Amnesty International, have been the main source of documentation on the specificities of warfare as experienced in the region, and, in Burundi, Ligue Iteka, has produced valuable source materials on the incidence and specific character of violence. The UN *Special Rapporteurs* and some western government embassies and agencies have also produced detailed reports of genocidal violence. These reports, along with newspaper articles and interview data, have provided essential source material for this chapter.

Conceptualizing the Civilian: A Note

> The civilian is like a bridge that everyone walks across. He never chooses to collaborate with one or the other but he is forced to do so. The big difference is that the others – soldiers and rebels – are armed. (Interview in Bujumbura, HRW, 2004a: 2)

The targeting of civilians is presented as a distinctive feature of post-Cold War non-conventional warfare. Kaldor and Luckham (2001) contend that, globally, the ratio of military to civilian casualties rose dramatically in the 1990s, and they estimate a 1:8 ratio of military to civilian casualties – the reverse of a century ago. Human rights organizations employ the distinction between civilians and combatants in international law to advocate for the cessation of hostilities. The 1949 Geneva Convention and the Additional Protocols aimed to enshrine the protection of civilians into the rules of modern warfare. Encoded in these international legislations is the principle that combatants fight wars and are therefore legitimate targets, while ordinary citizens or non-combatants have to be protected.

Contrary to attempts to interpret violence in Africa as the consequence of the re-traditionalization of African societies, a key contention of this text is that state-sponsored violence against 'citizens' forms part of the modern history of the region. In the case of Rwanda and Burundi, racialized and ethnicized discriminatory practices arising from the colonial period, and the increasing class differences between the educated *évolués* and their descendants, on the one hand, and the peasants on the other, helped to perpetuate the dehumanizing tendencies of the state's interactions with its people.[1]

---

[1] See Uvin (1998) for a discussion of the role of the *évolués* in laying the foundations for genocide in Rwanda.

The dichotomy between civilians and combatants, as in the liberal state, was never fully recognized in the region; in colonial wars, all civilians, unless they declared outright support for the state's project, were viewed as collaborators, rebels and insurgents. Even after the 1940s, warfare in Kenya, the Congo and Biafra resulted in vast numbers of civilian deaths (Hochschild, 1998; Elkins, 2005). In some parts of Africa, the period of the developmental state, temporally, involved a social pact between state and society. Indeed, in Central Africa, membership of this pact was highly exclusive. Moreover, in the last quarter of the twentieth century, development failure and neo-liberal economic policies helped to formalize the weakening of ties between the political elite and the wider citizenry, and has enabled the proliferation of violence whether state-sanctioned or via a state-promoted culture of impunity. Economically weak, and with rising militarism, such forms of the state result inevitably in the disintegration of the social fabric of the society.

Militarized Violence and Society in Burundi

The deepening militarization of Burundi society would not have occurred without considerable repercussions for the populace. An estimated 200,000 people were killed in 1972 and a further 20,000 in August 1988. Between 1993 and 2006, the civilian population was subjected to civil warfare waged by the military and government-backed militias against rebel groups and their supporters, killing an estimated 300,000 people, and forcing over 400,000 into exile.[2] In addition some 800,000 were internally displaced by the war and as part of the counterinsurgency strategies of the state.

Genocidal violence in Burundi has been pervasive. The persistent culture of impunity makes the violence both purposeful and random; enveloping most groups within the society, as perpetrators or victims. We cannot truly understand the nature of genocidal violence without taking into consideration the heterogeneity of the population, as the sequencing of political violence often reflects the fissures and fault lines within the society. While ethnicity constitutes a major fault line in Burundi and belligerents can rally groups under the ethnic banner by stoking xenophobia, and despite genocide being the clearest manifestation of violence, a vast proportion of violence takes place between members of the same ethnic group: Tutsi-Hima and Tutsi, Hutu and Hutu, northerners and southerners. Key distinctions across these groupings relate primarily to the timing of the execution of violence (some such as intellectuals are more likely to be killed first), the specific acts of violence to which people are subjected, and the institutional application of security measures – these often display the intersection of class, gender and race.

State-sponsored genocidal violence in Burundi followed a detectable pattern. It began invariably with attempts to exterminate the elite and potential elite; the primary threat to power in the context of the modern state: senior military officers, government ministers, politicians, intellec-

---

[2] IRC (2006) http://www.theirc.org/where/the_irc_in_burundi.html [accessed September 2006]

tuals, church leaders, civil servants, university students, professionals and school children. Basically, those with or acquiring the ability to participate at key institutional levels in modern society were often the first to be killed. Such crimes were usually perpetrated by state security services, the Tutsi-dominated military and the *gendarmerie*. This is how witnesses described the events between May and mid-June 1972:

> Local Tutsis, sometimes soldiers, sometimes civil servants, arrived and motioned Hutu teachers, church leaders, nurses, traders, civil servants into Landrovers with guns. ... In secondary schools teachers stood helpless as many of their Hutu pupils were removed ... Those arrested were usually dead the same night, stripped practically, clubbed to death in covered lorries on the way to prison, then finished off there with clubs at nightfall. Using bullets would have been wasteful.[3]

> ... The four Hutu members of the Cabinet, all the Hutu officers and virtually all the Hutu soldiers in the armed forces: half of Burundi's primary school teachers; and thousands of civil servants; At present (August) there is only one Hutu nurse left in the entire country, and only a thousand secondary school students survive.[4]

Twenty-two years later, in 1994, the pattern was not dissimilar; the UN Special Rapporteur for Burundi reported that:

> Hutu intellectuals, teachers, administrators and provincial governors have been killed since the beginning of the crisis. Ernest Kabushemeye (Minister of Mines and Energy), Fidele Muhizi (Governor of Muyinga), the administrator of Bwambarangwe and the administrator of the district of Kanyonesha, are a few examples. (UNESC 1995a: 9)

In another incident, on 4 June 1994, Amnesty International (1995a: 5) claimed that 'at least 15 unarmed Hutu students were killed and 13 injured ... during an attack by Tutsi students at Burengo secondary school.'

When Hutu rebels and militias perpetrated genocidal acts, they too focused first on the educated, as the case of Kibimba, Muramvya province, demonstrates. Seventy Tutsi school children were massacred as a reprisal for the assassination of Ndadaye in October 1993. The significance of western education for the reproduction of the modern elite places school children on the frontline of warfare. Throughout 1995, Tutsi and Hutu armed gangs threw grenades in schools in Muyinga, Kayanza and Bujumbura province, at critical times in the examination calendar. In June 1995, at the University of Bujumbura, 15 unarmed Hutu students were killed by fellow Tutsi students who were members of the militias '*Sans Échec*', *Sans Défaite* and SODEJEM (Nyamitwe, 2006; AI, 1995a). In reprisal Hutu gangs killed eight unarmed Tutsi students and

---

[3] Jeremy Greenland, 'Black Racism in Burundi', *New Blackfriars*, October 1973, quoted in Lemarchand and Martin (1974: 18).

[4] American Universities Field Staff Report on Burundi, 1972, quoted in Bowen *et al.* (1974: 6).

two university employees at Mutanga and Kiriri campus (AI, 1995a). In 2000, the Hutu-dominated rebel group, CNDD-FDD, targeted and killed several Tutsi candidates of ISCAM (*Institut Supérieur des Cadres Militaries* [Higher Training Military Institute] (ICG, 2000a). Getting a western education proved to be so life-threatening that, between 1993 and 1995, 20 per cent of school and university students were forced to discontinue their studies (UNESC, 1995b).

Another strategy that targeted elites focused on those who were members or alleged members of opposing political parties. In 1972, Micombero used the Hutu uprising to massacre his left-wing and moderate Tutsi challengers. After Ndadaye's murder, FRODEBU party members came under sustained onslaught from opposition political parties and militias; many were assassinated, forced into exile or to make political compromises, essentially forfeiting their democratic right to govern. Amnesty International (1996a) notes that over a dozen prominent citizens, mostly Hutu and Tutsi members of FRODEBU, were assassinated between October 1993 and January 2000.[5]

The relationship between state power and military dominance was such that the military could arrest unarmed civilians, even prominent ones and accuse them of being FRODEBU sympathisers or belonging to rebel movements – and, in many cases, they were either, illegally detained, tortured, summarily executed, or 'disappeared'. The security services perpetuated a 'culture of fear' and impunity. A US State Department report (1998: not numbered) notes, 'With their superior fire power and wide dispersion, the armed forces committed the most widespread abuses.' Violence by the military tended to take on an explicitly ethnic character during counter-reprisals, especially after the massacre of Tutsi civilians. The US Ambassador, Robert Kreuger, wrote, after visiting the scenes of military counter attacks:

> These tiny children were not members of any *Bandes Armées*. They were neither concealing weapons nor firing them. They are too small even to have held them. And yet their skulls were split open and their throats bayoneted. One child at the hospital had his arm broken by a man who stomped on it with a boot. (Press interview, Bujumbura, 27 January 1995)

In another incident, the military massacred between 200 and 300 Hutus after a CNDD/FDD incursion resulted in the death of 341 Tutsi civilians at Bugendana Municipality, Gitega region, on the 20 July 1996 (ICG, 1998a). In April 2003, Burundian soldiers turned their guns on civilians fleeing an attack by Palipehutu-FNL at a military post at Kabezi, south of Bujumbura (HRW, 2003). Again, in October 2003, when FNL murdered a soldier in the Kinama area of Bujumbura, soldiers killed three civilians, and the people were warned by the Military Commander of Socartic camp that if any further killings of officials were to take place, 'It was the population of Kinama that would pay. I will erase Kinama' (quoted in HRW, 2003: 20).

---

[5] For example, MP Gabriel Gisabwamana was assassinated on 1 January 2000.

Not all genocidal violence had political motives. It was often used by those seeking to acquire the property of others. HRW reports the case of one:

> administrative official who tried to extort produce from three families who refused to comply with his demands. According to witnesses ... the official then accused the young men from these families of being rebels; they were immediately arrested and subjected to severe ill-treatment. Two were later found dead. (HRW, 2000c: section VIII)

Soldiers, as representatives of the state, used the war to deepen the extractive economic practices of the state, appropriating by force goods and labour. Hutu civilians were forced to provide them with provisions such as firewood, food and water, to steal money and bicycles, to carry ammunition and water, and to run errands.

> In any case, the presence of the soldiers causes us insecurity. They ought to be spending their days at the battlefront, not going around where we live disturbing us. Besides having them always around makes the rebels think we are collaborating with them and then the rebels target us. (Human Rights Watch interview, 2003, Quoted in HRW, 2003: 31)

The state selectively militarized the population, reinforcing the public perception of the relationship between ethnicity. In the mid-1990s, sophisticated small arms and heavier weapons were distributed to Tutsi militias and ordinary civilians, some of whom were given weapon training by the military (UNESC; 1995b; HRW, 2004a). One report notes, 'Tutsi civilian extremists sometimes accompanied the armed forces during operations and the armed forces permitted them to engage in violence against Hutus' (US State Department, 1998: npn). These acts confirm the state's limited application of the terminology, 'civilians' (those who needed protection from the state) to refer essentially to the Tutsi ethnic group. The Hutu population were often subjected to collective punishment.

> In some cases, soldiers simply destroyed property, apparently to punish and humiliate the civilian population: they turned over pots full of food, broke jugs of beer, or dug up bananas that were being ripened to make beer ... "pull up the manioc growing in the fields and even stamp on the young shoots so that they will not grow". (Human Rights Watch interview in Bujumbura, HRW, 2004a: 9)

Young Hutus, often between the age of 15 and 30 years, were also armed as part of a state-sponsored paramilitary group – the *abajeunes* or *Gardiéns de la Paix,* which numbered 30,000 in 2001. This began in the northern province of Cibitoke in 1997 before spreading to Kayanza and to the southern provinces of Bururi and Makamba (HRW, 2001). After limited training of about a month, they were given a range of duties, which included patrolling their communities at night, manning road-blocks, supervising the provisioning of soldiers by local communities, participating in military raids, in the forced removal of people into camps and in the killing of civilians (AI, 2004e). Many youths joined because of pressure from local administrators.

> The Governor ordered that young men who are not in school should come and join the Guardians of the Peace. He made a speech ... and then the zone chiefs carried out the local organization. They distributed papers to write down the names of recruits. They said that those who are against this program will be punished. (Interview, quoted in HRW, 2001: 6)

Many observers interpreted this recruitment as a strategy to keep the adult Hutu men in a community accountable to the regime. Those who refused to join were considered 'supporters of the rebellion' and would invariably be arrested, tortured and killed (HRW, 1998). The only alternative was to run away and join the FDD and FNL rebels. The *Gardiéns de la Paix* were placed in the firing line, despite being ill-equipped for battle; they sustained high casualties. They received no material benefits from the state and many supported themselves by looting, armed robbery and extortion (HRW, 2001). In 2000, unemployed young Hutus were also recruited to patrol the poor urban districts of Kinama and Buterere in Bujumbura, whose residents were forced to pay a war tax of 500 Burundi Francs per month to support them (HRW, ibid.).

Once consequence of this state-promoted violence is that, during the 1990s, numerous Tutsi and Hutu armed groups emerged aligned to political parties or charismatic individuals, with names such as *Santiagos, Machinistes, Chicago Bulls* and *Intagohekas*. These militias replicated the violence being perpetrated by the military and were either affiliated to one rebel movement or another or pretended to belong to them (AI, 1996a; HRW, 2003). Widespread banditry was made easy by the availability of weapons – an AK47 assault rifle cost only US $20 (HRW, ibid.). Communities responded by forming vigilante groups and 'resorted to mob justice to avenge themselves' (HRW, ibid.: 50).[6]

After the signing of the peace agreement, the state's strategy for peace was the formation of multiethnic militia groups, *auto-défense solidaire* (self-defence in solidarity), to promote the poorer urban communities. Young people were forced to join and their practices of intimidation and brutalities did not differ from those of previous groups (HRW, 2001).

Lessons in Genocidal Violence: Young People and the War
As in other wars in Africa, the phenomenon of child soldiers was a dominant feature of warfare in Burundi. In 2004, the UN estimated that some 14,000 child soldiers had been recruited by government troops or armed opposition groups (HRW, 2004b). State mobilization of young men has long been a strategy of diffusing tensions caused by high levels of unemployment within the most volatile section of the population. Development brigades, as some were known, operated as a form of patronage that helped cement allegiance to the ruling party and the

---

[6] Ligue Iteka (2005a; 2006a) documents many cases of people being killed by vigilantes for alleged theft.

regime. The difference in Rwanda, and to some extent Burundi, was the way in which training focused on instilling ideologies of genocide and violent masculinities.

Richards (1996), in the context of Sierra Leone, interprets child soldiering as being linked to changes in the nature of patrimonialism, particularly its collapse under structural adjustment. Child soldiering, he argues, provides an alternative to traditional initiation ceremonies, where groups of young men are taught the skills of manhood; child soldiers appear to exhibit bonds of solidarity similar to those in age sets. In contrast, Kaldor and Luckham (2001) have queried whether official recruitment of paramilitary groups is due to a reluctance of the state to lose soldiers in the official army. Abdullah & Rashid (2004: 239) explore this labour thesis further by arguing that 'labour shortages and the nature and the character of the armed movements are therefore central to understanding the phenomenon of juvenile combatants'. They posit that the phenomenon of child soldiers reflects crises in the supply of available manpower, especially of 'able-bodied adults'. Where rebel movements lack a clear ideological focus, children and their families come to see the war as a form of employment. Writing on neighbouring Kivu Province in DRC, Van Acker and Vlassenroot (2000) contend that war offered youths opportunities for social mobility that had been denied them by the collapsed economic system.

In Burundi, numerous reports suggests that young men were drawn into the war machine by the prospect of employment, or for 'something to do', while others were abducted, or joined out of fear. The state also claimed that the children in the *Gardiéns de la Paix*, were former child soldiers who had become 'radical converts to non-violence' (UNCRC Burundi 1998: Para. 231). These children were said to be participating in 'civilian military work' (*travail civile militaire)*, which Human Rights Watch saw as 'an appropriate description for its ambiguous status' (HRW, 2001: 6).

Burundi has ratified the International Convention on the Rights of the Child and in its domestic laws is bound to protect children in emergencies, yet the state sanctioned the deliberate recruitment and use of children as helpers, guides and porters by the military and claimed that 'at least in this way, they are able to eat and survive' (UNCRC Burundi ibid.). From the children's perspective, especially those orphaned, military units may have appeared to provide sanctuary and an alternative family. Human Rights Watch reported:

> Most have no families or have found that their families cannot support them. They often wear cast-off shirts or pants from soldiers, enjoying the borrowed prestige of even a partial military uniform ... The boys themselves stated that they were happy to be working with the soldiers. One twelve-year-old said that the soldiers feed them well. Another, aged fourteen, said that he liked the guns. (HRW 2000c: section VII)

Nevertheless, empowering children through the gun instils militaristic values that may undermine the social fabric of society long after the war ends.

Hutu rebel movements also recruited and abducted school children to serve in youth wings such as Palipehutu-FNL's *Jeunesses Patriotiques Hutu* (JPH). Amnesty International (2004e: 5) claims that 'in November 2001, nearly 300 children were abducted from schools in Ruyigi and Kayanza provinces, many of them forced to carry equipment or assist wounded soldiers'. Children were often used in the firing line. As one recruit retold:

> They told us children were the best fighters. For example, if there was an attack, they would send us to stop the enemy advance. We were not afraid because we were all together and because they gave us special forms of protection. They weren't for everyone – diviners gave them only to those who were going to battle. (Interview quoted in HRW, 2003: 46)

Referring to a 16-year-old boy who had spent four years fighting for CNDD-FDD in Burundi and the DRC, Human Rights Watch states that:

> He had no idea what he and other FDD soldiers were supposed to be fighting for. He knew only that life was difficult, that the food was bad, that he was dressed in uniforms that were torn or in rags, that he was beaten, and that he slept outside. He said he was angry at 'the important leaders who are responsible for everything; it is their war. I have friends my age who are dead. (HRW, 2003: 46)

The rebel groups gave children ideological training; some were told that they were fighting for democracy and, in the case of Palipehutu-FNL, a religious cause. Historically, peasant protests among the Hutus have tended to take the form of secret religious cults; some were break-away Protestant sects, and those known as *Nanga Yivuza* flourished in Northern Burundi during the 1970s (Weinstein, 1974). Both the leadership of CNDD-FDD and Palipehutu/FNL represented themselves as Evangelical Christians, fighting a just cause, and living by the prescriptions of the bible.[7] Although they claimed that alcohol, drugs and sexual violence were prohibited, much evidence suggests that there were no differences in the type of atrocities committed by these groups.

Replicating State-Sponsored Violence: the Rebels
The scale of state-sponsored genocidal violence suggests that armed insurrection was the only counter to state power. However, this process has been far from straightforward. Despite incursions in the 1970s, the rebels only posed a real military challenge to the Burundi state in the late 1990s. Palipehutu was able to recruit within Burundi during the democratization process of the early 1990s (Ntibantunganya, 1999). Furthermore, all Burundian rebels were able to benefit from the war in the DRC and from globalization; the latter allowing greater ease of access to global networks for funds, weapons and trade in illegal goods. Both CNDD-FDD and Palipehutu-FNL gained refuge and support from the Laurent Kabila's regime in the DRC after the overthrow of President Mobutu who supported

---

[7] One branch of Palipehutu-FNL claims to be Seventh-Day Adventist; while Nkurunziza, who headed a faction of CNDD-FDD, is a born-again Christian.

the Burundian government (Chapter 7 & Table 7.2). Furthermore, the rebels were able to link up with local Bantu groups who were fighting Congolese Tutsis (*Africa Confidential*, 9 May 1997). Intense competition between the groups for recruitment in the refugee camps of Tanzania and in the Congo and differences over strategy meant that the rebels soon degenerated into factionalism, fighting each other and amongst themselves. Internecine violence became increasingly common as the rebel movements split into a multiplicity of factions. Palipehutu-FNL, it is claimed, attacked its own members who were seeking to flee the movement. Human Rights Watch (2000b) reports the massacre, in late 1999, of some two to three hundred Rwandan Hutu combatants, who had joined the FNL in 1997 and who were suspected of planning to return to Rwanda.

For many civilians, there was a lack of a clear enemy, as they were vulnerable to attacks even from those claiming to fight on the behalf of their ethnic group. The presence of rebel armies in an area provided no guarantee of security for Hutu communities who experienced looting, violence and destruction of property by rebels, the military and armed bandits alike. Rural communities were also subjected to additional taxes levied by the rebels. CNDD-FDD and Palipehutu-FNL forced peasants to provide them with provisions, and when people refused they were often accused of collaborating with the other rebel movement (HRW, 2000b & 2004a). FNL, reportedly, taxed peasants, 'ranging from US $0.50 to US $1.50 for one cow' (Irinnews.org, 20 September 2006: 1; Ligue Iteka, 2005b). CNDD-FDD also deployed extrajudicial judgements on the Hutu population (HRW, 2004a).

> In several cases, [CNDD-FDD] agents detained civilians in unofficial places of detention in private homes, accusing them of having supported FNL. CNDD-FDD representatives summarily settled various local conflicts, including questions involving land, marriage problems and failure to repay debts. According to several residents of these sectors, they imposed 'the politics of the stick,' meaning they beat persons whose personal or political behaviour they found unacceptable. (HRW, 2004a: 4)

The people became pawns, caught between state and non-state militarized groups. Human Rights Watch (1997a: 18) notes that 'the rebels became less discriminating in their raids using Hutu civilians as shield and thereby leaving the Hutu at the mercy of both sides in the war'.[8] Rebel violence against civilians intensified in late December 1999 and early January 2000 and seemed to correspond with developments in the Arusha peace talks, essentially the drafting of the peace agreement from which the rebels excluded themselves.

In early to mid-2003, CNDD-FDD targeted state officials, in particular communal administrators in order 'to demonstrate that government officials could not or would not protect the people of a given area' (HRW, 2003: 33). Numerous officials were killed or abducted. In June, local administrators were abducted in the provinces of Cankuzo, Kayanza,

---

[8] FDD and FNL fought in Cibitoke in 1997 (*Africa Confidential*, 17 April 1998), and Palipehutu and FROLINA fought each other in the northern provinces during April 1997 (HRW, 1998).

Mwaro, Bujumbura Rurale and Bubanza. The interests of state and rebels coalesced when CNDD-FDD joined the government later that year and amalgamated with the military to root out Palipehutu-FNL combatants and supporters from many communes, with the message 'FNL control is finished now' (HRW, 2004a: 4).

Numerous commonalities are apparent in the sequentiality and social character of the violence as perpetrated by state security and the rebels. In sum, genocidal thinking, along with a culture of impunity, has resulted in rebels sharing the state's disregard for the lives of the Burundi people, despite their advocacy of a political cause.

The Spatiality of Violence in Burundi

By studying the geography of violence, one seeks to understand the extent to which genocidal violence is differentiated according to hierarchies of space. Do the spatial binaries of rural/urban, regional/national and private/public have relevance in the Burundi context? Our understanding of political violence is that it constitutes struggles for territorial and institutional control of the space of politics. Although violence is likely to envelope the national space, it tends to have specific geographical attributes, depending on the origin and constituency of the perpetrators, the degree of support they receive from local communities and the physical terrain of the territory.

Recent geographical literature focuses on the emerging urbicide of recent wars, as in Bosnia and Iraq, where opponents seek to inflict maximum damage on urban areas because of their greater concentration of people; where the enemy cannot be clearly differentiated from the surrounding people, as in the 'war on terror' or where fundamentalist forces oppose the liberal modernity of the city (Graham, 2004 & 2007). African urban areas, especially the capital cities are centres of government and home to the political elite and are, therefore, well protected. Although subjected to bombing and grenade strikes, urban areas are rarely the scene of massacres on the scale that occur in rural communities. What McClintock (1996) terms 'the pathological geography of power that' that divided the colonial space are still pronounced in the post-colonial space. The security afforded by the colonial power varied according to geographical space and assumptions about modernity. Mamdani (1996) demonstrates how, during the colonial period, citizenship and rights resided in the city, the home of modernity, Europeans and urbanized Africans mimicked European ways and Africans who lived predominantly in rural areas were subjects, bound to a different legal system and a different set of rights. Africans were governed by 'tradition', a customary law codified by Europeans and their chiefs. In this bifurcated state, citizenship was the privilege of the civilized. This division not only allowed for different administrative regimes but also different regimes of violence and representations of violence. The promotion of difference and hierarchies of human beings gave authority to selected groups among the colonized to perpetrate violence on the inferior other. Here, they seek not to destroy the 'liberal modernity' of the city; it is the prize of the contestation, since it provides the organizational base for genocidal politics and economics.

Much has been written about the urban/rural dimensions of violence in post-colonial Africa, especially the scale of the violence meted out by armed groups against the peasantry (Keen, 2005; Mkandawire, 2002). Mkandawire (ibid.) postulates that most guerrilla movements in Africa have urban origins, and their grievances against the state are not shared by rural communities who still retain control over land and whose suffering from state exactions has been blunted by free-market structural adjustment policies. As a consequence, Mkandawire (ibid.: 182) argues, 'the social terrain of rural Africa [is unsuitable] for classical guerrilla warfare ... this generates self-defeating behaviour on the part of armed groups, and terrible suffering for rural populations.' This does not resonate in the Burundi case, where, according to Laely (1997), the state has retained a complex relationship with rural communities through a system of domination that involves 'personal bonds of dependency' or patron-client relationships and, where, as Oketch & Polzer (2002: 123) note, land pressure and struggle over land ownership, between the peasantry and 'powerful actors and groups' and between cattle-owners and agriculturalists, has fuelled rural discontent. Mkandawire's urban/rural dichotomy is perhaps too sharp for the movements under analysis; many of which voluntarily or even forcibly recruited from the countryside and had regional and urban strongholds. Hutu rebel groups initially targeted sites of maximum effect, mainly the capital city, the military or communities closely associated with the regime.

Urban-based political opponents tend to be the first to be arrested, yet they, simultaneously, have greater security due to the concentration of local and international human rights organizations and foreign embassies in the capital city. Their presence, however, did not prevent Bujumbura becoming a 'city of death', with frequent assassinations of political opponents. Where the centres of violence are effectively rural, this is often due to the state or the political elite having effective control over urban centres, particularly those that are ethnically homogeneous. When violence occurs in cities, variations in its intensity across urban space tend to reflect the spatiality of power and class, with poorer suburbs often bearing the brunt of the violence.

Ethnic Cleansing and Urban Theatres of War
It is commonly stated about Burundi that Hutu and Tutsi inhabit the same areas, but historical occupational differences, linked to geography and agro-ecological zones, meant that some areas, in the northern provinces, were more densely-settled by Hutu agriculturalists, whilst others, in central Burundi, for example, were more suitable for grazing and other activities. More detailed census on the distribution of Hutus and Tutsis are not available, yet one author claims that Hutus are in the majority in 110 communes, while Tutsis form the majority in only four: Gisoka and Rusaka in Maramvya Province, Mugongomanga in Bujumbura Rurale and Mugamba in Bururi (Ndarubayige, 1995). It is claimed that successive genocide, fear and hatred, and the protracted warfare have, inadvertently, led to greater spatial segregation of Burundians into Hutuland and Tutsiland, with the minority Tutsi becoming increasingly urbanised (Laely, 1997; Lemarchand, 1996).

There is clear evidence that state and military power in Burundi was also expressed in strategies aimed at the spatial reorganization and segregation of urban and rural communities as a mechanism to curtail support for the rebels. Between 1994 and 1996, the military and militias conducted ethnic cleansing in the capital, Bujumbura, and other urban centres in their *ville morte* (dead city) campaigns (Ntibantunganya, 1999). Military sweeps on predominantly Hutu districts resulted in the ousting of FNL rebels, the forced displacement of the population and enforced ethnic segregation.

> In June 1995, the military allegedly hunted down the population of Kamenge and Kimana in the Gishingano *collines*, on the outskirts of Bujumbura, where they had hidden. They reportedly used bayonets and hatchets to kill over 100, mostly women and children. It is said a pregnant woman was even disembowelled. (UNESC, 1995b: 20, para. 93)

Bujumbura's poorer peri-urban suburbs of Kinama and Kamenge became largely Hutu areas, and those of Nyakabiga and Ngagara essentially Tutsi (Map 3). By the late 1990s, FNL bases were located relatively close (not more than 50 km) to the capital city, such that between February and March 2001, they were able to occupy Kinama (ICG, 2001a). After the ceasefire agreement, in late 2003, CNDD-FDD took control of Kamenge and Kinama, and areas in Ngozi, Bubanza and Muramvya Province (Map 2). The inhabitants saw virtually no differences in the practices of the military and the rebels.

Human Rights Watch (2003: 37) notes that, in October 2003, some 20 people had been killed in clashes between FDD and FNL in Bujumbura and its suburbs. With the exception of a curfew, the authorities did little to stop the violence. While violence may have contributed to spatial segregation, ethnic demarcations are far from exact, and ignore the influence of class and power on residential segregation. Beyond the urban the geography of atrocities in Central Africa fits Mkandawire's representation of guerrilla groups as roving and partly stationary. Rebel bases are dependent not just on terrain, but supply chains and cross-border material support provided by neighbouring territories. ICG (2000a: 30) writes, in relation to Burundi, 'the rebellion is loosely knit and fluid: it has no front and no firm control of territory; it is a mobile guerrilla movement'. Consequently, in the 1970s, fighting in Burundi occurred mainly in the predominantly Hutu districts of southern provinces and the border regions, where guerrilla groups launched raids from bases in Tanzania and the army responded with reprisals against the Hutu population (Chapter 4). The violence of August 1988 took place in the Hutu-dominated northern provinces of Kirundo and Ngozi, following rebel strikes supposedly from across the border in Zaire.

When, in the 1990s, Palipehutu-FNL and CNDD-FDD found support in the DRC, their incursions into Burundi occurred in the Hutu-dominated northern provinces. After they were forced out of the DRC, FNL moved to Bujumbura Rurale, the province adjacent to the capital, where fighting was concentrated in the 2000s. In 1997 and 1998, after FNL ousted FDD from north-eastern Burundi, FDD shifted its operations to the southern and eastern provinces, mainly Bururi, Makamba and Ruyigi (HRW, 2000b). The central provinces of Cankuzo, Gitega, and Muramvya were also the scene of sporadic fighting in 1999 and early 2000. Intense rivalry between FDD and FNL led to factional fighting, causing the massacre and forced displacement of large numbers of civilians, both Hutus and Tutsis. Human Rights Watch (2000b) reports that FDD insurgents not only killed or kidnapped civilians, but looted and burnt houses, schools, health centres and communal offices in Kinyinya, Gisuru and Nyabitare. The primary purpose was to discourage refugees, especially those in Tanzania, from returning home by destabilizing the region. Not surprisingly, some 74,000 refugees fled to Tanzania. Within Burundi, even refugee camps under international protection, were not safe spaces. In August 2004, Palipehutu-FNL was able to support its Congolese allies by massacring 152 Congolese (Banyamulenge) refugees, mainly women and children, at the Gatumba refugee camp near the border with the DRC (UNSC, 2004; HRW, 2004c).

State-Sponsored Displacement: The Regroupement Camps
Forced encampment of rural communities became a counter-insurgency strategy of the Burundi state in 1996. It represented the coercive arm of state power over the people, especially Hutus, and a total disregard for their well-being. Between 1996 and 2000 the government established 57 *regroupement* camps, primarily in the south- eastern part of the country, on the pretext of protecting the people. There were no doubts among observers that the purpose of *regroupement* camps was to restrict the Hutu population's support for the rebels. Between 200,000 and 575,000 people (or 10 to 14 per cent of the population) were forced into encampments, and, in the province of Bujumbura Rurale, some 80 per cent (350,000) of the population were displaced into 53 camps in 1999; one camp, Kabezi, held some 40,000 people (HRW, 2000c). These camps were described by Nelson Mandela and FROBEDU/CNDD supporters as 'concentration camps'- akin to those of the Nazis.

Communities were given little or no warning of *regroupement*, and were expected to respond immediately to military orders to leave their homes. Many were forced to relocate without any possessions. Those who tried to flee were often cornered, and those who refused to move were declared accomplices of the rebels and liable to summary justice. According to Human Rights Watch (1998; 2000c), villages were destroyed in order to force people to move to camps. Witnesses report:

> We were burned out of our homes ... We were pursued by the soldiers. They did not want us to stay on our hills. They killed many people...The soldiers surrounded us and put us in the camps.[9] (HRW, 1998: 28)

In many camps the state made no provision to provide the inhabitants with water, food or shelter and, in some areas, they were often prevented from returning to their fields to cultivate. Dysentery and chronic malnutrition were pervasive. The existence of adult malnutrition signalled the extreme levels of impoverishment in the camps and in some rural

---

[9] HRW interview in Kayanza province, Dec. 1996, quoted in HRW (1998: 28).

communities (HRW, 2001). Camp inhabitants were subjected to forced labour, sexual violence and the looting of their property.

Camps were also ethnicized, with the state making a distinction between '*regroupement* camps', largely containing the Hutu population and Internally Displaced Peoples (IDPs) camps of mainly Tutsis, who, in some areas, were also forced to move to camps for their safety. IDP camps were better provisioned in that international relief agencies were given access to them, but were vulnerable to onslaughts from rebel movements (HRW, 2000c). As early as 1994, a report by the UN Special Representative, Francis Deng, found that:

> In most countries visited by the representative the displaced tend to be members of disadvantaged groups and in general do not enjoy a special favour from the system. In Burundi, however, the reverse is often true. The fact that Tutsi were in camps, rather than being evidence of their disfavour, was because they needed protection by the army. Paradoxically, however, being favoured has often been a source of misery for the displaced Tutsi. (UNESC, 1994: 27)

State protection did not necessarily translate into improved personal security. *Regroupement* camps of Hutus were sometimes placed strategically by the military in order for them to be used as human shields against rebel incursions – the rebels did likewise (HRW, 2000c). And, in camps such as Nyambuye & Kavumu (Bujumbura Rurale), the people were attacked by the military in reprisals for raids by Palipehutu-FNL. Freedom of movement was restricted for camp residents; those who left the camp to obtain foodstuffs or to access other services were accused of being rebels and were severely punished.

International and regional pressure was placed on the government to disband the *regroupement* camps. In June 2000, concessions made to the military regime as part of the peace agreement were conditional on the state disbanding the camps. Closures, however, proceeded very slowly and were compounded by the fact that many residents had their properties destroyed by soldiers and militias, or expropriated by Tutsis. Thousands of people sought refuge independent of the state, and fled to forests, marshland and other inaccessible locations and over 800,000 sought asylum in neighbouring countries.

Within the national territory, space intersected with ethnicity to produce distinct spatialities of violence that reflected hierarchies of space and class. Rural areas were militarized and subjected to extreme violence, whether committed by state actors or rebels, and poorer urban communities tended to bear the brunt of rebel activities or military retribution. Such violence was also gendered.

Masculinities and Gender-based Violence

The association of patriarchy and male dominance with militarism in the context of genocide leads to the proliferation of violence against those considered to being socially vulnerable, especially those lower down the gendered hierarchies. Militarized violence is a product of particular manifestations of patriarchy and its dependence on the linking of violent masculinity with the concept of individuality. Militarism, supported by hierarchical power relations, gives prestige, and filters power down to those legally sanctioned to hold weaponry. Arendt (2004: 237) quotes Jouvenel's 'a man feels himself more of a man when he is imposing himself and making others the instruments of his will.'[10] Enloe (1993: 47) and other feminists have shown us how militarism is embedded in the liberal state, and how 'masculinity and femininity are central to the creation and reproduction of militarism'. As state-actors, military men legitimate the institutionalization of masculine violence within society.

Connell's (1995 & 2000) assertion of masculinity as a historical product, linked to the rise of individualism, enables us to see how the modernizing state becomes an important site for the reproduction of violent masculinity. Linking colonial spatial differentiation with masculinity, McClintock (1996: 267) argues that 'the privileged national agents were urban, male, vanguardist and violent'. African men, forced to adopt a subordinate and marginalized masculinity both under colonialism and in the international arena, construct a more oppressive patriarchy, which relies on *authenticité* or a return to 'traditional' values in cultural practices, while employing modern technologies of war to maintain state domination of society. Militarism is associated with an extension of patriarchal control over women's sexuality as a means of shaping African men's sense of masculinity. The manifestation of marginalized masculinity in the twenty-first century, nevertheless, is qualitatively different from others in that its reference point also comes from globalized representations of hegemonic masculinity, in practice Rambo militarism confused with the emancipatory politics of Bob Marley.[11]

Twenty-eight years of successive military rule in Burundi have enabled military values that reinforced patriarchal tendencies and oppressive forms of masculinity to become entrenched in all areas of society. Locally, military men perform a violent form of masculinity that has become locally hegemonic. Being better-paid, having legitimate access to weaponry, and having the capacity to overthrow regimes give them a singularly superior status in society. Military officers, trained in elite military academies in France, Belgium and the USA, exhibit what Connell (2000) describes as a 'transnational military masculinity'. Represented as all-powerful masculine beings, they are able to exercise the power of control over life and death among enemy combatants and civilians. According to HRW (2004a: 11) one military mobile unit called itself the '*Bakanongwe*' or 'those who [dare even to] castrate leopards'.

Gendered Violence in Burundi

In traditional as well as modern Burundi society, violence was and continues to be gendered, with men being subjected to different forms of

[10] Bertrand de Jouvenel, 1952, 'Power: the Natural History of its Growth', quoted in Arendt (2004).

[11] Richards (1996) refers to Sierra Leonean rebels' fascination with the Rambo films and other violent videos. In contradiction, Bob Marley is simultaneously seen as a hero by young men.

violence from women. Here, Jones' (2000: 186) concept of 'gendercide' is instructive in explaining the differential treatment of men and women during genocide. He documents numerous cases globally where young men, even non-combatants, are singled out as 'targets of mass killing and genocidal slaughter as well as a host of lesser atrocities and abuses'. In Burundi, thousands of Hutu men lost their lives after having been suspected as rebels. Young men, in particular, were vulnerable to arbitrary arrest by military personnel or abduction by rebel groups, most often when carrying out livelihood activities such as farming and fishing, and returning home from work or school. Human Rights Watch relates the testimony of one woman:

> Soldiers beat young men especially harshly. She saw them beat one man, who seemed to be about twenty-five years old, so violently that he died on the spot. "After some time", she said, "He just stopped moving." Several others had their arms broken and remain disabled by their injuries six months later. (HRW, 2000c: section VI)

Jones (2000), in his criticism of the fact that so little attention is given to men as victims of genocidal slaughter, shows how women, in turn, are subjected to particular forms of violence that also constitute 'gendercide'. Jones' treatise is to put men-on-men violence back in the frame of analysis. In order to understand why violence is so differentiated we need to understand the patriarchal logic behind such acts. Power is the ability to dominate other men and women and is central to patriarchal societies.

The intersection of racial, ethnic and masculine hierarchies allowed for the perpetration of violence against men who are considered inferior or infidels with a certain degree of righteousness. Certain women, differentiated by race and ethnicity, who are seen as significantly lower down the human and feminine hierarchy, are exposed to forms of violence that defile their gender and person, as well as to torture and death. Women, especially older ones, are vulnerable to accusations of witchcraft and face death by popular justice; in Burundi, the latter occurred even in zones that were 'liberated' by rebels (Ligue Iteka, 2005a, 2006a). Between 2003 and 2006, several women were accused of collaborating with CNDD-FDD and killed by Palipehutu-FNL rebels (Ligue Iteka, 2006a).

Although the dominant narrative of women in wartime Burundi is that of victim, many women supported the wars by instigating violence, fighting or by supplying weapons. One of the main suppliers of weapons to CNDD-FDD was a woman known as Aziza Kulsum Gulamali, who was also involved in a range of illegal activities including gold, coltan and ivory trafficking (UNSC, 2001a). Demobilization data for the period August 2003 to July 2005 provide an indication of women's participation in the war as combatants (Bruchhaus, 2005). Of the 14,533 combatants demobilized, 3.5 per cent were women and they all belonged to rebel groups. Women constituted 8 per cent of demobilized CNDD-FDD's combatants and 2.6 per cent of Frolina. Women who joined rebel movements voluntarily reported gaining respect from their male comrades but, for the majority, close association with the military furthered their subordination (Bruchhaus, ibid.).

Because of their obvious vulnerability, I shall focus on women for the rest of this chapter. As Connell (1995: 83) notes, 'It is overwhelmingly the dominant gender who hold and use the means of violence.' Women's literal and physical disarmament by patriarchy makes their vulnerability to violence far greater than men's and, as their livelihood and caring activities sustain households and human bodies, it is critical that we investigate their distinct experience of violence.

Militarized Rape and the Sexualization of War

Rape has become like an epidemic[12]

Rape is the most common form of sexual violence suffered by women in the Great Lakes region. The war in the region is not only racialized and ethnicized, it is also sexualized. In spite of the silence surrounding male rape (Ligue Iteka noted seven cases in 2004), women suffered disproportionately from rape (AI, 2004b; Ligue Iteka 2005a). Young women have been, and continue to be, abducted, raped, exposed to sexually transmitted diseases and murdered because of their gender. In Burundi, reported cases of rape rise dramatically after the peace agreement. Numerous non-governmental organizations collect data on sexual violence. Ligue Iteka (2005b) saw cases rise from 983 in 2003 to 1,791 in 2005. Another NGO, Nturengaho, reported 93 cases in 2003 and 446 cases in 2004, 40 per cent of which were committed by armed personnel. Also Centre Seruka – a rape crisis centre – received 1,119 cases between September 2003 and 2004 (RoB, 2004). For the month of April 2006, ONUB (2006a) reported 42 cases of rape, 29 of which were committed against minors. Rape was by far the commonest violation of physical integrity. Despite the recent growth in NGOs dealing with sexual violence, there is still widespread under-reporting of rape in Burundi. This means that no accurate statistics can be provided, but they may not be significantly different from those for the Eastern Congo, where it has been estimated that over 40,000 women have been brutally raped, during and after the war, and some even by those charged to enforce the peace and protect civilians (HRW, 2005a).[13]

The geography of reported rape in Burundi suggests a strong correlation with areas of intense military activities, and also areas of greater sensitization to the criminality of sexual violence and available assistance to victims. The majority of rape cases therefore seems to take place in Bujumbura City (50–70 per cent), followed by Bujumbura Rurale (20 per cent), Ruyigi (15–20 per cent), Muramvya (10 per cent) and Rumonge (RoB, 2004). Perpetrators varied depending on the source of the data. Ligue Iteka reported that rape by military personnel amounted to only 9.2 per cent and that in 79 per cent of cases the perpetrators were known to the parents (RoB, 2004).

The motivations for rape vary considerably; rape can be institutionalized in the context of militarism and performed as a military strategy, or an act of reprisal, or it may simply reflect sheer brutality or abuses by men lacking sexual restraint. Militarized rape, according to Enloe, draws 'much of its

[12] A mother interviewed by Human Rights Watch, March 2004.
[13] UN peacekeepers were accused of raping local women in Eastern Congo.

rationale from an imaginings of societal conflict and/or the function of a formal institution such as the state's security or defence apparatus or an insurgency's military arm'... 'The male militarised rapist, in some ways, imposes his understandings of "enemy", "soldiering", "victory" and "defeat" on both the woman to be raped and on the act of sexual assault' (2000: 110). Militarized rape is not peculiar to African societies, as military men, worldwide, tend to be socialized into satisfying their sexual urges without penalty. Military hierarchies tolerate, if not encouraged, the use of extreme pornography by men under their command. Yet, not all military men rape, and not all those raped are women. Young men have also been victims of militarized rape – a topic virtually tabooed in Africa.

In Burundi, the military, armed opposition groups, criminal elements and individual men commit rape with impunity. One human rights organization described rape in Burundi as 'a strategy of war to terrorize, degrade and humiliate' (AI, 2004b: 11). Human Rights Watch also claims:

> The armed forces seem to use sexual violence against women as one of the means to subdue the population humiliating both the women and their families and contributing to a general atmosphere of fear. (HRW, 1998: 47)

As one case shows:

> I was going with three children to get water when a soldier stopped us on the road. The children managed to escape, but I fell and he caught me. He took me to a church, which they had turned into some kind of bar with food and alcohol everywhere. The soldier raped me in the church, and he told me I would be blessed because it was a holy place... Another one refused to rape me. The first soldier forced a bottle of beer inside of me. I started bleeding and shouting. The soldiers covered me with a military coat and left me outside the church to die. (Amélie, Widow, aged 30, in AI, 2004b: 7)

Even in the *regroupement* camps, where women constituted 80 per cent of the camp's population, women and children were unprotected and were therefore subjected to sexual abuse by government forces (AI, 2004b). Women, especially those in female-headed households, were particularly vulnerable in their homes at night. Many were forced to alter their daily patterns of activities if soldiers were known to be in the area. Amnesty International (2004b: 1) notes that 'whole families [were forced] to sleep outside and away from their homes ... rendering them still more vulnerable to malaria and other diseases.'

The association of the female body with the sanctity of the ethnic group, religion or nation has been seen as a critical factor in the frequency of rape in wartime; this is even more pertinent in the context of genocide (Baines, 2003; Cockburn, 2001; Enloe, 1993; Jones, 2002; McClintock, 1996; Peterson, 1992). Enloe (1993: 239) argues that the militarization of a nationalist movement inevitably affects conceptualizations of femininity and masculinity; men exerting their control over women 'becomes a man's way of protecting and reviving the nation ... rape and prostitution have been central to many men's construction of the nationalist cause'. Baines' (2003) study, in particular, highlights the interconnections between sexual violence against Tutsi women in the Rwandan genocide and Hutu ethnic nationalism. She argues that violence against Tutsi women was fundamental to binding Hutu men in the construction of the Hutu nation. Baines contends '... scripting the nation implies different acts of violence on men and women, ... reproductive capabilities and myths of feminine beauty mark some for extreme forms of gender violence over others' (Baines, 2003: 490). The marginalized masculinity of Hutu men was empowered by the ability to exert violence against women they believed to be their social superior. Tutsi women were subjected to extreme forms of mutilation. Assailants, according to Human Rights Watch 'cut off breasts, punctured the vagina with spears, arrows, or pointed sticks, or cut off or disfigured body parts that looked particularly "Tutsi", such as long fingers or thin noses' (1999a: 215). In contrast, in Burundi, Hutu women, presumably because of their inferior femininity, were not subjected to the same degree of bodily disfigurements, except that pregnant women were, in some cases, disembowelled. More recently, cases of mutilation of sexual organs leading to death have emerged.

> On 29 May 2004 around 5.30 am in Kinyinya-Kimana, in the Mubone zone, Commune Kabezi, a mobile battalion [Palipehutu-FNL] besieged the hills of Kinyinya and Kimana. The population of the immediate and surrounding areas fled towards Ruziba and seven people fell into the 'claws' of these soldiers who killed them in an atrocious manner. A 15 year old girl, named K.M., and a school girl in Year 6, was one of those killed. Before being killed, she was raped by a group of soldiers who after this first trial, pulled apart her legs and lashed them to separate bushes, inserting pieces of wood into her vagina. She died of haemorrhage. (Ligue Iteka, 2005a: 7)

Victims could not always identify whether their attackers were rebels or soldiers, and even when they could, justice was not forthcoming. As Twagiramariya and Turshen (1998) show with respect to Rwanda, Hutu women were raped by members of the Hutu militias and by the liberating Tutsi-dominated army. Similarly, in Burundi, the men in the rebel group CNDD-FDD raped both Hutu and Tutsi women. Tit-for-tat rape of Hutu and Tutsi women was also common. Amnesty International documented 'scores' of rape committed by government forces in Hutu areas in Ruyigi province in February and March 2003, and, in reprisal, Tutsi women were raped by CNDD/FDD in Ruhwago, Ruyigi Province (AI, 2004b: 11). Palipehutu-FNL claimed that as religious fighters rape was against their code of conduct, yet there were still reports of combatants committing rape (HRW, 2000b; Ligue Iteka, 2005a & 2006a).

While the gender and nationalism thesis assists in our understanding of the specific nature of sexual violence in the context of genocide, they do not explain its pervasiveness even after ceasefire agreements have been signed. Basically, abuse of women is frequently not viewed as a tactic of war or nation-building but simply as 'booty'. In most African societies, communities place limits on sexual intercourse and it usually has a cost associated with it; men pay bride prices for wives, money to prostitutes and 'sugar daddies' provide gifts to young women.

According to a report by the Burundi government (RoB, 2004), in Burundian culture, a married woman does not belong only to her husband but to all the men in her family (*Umugore n'uwumuryango*). Numerous cultural practices give emphasis to multiple sexual partners as a symbol of masculinity (*Impfizi ntiyimigwa*). Nevertheless, rape was still a socially unacceptable act. Some women were raped by people known to them who used the culture of impunity to exact revenge on women who had rejected marriage proposals, were beyond their social status or to just to satisfy sexual urges. The relationship between years of warfare and incidence of rape may also be significant. Most rapists were between the age of 16 and 30. An analysis, of Ligue Iteka's statistics for 2005, shows that 64 per cent of rapists were below the age of 30, and 22 per cent below the age of 20. These young men reached manhood in a climate where social norms and constraints were disintegrating and violation of women was the norm or went unpunished.

The rape of minors is largely committed by men who are known to the victims. Surveys by the NGOs, Nturengaho in 2003, and Ligue Iteka in 2004, found that children under ten years constituted 10.75 and 2.8 per cent respectively of recorded cases of rape, and that 43 per cent of rapes were committed against minors.[14] Ligue Iteka's (2006: 113) data demonstrate that in 2005, 16.5 per cent of victims were below the age of 10 and 28.9 per cent below 15 years. Social breakdown, the prominence of violent masculinity and the propagation of modern myths are all being used to explain what appears to be an increasingly high incidence of rape of minors. For example, one urban myth, emanating from South Africa, is that sex with young girls and infants is believed to provide protection against HIV/AIDS and to increase men's virility (Interview with Nturengaho, 2006; AI, 2004b).

Masculinized Violence and Development Failure
Turshen (2001) has attempted to understand the political economy of rape by linking it to women's productive and reproductive role in society. She argues that rape takes on immense significance in communities that regard women as property; where bride prices are paid in compensation for loss of labour, where only men are recognized as heads of household and where wives have no ownership of family assets. In her analysis 'the abduction of girls to serve as porters, farmers, cooks, cleaners, launderers, tailors and sex workers is perhaps the crudest form of asset transfer in civil war, in this case women's productive labour' (Turshen, 2001: 61). Turshen's link between rape and the commodification of women provides a useful framework to understand some cases, but it ignores matriarchal households and assumes that the wife becomes alienated property with the payment of bride price. As Diop (1989) argues, even under such circumstances, the wife belongs to her family and is not legally bound to her husband. Obviously, this arrangement has broken down in areas exposed to the dual forces of modernity and warfare. We, therefore, need to address rape within the context of a more dynamic political economy and its link to militarization.

---

[14] Ligue Iteka (2005c) *La Ligue Iteka organise un formation sur la prise en charge des victims des violences sexuelles*, Bujumbura, Burundi: Ligue Iteka. http://www.ligue-iteka.africa-web.org. [last accessed, 10 August 2006]. Nturengaho (2003) cited in RoB (2004).

African men have struggled to retain control of women's productive and reproductive capacities under conditions of colonialism and modernization in which the nature of their patriarchal role has been challenged. We need to know the extent to which the economic crises, the use of gender as conditionality and the collapse of patrimonial politics under SAP have aggravated the crisis of masculinity. Most accounts of the impact of SAP on gender focus on the ways in which women's labour has become intensified through the extension of their role as carers in the context of health charges and state retreat from service provisioning (Chachage & Mbilinyi, 2003). Women are often portrayed as the losers but men's loss of income earning opportunities may affect gender relations adversely. Jones (2002) refers to the loss of status felt by men following the political and economic gains made by pro-women policies in the 1980s and 1990s. Men, who are no longer able to use formal channels to secure their own well being and meet marital and other domestic obligations, might turn to illegal and militaristic activities. Regaining masculinized power, is partly tied up with the formation of guerrilla organizations; men and boys wielding guns are empowered in a destructive way. On the other hand by taking up guns, some men may be striving to repair the damage done to their communities in a revolutionary way.

Turshen's (2001) concept of asset transfers has resonance when we consider the reaction of husbands, families and households to rape. In Burundi, families seek recompense by demanding the rapist either marry the victim or pay compensation. For example, in Kayanza, in February 2004, the *Bashingantahe* ordered the payment of 27,000 FBU (US$ 2.7) for the rape of a 6 year old girl by a 16 year old boy (Ligue Iteka, 2005a: 56). Throughout Central Africa, women who survived such brutality suffer physical and psychological damage and social stigma, which leads to rejection by their husbands, families and communities.

> I don't know where my husband is. He left me and our children when he heard I'd been raped. I'm still in the camp – I have no where to go now. My house was destroyed by soldiers and anyway I think my husband wouldn't allow me to live there. I have no money. The children can't go to school. (Marie quoted in AI, 2004b: 7)

Reports of rejection following rape often point to local cultural perception of the diminished value of young girls in marriage transactions, and as wives and mothers, and implies, in a cultural relativist way, that 'traditionalism' and 'ignorance' are at the root of the problem. However, empirical evidence suggests that the fear of HIV/AIDS is now a common reason, plus the difficulty of socially incorporating unwanted or fatherless children into the household. This last factor has led to victims being forced to marry rapists, infanticide, child abandonment and forced abortions (Ligue Iteka, 2005a; Interview with Nturengaho, Bujumbura, 2006).

As well as being an intimate personal problem, rape is also a family, community, social, political, economic and health problem: it is simultaneously private and public. Sexual violence becomes widespread under conditions of hierarchical power relations in peace and war; it produces immense social disruption, increases people's exposure to sexually-transmitted and environmental diseases and its symptoms are aggravated under conditions of economic crisis, reducing access to health care and other ameliorative facilities. HIV/AIDS prevalence in Burundi varies geographically, averaging at an estimated 6.0 per cent of the population in 2002. Urban and semi-urban areas have higher prevalence rates, 10.9 per cent, and 12.1per cent than rural (3.2 per cent). While urban areas have shown some stabilization of infection rates. HIV prevalence rates for women (13.0 per cent) were higher than for men (5.5 per cent). For women between the ages of 15 and 54, the prevalence rate is twice as high as for men of comparable age.[15]

Securing Rights in the Context of the Militarized and Genocidal State

At the level of the state, the periodic legitimization of Burundi's coups and coup-makers has reinforced the historical acceptability of violence as the mechanism for state transformation, and somehow gives justification to all groups seeking to wrest control of the state through undemocratic means. Military regimes strengthen and expand the processes of militarization, which, linked to a culture of impunity, has allowed violence perpetrated by state and non-state actors to become endemic.

Numerous UN and NGO reports attest to the failure of the judicial system in Burundi to deal effectively with cases of genocidal violence and abuse. Terms such as 'alleged paralysis', 'biased' and 'Tutsi-dominated' were applied to the judicial system. The rule of law was applied selectively. Perpetrators of genocidal violence were often pursued if crimes were committed against the Tutsi group, but even the trials of those arrested did not follow due process (AI, 1998). Despite the incitement to genocide articulated by prominent Tutsi politicians, their arrest has often been, as in the case of Mathias Hitimana in 1994 and Jean-Baptiste Bagaza in 1997, for fomenting violence and alleged coup plotting. In practice, the judicial system affirms the conceptualization of Tutsis as citizens and Hutus and Twas as subjects, the latter two groups being subjected to arbitrary and extrajudicial violence.

Under military regimes, where political parties are often suppressed and the judiciary incapacitated, women's participation in politics tends to be extremely low and their rights are often marginal to the concerns of the regime. Interestingly enough, Micombero's regime established the Union of Burundi Women in 1972, while Bagaza's set up the Ministry for the Advancement of Women in 1983 and later in 1992, Buyoya ratified the *UN Convention on the Elimination of all Forms of Discrimination against Women* and signed the *Optional Protocol*, yet women's participation in politics was limited. According to the UN Committee on the Elimination of Discrimination against Women (CEDAW) (2000) report, in 1990, 2.6 per cent of political posts were held by women, increasing to 5.03 per cent after the democratic elections in 1993 and the appointment of a female prime minister from July 1993 to February 1994, but the figure fell back to 3.4 per

---

[15] Source: UNAIDS/WHO (2004) *Epidemiological Factsheet on HIV/AIDS and sexually transmitted infections: Burundi.*

cent in 1998, following Buyoya's second coup of 1996. The democratic elections of 2005, once again, led to an increase in women's representation as stipulated in the peace agreement. A female was appointed as second vice-president and women occupied seven of the 20 ministerial posts.

The experience in Burundi shows that it is only when the democratic space is opened up are women's rights addressed meaningfully. Both the revisions to the Burundi Code of the Person and Family, and the Labour Code to tackle issues of gender equity were carried out in the throes of the democratization process. The military seems both adept at promoting modernity while reinforcing patriarchal tendencies. The revisions to the family code, which on the surface promote equality for women, outlawed polygamy, bride price and fixed the age of marriage, actually reaffirmed the patriarchal state. According to Ntampaka (1999: 72), 'Article 122 [of the Burundi Family Code] which states, "The husband is the head of the family community", is a denial of equality. It exemplifies traditional [and patriarchal state's resistance [to gender equity]' (Ibid.). A key area of discrimination relates to the law on inheritance, with land pressure used by the state as a counter to women's demand for inheritance rights. Customary practices are also invoked to maintain women's subordination within the modern patriarchal state. This is reinforced in the initial report of the Burundi state to CEDAW, in which the government affirms the legitimacy of patriarchy:

> The traditional society is a patriarchal and patrilinear (sic.) one, in which a woman is constantly under the protection of a father, brother, uncle, husband or family council. Women have more duties than rights and must subordinate themselves to the customs and practices governing the relations between men. (UN CEDAW, 2000: 7 para. 1.3)

As the state and its military arm seem to have total life and death control over the people, it seems rather purgatory for the state to appeal to 'tradition' to justify its actions. Appeals to *authenticité* are often a way of deflecting criticisms of discriminatory practices.

The existence of legislation has not necessarily meant their reinforcement. For example, Article 385 of the Burundi Penal Code prohibits rape, yet women experienced immense difficulties in pressing rape charges. Of the 4449 cases documented by Ligue Iteka between 2003 and 2005, only 376 cases (8.45 per cent) went to court and only 46 per cent were resolved (Ligue Iteka, 2006a). According to Amnesty International, 'magistrates have ridiculed and humiliated women who have come forward, in one case a magistrate actually instructing a woman to deliver the summons to her alleged rapist' (2004b: 8). Although considerable resources are being used to sensitize law enforcement agencies to sexual violence, reports abound of victims and families who have failed to get justice via the judicial system – whether in the traditional or modern courts. The *Bashingantahe* and local military tribunals (*intahe yo ku mugina*) do not accept sexual violence as a crime, and often instruct the rapist to marry the victim. Such is the case of a 13 year old raped by a soldier on her way to school.[16] These factors often lead to under-reporting

---

[16] Ligue Iteka (2005d) *Le viol est-il un crime de guerre?* http://www.ligue-iteka.africa-web.org/article.php3?id_article=455 [last accessed 10 August 2006].

of rape cases, and those women brave enough to seek justice are not well-served by a judicial system that refuses to prosecute crimes perpetrated by the military or even to take abuse of women seriously. Clearly, the resurrection of the *Bashingantahe* has not led to the restitution of the recognition of women's well-being as a factor in community cohesion. With its conservative religious leaders appointed by the state, the *Bashingantahe* has become an instrument for maintaining the power of the genocidal state at the level of the community (Nindorera, c. 2000).

Amnesty International concluded that 'the experience of military trials in Burundi has repeatedly demonstrated that military jurisdictions are simply not capable of bringing to justice those accused of human rights violations' (2004b: 9). What is clear from the documentation of violence is the failure of successive Burundi regimes not just to respect its own internal laws, particularly its constitutions (of which there were eight between 1960 and 2005 and one amended convention of governance). For example, the state failed to fulfil 'its absolute obligation to respect and protect the human person' as written in Article 11 of the 1992 Constitution. Those with power, acquired through public office, often fail to recognize the existence of any limits to their power, whether they are military personnel, police, politicians or the judiciary.

Although, in the CEDAW report, the Burundi government acknowledged that the country had been experiencing 'socio-political crises' that had affected its ability to deliver on human and women's rights, it failed to mention domestic violence and the widespread nature of rape and sexual violence against women which were the direct results of the on-going civil war. The state's silences on these matters gave implicit support to violent behaviour, and reinforced the gender bias embedded in the ideology of national security (McClintock, 1996).

No Recourse to International Law

The state also has a certain disrespect for the international laws that it has ratified. Burundi is party to the 1949 Geneva Conventions and to the Additional Protocols. Protocol II of the Geneva Convention prohibits the recruitment of children under the age of 15 and the January 2000 *Optional Protocol to Convention on the Rights of the Child*, which Burundi has also ratified, prohibits the recruitment of children under 18 into the armed forces. Burundi became party to the UN's Guiding Principles on Internal Displacement that stipulated the humane treatment by sovereign governments of the displaced. In September 2004, Burundi ratified the Rome Statute of the International Criminal Court and is now obliged to investigate and persecute any person accused of acts of genocide, crimes against humanity and war crimes.[17] The Statute recognizes rape committed by combatants as a war crime.

[17] See Amnesty International, News Service 234, 23 September 2004, International Criminal Court: Burundi and Liberia – Ratification is an important commitment towards ending impunity. The ICC has announced that it will be investigating crimes under international law, including crimes against humanity and war crimes committed during the conflict.

International legal instruments appeared to have been ratified or signed at critical moments in Burundi's history, when the country seeks international legitimacy or acceptability, for example, during the period of the early 1990s when the country was in transition to democracy; in May 1990, the *International Covenant on Civil and Political Rights* and the *International Covenant on Economic, Social and Cultural Rights,* and the *Convention on the Rights of the Child* in August that year; in February 1991, Burundi became a signatory of the *World Declaration on the Survival, Protection and Development of Children,* and the *African Charter on Human and People's Rights;* and in January 1992, Burundi ratified the *Convention on the Elimination of all Forms of Discrimination Against Women,* and in 2003 signed the *African Union Protocol on the Rights of Women in Africa.* These international legal instruments provide the basis not just for the Burundi state to act against discrimination and genocidal violence, but also regional and international communities.

On a bureaucratic level, the Burundi government has complied with the submission of reports to the relevant UN Committees. In all cases, the inability of the state to act to ensure the extension and protection of rights has been blamed either 'on the social and political crisis' or 'the civil war' or on traditional values. The ICCPR Committee found gross violations of several articles of the Covenant. Burundi's delegation justified its failure to meet goals of equality of opportunities by claiming that it did not recognize the existence of a minority and majority population in Burundi (UN ICCPR, 1996).

Numerous UN reports and Security Council resolutions went unheeded by the Burundi government. In response to the UN criticism of the *regroupement* policy as a "humanitarian catastrophe" and calls for closure of the camps, President Buyoya retorted that the government 'did not have a *regroupement* policy' and 'that the measures taken were necessitated by security imperatives, and that their aim to was to ensure the security of the civilian population' (UNESC, 2000: 5). Since the president thought security had been improved, one can presume that the use of the word 'civilian' was a coded word for Tutsis, as the 'humanitarian and human rights needs of the affected population [Hutus] were not taken into consideration. Buyoya made it even clearer, when he declared:

> If you do not manage the security situation, chaos will come and you will disappear as the international community sits back and watches [sic]. The same community will later come and blame us for the massive killings and genocide, so we had to take up our responsibilities. (quoted in HRW, 2000c: section XII)

Both the international community and the Burundi state hid behind state sovereignty as reasons for inaction (UNESC, 2000). Two images of Burundi emerges from this study: one international – of a country beleaguered by civil war, where the state is doing its utmost to deliver on its obligations to the people; and another more salient national image, evident in the reports of human rights organizations and UN investigative teams, that shows a state complicit or unwilling to act when faced with gross violations of human rights. Like the colonial state before it, the post-colonial state performs on the international stage, as beneficent, constrained by the difficulty of its inheritance, meanwhile using violence as the means to retain power.

Conclusion

Several conclusions can be drawn from the various reports on violence in Burundi. Namely, how state power is closely associated with militarized violence, which is used instrumentally to retain hegemony and to prevent the emergence of oppositional forces. The presence of genocidal practices in a society is made more likely by the failure of the national integration project that sees all people as citizens and human beings with rights that have to be championed and protected.

Manifestations of violence reflect both an ethnic and non-ethnic character. That ethnicity is a major factor in political violence is not deniable, but ethnicity does not explain the myriad atrocities that are committed. In the political violence of Burundi, ethnicity determined who was killed first among the elite, especially in the capital city, and who had access to justice and the ability to secure rights within the national space.

In rural communities, ethnicity mattered in terms of the violence perpetrated by the military, but became less significant in terms of the exposure of children to militarized violence and in cases of gendered violence, which were both systematic and random. Most of the violence against civilians was random, done mainly because men in uniforms and possessing weapons had the power to do so.

By not acting to prevent gross human rights abuses, the state and the military and the international community contributed to a culture of impunity. Despite the genocidal character of some of the violence, there were clear cases of military units and individual soldiers who did not perpetrate human rights violations, suggesting that the tolerance of violations by the state (military courts and judiciary) ensures its perpetuation. In a militarized culture, local administrators often become co-opted or disempowered and the judiciary biased. The barrel of the gun becomes the determinant of justice. The pervasive militarization of Burundi's society is such that militarized violence remains prevalent, despite peace agreements and democratic elections. Militarized violence has become endemic and epidemic.

The key question, as put by Connell (2002), is how we can break down these hierarchies of violent masculinities. Since the majority of instances of genocidal violence are carried out by men in groups or 'collectivities', we need to consider the different ways in which, both through community and state action, good gender relations and non-violent social interaction can be promoted. This should be an essential component of any democratic transformation that claims to be participatory.

7

The Traditions | of Genocide
& Militarism
in the Region

Introduction

The genocidal state of Burundi is located in a region with a history and economics of genocide. An understanding of the regional and international dynamics behind the protractedness of warfare and genocidal violence in Burundi is of critical importance to those trying to move beyond the tribal narrative or 'failed state' theses as explanations of warfare, and especially to those in search of the modalities for peace. Tribal narratives present diversity as problematic in itself not, as Wamba dia Wamba contends, the consequence of an ethnically discriminatory state, which is well represented in the region. He notes:

> Regional leaders, directly or indirectly, contributed to keeping the war going by supporting, tolerating or being indifferent to the State-implemented criminal prescriptions originating from an extremist ruling minority. They do bear, to different degrees and in relation to their relative intervention capacity, geopolitical and moral responsibility for the genocide. Even those leaders who entertained refugee camps, by so doing contributed in helping the discriminatory states consolidate their repressive space. (Wamba dia Wamba 1997: 15)

Genocidal politics has been a regional phenomenon due to a common discriminatory, military and masculinist traditions embedded in the colonial and modernization experience and the post-colonial states' promotion of violence as the route to political power. From the late nineteenth century to the beginning of the twenty-first century the region and the seemingly insignificant Burundi have been interconnected and linked into global economic networks and international geo-politics.

The process of militarization discussed for Burundi applies in equal measure to the neighbouring states of Rwanda, Uganda and the Democratic Republic of Congo. The interrelationships between genocidal violence in the Central African region exemplify the problems with an analysis which focuses purely on the national scale. In this chapter the interrelatedness of regional warfare and its intersection with the global geo-political economy is examined, especially the impact in Burundi of the 1994 genocide in Rwanda, the 1998 war in the Democratic Republic of Congo (DRC), the cross-border transhipment to Burundi of illegally-acquired resources, and the material assistance obtained by Burundi rebels in neighbouring territories. Burundi's economy and society are so intertwined with neighbouring territories that the proposed way forward must envisage regional rather than national solutions to impoverishment, population pressure and the effects of differential resource endowment.

Regional Culture of Impunity for Acts of Genocide and Genocidal Violence

A survey of violence in regional states reveals a historical continuity of genocidal practices and a regional culture of impunity, from King Leopold's Congo Free State, Idi Amin's Uganda, Micombero's Burundi and Habyarimana's Rwanda, genocide has been part of the social landscape of the modern history of the region. The dehumanization of the African body in the Great Lakes region was fundamental to the early stage of globalization and imperial domination. The transatlantic slave trade decimated African communities as African bodies became chattel; bartered, violated and abused. African leaders who tried to resist this dehumanization were killed, expelled from their homeland or replaced with more willing supplicants. Hochschild (1998) relates the experience of King Alfonso I of Kongo (1506–c.1540), a Christian convert and a 'selective modernizer', attempting to adopt aspects of European culture whilst rejecting their political control and economic exactions. Alfonso's petitions to the Portuguese kings and the Pope were dismissed. He watched his powers eroded by modernization, 'while begging the Portuguese kings to send him teachers, pharmacists and doctors instead of [slave] traders' (Hochschild, 1998: 14). Colonial military and masculinist traditions eclipsed that of communities where women, such as Queen Nzinga (1583–1663) of Ndongo and Matamba (in present-day Angola), played a critical role in the defence of their people. Hochschild brought out the economics of genocide associated with the introduction of capitalist relations of production. Brutalities, such as beatings, the amputation of hands, the hostage taking of women and children, and the collection of skulls, which would today be described as 'barbaric' by some and genocide by others, were reproduced on a day-to-day basis.

Post-colonial Burundi's coup leaders have been schooled and socialized into the use of violence through their interactions with regional leaders, who themselves have not been democratically-elected. Burundi's rebel leaders also gain refuge, funding and·arms from neighbouring states, as well as being used as mercenaries to fight in other nation's wars. A regional masculinity of the 'strong man' mentality has dominated political culture and has implications for the widespread attacks on civilian populations and sexual violence that has emerged in recent years (HRW, 2005a; Puechguirbal, 2003). A consideration of genocidal practices in Rwanda, Uganda and the DRC and the historical relationships that these states had with successive Burundi regimes illustrate the complex regional dimensions of the problem.

The Spectre of Rwanda

Despite the similarities in ethnic groups and colonial experience, Burundi and Rwanda's post-colonial experience has been different. It would be impossible for people in two adjacent countries with similar political dynamics and with comparable ethnic composition and antagonism not to feel threatened by acts of violence carried out against those who share the same characteristics as themselves. Inevitably, genocidal violence in one state has had repercussions in the other. After each episode of Hutu-instigated genocidal violence in Rwanda, Burundi's Tutsis tightened their control over the state and the army.

Repressive militaristic acts were also aggravated by the periodic influxes of Tutsi refugees from Rwanda, who in the 1960s, amounted to some 40,000 and who, according to Prunier (1995: 8), 'contributed to an atmosphere of latent paranoia'.[1] Efforts were made by the state and the international community to relocate the refugees, especially unemployed young men, away from Bujumbura to Cankuzo on the border with Tanzania (Map 2). Rwandan Tutsis may have been also manipulated by foreign powers to instigate ethnic antagonism among the Barundi. Some claimed that this was the case with the American-employed Tutsi who murdered Prime Minister Ngendandumwe (Evanzz, 1992).

Although President Ndadaye was killed six months before the Rwandan genocide of April to July 1994, the failure of the international community to act to prevent the genocide of 750 people, while evacuating expatriate staff, provided a clear message to the region of the devaluation of African lives. The genocidal regime in Rwanda had already calculated that the UN, and especially key members of the Security Council, would not act to save African lives; this well-known but rarely acknowledged perception of African humanity on the global stage gave impetus to the *'génocidaires',* and constitutes an indictment of the UN.

The military victory of the Rwandan Patriotic Front (RPF) not only ended the genocide, but further entrenched militarist beliefs.[2] Because of its minority status and the presence of the routed genocidal army in neighbouring DRC, the post-genocide Tutsi-dominated regime has had to prioritize national security and the security of the Tutsi ethnic group, so both concerns have become synonymous. Through a combination of porous borders, regional support and international leniency members of the ex-Rwandan Army (FAR), the *interahamwe* militias and ex-government officials dispersed throughout the region and 'found refuge in Congo-Brazzaville, Angola, Central African Republic, Zambia, Malawi, Namibia, Tanzania and Kenya' (ICG, 2003c: 5). Some 30,000

---

[1] Lemarchand (1970: Chapter 15) documented the involvement of Banyarwanda refugees in Burundi politics, focusing on the 1964 plan to resettle 10,000 Banyarwanda refugees from the Murore area in Burundi to the Mwesi highlands in Tanzania. This plan was aborted due to changes in the ethnic composition of the Burundi government during 1964. The resettlement plans began under the government of the Hutu Prime Minister Ngendadumwe, and an agreement was reached with UNHCR and the Tanzanian state, however, the coming to power of a predominantly Tutsi government, under the leadership of Albain Nyamoya, led to a reversal of the decision, with the refugees receiving political and military support in their struggle against the Hutu government in Rwanda.

[2] The Tutsi-dominated Rwandan Patriotic Front (RPF) took power in July 1994.

were able to regroup in the Congo as the *Armée de la Libération Rwanda* (Rwanda Liberation Army – ALIR), and to launch attacks against post-genocide Rwanda from late 1996 onwards (OAU, 2000; Terry, 2002). Those displaced to Congo Brazzaville gained the support of President Sassou Nguessi, who enabled them to reorganize militarily and drew on their assistance in his campaign against his own rebels. They later transferred to the Congolese provinces of Katanga (Lubumbashi) and Equatorial and gained support from President Kabila, and from Zimbabwe and Angola (see Map 4).

For the RPF government in Kigali, sustainable peace in post-genocide Rwanda has meant an intensification of the process of militarization and the pursuance of military excursions into neighbouring DRC against the Hutu *génocidaires*. From November 1996 to May 1997 the Rwandan Army, under the umbrella of a Congolese liberation army, *Alliance des Forces Démocratiques pour la Libération du Congo* (AFDL), 'hunted down Hutus by the thousands, only some of whom were *génocidaires*'. An estimated 240,000 people were missing, allegedly massacred by RPA/AFDL forces (Emizet, 2000; Umutesi, 2000). A UN investigative team reported in July 1997 that:

> The killings by the AFDL and its allies, including elements of the Rwandan Patriotic Army, constitute crimes against humanity, as does the denial of humanitarian assistance to Rwandan Hutu refugees. The members of the team believe that some of the killings may constitute genocide, depending on their intent, and call for further investigation of those crimes and of their motivations. (Quoted in OAU, 2000: Para 20.39)

Yet, as the OAU (2000: Para 20.39) records, 'no further investigation was carried out'. Rwandan Hutu rebels have encountered mixed fortunes in the DRC. In 1998, the rebels formed the political party, Democratic Forces for the Liberation of Rwanda (FDLR), which included elements of the *Interahamwe* among the 15,000 to 20,000 men, and, who, according to ICG (2003c: 4), 'subscribe[d] to genocidal ideology'. After the Pretoria peace agreement of 30 July 2002, which stipulated the withdrawal of foreign troops from Congolese soil, the rebels received less direct support from the Congolese state.

The new Rwandan government seems bent on using its military muscle to ensure that the cry of 'never again' has meaning with respect to the lives of Tutsis. Observers of Rwanda have argued that this position has led to the return to a totalitarian state, dominated by a section of the Tutsi elite (Reyntjens, 2006). Nevertheless, President Kagame of Rwanda has been 'described' as being 'very supportive' of the efforts to find peace in Burundi, despite the inevitable coming to power of the Hutu democratic majority, and the continued presence in neighbouring countries of a re-established Hutu genocidal army.[3] Ethnicity has not been a factor in inter-governmental relationships. President Buyoya of Burundi was said to have had a good relationship with Rwanda's Hutu President, Juvenal Habyarimana, and did not actively support the Tutsi-dominated RPF.

---

[3] Interview with member of the Facilitation team, September 2005.

Uganda's Influence

Uganda is another country infamous for its massacres, under the military dictatorship of Idi Amin (1971–1979) and Milton Obote (1980–1985), and from rebel movements: Yoweri Museveni's National Resistance Army (NRA) (1981–1985), Alice Lakwena's Holy Spirit Battalion (1986–1987) and Joseph Kony's Lords Resistance Army (LRA)(1987–2006).

Although Burundi does not share a common border with Uganda, over the years, there has been reciprocal support among the respective military leaders. Idi Amin supported the Micombero regime, and, despite his protestations, it is alleged that, at the request of Micombero, he encouraged *Mwami* Ntare to return to Burundi, knowing that he would be killed (Chapter 4). Amin's reign of terror was matched by Micombero's in Burundi. Two decades later, President Yoweri Museveni, who came to power in 1986 after the National Resistance Movement captured power, received some financial support for his campaign from President Bagaza of Burundi.[4] Ousted members of Burundi's political and military elite have tended to find refuge in Uganda. After his overthrow in 1986, President Bagaza fled to Uganda before being offered asylum in Libya, while his family remained in Kampala. Bagaza thought Museveni would help him to return to power, instead, Museveni soon sought good relations with Buyoya. Under Buyoya, Burundi's military and Museveni's, National Resistance Army participated in joint training. In 1993, after the failed coup, some of Ndadaye's killers also found refuge in Uganda and were never expedited back to Burundi to face murder charges (UNESC, 1995a). As a consequence, Museveni's commitment to the Burundi peace process has been questioned. In 1999, in spite of the arms embargo, he released 28 containers of impounded arms and ammunition that were transiting Uganda en route to the Burundi army (Rwegayura, 2000).

Uganda's own post-colonial history is riddled with insurgent violence against the populace. The LRA, for example, has abducted an estimated 25,000 children, killed some 100,000, and forcedly displaced 200,000 people (HRW, 1997b). Museveni, a former rebel leader, affirmed rebel activity as a legitimate way to seek political change, by Uganda supporting the Rwandese Patriotic Front and military incursions into the Congo. In the 1980s, the Rwandans, who formed the RPF, fought with the army which brought Yoweri Museveni to power in Uganda, who, in turn, sponsored their 1990 war to return to Rwanda. President Museveni's historic speech to the OAU criticizing their myopia towards the near genocide committed under the Milton Obote regime in Uganda, had no impact and rang hollow, when Uganda under his presidency, he failed to condemn subsequent genocidal practices in the region and sanctioned the RPA's genocidal violence in Eastern Congo (Museveni, 1986).

The Uganda People's Defence Force (UPDF) was a key player in the Congolese wars of the 1990s on the side of the AFDL and the Kisangani wing of the *Rassemblement Congolais pour la Démocratie*. Members of Uganda's political elite and senior officers in the military have been implicated in the illegal extraction of natural resources from the Congo

---

[4] Museveni was supposed have received some US$150,000 and 100 million Burundi Francs from 1980 to 1986 (Rwegayura, 2000).

(UNSC, 2001a & b). Partly, in response, the Ugandan rebels, the LRA, formed links with the *interahamwe* and with Congolese rebels fighting the RCD. Other Ugandan rebel movements, the People's Redemption Army (PRA), the West Nile Bank Liberation Front (WNBLF) and the Allied Democratic Forces (ADF) have had bases in Zaire, and were supplied with weapons by the Sudanese, with the approval of the Mobutu regime (Prunier, 2004). These movements were remnants of the genocidal armies of Idi Amin and Milton Obote and comprised disaffected Catholics and Muslims (ADF & National Army for the Liberation of Uganda – NALU). The WNBF, led by Juma Oris, a former Minister in the Idi Amin government sought to return Amin to power. They committed atrocities largely against the civilian population. And, because of a lack of political base in Uganda, they dissipated in the early party of the twenty-first century. A similar situation would have befallen the LRA were it not for the support of the Sudanese government.

Congo/Zaire/DRC: the Pivot of Genocide
The proximity of Burundi's capital, Bujumbura, to the Congolese town of Uvira ties the country, its regimes and rebels inextricably into the economic and political life of the Eastern DRC, formally and informally. The DRC has been central to the militarization of the region. From its inception, power, authority and economic exaction have been closely associated with violence, both direct and structural.

To police the process of extraction during the colonial period, a colonial military force, the *Force Publique*, was used to 'repress and intimidate a defenceless population' (Nzongola-Natalaja, 2002). According to Hochschild (1998), millions of people died in killings of genocidal proportions. To supply labour to the plantations and mines, villages were exterminated, bodies mutilated and diseases spread on an epidemic scale. According to Wamba dia Wamba (2000: 1), what the Congolese call, '"Bula Matarisme" (to break stones, break everything, to destroy any resistance) or brute force, was the only method used to organize labour and was justified by elementary racism'. Even though the brutalizing excesses of global capitalism caused international outcry, the abuse of African labour continued, but more subtly under the guise of modernization and the 'civilizing mission'.

Rebellion during this era was prevalent not just from indigenous states, but often from among members of the *Force Publique*. Many Congolese soldiers refused to accept the processes of brutalization that working for the colonial regime entailed. Some rebellions, such as that of Kandolo, a former sergeant in the *Force Publique*, lasted many years (Hochschild, 1998). Rebels cited the inhumane practices of some white officers and the brutal treatment of women by the *Force Publique* as reasons for taking up arms against their former colleagues (ibid.). These forms of resistance to genocidal thinking need to be examined closely in the pursuit for spaces of peace.

Rather than eradicating colonial militarism, the traditions of the *Force Publique* was strengthened after colonialism under the guise of modernity; this received a boost when former colonial powers and Cold War superpowers competed to supply weapons to the Central Africa. In the early

1960s, Congo's transition to an independent state was marred by seces-sionist wars and Cold War rivalry leading to the brutal murder of its demo-cratically-elected prime minister, Patrice Lumumba; the latter purportedly carried out by Belgian and Congolese forces with the connivance of other western governments (De Witte, 2001). By replacing Lumumba with a former military man, Sergeant Joseph Mobutu, the West thwarted the struggle for self-determination and human dignity by the Congolese people.[5] Military leaders, like Mobutu, were legitimized by the interna-tional community who saw the military as the most modernized and, therefore, progressive elements in African societies. Mobutu, having trained in the West, was for 30 years 'America's [own] tyrant' (Kelly, 1993).

During the Cold War, the DRC was a highly militarized space; under the corrupt military dictatorship of the renamed Mobutu Sese Seko Kuku Ngbendu wa za Banga, the DRC became a staging post for the USA's anti-communist wars in Africa. The presence of the USA's military base at Kamina and their military support for the Angolan rebel movement, *União Nacional para a Independência Total de Angola* (National Union for the Total Independence of Angola) (UNITA), made Zaire the most militarized space in Africa. Mobutu benefited from US arms transfers, receiving between 1965 and 1997 more than $300 million in hardware, and training at a cost of over $100 million (Hartung & Moix, 2000). In a report for the influential World Policy Institute, Hartung and Moix surmise:

> US policy towards Mobutu was rationalized on the ground of fighting 'communism' and Soviet Union influence in Africa, but the US was clearly more concerned with securing its own interests in the region than helping foster a stable, secure, and peaceful future for the people of Central Africa. (Hartung & Moix, 2000: 11)

Mobutu ascended to power through violence and ruled for just over thirty years with violence. The Zairean military and numerous state-sponsored paramilitary forces conducted a reign of terror on the popu-lation, massacring students and campaigners for democratic change (Nzongola-Ntalaja, 2002).

Mobutu's regime continued with the economics of extraction and the politics of discrimination of the colonial regime. As in Rwanda and Burundi, the Belgian colonial power had constructed a divided state. With the aid of Christian theology, the colonial state refashioned local collectivities into hierarchies of human beings; racial, ethnic and regional hierarchies and in turn restructured gendered hierarchies of masculinities and femininities. In the Congo, the racial hierarchy included mulattoes, a group, not unlike the Tutsi who were privileged with mission education; they made up the bulk of the *évolués* or 'civi-lized Africans', and, as Hunt (1990) showed with respect to Burundi the *Foyer Sociale* was used to determine those sufficiently 'evolved' to deserve the award of a *carte du mérite civique* (civic merit card) or the *matriculation* as indication of their assimilation into colonial society (Nzongola-Natalaja, ibid.).

---

[5] Mobutu ruled Zaire from 1965 to 1997.

Mobutu attempted to obscure his autocratic and discriminatory practices by exhorting the Congolese people to practice *authenticité*, a return to traditional culture. Part of this *authenticité* practised by post-colonial African states involved a resurgence of the power of the patriarchal state to determine appropriate forms of masculinities and femininities. For African women, this resulted in attempts by the state and patriarchal men to control their sexuality through decrees on appropriate behaviour and dress codes. Women out on their own at night were deemed to be prostitutes and any man could (often violently) sanction those considered to be inappropriately dressed. These sanctions included Paul Kagame's (now the Rwandan President) violent criticism of the brazen display of mini-skirted sexuality by the Francophone-influenced Kigali women.[6]

The factors that contributed to the two wars that ravaged the country in 1996 and from 1998 to 2000 were, at one level, the outcome of an attempt to rid the country of kleptocratic regimes that sanctioned and supported genocide and ethnic discrimination and, at another level, an attempt by members of the regional and international community to reshape the politics of accumulation in the region in the post-Cold War era. The 1996 war was sparked off partly by the discriminatory practices of the Mobutu regime, amidst competition for resources between the different ethnic groups. The Eastern Congo has a diverse mix of local people, which in North Kivu includes the Banyarwanda (Hutus and Tutsis) who migrated originally from Rwanda and settled in the region over a century ago, though some were resettled there by the Belgian colonial government in the 1930s. In South Kivu, residents include a Tutsi group known as the Banyamulenge, or people from the Mulenge hills. Over the years, the state bought local loyalties by manipulating regional identity politics to secure or deny access to resources in areas where competition was intense. In Eastern Congo, this led to challenges from the indigenous peoples over the Banyarwanda's and Banyamulenge's access to land and rights, especially those accorded by citizenship. In 1981, they were effectively disenfranchised by the Mobutu regime and subjected to constant hostilities from indigenous communities.[7] Violence flared up North Kivu in 1993. *Mai Mai* militias from the Hunde, Nyange and Nande ethnic groups, sponsored by local politicians, attacked Banyarwanda (mainly Hutus) who responded by forming their own militias. Violence escalated into outright war in 1994 following the arrival of the Rwandan Hutu refugees, comprising *génocidaires* and members of the routed Rwandan army. In North Kivu, armed Rwandan Hutus linked up with Zairean Hutus to attack the *Mai Mai* as well as the Zairean Tutsis, inciting the Hutus to ethnically cleanse communities in the Masisi area, massacring some 6,000 people and forcibly displacing a further 250,000 (OAU, 2000). Observers note the complicity of the Zairean government, especially the local political elite, in promoting genocidal violence (HRW, 1996).

---

[6] Interview with informant, Kigali, August 1995.

[7] In June 1981 – Law N81–002 granted Zairean nationality only to those who could prove that their families resided in the boundaries of Zaire when it was drawn up by colonial powers in 1885.

Mobutu's disregard for the humanity of Africans was shown in his backing, firstly, for the Micombero regime in Burundi. In 1972, he supplied weapons and helicopters to put down the 'uprising', partly to undermine support for Zairean rebels, some of whom operated out of Bujumbura (Bowen *et al.*, 1974). Later on, he gave military support to the genocidal Rwandan regime; in 1991, he provided weapons for the war against the RPF and, after the 1994 genocide, offered refuge to the *génocidaires*, allowing some 18,000 members of the ex-Rwandan army, *Forces Armée Rwandaise (FAR)*, to regroup. He also incorporated some of them, along with the *interahamwe,* into the Zairean forces (UNSC, 2001a). More evidence is provided by Fiona Terry's (2002) evaluation of the role of international aid to the *génocidaires*, and the support given by Mobutu and his regional and international associates (South African, Israeli, Albanian, Chinese and French) to the exiled Rwandan government and to the rearmament of the FAR. Once armed, the *génocidaires* were able to launch attacks against the RPF's Rwanda, killing both Hutu and Tutsi civilians. Mobutu's inhumanity was shown by his willingness to use Hutu refugees as pawns, when in August 1995, he forcibly repatriated some 11,000 Hutus and blamed the expulsion on the lifting of the international arms embargo on Rwanda. The international community gave him US $1.5 million to allow the bulk of the refugees to remain.[8]

The 1996 Congolese war was started by anti-Mobutu rebels under the umbrella of *Alliance des Forces Démocratiques pour la Libération du Congo* (AFDL) backed by Uganda, Burundi and Rwanda, who were looking for a way to tackle their own rebels hiding out in the Eastern Congo.[9] Laurent-Désiré Kabila, a Congolese rebel leader of the 1960s, was selected as a figure-head leader. Tragically, Kabila, who took over the presidency after Mobutu's demise in 1997, maintained some of the corrupt practices of the previous regime. His government failed to break the genocidal and discriminatory traditions of the Congolese state. In 1998, he sought independence from his Rwandan and Ugandan king-makers by appealing to the Congolese people to kill all Tutsis. In a radio message the people were exhorted to:

> bring a machete, a spear, an arrow, a hoe, spades, rakes, nails, truncheons, electric irons, barbed wire, stones and the like in order, dear listeners, to kill Rwandan Tutsis ... wherever you see a Rwandan Tutsi, regard him as your enemy. We shall do everything possible to free ourselves from the grip of the Tutsis. (Laurent-Desirée Kabila quoted in *The Times*, 14 August, 1998: 13)

This speech has to be placed within the historical and regional context of violence and enmity against Congolese of Banyarwanda descent.

Movements against the continuation of Mobutuism caused what some have described as Africa's First World War. Between 1998 and 2000, insurgency in the Eastern Congo by the *Rassemblement Congolais pour la Démocratie,* again supported by Rwanda and Uganda, led to Kabila

---

[8] Interview, UNHCR Representative, Kigali, 1995.
[9] Burundi was also interested in protecting its trade routes through the Congo and Lake Tanganyika (Irinnews.org, 9 January 2002 'Burundi-DRC: Bujumbura to withdraw troops from Congo').

requesting military support from his southern African neighbours, Angola, Namibia and Zimbabwe. Other countries, many outside of the Central African region, got involved: Sudan, Libya South Africa, Chad, Egypt, Congo-Brazzaville, Eritrea, Ethiopia and Tanzania, in what the OAU (2000: Para 20.45) describes as 'a series of bewildering and often unexpected alliances with various governments'. Zimbabwe assisted the Kabila regime by providing training and weapons for Burundi's CNDD-FDD, which was used to fight against Rwandan and Ugandan backed forces in Lubumbashi (OAU, 2000). The agenda for many of these countries and rebel movements was not peace; some had vested interests in capturing the rich resources of the territory.

In the 1990s, numerous rebel groups and militias operated in the eastern Congo. The OAU (2000) notes the presence of 'several competing anti-Kabila rebel groups; UNITA, well-armed Mobutu generals, ex-FAR and *Interahamwe...*' Behind some of the rebel movements and 'rogue gangs' were:

> ... often found foreign patrons, some of them legitimate corporations, others more shadowy enterprises, and quietly behind them can be found foreign governments watching out for the interests of their citizens ... Powerful companies with interests in the DRC have home bases in South Africa, Zimbabwe, the US, Britain, and Canada. (OAU, 2000: 20.51)

Contemporary economistic explanations of 'resource driven' wars seem to fit the scenario in the Democratic Republic of Congo, where rebel armies, sometimes with the collaboration of neighbouring states and international companies, armed and enriched themselves through informal timber and mineral extraction (Taylor, 2003; UNSC 2001a & b; UNSC, 2003). Nonetheless, 'greed' on its own cannot explain the reasons why peasants, particularly young men, would join 'warlords' to perpetrate violence of genocidal proportions against neighbouring communities. Analysts of the late twentieth-century DRC have yet to produce detailed empirical work that interrogates the political culture, its military traditions and its global networks.

From the inception of the post-colonial Congolese state, the exploitation of natural resources has been a threat to its territorial integrity. In 1960, by funding secessionists, the Belgian Company, *Union Minérie,* was prepared to fragment the country in order to retain control of copper mines in Katanga, now Shaba region. The country's abundance of strategic minerals such as uranium, diamonds and coltan has led to intense competition between world powers for influence over its government and access to its resources (Moyroud & Katunga, 2002). The West, triumphant with the installation of Mobutu, ignored his undemocratic practices. Mobutu's regime used patrimonial politics to control the vast territory and amassed $12 billion in foreign debt, obtained ostensibly to support development programmes, in spite of the billions accrued through national resource exploitation. In turn, Kabila used the country's resources to obtain military assistance and training, and subsidized the costs of his allies' intervention by giving mineral and timber concessions in the DRC to Zimbabwean and Namibian companies (UNSC, 2001b).[10]

The trans-national corporations from the US, Canada, Belgium and South Africa that were allowed to operate lucrative extractive concerns in the country under Mobutu, sought new deals with Kabila and hastily signed contracts with him, but when he failed to honour them, he became an impediment to Western interests (UNSC, 2001a & b). The assassination of Kabila in 1999 and the West's quick recognition of his son, Joseph Kabila, as the new president, reflected an urgency to pursue business as usual, despite the prevailing rhetoric of instilling democratic governance in Africa. A specially commissioned UN Panel of Experts investigating the *Illegal Exploitation of Natural Resources and Other Forms of Wealth of the DRC*, found that the 'lootability' of strategic minerals such as diamonds and coltan has generated considerable competition for the control of resource-endowed areas and led to the 'unsustainable and environmentally hazardous' illegal exploitation of resources by rebel movements and companies attached to regimes in Uganda, Rwanda and Burundi (UNSC, 2001a & b). The report claims that 'over one-third of the total rough diamond production of the Congo, valued at $300 million a year, is smuggled annually via the Central African Republic and the Republic of Congo' (UNSC, 2001b: 10). While, the first report named and shamed many individuals and companies, both regional and trans-national, the Commission's final report (UNSC, 2003) seems to suggest a compromise, by claiming that the transnationals named had 'resolved' their problems, and proceeded to argue for their increased role in the exploitation of natural resources. The report (2003: Para. 56) notes that 'large international mining and oil companies have been shown to contribute more to the countries in which they operate than their smaller competitors.' The historical evidence from the Congo suggests otherwise.

So high are the economic stakes in the Congo that sustainable regional peace is unattainable without firstly a resolution of warfare in that country. The Lusaka Peace Accord, signed in 1999, ended the war but has not stemmed the violence. The Peace Accord was essentially a ceasefire agreement without a peace agreement which led to neither a ceasefire nor peace. Despite the agreement, the government embarked on considerable foot-dragging before finally agreeing, in January 2001, to talks with rebel movements. The peace agreement of 2002 was a transitional power-sharing arrangement that laid the framework for democratic elections in 2006. At the formal state level the agreements led to the withdrawal of foreign troops from Congolese territory, but they have not stopped foreign complicity in the illegal extraction of valuable strategic minerals (Campbell, 2002; HRW, 2005b). Nor have they ended the fighting, as factionalism within the rebel movement and the militarization of local communities, coupled with the poor infrastructure, combine to reduce state effectiveness in policing the territory. Local militias and foreign

---

[10] Kabila gave International Diamond Industries a monopoly for the commercialization of diamonds in exchange for $20 million and military equipment. According to the UN, IDI paid only $2 million and provided no military equipment.

rebel groups have continued to operate in the Eastern Congo, despite the UN peace-keeping force's efforts at disarmament in line with the requirements of the Peace Accord.

The Role of International Actors in the Militarization of the Region

In line with realist conceptions of militarism, the modern state formed out of the brutalization of the populace, pursued a programme of formal militarization, aided and abetted by foreign governments, both communist and capitalist, which sought markets to sustain their industrial-military complexes, and perceived military strength as providing the basis for the peace and stability necessary to protect their economic interests.

Western governments have a history of being implicated in African regional warfare. Their complicity in the militarization of the region is to be found in a) the installation or support for military dictators attuned to their interests; b) the establishment of military accords for the supply of weaponry and the training of military personnel even though military equipment and knowledge were often directed at the repression of citizens; and c) the use of Africa as a theatre in which to fight proxy wars during the Cold War or in the 'war on terror' of the early twenty-first century and d) the support for anti-Marxist secessionist movements in the region. Belgian and US intervention in the first UN peace-keeping mission in Africa was against Patrice Lumumba, for fear of him receiving support from the Soviet Union. US pursuance of the Cold War, using the territory of the region, benefited states that sought weapons for their own international security and national loans and aid for the leaders' personal enrichment. American's overt and covert arms transfers to UNITA helped to sustain the Angolan war. Military accords with the US, France and Israel, in particular, often resulted in them selling weapons to Central African regimes, unnecessary for the maintenance of national security and for which there was no domestic expertise (Bizimana, 1999; Hartung & Moix, 2000). In 1998, US weapons sales to Africa totalled $12.5 billion dollars (Hartung & Moix, 2000).

The training of military officers was another strategy used by the West to ensure continuation of friendly regimes in the region. Between 1997 and 1998, the US provided military training to six of the countries that fought in the Congo in 1998 (Hartung & Moix, 2000). In the late 1960s and 1970s, France signed military agreements with Burundi and Rwanda to provide training and weaponry. When the RPF began their campaign in 1990 against Rwanda, the French sent military assistance to the Rwandan regime and the USA supplied the RPF via Uganda. France has been accused of being complicit in the 1994 genocide, when it used a supposedly humanitarian mission, the creation of a safe haven under 'Operation Turquoise', to enable the perpetrators to escape. Indeed, France's self-interest is often inseparable from its professed humanitarian actions.

Table 7.1: Suppliers and value of arms transfer to countries of the Great Lakes Region (1997–1999) (Millions US$)*

Supplier Country	Total Millions US$	USA	Eastern Europe	China	Middle East	East Asia	Others
Burundi	25		5		25		
Congo (Brazzaville)	20						
DRC	235		30	100		30	
Rwanda	55	10	10				10
Uganda	115	10	40	50		10	5
Tanzania	20						20
Zimbabwe	80			70			

Source: US Arms Control and Disarmament Agency, *World Military Expenditure and Arms Transfer*, 1999.
* This table shows known official arms transactions.

After the Rwandan genocide, Western governments that supported directly or indirectly genocidal regimes, found themselves struggling to maintain their hegemony in the region. Following the RPF's victory, France and Belgium proposed that the RPF government should hold a national conference of dialogue with exiled members of the genocidal regime as a condition for giving financial assistance.[11] Consequently, they lost their influence over Rwanda and were replaced by Britain and the USA; the latter almost immediately started a training programme for the post-genocide Rwandan army. These governments have come under criticism for tolerating an increasingly undemocratic Rwandan regime (Melvern & Williams, 2004; Uvin, 2001). Burundi suddenly found itself with lots of international 'friends', many lobbying for their own national interests and jostling with regional powers. The USA's involvement in supplying weapons to anti-Mobutu and anti-Kabila forces was determined more by America's desire to retain its influence in the region amidst the growing unpopularity of the Presidents than any real interest in dethroning repressive regimes. As the OAU (2000) remarks European powers were also 'active behind the scenes'.

Lacking the commitment to stop genocide, yet seeking to continue western military investment and influence in the region, the US and France, in particular, embarked on establishing programmes to enhance African peace-keeping capacity. In 1996, Warren Christopher, US Secretary of State for Africa, called for the creation of an African crisis response force so that 'the continent will have the ability to respond rapidly and effectively to crises in Africa and beyond.'[12] This manifested into the establishment of the US's African Crisis Response Initiative

---

[11] Interview with UNHCR Representative, Kigali, 1995.
[12] Statement made by Warren Christopher, US Secretary of State for Africa, Arusha, Tanzania, 11 October 1996.

(ACRI, 1997–2001) by the Clinton administration, which provided military training and sophisticated weaponry to American allies, in order to train an African rapid-deployment peace-keeping force as substitute for American soldiers in the event of another Rwanda on the continent. (Omach, 2000).[13] In 2002, and after the events of September 11, 2001, the Bush administration replaced ACRI with the African Contingency Operations Training and Assistance (ACOTA) and incorporated it into its 'war on terror'. ACOTA was an expanded programme with a more 'robust' mandate, which included the training and equipping of African armies for 'offensive military operation' (Keenan, 2004; Volman, 2003). ACOTA enables African states to enhance their military capacity, at a time when most have been criticized for increased military expenditure.

The French established *Renforcement des Capacités Africaines de Maintien de la Paix* – Reinforcement of African Peace-Keeping Facilities (RECAMP), its own training programme for African peace-keepers in 1996. According to the French Ministry of Defence, 'RECAMP reflects a new commitment to Africa by France in the interest of security on the continent'. To this effect, France has 'refocused its defence cooperation with these states towards reinforcing their own peace-keeping capacity.'[14] By establishing RECAMP, France was able move out of its Francophonie African base to extend its influence to Anglophone and Lusophone countries in co-ordination with regional organizations such as ECOWAS, SADC and the African Union. Since its inception, there have been five RECAMP exercises, costing over 50 million Euros: RECAMP I (Guidimakha) with ECOWAS from 1996 to 1998 involved cross-border exercises between Senegal, Mali and Mauritania; RECAMP II in Gabon in 2000 for Central African countries; RECAMP III 'Tanzanite' in 2002 for SADC countries;[15] RECAMP IV for ECOWAS countries in Benin in 2004, and RECAMP V in 2005 for *Communauté Economique des 'États d'Afrique Centrale* (CEEAC) in Gabon, Cameroon and Congo (Brazzaville). Individual training of military personnel took place at France's training facilities in Mali and in mainland France. RECAMP has enough equipment for three battalions, 'pre-positioned' on French bases in Africa, which, theoretically, Africans can draw on to support peace-keeping exercises.

'Non-State Actors' in Regional Militarism

The post-Cold War privatization and decentralization of state authority inevitably includes the privatization and de-regulation of war, an informal militarization, which the state and political elite try to control through the creation of their own firms, paramilitary force, militias or rebel movements. Private global networks of arms sales rose at the same

---

[13] See http://usinfo.state.gov/regional/af/acri/
[14] See RECAMP at http://www.un.int/france/frame_anglais/france_and_un/france_and_peacekeeping/recamp_eng.htm [last Accessed 8 September 2006].
[15] (All Africa.com, *President Appeal for End to Conflicts*, article by Ofeiba Quist-Arcton, 23 May 2001).

speed as private military contractors (PMCs), providing protection for western governments, multilateral agencies and NGOs, and for trans-national corporations working in resource-endowed conflict zones and bolstering the reign of undemocratic African leaders (Leander, 2003). Directors of these 'private' military organizations move between state and non-state spheres.

Some PMCs have organized themselves into euphemistically named 'International Peace Operations Organizations' and have already replaced multilateral peace-keepers constrained by 'lofty mandates'. Using the rhetoric that the private sector is 'faster, better and cheaper compared to state efforts', they seek to act as surrogates for absent western military capabilities in African peace operations'.[16] PMCs position themselves to fill a gap made vacant by western governments' unwillingness to face the political repercussions of military intervention in African warfare. The activities of private military companies, such as Dyncorp International and Pacific Architects and Engineers, in Liberia, Sierra Leone and Darfur indicate the scale of the formal links between PMCs and Western states. More specifically, Dyncorp International had a US $35 million contract from the US government to train the Liberian police and has similar assignments in Southern Sudan. These organizations exist in a sphere of unaccountability and are not subjected to the international regulations relating to peace-keeping and the treatment of local communities.

The growth of PMCs occurs simultaneously with the de-regulation of arms sales and the proliferation of arms transfers outside of the control of states and their contracting agencies (Musah, 2002). Illicit arms in Central Africa come from diverse sources, from the US, UK, Belgium, France, China, Israel, North Korea and South Africa. Muslims from Iran, Iraq, Saudi Arabia, Pakistan and Sudan have provided financial backing for groups with Muslim leaders, and Western evangelical movements and Catholics have also supported groups associated with their religious denomination (HRW, 1997a).

Within the Central African region the relatively porosity of borders has allowed the uncontrolled movement of arms and armed combatants. Inaccessible areas in eastern DRC have become havens for rebel groups, hosting, in 2001, over nine foreign rebel movements (Table 7.2). Consequently, a theoretical separation of state from non-state actors is fraught with difficulties due to many states providing direct and indirect sponsorship of rebel movements from neighbouring territories, and even creating some within their own, supposedly to cause disunity among the real opposition. The Zaire/Congolese regimes provided sanctuary for rebel movements from Angola, Congo-Brazzaville and later from Rwanda and Burundi. Numerous rebel groups formed transnational alliances to pursue war in the region. In the case of Burundi, in January 1997, CNDD/FDD, Frolina and Palipehutu signed an agreement with the Congolese rebel group, *Conséil Nationale de Résistance du Kivu* (CNRK), to pursue jointly the war against Laurent Kabila's DRC and the Burundi (*Africa Confidential*, 9 May 1997).

[16] Doug Brooks, President of the International Peace Operations Association, before the US House of Representatives, Committee on International Relations Sub-Committee on Africa, Friday, 8 October 2004.

Table 7.2: Armed Groups and Rebel Movements in the Great Lakes Region since the 1980s

Country of origin & name	Date of inception and Leadership	Military Strength (estimated)	Geographical area of activity	Regional Support
Rwanda Rwandese Patriotic Front (RPF)	(1987–1994) Formed in Uganda and headed by Paul Kagame, who became head of state – RPF converted to the Rwandan Defence Forces (RDF)	25,000–30,000	Rwanda	Based in Uganda RDF fell out with Uganda over involvement in the DRC
Forces Armées Rwandaises (FAR)	Members of the ex-Rwandan army that fled to the Congo in 1994		DRC – some returned to Rwanda after 2002	DRC
Interahamwe (those who fight together)	Rwandan state-sponsored militia, carried out the 1994 genocide			DRC/Central African Republic
Armée pour la Libération du Rwanda (ALIR)	ex-FAR and militia members formed in 1996, head of military operations Paul Rwarakabije Separated into breakaway groups ALIR I, II & III Merged with FDLR in 2000	10,000–15,000	North and South Kivu and Katanga fighting RCD-Goma and RDF Some members fought in Burundi on the side of Palipehutu-FNL	DRC under Laurent-Désirée Kabila
Democratic Forces for the Liberation of Rwanda (FDLR)	Formed in 1998 from ex-FAR and *Interahamwe génocidaires*, merged with ALIR in September	15,000–22,000	Based at Kamina in Katanga (1999–2002) and Kivu province,	Supported militarily by Kinshasa After 2005 – some

Group		Numbers	Operations/Location	Support/Weapons
	2000, and headed by Dr Ignace Muramashyaka		DRC Military operations in Rwanda	repatriated to Rwanda by MUNDOC
Burundi	Details of these Burundi groups are to be found in Table 5.1			
Conseil National Pour la Défense de la Démocratie – Forces pour la Défense de la Démocratie National Council for Defence and Democracy – Forces for Defence and Democracy (CNDD-FDD)	1993–2003	10,000–16,000	Eastern Congo under Laurent Kabila, Burundi	Zimbabwe, DRC, and assorted arms dealers supplied weapons
Parti Pour la Libération Du Peuple Hutu/Forces Nationales pour la Libération (Palipehutu- FNL)	1980–2006	Karatasi – 1,000 FNL-Rwasa – 3,000 FNL-Mugabarabona – 1,000	Bases in the Congo, Burundi and Tanzania	Support from a variety of sources, including the Middle East, and Evangelical Churches
Front Pour la Libération National (Frolina)	1989–2000	1,000	Operated in central and Southern Burundi; bases in Tanzania	Indirect support from Tanzania
Gardiens de la Paix (1998–2005)	Paramilitary group established by the Burundi government to fight the rebels and maintain security	25,000–30,000	In Burundi, but some members fought in the DRC	Supported by the Burundi government
DRC				
Alliance des Forces Démocratiques pour la Libération du Congo (AFDL)	Formed in 1996 as an anti-Mobutu force and headed by Laurent-Desirée Kabila – deposed Mobutu and took power	n/a	Eastern Zaire	Supported by Rwanda and Uganda

Country of origin & name	Date of inception and Leadership	Military Strength (estimated)	Geographical area of activity	Regional Support
Rassemblement Congolais pour la Démocratie (RCD)	Created in 1998 in Kigali of anti-Kabila Congolese forces; Split in 1999 to form: RCD-Goma headed by Emile Ilunga Onusumba then Azarias Ruberwa) and RCD-Kisangani/ Mouvement de Libération (K/ML) (headed first by Wamba dia Wamba and later by Mbusa Nyamwisi – signed peace agreement in 2002	n/a	Eastern DRC By 2002 RCD-Goma reached Kasai, Kivus, Maniema, Orientale and parts of Katanga	Supported by Rwanda and Uganda financially and militarily RCD-Kinsangani had strong moral support from Tanzania and Mozambique.
Mouvement de Libération du Congo/MLC – merged with RCD Kisangani to form MLC/FLC (Forces for the Liberation of the Congo)	(1998–2002) Congolese Liberation Movement headed by Jean-Pierre Bemba	n/a	North-West Congo, with HQ at Gbadolite	Supported by Uganda
Conséil Nationale de la Résistance du Kivu (CNRK)/	Formed in 1997, led by Asema Bin Amisi of Bembe origin	n/a	Kivu region of Eastern DRC	
Mai-Mai	Formed in 1996 by General Dunia, opposed to the presence of foreign troops in the AFDL; many factions	n/a	Kizi District (Eastern DRC)	Middle East
Union of Patriotic Congolese (UPC)	Formed in 2002 by Congolese of Hema ethnicity and headed by Thomas Lubanga, who in August 2006 became the first Congolese to be charged with	n/a	Eastern DRC	Supported first by Uganda, and after 2002 by Rwanda; fought with RCD Goma

Front Contre L'Occupation Tutsie (FLOT) / *Union des Forces vives pour la Libération et la Démocratie en RDC-Zaire* (UFLD)	war crimes at the International Criminal Court. Anti-Tutsi group active in 1997 and 1998	n/a	Eastern DRC	
RCD-National: Congolese Rally for Democracy	Formed c2000 and headed by Roger Lumbala	n/a	Operates in Ituri district	Supported by the Ugandans
Popular Force for Democracy in Congo (FPDC)	Political party created in 2002 with its own militia		Operates in the Aru and Mahagi area of Eastern Congo	Supported by Ugandans
Patriotic Force for Resistance in Ituri (FRPI)	Formed in November 2002 by the political party (FRPI) – made up of Ngitis	9,000 (est.)	Ituri district of Eastern Congo	Has links with Ugandans
People's Armed Forced of Congo (FAPC)	Formed in March 2003	n/a	Operates in the Aru and Mahagi area of Eastern Congo	Supported at various times by Ugandans, UPC, RCD-ML & RCD-National
Front for National Integration (FNI)	Political party belonging to Lendu ethnic group with its own militia	n/a	Operates in Ituri district	Supported by Ugandans, then RCD-ML and Congolese government
Uganda				
National Resistance Army/ Movement (NRA/NRM)	1981–1986, Headed by Yoweri Museveni who overthrew Tito Okello to become head of state; NRA/NRM achieved victory in 1986 and formed the government.			
Holy Spirit Battalion	1986–1987 started by a spiritualist Alice Lakwena	n/a		

Country of origin & name	Date of inception and Leadership	Military Strength (estimated)	Geographical area of activity	Regional Support
Lord's Resistance Army (LRA)	1987–2006, started by Joseph Kony, former Ugandan army officer and Lakwena's nephew after her defeat	n/a	Acholi districts of Northern Uganda	Supported by Sudan
People's Redemption Army (PRA)	2004–	3,000	Bases in the DRC; Attacks in West Nile District	Reportedly trained in Rwanda
West Nile Bank Front (WNBF)	1994–1998	Hundreds	Bases in the DRC	Fought in the 1998 Congolese war
Allied Democratic Forces/ National Army for the Liberation of Uganda (ADF/NALU)	1988–2005, comprised forces opposed to Museveni's UPDF	3,000	Bases in North Eastern DRC attacked civilian targets	Supported by Sudan
Angola *União Nacional para a Independência Total de Angola* (National Union for the Total Independence of Angola) (UNITA)	1975–2002 Headed by Joseph Savimbi until his death in 2002	n/a	Bases were in the DRC	Supported by the apartheid state of South Africa and the United States of America during the Cold War
Front for Liberation of the State of Cabinda (FLEC)	Separatist movement from the province of Cabinda, started in 1975 and headed by Commandant António Luís Lopes; split in the 1980s into FLEC-FAC and FLEC Renovada	n/a	Bases in the DRC & Congo-Brazzaville	Supported by Congo-Brazzaville before 1997 & Zaire under Mobutu

Sources: UNSC 2001a; ICG (2003) *Rwandan Hutu Rebels in the Congo: A New Approach to Disarmament and Reintegration*, ICG Africa Report no.63, Nairobi/Brussels; Human Rights Watch (2003) *Ituri: Bloodiest Corner of Congo*; Correspondence with Wamba dia Wamba.

Some would argue that the protracted nature of the conflict was due to the ability of opposition forces to regroup and receive military support in neighbouring countries. State recognition of these forces have enabled them to transform into formal political movements and gain international credibility, one such group was the ex-FAR who renamed themselves the Democratic Forces for the Liberation of Rwanda (FDLR) and sought political party status.[17]

Burundi Refugees and Tanzania/Burundi Relationship

Tanzania is the only country in the region that was not directly involved in genocidal violence, though it has shown with the invasion of Amin's Uganda in 1979 that it is not afraid of interfering militarily in the internal affairs of neighbouring states, if they threatened its own national security. Its progressive stance in supporting freedom fighters was directed primarily at those Africans involved in anti-colonial struggles and this position attracted refugees from independent states seeking support from repressive regimes. Tanzania's proximity to Rwanda and Burundi has also meant that warfare in those two countries has resulted invariably in an increase in its refugee burden. During the Cold War, Tanzania entered into an agreement with the UNHCR and the regional governments that relocated refugees to a distance of more than 50 miles from the border. From the 1970s, successive Burundi regimes have accused Tanzania of supporting rebel movements, which officially Tanzania has always denied. Tanzania, in response, has repeatedly cautioned refugees about the effects of their subversion on its relationship with Burundi (Chapter 8).

Throughout the 1972 genocide, although Tanzania bore the brunt of the Barundi refugee problem, the Tanzanian leadership never publicly expressed concern about the situation in Burundi. Even after Burundi troops in pursuit of refugees, bombed Tanzanian border villages from March to June 1973, killing 52 Tanzanian citizens, and the dock workers boycotted goods destined for Burundi, President Nyerere decided to rely on diplomacy and merely warned Micombero during 'good-neighbourly' talks (*Daily News*, 23.7.1973). Nyerere affirmed the absence of conflict between Tanzania and Burundi, and argued that there was no need for outside mediation (*Daily News*, 17.7.1973). Burundi agreed to pay 3.4 million shillings compensation to Tanzania. At least once a year during the 1980s, a senior member of the Tanzanian government would issue a warning to the refugees. In 1985, President Julius Nyerere and the minister of home affairs separately cautioned refugees not to involve themselves in activities designed to overthrow the Burundi government (*Daily News*, 12.7.1985; *Daily News*, 11.4.1986).

During the 1990s, with a refugee population of over a million, compounded by the destabilizing impact of the presence of *génocidaires* from Rwanda and rebels from Burundi, Tanzania became less of a benevolent host. At the same time the Burundi government intensified its

---

[17] BBC News Africa: *Living with Hutu Rebels*, 16 June 2005.

propaganda against Tanzania for harbouring, training and arming rebels. In 2001, President Buyoya claimed that Burundi was 'almost in an open state of war' with Tanzania (Reliefweb, 16 June 2001). Despite Tanzania's professed innocence, NGO research has unearthed numerous instances of its tolerance of Burundi rebel activities on its territory (HRW, 1997a; ICG, 1999c). According to International Crisis Group:

> Western Tanzania is a focal point for key activities of the rebellion including: military mobilization, recruitment, training, fund-raising, political strategizing, communications, arms trafficking, resource distribution, medical treatment, naval operations and the launching of cross-border attacks. (ICG, 1999c: 10)

Three years later, in what appeared to be a diplomatic volte face, the same International Crisis Group could state that 'there is no credible confirmation of Tanzanian logistical support or direct Tanzanian involvement' (ICG, 2002b: 12). There is no doubt that Tanzania provided tacit support in terms of giving sanctuary to FRODEBU exiles and allowing FROLINA and Palipehutu/FNL to operate clandestinely within western Tanzania, but the degree of actual state involvement is still unproven.

The Tanzanian government seems to have taken up two positions based on the potential threat that the presence of refugees posed to national security. During the Cold War and the presidency of Nyerere, Tanzania gained considerable international kudos for its benevolence towards refugees, yet the state was always concerned about compromising its own security, allowing local and regional officials to reinforce, periodically, the power of the state over refugees within its territory. This involved restrictions on movement, confinement to settlement, round-ups in towns and villages, and forced repatriation. In 1996, Tanzania called for the creation of safe zones within Burundi to reinforce the rights of citizenship, to keep the problem within its country of origin and 'as a confidence building measure' to minimize disruption to refugees (RoT, 1995: Para. 12).[18] Nevertheless, a certain degree of sympathy for the Burundi cause has prevented the mass forced repatriation that the state visited on the Rwandans in December 1996. Instead, Tanzania was persistent in its pressure on the Burundi government to seek a peaceful solution to its problems, and was openly hostile to the 1996 Buyoya coup.

Many observers in the international community were suspicious of Tanzania's strategic and economic interests in Burundi, and acted to undermine and minimize its involvement in efforts to end genocidal violence (Chapter 9) (ICG, 2001b & 2002b). Tanzania appeared keen to play a major role in the region and, in 2004, hosted the 'Great Lakes International Conference on Peace, Security, Democracy and Development', a meeting of donors, regional heads of state and NGOs.

---

[18] Quoted in Bonaventure Rutinwa (1999).

Regional Organizations: Approaches to Genocide

For almost four decades after its formation, the leaders of the OAU were reluctant to condemn genocide, hiding behind the principle of non-interference in the internal affairs of member states embodied in Article III (2) of its 1969 Charter and reflecting UN Cold War policy. This was an agreement made between heads of states, and the strict allegiance that successive leaders have paid to it reflects their narrow conceptualization of what constitutes the political community. Defining citizenship and rights as existing purely within the boundaries of the nation-state has placed the majority of people in the region at the mercy of discriminatory states that perceive rights and citizenship as applying to a select few.

During the 1972 genocide in Burundi, the OAU sent a message of support to Micombero. Presidents Nyerere and Mobutu were encouraged by some western powers and the UN to talk privately to him – but to no avail (Bowen *et al.*, 1974). In 1999, well after a number of international investigations had taken place, the OAU commissioned an International Panel of Eminent Personalities to conduct its own 'investigation into the 1994 Rwandan genocide and the surrounding events'. Although it came six years after the genocide, the report presented a distinctively informed African interpretation of events and concluded that 'the facts are not in question: a small number of major actors could have directly prevented, halted, or reduced the slaughter; they include France in Rwanda itself, the US in the Security Council; Belgium ... and Rwanda's church leaders' (Para. ES.44). The report seemed to absolve the OAU itself of blame, commenting that its 'well-meant initiatives' came to nought, because it had 'the resources and the power to do nothing more than bring adversaries together' (Para. ES.19).

It was not until 2002, after successive genocidal violence in the Great Lakes region and elsewhere on the continent that member states of the OAU's successor organization, the African Union (AU), agreed to the principle of:

> ... the right of the Union to intervene in a member state pursuant to a decision of the Assembly in respect of grave circumstances, namely: war crimes, genocide and crimes against humanity.[19]

Yet, as the conflict (2004–) in the Darfur region of Sudan has shown, African leaders are still reluctant to act to save people's lives, and some countries, such as Tanzania, are not signatory to the UN's Genocide Convention. Nevertheless, the AU's refusal to recognize the transfer of power by undemocratic means marked a significant milestone in African political culture. Consequently, the AU has been mobilized to support the various peace initiatives in the region.[20]

---

[19] African Union, *Protocol Relating to the Establishment of the Peace and Security Council of the African Union*, Adopted in Durban, South Africa, July 2002, Article 4. (J).
[20] With respect to Burundi, there was an unwritten agreement (3 plus 1 mechanism) that the Republic of South Africa, Tanzania and Uganda, supported by the UN/AU, would oversee the Burundi peace process.

The Question of Regional Citizenship

The persistence of thousands of non-indigenous communities in neighbouring states has rekindled the debate on the principle of regional citizenship. The discriminatory and competitive politics of the state has
served to externalize opposition groups and individuals, many of whom
have found their lives threatened or have been subjected to genocide.
These racist practices have intensified with the introduction of competitive politics and because of the inequalities generated by market-driven
processes of accumulation. Numerous victorious politicians in democratic elections have found their citizenship challenged in the courts by
the opposition.[21] As the territorial boundaries of the nation-state appear
incapable of containing these divisive forces in ways that would protect
the rights of citizenship, we need to think beyond state sovereignty and
conceptualize political identities beyond national boundaries – finding a
regional solution as opposed to a national one (Peterson, 1992). Should
Africa remain a slave to arbitrary colonial borders that instilled violence
on communities and continue to generate refugees and citizenship
problems in the post-colonial era?

The history of migration and mass movement of people in the region
needs to be discussed in the context of a broader understanding of
national security and peace. In the mid-1990s there were some 10 million
refugees on the continent, may of whom lived for years in protracted
refugee situations, with two or three generations born in exile. These
people lived in limbo, stateless, in fear of forced repatriation and
subjected to the marginalizing policies of their host states. It is these
policies that have forced many to form rebel movements to return to their
home countries. Many Rwandans, Burundians, Congolese and Ugandans
have grown up in neighbouring countries, and have an understanding of
regional space which is beyond the comprehension of small national
elites whose power is determined by defining who does or does not
belong to the sovereign space. As regional states and the international
community, for fear of secessionist and revanchist claims, have refused
steadfastly to sanction alterations of colonial boundaries, a federated
regional grouping may appear be more plausible.

One solution is to allow refugees to settle permanently in host states. In
1980, Tanzania granted citizenship by presidential decree to 36,000
Rwandan refugees who had resided in the country since 1964; by this
time over 15,000 of them had already applied for citizenship taking
advantage of the seven-year residency requirements under the 1972
Immigration Act (*Daily News*, 29.9.1978). Despite the decree, Rwandan
refugees had to go through the same procedure as before, and many were
refused citizenship seemingly at the whim of local and regional party
officials, only 950 naturalized (AI, 2005). Those refugees who refused to
naturalize were not treated favourably by Tanzanian officials, who were

---

[21] In Tanzania, there were several cases, especially following the 1996 elections. Azim Premji
of Kigoma Urban (*Daily News*, 23 November 1996); Iddi Simba, Ilala's CCM political
candidate, was accused of being of Burundi origin (*Daily News*, 15 June 1996) and Arcada
Ntagazawa CCM member of Parliament for Kibondo district was declared not to be a
Tanzanian citizen (*Daily News*, 23 November 1996).

affronted when, in the mid-1990s, some Rwandans gave up their citizenship to return to Rwanda after the RPF's victory.

The 1972 cohort of Barundi refugees in Tanzania were also eligible to apply for citizenship, yet the number of applications was significantly smaller and those approved smaller still (*Daily News*, 19.6.1996). According to Amnesty International (2005), between 1970 and 2004, only 1068 Burundians had been naturalized. There were several possible explanations; their commitment to political change in Burundi: the cost of citizenship application (US $800 in 2005) coupled to the high possibility of failure. Tanzanians made it extremely difficult for people to naturalize putting in place 'lengthy bureaucratic procedures' (AI, 2005: 31). More importantly, this led to a profound distrust of the Tanzanian authorities, who, despite the country's generosity', were not viewed positively by the refugee population.

The economic and political benefits of a United States of Africa were proposed by Kwame Nkrumah in the 1960s, but opposed vehemently by those leaders of states that were aligned to the West. The OAU, formed as a compromise in 1963, showed itself incapable of championing the rights of the people. Since the 1960s, numerous regional economic groupings have included in their charters the principle of the free movement of people, but few have operationalized it, and many have introduced restrictive national legislation akin to those in the Europe, aimed at hindering cross-border migration from neighbouring territories. In eastern and southern Africa states accept a regional hierarchy of states and of citizens that, for example, value the life of a South African more than that of a Mozambican.

It is not just national elites that fear diminishing influence in a federated region. Many global corporations and their respective home countries would have difficulty negotiating lucrative contracts with a more empowered regional economic grouping. These reasons have been central to efforts in East and Central Africa to de-rail proposals to establish viable economic units. Burundi hostility to Tanzania comes not just from its hosting of rebel movements, but relates back to pre-independence negotiations between Prince Rwagasore and Julius Nyerere to establish an East African Federation. Periodically, there have been suggestions that the Hutu/Tutsi ethnic imbalance would dissipate if Rwanda and Burundi were incorporated into larger political and economic units.[22] Many of the economic groupings that exist are dependent on alliances with former colonial powers or fit into imperialist agendas for trade and co-operation. One such group was the now moribund French-sponsored Great Lakes Economic Community, comprising of Zaire, Rwanda and Burundi, which France used to pursue its interests in the region.

This fear of regional strictures has helped genocidal Burundi regimes to attract international support and Hutu rebels to find allies among indigenous Bantu groups throughout the region. An accusation, which was used as propaganda by the Hutu groups, was that Museveni, Nyerere, Buyoya and Kagame were involved in a conspiracy to establish a Tutsi-

---

[22] Rwanda and Burundi have since joined the regenerated East African community.

Hima empire throughout East and Central Africa. Its potency was such that it warranted a mention in the OAU's report on the Rwandan genocide. People of diverse cultural and ethnic background are being attributed political identities that are already conflictual and that threaten to engulf the region in genocidal violence. The report refers to broadcasts from a radio station in Eastern Congo, that urged Bantus 'to rise as one to combat Tutsi, who are described as 'Ethiopians and Egyptians' and to help 'their Bahutu brothers to re-conquer Burundi and Rwanda'.[23] Regional leaders have a duty to counteract such negativities by promoting alternative understandings of citizenship and political identity. In the context of Central Africa, the concept of national security as a part of state sovereignty has been made redundant by the conduct of warfare within the region.

A Regional End to Impunity

The issue of impunity for those who have committed crimes against humanity is not just an issue of national legislation; it could be tackled at the regional and global scale. According to Article 4 of *The African Charter on Human and People's Rights*, 'Humans are inviolable. Every human being shall be entitled to respect for his life and the integrity of his person', and Article 5 states, 'All forms of exploitation and degradation of man particularly slavery, slave trade, torture, cruel, inhuman or degrading punishment and treatment shall be prohibited.' As shown, most perpetrators of genocide and other crimes against humanity are able to find safe havens in neighbouring countries. The presence of a militarized culture throughout the region and the devaluation of African lives, means that the moral compulsion that would have forced regional states to act in cases of genocidal violence has not been present. In cases of forced repatriation, due legal process is often not applied by home states. For example, according to Amnesty International (1996b), in 1996, Tutsi-led groups in Zaire handed over Hutu refugees to the Burundi government. These refugees were massacred or 'disappeared' after being sent back to Burundi, with most of the killings being committed by the Burundi armed forces.

Throughout the region, massacres and sexual violence have reached epidemic proportions. A World Health Organization report estimated that in two provinces of Eastern Congo 40,000 women were raped during the war by soldiers, militias, criminal gangs and individuals with guns.[24] Cross-border movements of armies and militias, means that once a ceasefire or peace agreement has been signed many of those returning to join the new national armed force are guilty of crimes committed in neighbouring states. Custom and tradition appear to be a great hindrance to women seeking help on a national stage; a regional culture founded on the concept of a trans-national citizenship would enable women's organizations to campaign to change regional and national perceptions of rape, in much the same way as current HIV/AIDS campaigns on the continent.

---

[23] *Voix du Patriote* (Voice of the Patriot), 1997/8, quoted in OAU, 2000: Para 20.75.
[24] *Mail & Guardian online*, Thousands raped in the Congo, 8 March 2005. www.mg.co.za

Conclusion

This chapter has shown that warfare in Burundi is not an isolated affair, but fits into a regional history and practice of genocidal violence and undemocratic regimes, linked to the devaluation of African lives. States throughout the region were built and are sustained by discriminatory and violent practices based on racial, ethnic and regional differences. Post-colonial states have not been able to transcend this colonial legacy, and instead have no qualms about promoting such practices abroad, even if it means the incitement to genocide. This regional and international tolerance of genocidal violence against African people is partly the cause of the protractedness of regional warfare. Equally important are the growing militarization of the region and the complicity of foreign powers through the process of extraction, the sale of weaponry and the training of military personnel, making the concept of the civil war, as we have seen in Eastern Congo, a geographically limiting term. In the twenty-first century, the US 'war on terror' and international policies regarding peace-keeping suggest that Africa is set to be an even more militarized space. The fact that nations that represent themselves as being morally superior are implicated in the violence is worrying for the ordinary African searching for spaces of peace.

By the beginning of the twenty-first century the peace imperative appears to have been lost, as most regional states embarked on militarist adventures and those that claimed to have intervened on the part of peace seem to be promoting vested national interests. Since national security is conceptualized in militarized ways and state power is defined by its ability to wield military might, which often translates into repression of the populace, those seeking peace may want to look to the possibility of non-sovereign concepts of territorial space for the protection of their right to claim humanity. The gross imbalance between military and social welfare expenditure reflects the entrenchment of a deformed masculinity that prioritizes weapons over human wellbeing.

Within the regional space are a number of refugee communities, disen-franchized by their home countries, whose movements transcend the territorial logic of the nation-state and who have the potentialities of forming progressive trans-border communities, if their productive capac-ities can be harnessed by host states frightened of their lack of political and national allegiances. This is not to forget those criminal and geno-cidal elements among such communities, but a concerted effort by states to rid the region of such elements would diminish, if not eliminate, any threat they might pose.

8

Global Humanitarianism & the Dehumanization of African Refugees

Introduction

This chapter discusses the ways in which Cold War and post-Cold War geo-politics have shaped the refugee discourse and the response of both humanitarian agencies and African states to forced migration. The historical experience of Burundian refugees in Tanzania will be used to demonstrate how the extension of the international refugee conventions to Africa and the accompanied humanitarian regime has contributed to the undermining of human inviolability. Recast as 'victims' needing expensive international aid, African refugees have been both commoditized and externalized from the body politic. It is argued that humanitarianism, in perpetuating the existence of alienated communities in African countries, is complicit in the production of a refugee discourse that is both depoliticizing and dehumanizing. In addition, the use of international assistance to sustain protracted refugee situations prevented many African governments from seeking long-term regional solutions to the refugee problem, whether in terms of a commitment to resolve the causes of flight or the integration of refugees into host societies. Aid enabled the construction of the refugee as a problem and as an alien 'other', outside the realms of the sovereign state. The convergence of aid with neo-liberal democracy undermined elements in African societies who used xenophobic attacks on refugees to bolster political ambitions.

In the mid-1990s the Great Lakes region of Africa was brought to world attention by the spectre of genocide, the mass displacements of its population and mass deaths from disease epidemics. Some three million Rwandans, mainly Hutus, fled the country after the genocide and joined some 800,000 Burundians; by 2003 some 450,000 Congolese were in exile and over two million internally-displaced (Figure 4).

Since 1964, international humanitarian organizations, including the UN system and international, regional and local NGOs, have striven to provide emergency assistance to the affected populations. The region was host to some of the first post-colonial African refugees when Rwandan Tutsis fled the Hutu revolution of 1959 and found asylum in Tanzania, Burundi, the Congo and Uganda. Similarly, the Burundian refugees of the 1960s, 1972 and 1988 found refuge mainly in Tanzania, Rwanda and the Congo. The intractability of the political problems meant that many Rwandans and Burundians remained in exile for decades and, in the case of those Burundians in Tanzania, were provided with international aid for more than three decades. The 1994 humanitarian crisis arising from the genocide in Rwanda brought to the fore challenging questions relating to the relevance of humanitarian intervention.

It is no longer churlish to analyse critically the role of humanitarian organizations in Africa even under conditions of war. The increasing incidence of wars has allowed humanitarian and non-governmental organizations (NGOs) to intensify their work on the continent. Their presence has led to numerous questions about their agenda and their relationship with the state and civil society; with budgets greater than most post-conflict governments, how have NGOs dealt with issues of violence and identity? In the context of genocidal violence in Central Africa or 'complex humanitarian emergencies', to what extent have these organizations helped to ease the suffering and/or slow the pace of militarization? The need for political legitimization, in the context of a democratic deficit, led many agencies to articulate civil society empowerment as a primary goal, which somehow has not resulted in greater political participation of the people. Of issue should be the relationship between western humanitarianism and the protection of the human in Africa and the extent to which humanitarian action has transcended the hierarchies of race.

What Humanitarianism?

Humanitarianism suggests an ethical interest in alleviating the suffering of human beings and the general human welfare of people. In times of crisis, as in war-torn situations, those with the necessary means should offer assistance to ameliorate the wretched conditions of their fellow humans. Humanitarian action is a fundamental part of human behaviour. In the twentieth century, humanitarianism became organized and institutionalized with the establishment of regional and global networks of relief providers. Throughout much of this century, humanitarian action was considered to be intrinsically good and politically neutral. Formal humanitarian organizations, originating predominantly from northern developed countries, dispensed assistance to those unfortunate enough to live in disaster-prone areas. The message was that in the alleviation of suffering, we all belonged to a common humanity. Humanitarians were perceived by themselves and by their supporters as operating independently of states, intervening to help those abandoned by their governments.

Understanding contemporary humanitarian action in Africa demands an historical perspective on the relationship between humanitarians and imperialism on the continent. David Livingstone and other nineteenth century missionaries thought the souls of African people could be saved through being bonded to Christianity and commerce. This perspective did not disappear with decolonization, instead, it retreated in the face of independent Africans asserting their own humanity, and their right to be treated as equal members of the human race.

The stridency of African states in asserting their sovereignty meant that states could exercise their power to determine which organizations operated in their territories, and those allowed in shifted from a civilizing to a developmental agenda and functioned in the background. This position fitted well with Cold War geo-politics, when western and communist governments would court states and were reluctant to criticize human rights abuse. As African Rights (1994b: 4) note, humanitarians occupied a 'sharply circumscribed space' that '...was defined by western governments and host governments, in ways that suited their political interests'. Historically, western humanitarian agencies in Africa have always worked within parameters defined by the state, and operated essentially as a sticking plaster to the brutality of the localized impacts of imperialism and superpower rivalry.

The mid-1980s saw marked transformations in the nature of the humanitarian regime; these were consolidated in the 1990s. The major changes were in terms of a rapid increase in the actual number of organizations; in their patterns of funding, especially that coming directly from home governments and the adoption of a more overt political stance. Some authors link these changes to the 1984/5 Ethiopian and Sahelian famines and to the 1994 Rwandan genocide (African Rights, 1994b; De Waal, 2000; Duffield, 2001; Kathina and Suhrke, 2002). The rise in the number of relief organizations was not purely consequential on the media spectacle in the representation of the disasters, though that too played a role, but reflected more fundamental transformations in global geo-politics and global economic restructuring under neo-liberalism. As part of the economic subjugation of African states to the market-oriented neo-liberal policies of the World Bank and IMF many states were discouraged from providing basic welfare services to their already impoverished citizens. The social fall-out of the economic crisis and state retreat created numerous problems, including an intensification of violence, both in the private and public spheres.

The post-Cold War rise of NGOs was palliative to the erosion of state provision of welfare services under neo-liberalism. This was effectuated by the shifting of development and humanitarian aid away from states to international NGOs, many of which promoted their comparative advantage, vis à vis the state, in delivering services to the poorest of the poor. The material gains arising from the redirection of aid away from state institutions to international and local non-governmental agencies created a competitive environment in service provisioning that became intensified in situations of mass and protracted human suffering as existed in the Great Lakes region. This rise in humanitarian agencies is exemplified by the 200 relief agencies that operated in the Rwandan refugee camps in Eastern Zaire between 1994 and 1996. Humanitarian action became a veritable business for western and some local entrepreneurs and careerists. In line with their enhanced status, humanitarian organizations bureaucratized themselves into simulacra of state institutions, taking over the role once played by states, endowed with more resources and organizational capacity than the local, regional or even national state (Waters, 2001).

International humanitarianism sets itself above criticism by universalizing western principles of individual human rights. Duffield (2001) claims this was a Cold War phenomenon, deployed by humanitarians to raise themselves above the fray of superpower politics. The discourse of universal human rights is still evident in many policy circles as part of the rights-based approaches that promote the implementation of international human rights legislation in the process of humanitarian action. In contrast, De Waal (2000) makes a distinction between international humanitarian law that evolved after the Second World War that includes the Genocide Convention of 1948, Geneva Conventions of 1949 and the 1951 Refugee Convention, and the humanitarian principles being expounded by contemporary humanitarian agencies. These agencies, he contends, give emphasis to securing the delivery of aid, the protection of international staff, aid-coordination, and negotiated access to victims at the expense of laws aimed at protecting the human even in the context of war. The focus on principles has led to a close alliance between humanitarianism and militarism.

The Rwandan genocide is supposed to have marked a sea-change in the philosophical approach of humanitarian organizations. Many of which were severely criticized for taking a political stance during the genocide which might have resulted in more people being killed; for their role in sustaining the *génocidaires* of the ex-Rwandan army and *interahamwe* in the camps in Eastern Zaire; and for the inappropriateness of some of the aid delivered, some have argued, after much soul searching and the publication of a 'code of conduct', that a 'new humanitarianism' has emerged. Duffield (ibid.) claims that humanitarians recognized the inadequacy of their apolitical stance in the context of complex humanitarian emergencies when whatever they do can have good or bad outcomes. He attempts to make a case for the emergence of what he labels as 'new political humanitarianism'; a humanitarianism that realizes that politics is not bad, and 'that neutrality is impossible in the new wars, since any assistance necessarily has political effects' (Duffield, ibid.: 75). Politics, he continues, has 'a legitimate concern with relief and suffering, the restoration of peace and securing justice' (ibid.: 87). Therefore, the new political humanitarianism 'reinforces earlier policy commitments to linking relief and development, conflict resolution and societal reconstruction' (ibid.: 75). Many in Central Africa would not dispute the purpose of politics; the issue is who constitutes the political community and who decides the priorities of the state.

What this new label does is to give clarity to what has been the practice on the ground. The 'new political humanitarianism', which could be equally termed 'neo-liberal humanitarianism', is much more interventionist. Neo-liberal humanitarianism bears the hallmarks of other neo-liberal agencies; being largely externally funded and managed, they have problems of local accountability. Furthermore, in their roles as problem-solvers and interlocutors for the voiceless, they infantilize and victimize recipients of aid (Campbell, 1996; Uvin, 1998). Their professed strengths and longevity seem to be conditional on the perpetuation of the conditions of human suffering in Africa (Chaulia, 2006). Simultaneously, neo-liberal humanitarians reinforce the nefarious political elite through the input of foreign exchange into the economy, while undermining state and regional sovereignty, the very mechanisms that are likely to bring about real improvements in people's well being. In its institutional practices, humanitarian action strengthens the characteristics of the discriminatory state, privileging one social group above the other.

Kathina and Suhrke (2002: 14) in their edited volume on, *Eroding Local Capacity*, unveil the disempowering impacts of international humanitarian action in Eastern Africa, where it 'devalues local actors in both the public administration and civil society.' Like Duffield (2001), the authors argue that humanitarian organizations responded to these criticisms by changing the discourse of intervention to focus on building capacity by merging the short-term goals of relief work to longer term developmental ones. This step is even more problematic for Africans because, historically, the ideas of development have been highly contested. Certainly, there is much doubt as to whether humanitarian agencies, acting in consort with western donor agencies and the UN, can deliver, as Duffield (ibid.: 101) purports, 'a sustainable process of self-management that has economic self-sufficiency at its core'. Since the 1980s, grounded evidence indicates that the development policies purveyed by the neo-liberal organizations have had the effect of intensifying rather than alleviating the impoverishment of African people.

While they advocated universal principles of human rights at a global level, western governments have always exercised differences in their regional application, pointing to the existence of an unspoken ideology of a hierarchy of human beings. Hidden in western international geopolitical discourse is the assumption that some people are 'more human than others' (Dallaire, 2003: 522). Despite their professed humanistic foundations, the actions of western humanitarian agencies are often underpinned by social Darwinian ideology, especially at the point of aid delivery. Of note is the imbalance of power and wages in aid projects between white westerners and African humanitarian workers; the public prostitution of images of disaster victims; the infantilization of refugees, and the evacuation of westerners during the Rwandan genocide and other conflict situations. Humanitarianism contributes, maybe unwittingly, to the reproduction of, and the persistence of, racial hierarchies and particularistic identities, be they ethnic, regional or gender based – a characteristic it shares with military institutions. Humanitarian action can help further the process of militarization, as aggrieved communities who are unable to avail themselves of the rights of citizenship, especially when subjected to state-sponsored violence, tend to seek resolution in non-state and less formalized orchestrations of violence.

Another post-Cold War trend in humanitarian intervention is the close association of western militaries and private military contractors in humanitarian work. Towards the end of the twentieth century, an alliance emerged between western militaries and some western humanitarian agencies; the latter becoming reliant on western military intervention to ensure their ability to deliver aid to the suffering, while the militaries sought post-Cold War use for their hardware and manpower. Military humanitarianism has become part of the general discourse, with some observers advocating greater liaison between the military in their peace-keeping capacities and NGOs (Slim, 2003). Certainly, military leaders are keen to extend the military's role in post-conflict reconstruction. One American colonel posits that the US military could fill what he describes as the 'reconstruction gap' between peace-keeping and NGO peace-building (Williams, 2005).

In militarist ideology the notion of 'us and them' involves an 'othering' of the enemy that justifies and facilitates his/her elimination. Military humanitarianism is a contradiction in itself, and only works if the beneficiaries (victims) are perceived as not belonging to the same human family or as being so brutalized that the institution whose norms are responsible for their suffering can re-present itself as angels of mercy, whether in the blue helmets of the UN or the garb of the national army (Enloe, 2002). Now, let us turn to the plight of Burundi refugees, mainly in Tanzania, and illustrate how the changing dynamics of humanitarian action intersects with regional states and affect refugee communities.

The Cold War and the Internationalization of the African Refugee Problem

During the 1960s, while independent Tanzania was confronted for the first time with a refugee problem,[1] various international humanitarian organizations and western governments were also expressing their concern about the new wave of refugees on the continent. Political instability arising from the decolonization process led to fears of dissidents forming alliances with communist groups. It became necessary for this new African reality to be speedily included in the internationally-recognized legal conventions in order to monitor, control and direct the movement, and so prevent such alignments.

Three major international conferences, one in 1966 and two in 1967, addressed the issue,[2] and were influential in that their recommendations were later incorporated into the *1969 OAU Convention Governing Specific Aspects of Refugee Problems in Africa*. Earlier, in January 1967, the UN had adopted its protocol which enabled the 1951 Convention to cover the whole world; thus extending the mandate of the United Nations High Commissioner for Refugees (UNHCR). The internationalization of the African refugee problem meant that refugees could no longer move undetected into neighbouring states. Aid, provided by western governments and coordinated by UNHCR became a strategy to control them. The activities of the UN and its refugee organ, UNHCR, were described in 1967 as providing:

> Obscure moral support for liberation, while at the same time pursuing programs which encourage a posture of rehabilitation with the promise of a new life, serving free Africa, and not the cause of the liberation for which they seek support. (Metcalfe 1967 in Brooks & El Ayouty, 1970: 74)

---

[1] In 1963–64 the first refugee groups from Rwanda and Zaire sought refuge in Tanzania.
[2] The most influential was the conference on the Legal, Economic and Social Aspects of the African Refugee Problems, 9–18 October 1967, sponsored by UNHCR, ECA, Dag Hammarskjold Foundation and the OAU. Also in November 1967, a similar conference was held at St. John's University, New York. In 1966, SIAS Uppsala, organized the first international conference on African refugees, looking at 'Refugee problems in Southern and Central Africa', sponsored by the Swedish government.

The UN was well aware of the potentially negative and self-destructive effect of asylum on refugees; despondency, indifference and a confusion of identity and purpose. African states did not have to be coerced into enforcing policies that depoliticized refugees, separating them from their cause, and generally maintaining the political status quo within the region. With their own legitimacy open to question, Africa's ruling elite found it beneficial to have such an approach universally accepted. In a speech to the 1967 conference, Diallo Telli, then the Administrative Secretary of the OAU, described the refugee problem as an international problem, because of 'the potential threats which it holds to stability, peace and security in Africa and the world'. Fundamental to the OAU's refugee policy were strategies to prevent refugees committing acts of subversion against their country of origin. Member states demanded:

> Refugees must in no case be allowed to attack their country of origin, either through the media of press, or radio, or by the use of arms. In the same way, the countries of origin must not consider the harbouring of refugees as an unfriendly gesture; and refugees must desist from any attack on the countries of origin through the media of press or radio or by resorting to arms.[3]

These principles were encapsulated in the 1969 Refugee Convention. In this way, international assistance was guaranteed and it would, additionally, be under the guidance of the UN system:

> Since the states of asylum in Africa are not generally equipped to handle the economic and political problems for refugees alone, this work of the United Nations is important. By channeling the problem of refugee settlement through the UN, a multi-lateral solution can be financed and executed in the overall interests of maintaining international order in the face of potential crisis situations caused by refugee displacement. (Metcalfe, 1967 in Brooks & El Ayouty, 1970: 76)

Initially the UNHCR imposed a set of criteria that African states had to satisfy before receiving aid. Recognizing their sovereignty, African governments must officially request assistance; secondly the problem must be of such a magnitude that it cannot be solved by the government; and, finally and more importantly, the solutions proposed by the host government for the refugees should be practical and based on humanitarian and social considerations, thus removing the problem from its political context (Holborn, 1975). This dependence on external aid compelled African states to rely on western-derived solutions to the refugee problem, principally the concept of voluntary repatriation, as the best solution to refugee problems, and in its absence, land settlement, through long-term refugee programmes and projects. In the 1990s, states have become less willing to settle refugees, and repatriation, forced or voluntary, has become the preferred solution (Black & Koser, 1999).

---

[3] OAU principles contained in the speech of Diallo Telli, Administrative Secretary-General to the 1967 conference.

African states actively sought internationally-provided material assistance for refugees, presenting their countries as making enormous 'sacrifices' by accommodating refugees. President Nyerere of Tanzania iterated this position several times. In 1979, he declared:

> Our resources are very limited, and the demands made upon us are very large. But I do not believe that dealing with the problems of 3.5 million people and giving them a chance to rebuild their dignity and their lives, is an impossible task for 46 nations and 350 million inhabitants. (Nyerere, 1979: 14)

The underdeveloped character of many post-colonial African states meant that African refugees could not achieve improved status without significant inputs of international aid, which for about three decades, helped to sustain permanent refugee communities. UNHCR and its implementing NGOs came to dominate refugee relief, often providing a standard of service that was beyond that available to local communities from the crisis-ridden national state. This disparity in resource access created antagonism from local elites and increased the financial burden on UNHCR. In the mid-1980s the discourse of refugee aid became focused on minimizing an assumed dependency of refugees on international support through promoting self-sufficiency and their local integration in host countries.

This was not a new development. The 1967 conference on African refugees also recommended the promotion of zonal-integrated development schemes, which would enable the integration of refugee communities into the social and economic structure of the host society. Both the refugee community and the local population would, therefore, share in the benefits accruing from the new financial investments in the area, thus avoiding friction between the two groups. Donors were unwilling to initiate projects on zonal-integrated development in the 1970s, due to the worldwide economic crisis, and in the Tanzanian case, to the high capital outlay and widespread failure of such schemes. UNHCR emphasized the 'non-operational' component of its statute, which excludes its direct involvement in development activities. However, in the 1980s, UNHCR and the donors, in trying to avoid long-term maintenance of refugees on schemes, revived the discourse on integration into the host society.

Concurrent with the development of ideas about integration, African governments reinforced their call for further assistance to cope with the rapidly increasing number of refugees. In 1979, an African-inspired conference was convened in Arusha, Tanzania, to address this issue. African states, noting the disparity between the levels of assistance to Asia and Europe, demanded more aid, while at the same time making some concessions on human rights, detention, imprisonment and forced repatriation (Eriksson *et al.*, 1979 (1981)).

Burden-sharing among African states, as espoused in the 1967 conference, failed to materialize. The notion of 'burden-sharing' was originally used by the OAU to encourage member countries with few refugees to assist those with a large refugee population. By the late 1970s, as a reaction to their restrictive immigration policies, western countries began to promote African-based solutions to the African refugee problem. African states have insisted that the West share the burden by providing material assistance. Their position was succinctly put by President Nyerere in 1983:

> We recognize that Africa's refugees are primarily an African problem and responsibility. Yet we have no false modesty which requires us to reject outside help. Indeed we feel that we have some right to claim it. Quite apart from the common humanity of mankind, there can be few refugee situations in Africa which have not been in some way worsened by the political, commercial, or military activities of more powerful and wealthy nations in the world. (Nyerere, 1983: 8)[4]

Thus, by 1987, Barry Stein could define the concept of burden-sharing as 'international assistance given to a heavily burdened refugee asylum country to lighten its load' (Stein, 1987: 48).

UNHCR responded with The First International Conference on Assistance to African Refugees (ICARA I) in 1981 and ICARA II in 1984. The former was, according to the organizers, to draw public attention to the scale of the refugee problem in Africa, while ICARA II was primarily concerned with the impact of refugees on the host communities and with creating practical links between assistance and [infrastructural] development. As shown earlier, the idea of linking refugee aid with development dates back to the 1967 conference, in addition to the 'durable' solutions.[5] In the context of ICARA II,

> A durable solution means helping the refugees to become self-sufficient, and enabling them to integrate and participate fully in the social and economic life of their new country or of their homelands, if they repatriate. (Stein, 1987: 48)

ICARA II was an attempt to get other UN bodies: FAO, ILO, UNDP, UNFPA, to participate in development-related refugee assistance. Betts (1984) outlines some of the planning procedures for such forms of assistance. Although suggesting that such projects should be integrated into national and local development plans, he conceives that they would often mean a revision of the government's rural development approaches within the affected area. This is at variance with the proposal of the 1967 conference where the plans were to be drawn up and executed by host governments. In practice, UNHCR not only provided the financial assistance, but was influential in the selection and execution of the plans. Pierre Coat, a UNHCR Senior Planning Officer, outlined the organization's policy:

> Clearly the host country enjoyed full sovereignty and UNHCR would not impose the settlement site, but to what extent should it resist a bad choice?

---

[4] President J.K. Nyerere, Speech at Geneva, 3 October 1983, when receiving the Nansen medal for services to the cause of refugees. Nansen had been the Commissioner for refugees in the League of Nations, the forerunner of UNHCR, following the First World War.

[5] Durable solutions refer to the three suggested in the recommendations of the 1967 conference, voluntary repatriation, resettlement in a second country of asylum or systematic land settlement in the first country of asylum.

> UNHCR should avoid placing itself in a position of confrontation and should negotiate and insist on independent technical advice. Should that fail, UNHCR should refuse to sponsor such projects while promoting other alternatives. (Coat, 1978, quoted in Betts, 1984: 14)

Betts (1984) also advocated the use of 'neutral' implementing agencies as opposed to government ministries, in order to overcome problems arising from changes in government. Clearly both the above proposals have implications for sovereignty, and reflect the increasingly weak and ineffectual character of the post-colonial African state in the context of an emerging neo-liberalism. Fourteen African countries submitted projects for funding to ICARA II. Not surprisingly, those projects for which aid was forthcoming were confined to activities within the existing settlements, and did not involve the local people.

Having discovered the capital-intensive nature of schemes, the donors promoted the proliferation of the concept of 'self-sufficiency' in refugee literature/terminology. At the same time, the notion of the 'dependency syndrome' was promulgated. Lance Clark (1986) describes refugee dependency syndrome:

> as a term used by non-refugees, by those in the international assistance system and by host and donor country officials, to describe the personality characteristics of refugees. Refugees are often described as unmotivated, lacking in initiative, as being unappreciative of the kind of assistance given, to them, looking to others to solve their problems. (Clark, *Refugee Magazine*, May 1986: 35)

Refugees were said to be over-reliant on the donors, and especially on donated food. Sydney Waldron (1987), in his article, *Blaming the Refugee*, tried to explain the origin of this stereotype by applying the concept of the 'total institution' to understand the structures of administration of camps/settlements and to provide insights into the management and perception of expatriate bureaucrats, from whom such negative statements about refugees originated. Waldron concludes that refugee settlements:

> ... are institutionally structured residential populations which are ruled from top down. Life is planned and scheduled by those in control of the basic resources of the population; the domain of the residential community is coincident with the domain of control; and the boundaries of social and economic action are formally circumscribed ... [therefore], the common denominator of refugee behaviour is learned or spontaneously developed in situ as involuntary migrants become exposed upon entry to the social, psychological and economic order of the refugee camp ... [thus] the tendency to stereotype 'inmates'... results from a repetitive handling of a mass number of 'cases', where individual differences are hidden and the commonality which produces stereotypes derives from the bureaucratically derived definition which structures role behaviour between 'staff' and 'inmate'. (Waldron, 1987: 2/3)

The collaboration between humanitarian agencies and African govern-ments resulted in a policy framework aimed first at depoliticizing refugees from post-colonial African countries; reframing them as 'victims' who are worthy beneficiaries of humanitarian aid and second at externalizing protection and assistance to African refugees, inadvertently creating a new political identity of the 'refugee' in contemporary African countries. In contrast, those fleeing communist regimes to the asylum countries of the West, were deemed to be 'political refugees' or 'dissi-dents', and though considered worthy of assistance and a better life, were not prevented from conducting political action against their countries of origin. Throughout the Cold War, humanitarian assistance was used to maintain a dichotomy between innocent refugees and belligerents, which became even more unworkable from the 1990s onwards.

The Post-Cold War Humanitarian Regime in Africa

The refugee regime of the 1990s was qualitatively different from that of previous decades. The new policy reflected the reluctance of UNHCR to embark on further long-term settlement programmes, due to the financial burden linked to the increasing scarcity of donor funds. The ending of the Cold War also meant the ending of support for proxy wars on the continent, which resulted in the signing of peace agreements and the repatriation of many refugee communities. During the 1990s UNHCR was able to proclaim repatriation as the preferred solution and initiated repatriation programmes to Eritrea, Mozambique, Angola and Namibia. The end of superpower politics meant that there was no longer a justifi-cation for the maintenance of long-term refugee communities. Refugees, no longer potential pawns in the ideological game, could be repatriated irrespective of political change in their countries of origin. *Refoulement* or forced repatriation no longer resulted in international repudiation. More importantly, the anti-asylum stance of most western governments spread globally and, in Africa, manifested in states once renowned for their hospitality, resulting in pernicious anti-refugee discourse.

Black & Koser (1999) question the appropriateness of the international discourse which focused on repatriation and reconstruction as the end to the refugee cycle, noting how the lived realities of refugee communities do not fit with international organizations' conceptualization of home and the role of migrants in reconstruction. If there were any doubts in the minds of African governments as to the legality or appropriateness of repatriation, these were dissipated with the presence of over two million Rwandese refugees in 1994 – some of whom were *génocidaires*. The horrors of the genocide and cholera-related deaths in the makeshift camps precipitated a humanitarian effort of a magnitude unseen in modern times.

The desire to assist the 'victims' resulted in aid agencies establishing temporary camps in neighbouring Zaire and Tanzania and spending some two billion US dollars sustaining the refugees from April 1994 to December 1996. The international media were complicit in the construction of the refugees as 'victims', thus enabling one of the largest funding drives of the decade. As a reflection of the competitive environment that aid agencies found themselves in, one humanitarian worker was quoted as saying that the imperative was to 'be there or die' (JEEAR, 1996: 152). By framing all refugees as victims they, inadvertently, supported those who had committed acts of genocide (Nzongola-Ntalaja, 2002; Terry, 2002).

It was the militarization of the camps and the regional security threat posed by *génocidaires* and members of the ex-Rwandan army *(Forces Armées Rwandaises)* based in the camps that resulted in their closure and the forced repatriation of the refugees (Adelman, 2003). The support by the international community of up to 225,000 *génocidaires* and their families challenged the prevailing assumptions of asylum and security. How could one separate the genuine refugee from combatants? Was there total ignorance of the presence of *génocidaires* or did the economic logic behind the humanitarian imperative overrule issues of ethics? Adelman (2003) suggests the latter, noting that UNHCR had knowledge of the presence of ex-FAR soldiers and *interahamwe* militias in the camps. They received 'arms shipments ... conducted military training exercises, recruited combatants, and planned a "final victory" and solution to Hutu-Tutsi antagonisms' (Adelman, 2003: 104). His argument is that the international agencies, through ignorance, continued to frame the refugees as victims, thus enabling them to regroup in exile, and to pose a threat to long-term peace and stability in the region.

While international humanitarian organizations may have learnt their lessons and have changed course, the consequence of their actions for locals and refugee communities were still evident in the 2000s. The failure to make a distinction between refugees and combatants, even when certain camps were evidently militarized, led to greater antagonism by states and indigenous communities towards refugees, and the criminalization of all, including women and children, as potential rebels.

Burundi Refugees in Tanzania: The *Longue Durée*

As a refugee-receiving as opposed to a refugee-generating state, Tanzania provides a classic opportunity to explore historically the changing approaches to African refugees and the interconnectivity between international aid, donor governments and the national state in the context of global militarism.

African governments, such as Tanzania, who were committed to anti-colonial struggles, provided secure spaces wherein refugee members of liberation movements could operate even when it compromised their own national security. It was this open-door political policy that enabled Rwandan and Burundian refugees, fleeing genocidal violence in post-colonial states, to be welcomed by Tanzanians (Chaulia, 2003; Daley, 1989). The country has been host to two distinct cohorts of predominantly Hutu refugees from Burundi: those who fled after the 1972 genocide (often referred to by international humanitarian agencies as 'old caseload') and those who fled after the murder of Ndadaye in 1993, the intensification of warfare in 1994 and during the *regroupement* exercises from 1997 to 2000.

Estimates of the total refugee population vary by several thousands, with about 200,000 of the old caseload living in purpose-built settlements in Rukwa and Tabora regions and in villages around Kigoma town. The new caseload, at its peak in the year 2000, amounted to an estimated 364,000 and throughout the duration of their asylum remained in holding camps in Kigoma and Kagera regions (Map 5).

The differences in Tanzania's approach to these two cohorts of refugees reflect changes in the global political economy and, correspondingly, in the humanitarian regimes. The 140,000 refugees fleeing the 1972 genocide were welcomed by the Tanzanian authorities, who with international humanitarian assistance, made efforts to minimize the security risk by moving them to a distance of more than 50 miles from the border, and ensured their self-sufficiency by settling them in agricultural settlement schemes with the assumption that they would start a new life in Tanzania and refrain from political action against the Burundi government.

Table 8.1: Estimated Number of Burundian Refugees in Neighbouring Countries, April 2000

Country	Region (s)	Population
Republic of Tanzania	Ngara, Kibondo, Kigoma & Kasulu	340,542
	Rukwa & Tabora	200,000*
Rwanda		1,207
Congo-Brazzaville		
DRC	Kivu	20,000
Zambia		1,164
Angola		150
Malawi		200
Cameroon		270
Total		364,000

*1972 cohort
Source: adapted from the Arusha Peace and Reconciliation Agreement for Burundi, 2000.

In practice, this approach did little to integrate refugees into Tanzanian society. Refugees were settled in isolated tsetse-infested areas in Tabora and Rukwa regions some 200 miles from the border with Burundi. Tanzania's national refugee law required them to live in camps and permits were needed to travel beyond camp boundaries. While as peasants they contributed to an increase in the agricultural productivity of the regions and participated in labour migration to cash-crop producing areas, their possession of the label 'refugee' meant living in extended exile for some 30 years and lacking the rights of citizens such as freedom of movement and access to education and employment outside the settlement (Daley, 1992 & 1993).

International aid enabled the Tanzanian state to develop a model of refugee assistance that was duplicated elsewhere, but conspired to keep the refugee communities in a protracted state of asylum. Humanitarian agencies attributed the persistence of aid to refugees to the presence of the 'dependency syndrome' among the refugee population. This is in contrast to the discourse of the hardworking, industrious refugees, which is used simultaneously to describe Burundi refugees. Furthermore, there are significant qualitative and quantitative differences between the aid requested by settlers and that provided by the donors. The whole process of applying for aid was complex, and was at the discretion of the Tanzanian state. Aid applications had to be approved, processed and formally requested by the Ministry of Home Affairs. In most instances, the Tanzanian state actually lacked this power as the donors autonomously selected their own projects, and sought only final approval from the government.

Tanzania and Refugees in the Post-Cold War Era
The situation of the 1990s post-Cold War cohort of Burundi refugees in Tanzania was markedly different. A number of factors came into play: transformations in global geo-politics dictated a new international refugee order in which asylum was no longer a necessary right, while the emergence of multi-party politics in Tanzania and elsewhere in the region intensified political competition, which, in turn led to the polar-ization of identities and xenophobic and anti-refugee sentiments among host communities, incited by politicians, particularly those from the affected regions.

These factors were compounded and took on resonance with the influx of 500,000 Rwandan refugees, militias and ex-FAR after the 1994 genocide. Some 500,000 Barundi refugees fled to Tanzania after the overthrow of the democratically-elected government in October 1993 and further influxes occurred in 1994 and 1996 with the intensification of the violence. Throughout the remainder of the 1990s and in 2000s protracted warfare ensured a steady flow of refugees into Western Tanzania. Holding camps were established for Burundian and Rwandan refugees in Kagera and Kigoma regions (Map 5). As with previous camps, humanitarian relief was coordinated by the Ministry of Home Affairs and UNHCR and implemented by predominantly international relief agencies. Despite the Tanzanian camps being better run than their Zairean counterparts, the issue of security was paramount.

Elements of the genocidal Rwandan army and the Hutu militias also fled to western Tanzania leading to a proliferation of arms in the region and producing a climate of insecurity. Refugees were accused of banditry, rape, murder, theft and of causing food shortages and environmental degradation (*Daily News*, 3.8.1994).[6] The Tanzanian state took several steps to resolve this problem. First, it closed its borders, supposedly, according to one UNHCR official 'with a humanitarian face'. The border closure was in name only, in reality it was an impossible task, since the state lacked the capacity to patrol the vast territory. Second, it requested international assistance to help disarm the refugees, but this request occurred at a time when many western governments were unwilling to lose personnel in African warfare (*Daily News*, 20.3.1996). When help

---

[6] 'Rwandese refugees bring water and soil erosion', *Daily News*, 3 August 1994.

was unforthcoming, the government embarked on a strategy of forced repatriation.

Host Government Fatigue and Repatriation of Refugees
Despite being signatory to international refugee law, the Tanzanian state has always exercised its sovereign right to deny entry by closing its borders with refugee-producing countries or repatriate forcibly refugees from its territory. For many years, the protracted nature of warfare in Rwanda and Burundi forestalled any mass voluntary repatriation programmes, despite periodic surveys conducted to determine refugee willingness for repatriation.

Therefore, at the sign of any stability in Burundi, Tanzanian officials have sought to pursue repatriation. International optimism during the democratization process of the early 1990s led to refugees being encouraged to return home voluntarily, and UNHCR assisted in a programme of repatriation and rehabilitation. The ensuing and protracted warfare that followed hardened rather than soften Tanzania's stance with regards to repatriation and the government declared 1996 as the year of voluntary repatriation (*Daily News*, 24.5.1996). A position Jakaya Kikwete, the foreign minister, confirmed when in March 1996 he was reported to have declared that 'the attitude of Tanzania is slightly different from what it was in 1965, 1969, 1972 and 1987.' This he attributed to 'increasing crime, negative environmental impact and pressure on services' caused by refugees.[7]

After failing to get international support to disarm the refugees amidst internal pressure for greater security, Tanzania forcibly repatriated over 500,000 Rwandan Hutu refugees in December 1996, after they had spent almost two years in the country. A UNHCR representative described it as 'a purely military operation that took less than two weeks'.[8] Police and the military used UNHCR-sponsored vehicles to ferry people to the Rwandan border. Humanitarian agencies were complicit in the repatriation exercise. UNHCR signed a memorandum of understanding to repatriate all the refugees, and the Tanzanian government had the support of donors, unwilling to support refugees in extended exile (Whitaker, 2002). After the departure of the refugees, western donors pledged some $25 million for the rehabilitation of Kigoma region. While forced repatriation largely solved the Rwandan refugee problem, the government was unwilling to conduct a similar exercise for the Burundians. Instead, numerous agreements were reached with successive Burundi governments to allow repatriation. When surveyed, refugees predominantly cited the lack of security in Burundi as the primary factor in their unwillingness to return. To counter this claim, UNHCR often stated that refugees were being sent home to only regions considered to be safe.

Notwithstanding its renowned humanitarian credentials, Tanzania has a long history of forcibly repatriating individual refugees (*refoulement*).[9]

---

[7] *Daily News*, 'Kikwete restates Tanzania's stance on refugees', 2 March 1996.
[8] Interview with UNHCR official, Dar es Salaam, 1997.
[9] In April 1987, the Tanzanian government forcedly repatriated Barundi refugees living in Kigoma region, on the basis that they were economic migrants not refugees (*Daily News*, 6 April 1987).

Throughout the period of warfare in Burundi, human rights groups reported the *refoulement* of Burundi refugees by the Tanzanian government. From February to May 2000, Tanzania repatriated 80 Rwandese and 580 Burundians living in Biharamulo and Ngara districts, some of whom have been in the country since 1960 and 1972 (AI, 2000). In 2002, President Mkapa called for the setting up of 'safe havens' in Burundi.[10] During this period, returnees faced persecution and even death on their return to Burundi. Many were accused by the army, militias or member of the local communities as belonging to rebel groups and of committing genocide. One refugee told the United States Committee for Refugees (USCR, 1993: 22), 'The UNHCR should not have sent us to be massacred.' Forced repatriation by the Tanzanian government, with the tacit approval of UNHCR, violates the basic law under which refugees' rights are supposedly safeguarded, and highlights the acceptance of western donors of the undemocratic practices of the Burundi state.

Changing Refugee Legislation in Tanzania

Another strategy adopted by the Tanzanian state was to introduce new legislation. Until the beginning of the 1990s, Tanzania's Refugee (Control) Act (1966) – an amalgam of earlier colonial laws – was oriented towards controlling alien populations. It was relatively effective in the context of a strong state and concerted regional effort to contain refugee activities. In November 1986, at a summit meeting in Kigali, the leaders of Tanzania, Kenya, Burundi, Zaire, Uganda, Sudan and Rwanda, agreed to create border buffer zones separating refugees from their countries of origin, to disarm and to prohibit them from forming military units (*Daily News*, 29 November 1986). Tanzanian legislation made it illegal for refugees to live outside their specific settlements without a permit and camps were normally run by a military commandant.

The events of the 1990s and the weakening of the central state, the result of economic crises, multi-party democratization and over a million refugees led to the formulation of new legislation with a strong security component. The new Refugee Act (1998) which came into force in February 1999 reinforced the state's dependence on the United Nations and introduced measures for individual as opposed to group recognition of asylum status (RoT, 1998). Overall, according to Kamanga (2001), the Act will lead to greater covert rather than overt control of refugee movements. Kamanga (2001: 14) writes, 'The Act eschews explicit reference to neither 'local integration' or a refugee's right to seek naturalization and has confined itself to acknowledging only the other two known durable solutions, that is to say, repatriation and settlement.' Among the objectives of the 1998 Act, he claims, were the need:

> a) ... to signal disengagement from the open door policy of the Nyerere administration with a view to making Tanzania a less 'attractive' destination for asylum seekers hand in hand with sending a deterrent message to wilful authorities in particular refugee-generating countries; b) to convey to

---

[10] Tanzanian *Guardian*, 'Refugees unbearable burden to Tanzania, Mpaka tells diplomats', 11 January 2002 by Peter Tindwa.

the international community disenchantment with the international humanitarian assistance delivery system for being not sufficiently troubled by the impact of refugees on poor fragile Tanzania; c) to assure the populace that the government is determined to address the 'problem' of seemingly endless refugee influxes that are a direct cause of insecurity, environmental degradation, unemployment, moral decadence and electoral tensions. (Kamanga, 2001: 22)

Interpretations of the act varied with local government authorities, who had considerable discretion. For example, the military authorities in Kagera region ordered all refugees to go to camps or face six months imprisonment (AI, 2000). Similarly, the Kibondo district commissioner restricted refugee movement to a four kilometre radius around the camps (*Refugees International*, 2004). Local Tanzanian militias (*Sungu Sungu*) perceived this policy as an opportunity to strip refugees of their material goods. There was often no discrimination made between old caseload refugees and the post-1990 arrivals. Many of the former were forcibly moved to camps, losing livelihoods and property, and were separated from their families (HRW, 1999b).

The final strategy of the Tanzanians was to pursue a peace initiative (Chapter 9). Convinced that the Burundi problem 'was political and not humanitarian', the ruling party, *Chama Cha Mapinduzi* (CCM), incorporated a commitment in its 1995 election manifesto (para. 36) to seek solutions to the Burundi and Rwanda refugee issues. Since the early 1990s, most political parties, when campaigning in the western region, used repatriation as part of their electioneering rhetoric.

The Arusha Peace and Reconciliation Agreement for Burundi of 2000 specified the conditions under which refugees should be returned to the country. Protocol IV of the Agreement called for the establishment of a specific agency, the National Commission for the Rehabilitation of *Sinistrés* (CNRS), which would, with the assistance of UNHCR and NGOs, 'ensure the social and economic re-integration' of the returnees, to include 'food aid, material support and assistance with health, education, agriculture and reconstruction until they are sufficient'. The Protocol also required the establishment of a Land Commission to help refugees to either recover their land and property or be given compensation, and to settle disputes and ensure equity and transparency in redistribution. The Transitional Government in Burundi established the CNRS in March 2003, but it was subsumed under the Ministry for the Reintegration and Rehabilitation of Displaced Peoples and Refugees, without the power envisaged in the peace agreement (ICG, 2003b).

On 8 May 2001, a tripartite agreement was signed between the governments of Tanzania, Burundi and UNHCR to put in place a programme for the repatriation of refugees. Visits were made by Burundian and Tanzanian ministers to the camps to exert pressure on the refugees to repatriate. At the end of the year less than half the refugees had registered for repatriation (ICG, 2003b). A survey by UNHCR in December 2002, estimated that 370, 861 Burundi refugees were still residing in camps in Western Tanzania (UNHCR, Tanzania, 2002). An estimated 250,000 returned after 2002, many returning to northern and north-eastern provinces. In 2004, UNHCR devised a four-year plan for the repatriation of the refugees (120–150,000 in 2004; 200,000 in 2005; 100,000 in 2006 & 50,000 in 2007) and requested a budget of US $60–85 million for their return and reintegration.[11] Refugees, caught between a rock and a hard place, resigned themselves to repatriation.

> I am going home because I don't know what else to do. I used to go to the bush for wood and sell it to make some money. Nowadays we are restricted. If we are caught outside, we are forced back to our country. The thing I was doing to make a living has been taken away from me. (Burundi Refugee, Ngara district, Tanzania, quoted in IRIN *Special Report on Returning Burundi Refugees*, 8 May 2002)

> I will go back to Burundi, because the government of Tanzania is insisting that no-one stays here. (Refugee Woman, Ngara district, Tanzania, quoted in *IRIN Special Report on Returning Burundi Refugees*, 8 May 2002)

Despite the peace agreement, refugees continue to flee from Burundi, claiming insecurity, harassment by rebel groups and political parties as the reasons for flight. In 2002, an estimated 29,000 refugees entered Tanzania. A process of 'recyling' existed throughout the period 1991 to 2005. ICG (1999b: 10) found that, 'most of the recyclers … returned because they found their local *collines* too dangerous or difficult, particularly if their houses had been destroyed, their land seized, or if they have been accused of colluding with rebels.' In 2004, the Burundi refugee population in neighbouring states was estimated at about 777,000, with 400,000 (including the 1972 cohort) in Tanzania (UNHCR, 2004 & 2005). Between 2001 and 2005, an estimated 285,000 returned to Burundi, with border provinces such as Ruyigi receiving the largest number (UNHCR, 2004 & 2005).

The issue of access to land or return of property is of critical importance both for refugees and those internally displaced. Many returning to their home areas have found their land reallocated or in use by others, most of whom are reluctant to give up occupancy. This situation was more acute for those refugees who fled in 1972. As Amnesty International (2005: 44) notes, 'A number of returnees have faced threats, violence or imprisonment when they attempted to reclaim their land.' Kamungi *et al.* (2004) note the difficult disputes that refugees and displaced people encounter when trying to acquire land and the fact that land left unoccupied has been reallocated by the government to businessmen and members of the politico-military oligarchy. Oketch claims that the Land Commission established in April 2003, was a battleground between the various political groupings seeking to control its resources.

> The huge financial outlay for the Commission's programme is the target of politicians who seek to benefit from contacts and therefore the activities of the Commission are likely to be further politicized to the detriment of IDPs and refugees. (Oketch, 2004: 28)

[11] UNHCR Draft operation plan for the Repatriation and Reintegration of Burundian Refugees, Bujumbura, February 2004, cited in Oketch, 2004).

Returnees, without access to land, were forced to reside in camps for the internally displaced; in 2004, over 196 households were affected (AI, 2005). Female-headed households, estimated to constitute about 44 per cent of households in the displaced camps, were particularly vulnerable (Kamungi *et al.*, 2004). Their access to land was restricted by gender biases in succession laws and in the communities.

Global Humanitarianism, Victimization and Militarism in Refugee Communities

Although the Tanzanian state is able to exert its authority when dealing with refugees, it is less powerful in relation to international humanitarian organizations. During the Cold War, the government was compelled to participate in tripartite agreements with UNHCR and an international NGO, namely the Tanganyika Christian Refugee Council – the local agent of the Lutheran World Federation. From the 1960s, a premise was established whereby external aid was considered fundamental to the success of any refugee programme. The distribution of responsibilities was such that the government was required to provide the land, an officer to take charge of the security of the settlement/camps (army officer), the NGOs role was to register refugees and provide the staff plus, food, medical, educational and other social services. UNHCR arranged for the movement of refugees, financed the project and liaised with the providers. Within this arrangement was a hierarchy of roles, which led to an undemocratic structure of refugee assistance with a hierarchy of subordinate relationships in the order of donors, NGOs, State and refugees. From the time the refugees entered the humanitarian umbrella, they entered a dependent relationship with little or no control over the forces of their own social reproduction.

The practice of encampment, with its restrictions on mobility, on farming outside the camps and food rationing involved clearly defined hierarchical authority and power structures. The refugee experienced what Rodney (1972: 30) describes as a psychological crisis whereby 'the African himself has doubts about his capacity to transform and develop his natural environment.' A situation of dependency is created where the refugee's very existence is dependent on the presence of humanitarian action in the camps, to such an extent that governments and agencies can decide when to reduce food rations as an inducement for repatriation. However, for entrepreneurial agencies, the dependency is two-way. After the departure of the Rwandans in 1996, UNHCR began a process of aid rationalization, which meant closing some camps and projects. This was considered a 'very painful exercise for NGOs ... many did not want to give up'.[12]

Viewed as a homogenous mass from the 1960s to the 1990s, little or no account was taken of the differences among refugees, whether regional, social or gender. Only their ethnic identities, the presumed cause of flight, were singled out. Refugees were victims on whom 'aid was

---

[12] Interview with UNHCR representative, Dar es Salaam, 1998.

imposed' (Harrell-Bond, 1985). Control over the material and social aspects of refugee well-being became the preserve of donors. By the 1990s, sustained criticisms of the practices of humanitarian organizations in various refugee contexts led to more nuanced and differentiated approaches, particularly recognition of the significance of gender in determining the livelihood chances of households (Turner, 2004).

Women and children constitute some 60 to 75 per cent of most displaced and refugee populations. As vulnerable social categories, they occupy special moral spaces in global humanitarian law and policy frameworks. Special programmes are designed specifically to target them.[13] Gender mainstreaming, for example, requires camp design to take account of the gendered use of space, such as location of water points and washing areas to minimize sexual violence against women (Oxfam, 2002a). These programmes have implications for how the patriarchal host state and the marginalized masculinity of men in the refugee camps perceive refugee women and children.

Evidentially, marginalized masculinity in Africa feels beleaguered by the mainstreaming of gender issues in development policy and humanitarian aid. HRW (2000a) found that the targeting of women by aid organizations created resentment among men, who used domestic and sexual violence as a means of asserting their masculinity. Turner (2004) also reports that patriarchal relations and the structure of the family unit were presumed by men to be under threat in the camps. Reflecting the men's sentiments, he reports: 'when the men can no longer provide for their wives, these women consider UNHCR or the "white man to be a better husband" and don't respect the men as they used to or ought to do' (Turner, 2004: 94). Women were still vulnerable, even under the protection of UN agencies.

Gender struggles may partly explain why neither the refugee men, nor the Tanzanian authorities took violence against women seriously. In the *Bashingantahe* (community) courts, accused men would normally pay compensation to the victim's family; which could be as minor as a piece of cloth (*khanga*) or a goat. Rutinwa (2005) notes that pregnant women were often required to pay compensation to their husbands, if they were unable to identify the perpetrator. A Tanzanian judge was reported to have acquitted ten Tanzanian men who were alleged to have raped 24 Burundian women and girls, because the prosecutor was 75 minutes late (AI, 2000).

Moreover, a UNHCR study of domestic violence and food rationing in camps in Tanzania between March 2004 and June 2005 found a positive correlation between increases in violence and food rationing.[14] The period of ration cut, October 2004 to June 2005, when rations were reduced from 1,857 Kcal. to 1,252 Kcal., saw just over a 100 per cent rise in domestic violence.[15] According to UNHCR, the ration remained below the minimum needed for a healthy living (2,100 Kcal.):

[13] See UNHCR, *Guidelines for the Protection of Refugee Women*, Geneva, July 1991 enabling the establishment of Women's Crisis Centres and Drop in Centres. Some camps have child care protection units, with Children Committees and a Children's Parliament.

[14] UNHCR Tanzania, Monthly Updates, 2005.

[15] See UNHCR, Tanzania, *Refugee Situation Update*, July 2005.

> Shortage of food and non-food items [clothing, water buckets, sanitary towels] at the time when refugees are restricted from engaging in food production and income generation outside [the] camps has multiple adverse impacts on protection including affecting the nutritional status of refugees, compelling some of them to engage in criminal activities in order to make ends meet and exposing women to sexual exploitation. (Rutinwa, 2005: 45, Para. 217)

This provision of inadequate food and its gendered consequences, in the context of limited employment or livelihood activities, seems at variance with the prevailing rights-based discourse of humanitarian agencies. Human rights discourse, focusing on the individualized experience of women, children and the elderly can, in conditions of crisis, lead to an atomization of communities. This may be a good thing when communities are led by *génocidaires*, but, as shown in western Tanzania, international agencies cannot provide for all the needs of refugees, who often have to fall back on kinship ties and social networks.

Refugee Militarism

There is overwhelming evidence that refugee communities have become increasingly militarized, especially after 1996 and the start of the war in the Congo. The proliferation of weapons in the hands of non-state actors has speeded up the processes of militarization in communities. This has implications for the nature of violence not just in home communities but also in those of the internally displaced and refugees. An Oxfam report (2002a: 13), on protection in the camps, notes the high incidence of rape, sexual harassment and murder; the latter was often 'linked to political disagreements, criminal activity and domestic or business disputes'. The rampant violence and criminal activities reported in ethnically homogenous refugee communities that were under the protection of international agencies, signalled a more generalized international acceptance of a lower standard of African well being and the culture of impunity prevalent in the region.

Displacement and prolonged encampment may lead to unintended results. Liisa Malkki's (1995) fieldwork among 'old caseload' Burundian Hutu refugees highlights how the process of displacement produces particular mythico-historical narratives of violence and victimhood that contribute to the dehumanization of both Hutu and Tutsi. Recounting the episodes of violence depicted by the refugees, she remarks:

> These accounts together documented a process of profound dehumanization of the Hutu as a people, of their objectification as something less than human and 'natural'. However, simultaneously, as these events and techniques were being described in the mythico-history by the refugees themselves, the dehumanizing gaze was necessarily turned against those who were considered to have produced and deployed the techniques of human destruction described. Thus, it was not specific individual perpe-

trators, but 'the Tutsi' as a homogeneous category that had created the violence, perversity and defilement. (Malkki, 1995: 93)

Malkki's research shows how militaristic ideology can be used to mobilize and promote solidarity among victimised groups. Constructions of the violent 'other' acted as a mechanism for empowering Hutus in the demasculinizing, disempowering contexts of camps, enabling the creation of militarized communities where wars and memories of violence are relived. These give impetus to the formation of exile political parties and guerrilla armies, with the explicit goal of using force to return to their homeland. Such disaffected communities, forced to remain in camps, can provide fertile ground for the recruitment of combatants.

In war and post-war societies, international aid has a wealth-generating dynamic of its own. It has helped inadvertently to sustain regimes of violence in Africa. In Burundi, state policy of *regroupement* (Chapter 6), drew on the knowledge that international humanitarian organization would not allow the encamped population to starve. Humanitarian provisioning then became part of the genocidal strategy of the Burundi state. In the province of Bujumbura Rurale alone, more than 15 NGOs provided assistance to over 300,000 people regrouped by the government on 52 sites (OCHA, 1999). A study by the US Committee for Refugees found that the military had 'profited from [an] inflated food distribution list' (USCR, 1998: 41).

In devastated economies, the arrival of humanitarian aid can often stimulate illegal and legal networks of service provisioning and consumer markets. Aid provides cover for the trans-border movements of illicit consumer goods and weaponry. In some countries, where the formal economy has been virtually extinguished, foreign aid enables a rapacious political elite to accrue wealth in the early post-war period.

Conclusion

African refugees became a 'problem' in the era of the Cold War and in a period when attempts were being made to build nation-states on the continent. Refugees became caught up in the discourse of sovereignty as expounded by states and multilateral institutions and that of victimhood as propounded by humanitarian agencies. As shown by my examination of the plight of Burundi refugees in Western Tanzania this was not coincidental.

Refugees' experience in exile simultaneously reinforces and threatens the territorial logic on which the international community is based. This is most evident in the impact of geopolitics on refugee communities. Cold War geopolitics produced a particular refugee regime, which was no longer necessary once the communist threat had disappeared. Through its refugee population, Tanzania became affected by the intensification of the processes of militarization in Burundi and in the region. Its inability to cope, in the 1990s, reflects not just the magnitude of the refugee communities, but also the declining power of the central state under multi-party politics and electoral democracy.

Refugees, already isolated through encampment, occupied an ambiguous position. While the state courted international favour and financial resources through their presence, its policies and practices towards them became increasingly draconian. Tanzanian authorities appear to want refugees only if the international community can support them in perpetuity; this seems to be a major factor in the state's reluctance to integrate refugees into local communities. With the ending of the Cold War, African refugees rank even lower in western priorities and aid transfers have shown a downward trend. Consequently, the international community's unwillingness to meet the financial conditions set by the Tanzania state will lead to the situation of refugees becoming more precarious. The Tanzanian state, powerless in the context of neo-liberal humanitarianism, embarked on exacting its revenge on the beneficiaries of humanitarian assistance.

To sum up, humanitarian action has created a population whose rights are international, as neither the host state nor the home state has sought to extend and protect the rights of asylum or of citizenship. I have to concur with Soguk, when he notes that:

> [The] refugee problematizations affirm and privilege the postulated hierarchy of citizen/nation/state constellation by conditioning and limiting the possibilities of actions and their meanings as to who is a citizen or who is a refugee or what the boundaries of sovereign statehood are or should be. (Soguk, 1999: 18)

The presence of international aid affirms this hierarchy and undermines the possibilities of an emerging social contract between states and refugees. Aid, deployed largely independent of states, is filtered through equally salient networks and hierarchies of power. Neo-liberal humanitarian agencies' excursion into politics and development challenges African peoples' right to be part of a broader political community and to play a role in determining the course of history.

9

Challenging Genocide Local, Regional & International Peace Initiatives

Introduction

> The conception of peace that dominates in the world is more like peace brought from without. It's a peace that responds to the demands of those who threaten peace, not the demands of the victims. So it ended up saying, look, we must satisfy the actors, those who may resume or want to continue the war. If they stop fighting, the victims also benefit because there is no war, but the victims are not necessarily the starting point in terms of what kind of peace we want.[1] (Wamba dia Wamba, 2004)

Wamba dia Wamba is not alone in articulating the imposition on Africans of western conceptualization of peace. Like development theory, peace theory and its application in Africa is largely determined by the prevailing international power relations and policy framework. Steans (1998: 106/7) points out that in classical realist thought the concept of peace was essentially 'negative peace' as peace and security were seen as attainable by 'shifting alliances which preserved a balance of power among states'. In neo-realist thought, she continues, 'Hegemonic states dominate international institutions and, in this way, 'manage' international security, [assuming that] the security of one state is closely, inextricably even, linked with the security of other states.' Neo-realism dominates contemporary approach to international peace-keeping. Since the Second World War, the United Nations has established international norms governing the establishment of peace and stability, which, in practice, means different things in hegemonic and weak states. Westerners' perception of threats to global peace varies historically; for example, during the Cold War it was nuclear proliferation, then, after 11 September 2001, 'terrorists'.

Throughout much of Africa's modern history, European conceptions of peace have predominated and were an integral part of the regime of violence that came with colonial rule. In Chapter 2, I discussed how violence against natives, often carried out by representatives of the colonial state, was brutal in the extreme, sometimes involving the wholesale destruction of communities, especially at the point of conquest when the colonial state pacified rebellious groups or enemies. Pacification

---

[1] Ernest Wamba dia Wamba, Conversation with History Interview with Harry Kreisler, UC Berkeley, Institute of International Studies, 17 March 2004.

was often constituted as a violent act, whereby, through violence, the powerful could instil fear as a means of domination. For many Africans, the externally imposed peace that came with pacification meant the loss of control over territory and the subjugation of the people to foreign rule. The nation-state idea, which emanated from Europe, embodies within it its own vision of peace which emphasizes racial and cultural homogeneity as a prerequisite for a peaceful society. Consequently, political and social mechanisms to deal with diversity are underdeveloped theoretically. This vacuum has led to the dominance of models of the state that rest upon supposedly normative practices of discrimination.

In Africa, peace and stability have not necessarily implied the absence of direct and structural violence. Violence on the continent of Africa, including proxy wars during the Cold War, helped to maintain the peace in Europe and North America. A stable state implied the dominance of a militaristic state, using force to repress popular demands for representation and improved well-being. The West represented this concept of peace in Africa as peculiar to African politics. Emmanuel Hansen (1987) entreats Africans to reject a position on peace that sees peace as the peace of Europe and North America, replacing it with an 'African perspective', which is concerned not only with 'the resolution of conflicts [but with] the transformation of the extant social systems at both national and international levels'. For Africans, therefore, peace should be conceptualized as 'a certain minimum condition of security, economic welfare, political efficacy and psychic well being' (Hansen, 1987: 7). Hansen's proposal of an African perspective on peace is similar to those of feminist and peace theorists who seek alternatives that have far-reaching social and political consequences than those advocated by normative models.

This chapter demonstrates how the Burundi peace negotiations (1996–2000) and the ceasefire negotiations and political settlement, whilst portrayed as a regional initiative, have been informed by the Eurocentric and masculinized concepts of national security and peace. It begins with a discussion of the region's experience with conflict resolution, followed by an exploration of how a feminist conceptualization of peace can help us understand the peace that has been promoted in Africa. The chapter then focuses on the emergence of a regional thrust for peace in Burundi through the interventions of Julius Nyerere, Yoweri Museveni, Benjamin Mkapa and Nelson Mandela, their efforts to get participants to the talks and the issues that stalled the talks. The contributions of a multiplicity of actors to the peace process are examined: the political parties, western donors, multilateral organizations, peace consultants, international NGOs and civil society organizations, especially Burundi women, in light of UN Security Council Resolution 1325. The chapter concludes with a discussion of the contradictory role played by external donors and international actors in the peace process.

International Conflict Resolution in Africa

Prevailing conflict resolution models adopt the minimalist interpretation of peace. They have tended to be formulaic and applied universally.

Implicit in these models are interpretations of the causes of conflicts. Not only has the ending of the Cold War affected how we perceive peace, but also our understanding of the nature of warfare. In the case of warfare in the Great Lakes region of Africa, conflict models tend to retraditionalize wars by employing the popular discourse that represents wars as essentially tribal, often arising from age-old enmities, or entrenched inequalities based on ethnicity, race or religion. Even when the interpretation attempts to avoid ethnic reductionism, it does so by linking ethnicity with simplistic arguments about greed and grievance harboured by conflicting parties (Chapter 1). Another viewpoint represents war in the post-Cold War period as 'new'; non-ideological and fuelled by the avariciousness of patrons or 'warlords', aiming to capture state resources for private gain. While the causes of the conflict and the nature of reforms are sometimes debated, the solutions appear fixed. They address issues of political reform by way of power sharing between warring factions, with the intention of instituting liberal democracy as well as economic and social reforms.

Power-sharing has become a popular post-Cold War solution to the problem of multi-ethnicity and other forms of difference in Africa (Spears, 2000 & 2002; Tull & Mehler, 2005). Power-sharing often means dividing the transitional institutions of governance between political parties and rebel movements to be followed at a specified period with a new constitution and democratic elections. This peace trajectory includes the establishment of a broad-based transitional government made up of different political parties, the reform of the national security apparatus to include the demobilisation of rebel armies and militias and the creation of a truly national army; the repatriation of refugees and the resettlement of displaced people, coupled with measures to kick-start the economy. But, in practice, power-sharing does not lead to any radical changes in the nature of the state and may encourage the 'insurgent violence' (Tull & Mehler, 2005). This is why Mafege's (1995) assertions that the liberal concept of conflict resolution by power sharing only serves to regularize the established set-up, leaving the contradictions within the society unresolved.

The notion of post-war reconstruction which includes reconciliation and demilitarization has become part of the policy framework for conflict resolution. In the last two decades, the global dominance of neo-liberalism, its political prescriptions and free market economic models have limited the discussion of alternative frameworks for peace and reconstruction. The latter implies a return to a state of security and stability, which, from a national security perspective, requires the reformalization of state monopoly on violence. Thus, peace-building projects prioritize the security as opposed to the political and gendered aspects of demilitarization and reconstruction.

Reconstruction is thus a problematic term; back to what one might ask? It may have resonance where social/economic breakdown has been dramatic and the freedoms enjoyed prior to conflict can be reinstituted. Unfortunately, the political and economic realities in Africa suggest that transformation not reconstruction is necessary for long-term peace and stability. Yet the individualism of market liberalism is promoted as the natural order of things, as opposed to the kind of redistributive justice needed to sustain 'positive' peace.

In the post-Cold War neo-liberal era, two further significant changes can be noted in relation to conflict resolution; the proliferation of non-state organizations and individuals involved in mediation and the inclusion among the protagonist of a multiplicity of non-state actors. Clapham (1998: 205), writing on the Rwanda peace negotiations of the early 1990s points out that any protagonist 'who could muster evident support now had to be admitted to ... on terms of broad equality with existing regimes' and were given a status 'that only very inadequately reflected their popular support or military strength'. Invariably, establishing political parties and rebel movements guarantees access to political power. These developments have had considerable implications for the nature of the peace deal.

Humanitarianism in the neo-liberal era encompasses a more interventionist role in peace making and peace building for a range of regional and international actors, turning peace into a veritable industry. Multilateral and regional organizations, such as the African Union, have set up organizational arms focusing on peace. Many western governments have peace initiatives outside of the UN and AU peace process, trying to broker deals that will increase their influence with the post-conflict regimes. Furthermore, the dominance of neo-liberal ideas in reconstruction has led to increasing attempts to involve the private sector (security firms and multinational corporations) in the drawing up of blueprints for post-war societies (Chapter 7).[2]

Similarly, international, regional and local NGOs have been active in formulating and promoting peace initiatives. The nature of the peace problematic is such that the motivations of individual actors beg investigation. Evidence from Central Africa suggests that they do not necessarily share a common understanding of the complex dynamics of the violence and, although, the solutions appear universal, they often seek to champion particular individuals or groups, and even enter the process for their own vested interest. Consequently, the proliferation of mediators seems to protract warfare rather than lead to swift resolutions. Clapham's (1998: 209) conclusion in relation to Rwanda is worth noting here.

> The mediators are not merely bystanders to the conflict which they are attempting to resolve, but participants, whose involvement weakens or strengthens the position of different internal parties, and may indeed even strengthen the position of those domestic factions which are most adamantly opposed to the negotiated settlement which the mediators are attempting to bring about. (Clapham 1998: 209)

Conflict resolution models can contain inflated assumptions about the commitment of the belligerents to the peace process. Explanations for the failure of peace agreements point to the lack of political will on the part

---

[2] The energy multinational, Bechtel Corporation, has drawn up its own reconstruction package for the Congo. See Bechtel Corporation, 1997, *An Approach to National Development in the Democratic Republic of Congo.*

of the signatories. It is argued that the 'spoilers' see war as more profitable than peace. Even among those who do not opt to pursue violence as a means of gaining political advantage, there is a reluctant acceptance of electoral democracy as a means of determining political composition of governments. With the advent of power-sharing as opposed to winner-takes-all elections, many parties prefer to gain political advantage through negotiations before committing themselves to the electorate.

Implicit in contemporary conflict resolution models is a perception of African societies that denies agency to African people. In spite of the accommodation of a multiplicity of actors, they still fail to envisage the masses as belonging to the political community. They find no role for the people except as victims of rapacious elites and warlords. In such scenarios, the victims become the responsibility of humanitarian agencies and politics the sole preserve of representatives of political parties. If one argues that popular participation in politics is universally desirable, and that the electoral democracy of western liberal society is unable to deliver the political commitment from belligerents as well as the social transformation that is required for sustained peace, then we need to consider ways of incorporating the body politic into the peace process.

Engendering Peace in Africa

To feminists, the ending of direct violence can only come about through the use of progressive definitions of peace that advocate radical transformations in society. Peace in realist approaches refers to the reassertion of the patriarchal state. Sexual violence in warfare reflects peace time perception of women's role in society. The marginalization of women from politics within the modern liberal state signifies politics as an exclusively male sphere of activity, despite the incorporation of women as 'fighters' during war time.

In Chapter 2, I considered the significance of the interconnectedness between the concept of national security and women's subordination. A militarized interpretation of national security has implications for the well-being of citizens and may further the bureaucratization of violence. A system in which national security and maintaining the peace necessitates the formalization of violence, the concept of peace then becomes a militarized one. A militarized peace has become hegemonic in the international system and, as we have seen in Chapter 7, it is almost forced by western governments on many African countries.

At the turn of the twenty-first century, international discourse altered to incorporate women as agents of peace and to mainstream principles of gender equality into international peace-keeping (Chinkin, 2003). This new policy framework is reflected in UN Security Council Resolution 1325 (2000), which gives emphasis to gender-based violence and the role of women in peace-keeping. It urges states to end impunity and to prosecute those responsible for sexual violence and other forms of violence against women and girls. Resolution 1325 has enabled UN agencies to support African women's organizations already mobilizing for peace in Burundi and in the Congo (Burke *et al.*, 2001; Puechguirbal, 2003).

The diverse war experience of Burundian women exemplifies the danger of essentializing women. Equally, their interpretation of peace may also be quite differentiated. Blanchard's (2003: 1290) suggestion that 'the identification of women with peace be balanced by recognition of the participation, support and inspiration women have given to war making', is worth much consideration. There is evidence of African women having been active participants in genocidal violence in Rwanda and to a lesser extent Burundi. African Rights (1995: 2) documents how Hutu women in Rwanda identified the people to be killed. Educated women, who held government positions, bore 'a special responsibility for the breadth and depth of women's participation in the killings'. Women parliamentarians, councillors and mayors were willing to order the killing of Tutsi girls and the Tutsi children of Hutu women married to Tutsi men.

> Léoncie went looking for lists and communal documents to enable her to draw up an exhaustive list of people to kill. She was therefore able to identify Hutu women who had married Tutsis and had children with them. The first time the two women put out the order to kill Tutsis girls, descendants of Hutu mothers, it was applied in certain cellules like Ndora and Uruyange. (African Rights, 1995: 38)

After the genocide, Hutu women took 'advantage of the blanket cover of their 'innocence' to return to Rwanda and 'provide information to their men folk on their reconnaissance visits' (African Rights, 1995: 3). Despite the popularity of the discourse on African women as victims in wartime, there is widespread evidence to suggest that some women were able to take on very proactive roles, as fighters and community leaders. As Peuchguirbal (2003: 1274) notes, 'war provided Congolese women with opportunities as well as burdens. They took up leadership positions and revived local networks. They were not mere victims as they fought for their survival'. In the absence of men, war can liberate women from the patriarchal straitjacket.

African women's campaign for greater participation in the peace process has tended to perpetuate essentialist notions of women as natural peace-makers, claiming, as Diop (2002: 143) does, that 'women are better equipped than men to prevent or resolve conflicts' because they 'are excessively affected by war and should be playing a fundamental role in reconciliation, reconstruction and rehabilitation', thereby implying that women possess some innate suitability for peace negotiations. The Kigali Plan of Action of 1997 calls for recognition of women's traditional peace-making roles and their rights to equal involvement in all peace initiatives including early warning mechanisms and swift responses at national and international levels.[3] Women's involvement in peace-keeping is long overdue, but from what perspective? African feminist scholars have criticised the disempowering role of elite women who have been coopted

---

[3] Kigali Declaration on Peace was adopted by A Pan-African Conference on Peace, Gender and Development on 3 March 1997, organized by the Government of Rwanda, ECA and the Organization of African Unity (OAU), development and gender equality.

into militarized institutions.[4] Accepting women's uncritical involvement in peace-making may not produce transformative results. Although it may go some way to breaking down the norm that politics is a masculine sphere, and may counter, De Waal's (2002: 103) scepticism of African women playing a significant role in peace-making, because, he claims, 'peace is made between those who control armed forces' and women don't 'have the power to deliver it'.

Giving space to gender equality in peace-making and post-war reconstruction can help to kick-start some of the changes necessary to tackle violence across the spectrum. However, more profound and lasting transformation requires an emancipatory feminist perspective on the causes of violent conflict and the conditions for peace. As we have seen, wars expose the false dichotomy between the public and the private, and force women and their interests into the spotlight. Peace and de-militarization, in feminist theory, necessitates concomitant transformation in the socio-economic system that promotes different forms of state/society relationships and alternative forms of masculinity. Women have the capacity to articulate a post-war society that gives prominence to the well-being of all 'African people', challenging the dehumanizing violence that people have been socialized into accepting as the norm and spearheading the incorporation of the voices of the dispossessed and disenfranchised.

International Peace-Making in the Central African Region

International regional organizations have acted as brokers of peace within Africa with varying degrees of success. It is almost a dictum that external intervention to resolve internal conflicts in African states can be interpreted as 'too little too late'. Observers, in assessing the relative ineffectiveness of modern, in particular, Cold War, peacemaking tend to point to three main causations; first that the principles in the Organization of African Unity's Charter of non-interference in the internal affairs of member states and respect for their territorial integrity partly accounted for the foot-dragging that preceded most peace initiatives. However, the genocidal events of the 1990s spurred the OAU to introduce its *Mechanism for Conflict Prevention, Management and Resolution* and its successor, the African Union, to set up in 2002 a *Peace and Security Council* with a more interventionist mandate. The Union's refusal to recognize the transfer of power by undemocratic means marked a significant milestone in African political culture.

Second, although troops from independent African states were used in the first UN peacekeeping mission in Africa (Congo in 1960s), African states have never committed adequate resources for support of regional missions. To date the OAU/African Union has been active in four regional initiatives for peace, spearheading peacekeeping missions in the form of the Neutral Military Observer Group (NMoG) in Rwanda (1993),

---

[4] For example, the UN Commission on the Status of Women and the OAU cosponsored the organization of the *First Summit of First Ladies for Peace and Humanitarian Issues*, held in Abuja, Nigeria, 5–7 May 1997.

African Mission in Burundi (AMIB) with troops from South Africa, Ethiopia & Mozambique (2000), and the OAU/UN mission in the DRC (2000) prior to the United Nations mission's MUNOC (2001) and in Darfur, Sudan (2004). Historically, lack of funds and poor logistical support has reduced the effectiveness of regional missions, which are often handed over to the UN, and prompted some western governments to establish their own African peace-keeping initiatives (Chapter 7).

Finally, the third factor leading to the delayed response relates to the duplicitous role of the international community. Western governments have a history of being implicated in warfare in the region, and, as shown in Chapter 7, not necessarily on the side of peace, but for their own national or geo-political interests. Even the UN has not been a model of peace in the region, having sullied its credentials in the Congo it also came off unfavourably in the Rwandan genocide. While supporting the Arusha Peace Agreement with Security Council Resolution 868 of 29 September 2003 and the despatch of 2700 troops in a peacekeeping mission (UNAMIR), it lacked the mandate to intervene in the genocide and reduced its troops to 270 at a critical moment when it could have saved lives (Melvern, 2000).

The UN's operations in Burundi (United Nations Operation in Burundi (ONUB) and in the DRC (United Nations Mission in DR Congo (MUNOC)), were not able to avert the massacres of 152 refugees in Gatumba, Burundi (August 2004) and 1000 people in Ituri, DRC (April 2003).[5] MUNOC with a contingent of 16,000 peace-keepers in 2005 was deployed earlier in November 1999 to facilitate the implementation of the Lusaka Peace Accord and the 2002 ceasefire agreements. The limited Chapter VI mandate of MUNOC meant that it was not able to intervene to stop the killings. International condemnation led the Security Council (Resolution 1493) to approve the launch of the Ituri Brigade, a 3,500 branch of MUNOC. The Brigade, known as Operation Artemis and spearheaded by the French-led EU Interim Emergency Multinational Force (IEMF), was given a Chapter VII mandate and a 'much more robust posture', which should have enabled it to disarm militias in the district, yet the fighting persists.

In effect, limited mandates and inadequate resources of peacekeeping missions have meant that they have rarely kept the peace. The particular failures of the UN, throughout the 1990s, have led to questions about the commitment of Security Council members to peace in terms of mandates and the availability of resources for conflict management (Jones, 2001). Chopra (1996), among others, sees the problem as one of too little intervention and calls for a widening of the UN mandate to include activities to build peace, which encompasses more comprehensive peace-building activities. Chopra's revised UN mandate would have the organization acting as a transition government, with governorship and direct control of territory. Similar viewpoints have arisen from western proponents of the 'failed states' thesis, claiming that UN trusteeship will involve better governance and a return to peace (Caplan, 2007).

[5] See UNOB, UNOM, DRC and UNHCHR, 2004, *Regarding the events that occurred at Gatumba*, presented to UNSC, 18 October 2004, and ICG (2004) *Maintaining Momentum in the Congo: The Ituri Problem*, Africa Report 84, Nairobi/Brussels: ICG.

The fundamental issue is not to do with mandates, but the hegemony of a conceptualization of conflict resolution and peace that focuses on strengthening the military arm of the central state, while excluding non-violent alternatives. Basically, this narrow definition of peace ends up aiding the embeddedness of a militarized culture. No wonder genocidal violence continues to be perpetuated after peace and ceasefire agreements have been signed.

The Burundi Peace Process: The Regional Thrust for Peace

The Burundi peace negotiations, spearheaded by Tanzania and with the critical initial sponsorship of the Atlanta-based Carter Centre, arose from a regional initiative by neighbouring states concerned about the protracted nature of the conflict and its destabilizing impact on the region. The Organization of African Unity (OAU) gave its approval with declarations at two summit meetings. First, the Cairo Declaration on the Great Lakes Region signed by Mobutu Sese Seko, Yoweri Museveni, Pasteur Bizimungu and Sylvestre Ntibantunganya on 29 November 1995 and secondly, at the Tunis meeting in March 1996. At both meetings International support was given in UN Security Council Resolution 1049 (5 March 1996) and 1072 (30 August 1996). In the latter, the Security Council condemned the coup and called for the immediate resumption of dialogue. Regional states (Uganda, Tanzania, Kenya, Zaire (DRC) provided funds, and their leaders acted as ultimate arbitrators. The negotiations began first in the northern Tanzanian town of Mwanza in April 1996 and shifted to Arusha in June 1998. Talks were scheduled to coincide with the Summits of regional heads of states to ensure full regional consultation and to keep them on track. Between June 1996 and December 1999, there were six regional summits on Burundi aimed at maintaining a regional consensus and tackling problematic issues that were de-railing the talks.

After the first regional summit (Arusha I) on 25 June 1996, regional heads of state issued a communiqué advocating a negotiated settlement to the crisis in Burundi and national reconciliation; they called for an arms embargo and the denial of visas to those opposed to peace. The Tutsi officers' coup of 25 July 1996 that returned to power Pierre Buyoya, a former Tutsi president and coup-leader, was widely condemned by regional leaders at the second Regional Summit of 31 July 1996. The summit focused on measures aimed at returning Burundi to constitutional order and called for the immediate restoration of the National Assembly and the lifting of the ban on political parties. Economic sanctions were imposed on the government in Burundi and, in September 1996, the OAU declared the military junta illegal.

> For the first time a group of leaders declared that they would no longer accept an individual who came to power through a *coup d'état* as a legitimate Head of State. It was a significant shift not only because it departed from the previous trade unionism of Heads of State, but because it also set out new criteria for legitimization and acceptance. (Bunting *et al.*, 1999)

These actions were significant from the point of view of those who demanded a new mode of politics in Africa; one that recognized and uphold the democratic rights of African people.

Issues that Stalled the Talks

It took four years from the beginning of the talks before the peace agreement was reached. This protractedness was partly due to the factionalism among the principal actors, delaying tactics and disputes over procedures, and the Burundi government's opposition to what was seen as regional interference, especially sanctions and the intervention of a regional peace-keeping force.

The first and second peace talks or Mwanza 1 and II ran from 22 to 26 April 1996 and from 3 to 9 June 1996 respectively, and involved UPRONA, aligned to the coup leaders and the main Tutsi-dominated party, FRODEBU (*Front Pour la Démocratie au Burundi*), the assassinated President's party, and the leading Hutu-dominated political party and its then military wing, CNDD (*Conseil National Pour la Défense de la Démocratie*). Nyerere tried to forge a closer relationship between FRODEBU and UPRONA, with the intention of sidelining the smaller parties. However, UPRONA was against returning to the constitution and sought commitment from FRODEBU to disband CNDD – then its military wing. According to Bunting *et al.* (1999: 3) the meetings were 'intensive and acrimonious'. Nyerere drafted a statement in which the party leaders would declare commitment to the peace process, agreeing that:

> There cannot be a solution to the conflict in Burundi through the use of arms or other forms of violence, because the nature of the conflict is political [Para. 3c];

> They condemn violence, political killings and assassinations as means of achieving or returning political power or settling differences with political opponents [Para. 4a];

And:

> Reiterate [their] total commitment and adherence to the use of political and constitutional means for the achievement of political objectives [Para. 4c]. (Quoted in Bunting *et al.*, 1999)

The Mwanza talks adjourned in both cases because UPRONA, led by a Hutu, Charles Mukasi, refused to sign the statement committing the party to externally-mediated talks. Nyerere rejected UPRONA's demand for the word convention to be added as one of the means to 4c. Evidently, UPRONA was not interested in a regionally negotiated settlement as it was already committed to the internal cross-party alliance in the faltering UN-brokered Convention of Government.

Five regional summits were held before the Burundi government was prepared to participate in the talks, citing its opposition to the regionally-imposed sanctions and to foreign intervention.

The Question of Military Intervention
A major area of contention was the issue of military intervention to stop the killings that escalated after October 1993 and to prevent 'another Rwanda'. At the Regional Summit of 25 June 1996, attended by Kenya, Uganda, Zaire, Ethiopia, Rwanda and Tanzania, Burundian President, Sylvestre Ntibantunganya and Prime Minister, Antoine Nduwayo, requested the formation of an intervention military and police force (MIPROBU – International Mission of Protection and Observation for the Reestablishment of Confidence in Burundi), which was to have 180 soldiers and 30 civilians. Ethiopia, Tanzania and Uganda offered to provide troops, and the USA offered logistical support (*Daily News*, 19 January 1996).[6] Regional heads of states agreed to set up a Technical Commission headed by Tanzania to decide on the form and scale of the military assistance. On their return to Burundi, Ntibantunganya and Nduwayo were unable to persuade the military and the political class to accept the proposal (Bunting *et al.*, 1999). Nduwayo, a Tutsi, later distanced himself from the plan, accusing the President of plotting to neutralise the powerful Tutsi-dominated army.

The Burundi state, the military and Tutsi-dominated parties had always opposed an external intervention force, especially from neighbouring countries, even though they tolerated the presence of the 47 members of MIOB (International Observer Mission to Burundi) who had been in the country since Ndadaye's death; again France supported their stance. Indeed, Tutsi political parties and their leaders, such as former president Bagaza, called for protest against any military intervention and sought to make the country ungovernable. Many represented the presence of such a force as colonial occupation. The first three weeks of July 1996 saw student demonstrations, mob violence, massacres of both Hutus and Tutsis, incitement to violence and strike-calls by Tutsi politicians, while the Tutsi prime minister, Antoine Nduwayo, openly declared his opposition to military intervention and accused the Hutu president of 'a hidden agenda' to neutralize the army' (*Radio Burundi*, 4 July 1996). Hundreds of their supporters took to the streets and the country was thrown into the chaos that culminated in the July 1996 *coup d'état*. In contrast, Hutus in exile, such as Jean Minani, leader of the external wing of FRODEBU, supported what he termed a 'peace observer force'.

While the issue of a humanitarian force was being discussed at the UN Security Council, there was no real appetite in the West to commit troops for military intervention, bearing in mind the 1992 debacle in Somalia.[7] Certainly, the French and the USA were against such an intervention; the

---

[6] The Technical Commission met in Arusha in early July 1996 (Kenya was an observer and Zaire was not represented). The Burundian delegation was incomplete and represented by the ministers of foreign affairs, justice and agriculture, and heads of the offices of the president and prime minister.

[7] See UNSC, 15 February 1996, Report of the Secretary-General on the Situation in Burundi, S/1996/116.

latter, under pressure from domestic lobbies, responded with proposals for the creation of a regional peace-keeping force – ACRI (Chapter 7). The OAU and regional governments gave serious consideration to the military option, but were constrained, according to Maundi (2004: 311), by 'lack of acceptability' on the ground and 'lack of logistical capability'. In the end, the OAU's mission was a smaller observer force (OMIB) consisting of 46 civilians and 'unarmed military personnel', that, Maundi (ibid. 309) notes, 'was in no way capable of protecting the government leaders or preventing killings, let alone reinstating constitutional legality' – the reasons originally adopted for military intervention.

Regional Sanctions
Regional governments responded to the coup of July 1996 by introducing sanctions to pressure the government to restore constitutional order.[8] Historically, Tanzania already had experience of imposing an embargo against Burundi. In 1973, it blocked goods travelling to Burundi from the port of Dar es Salaam in protest at incursions of the Burundi army into its territory and the massacre of its citizens (*Le Monde*, 19.7.1973). The embargo was in place from October 1996 to January 1999. Enforced by Tanzania, Uganda, Kenya, Eritrea and Rwanda, it involved the sealing of road, rail and air links to land-locked Burundi.

There were a number of question marks over the effectiveness of sanctions considering the porosity of the borders with neighbouring countries. ICG (1998a: 39) claimed its effects 'were felt in the first six months'. Throughout the period of sanctions Burundi was reported to be a 'gold mine for profiteers' (*The East African*, 11 March 1998). Numerous reports pointed to sanctions-busting and the growth of the informal economy. France continued to supply the country with goods and weapons. Oil and dry bulk cargo were reported to have been secretly hauled through neighbouring states, malt for beer brewing came from Zimbabwe, and coffee was exported via Lake Tanganyika and South Africa, after 'deals were struck with Israeli businessmen' (*Daily News*, 15.5.1997; ICG, 1998a: 39). Sanctions were also violated through eastern DRC and by daily flights to and from Belgium, France and other EU countries and in August 1997, Kenyan Airlines resumed flights to Bujumbura (*The East African*, 18–24.8.1997). Regional heads of state were accused of 'turning a blind-eye to sanctions busting', because sanctions were damaging their 'economic interests' (ICG, 1998a: 40).

Even though the sanctions were relatively ineffectively applied, they marked an important step in the move by African states to find regional solutions to their problems, and were the mechanisms by which they were able to draw the Burundi government to the negotiation table. However, this was not a smooth process, with opposition from the Burundi and western governments, and international NGOs, (ICG, 1998a). The issue of sanctions divided the international community (western governments and NGOs) and countries of the region. Regional leaders saw sanctions as 'the only viable alternative to remaining passive

---

[8] Sanctions were agreed at the regional Summit of 31 July 1996.

or intervening militarily – an option envisaged in some circles, but which the Security Council was not prepared to accept'.[9]

With the help of an American advertising agency, the Burundi government launched an international campaign to get the sanctions lifted, arguing that it was the poorest of the poor who suffered more from sanctions, even though evidence showed that essential goods and weapons were still reaching the country. The Burundi government's 'diplomacy, which was, according to Bunting *et al.* (1999: not numbered), 'dynamic, aggressive and effective', had the support of western countries and NGOs. France complained that they should have been consulted. The French ambassador to Tanzania, Jacques Migozzi, was reported to have said 'the blockade does not resemble those placed against Iraq and Libya. This was decided by heads of state in the region. They lack global status' (Baraka & Mfinange, 1998). France, Italy and the Vatican's objection to the embargo seems to rest on the fact that it was a purely African initiative, but also because sanctions undermined neo-liberal free market ideology and affected business interests. The European Union punished Tanzania by calling for a financial audit of monies spent on the peace talks and by giving the facilitator less money for the sessions.[10] The special envoys from the USA, EU, Belgium and Canada campaigned at the Regional Summit of June 1998 for the sanctions to be lifted and for the peace negotiations to be shifted from Tanzania. According to Julius Nyerere, the then mediator:

> We have to balance the significance of their financial contribution, the power of the governments and multilateral organizations they represent and the amount of damage the pursuit of their own parochial interests can cause to the process. This should be measured against the need for the funding, diplomatic relations with the countries and the institutions they represent and the overall peace process. (Burundi Peace Negotiations, 1998: 14–15)

The financial shortfall was filled by regional governments and the OAU, which wanted to keep the talks going. Almost in retaliation against regional stubbornness, several western countries increased 'humanitarian' aid to Burundi.

Aid agencies, including the World Bank, the UN and western countries also campaigned aggressively for the lifting of sanctions, claiming that they were having 'devastating consequences' on the population. Reports by UNDP, international NGOs, Action Aid and International Crisis Group were very critical of the regional initiative (ICG, 1998a; Mthembu-Salter, 1998; Irinnew.org., 16 December 1998). At the request of NGOs and agencies operating in Burundi sanctions were eased twice, firstly to enable importation of fuel, medicines and other supplies and, in April 1997, at the fourth regional summit on Burundi, sanctions were again eased to include 'all food and food products, all items relating to education, construction

---

[9] Speech by Walter Bgoya, at Workshop on Confidence Building and the establishment of links between the Arusha process and the peace initiatives within Burundi, 21–23 June 1999, quoted in ICG (2000a: 13).

[10] According to Maundi (2004) almost 15 million US dollars were committed to the talks, the bulk of which came from western donors.

materials as well as all types of medicines, agricultural items and inputs'.[11]
There was considerable evidence to indicate that food shortages among the
population were the consequences of the war and the government's policy
of *regroupement* (forced villagization). Regional leaders had called on the
government to disband the *regroupement* camps. According to one
Burundian exile 'Sanctions impacted more on the population of
Bujumbura than on those in the villages, who had virtually no access to
imported food or medicines.'[12] Despite the opposition, regional leaders
and some international observers claimed that the sanctions worked in
that they made the Burundi government ready to talk, even if not immediately (Pendergast & Smock, 1999). Sanctions were not just symbolic; they
prevented certain governments from selling arms to Burundi, limited the
travelling of the political elite, and, in the end, forced the Burundi
government to give the impression, internationally, that it was seeking its
own multi-ethnic internal solution.

Internal Peace Talks
Buyoya sought to undermine the regional peace initiative by refusing to
participate in the negotiations and by starting the *Partenariat Intérieur
pour la Paix* (Internal Partnership for Peace), backed by international
actors such as France (Chapter 5). His ability to negotiate with the opposition reflected the differences between representatives of the Hutu
parties internally and externally. Internal FRODEBU, under the leadership of Augustin Nzojibwami – of Bururi origin, sought to regain some
of the democratic power it lost through accommodation with Buyoya. On
25 January 1997, six months after taking power, Buyoya re-opened the
National Assembly, which he enlarged from 81 to 121 members, to
include 12 representatives from political parties and 28 from civil
society, all selected by him and the President of the National Assembly
(ICG, 1998b). He also lifted the ban on political parties, legalizing those
parties that formed after the 1993 elections – many of them Tutsi-dominated.[13] The parties later, on 6 June, signed an agreement supporting the
regime in its three-year transitional process that was to include a national
debate, which would exclude Hutu rebels. The internal partnership,
which reversed the dominance of the democratically-elected parties was
beneficial to the Tutsi parties, many of them that campaigned vigorously,
and sometimes violently, against '*génocidaires*' in FRODEBU being in
government soon came to accept political figures who they once claimed
supported genocide (ICG, 1998b). In the end, the internal peace process
could not succeed due to the absence of prominent exiled Hutu politicians and the commitment of regional leaders to finding a long term
solution. Many western governments and opportunistic individuals
supported the internal peace talks. A report by the donor-funded
International Crisis Group (ICG) declared that it was only once the
'Internal Partnership for Peace' had started in June 1998 that 'negotiations can be regarded as having really began' (ICG, 1999a: 7).

[11] *The Tanzanian Guardian*, 18 April 1997.
[12] Interview with Burundian politician, Brussels, 1997.
[13] Article 6 (30 of the Constitutional Act for transition – decree law no1/008, June 1998)
forbade political parties form holding rallies and meeting (ICG, 2000a).

The Participants in the Peace Process
The success of the regional initiative was dependent primarily on the principle reputation of the two leading mediators; former Presidents, Julius Nyerere of Tanzania and Nelson Mandela of South Africa; both highly respected regionally and internationally. Nyerere's leadership was overwhelmingly supported by regional leaders. He also gained the support of Buyoya in a speech made at the Great Lakes Forum of the Washington-based Centre for Preventive Action and who was consulted by Nyerere prior to the July coup (Bunting *et al.*, 1999; ICG (2000a).

Many Burundians, Hutus and Tutsis, as well as external observers, questioned the motivations behind the involvement of Nyerere and the Tanzanian government and accused them of bias due to Tanzania's historical knowledge of the issues and relationship with Burundi. Nyerere, who was close to the first elected leader of Burundi, Prince Louis Rwagasore – a Pan-Africanist, was sympathetic to the plight of the refugees, and was also opposed to the coup that reinstated Pierre Buyoya as President. Reportedly, Nyerere said, 'all those at Arusha have been democratically elected regardless of how they won election ... Africa is no longer willing to accept military regimes' (*Le Monde*, August 1996, quoted in ICG, 1998a: 9). Given the narrow political base of the military leadership in Burundi under Buyoya, any attempt to foster peace and negotiations was interpreted as support for rebels. Nyerere and the Tanzanian government had a vested interest in attaining peace, to enable the repatriation of refugees and to prevent the potentially destabilizing tensions caused by their presence on its territory.

Nyerere also came under suspicion from Hutus. Some talked of a conspiracy between him and the leaders of Uganda and Rwanda to establish a Hima empire across Central Africa (OAU, 2000).[14] Clearly, Nyerere understood the fears of the Tutsi while recognizing the grievances of the Hutus and the inevitability of majority rule (Butiku, 2004).[15] Nevertheless, he felt that his facilitation could only be effective if he had the support of the Burundians, and visited Burundi from 27 to 30 December 1995 (Bunting *et al.*, 1999). In Bujumbura, he met with a cross-section of Burundi's political class and military and with members of the international community, UN representatives and ambassadors from France, Belgian and the USA. He, then, through the Mwalimu Nyerere Foundation, established a regional facilitation team, which included experts on the Burundi crisis, French and Kirundi speakers, academics, top judges and representatives from donor countries. He used his *mzee* (elder) statesman's status to mobilize and retain the support of regional leaders, even though some were not predisposed to be sympathetic to the plight of the Burundi people.

After Nyerere's death on 14 October 1999, the Burundi government, along with international peace advisers and the USA, supported a South African mediation with former President Nelson Mandela as facilitator (Irinnews.org, 19 October 1999). The Burundi government argued that 'a South African mediation would correct 'a number of weaknesses

---

[14] Interview with Burundi embassy attaché, 2000.
[15] Interview with member of facilitation team, Dar es Salaam, 2000.

observed in the methodology and management' (Irinnews.org., 19 October 1999). Mandela took over as facilitator in December 2000 and lambasted the Burundi politicians, entreating them with, 'please join the modern world. Why do you allow yourselves to be regarded as leaders without talent, leaders without vision?' He also argued that 'the [peace] process must be all-inclusive otherwise there can be no guarantee that the decision of the people here, even if it is unanimous, will be respected by the armed groups on the ground' (*BBC News*, 16.1.2000).

Indeed, Mandela's facilitation was considered a success, more so since it culminated in the signing of the peace agreement in 2000 (Bentley & Southall, 2005: Mpangala & Mwansasu, 2004). Coming from a regional superpower, Mandela was considered to have brought 'a lot of clout' to the negotiations, as South Africa 'had the military capacity to support any agreement'.[16] One manifestation of the clout that Mandela brought was that numerous presidents, including Bill Clinton of the USA went to the signing of the agreement. However, Mandela's methodology was criticized for being 'extremely personalized' and unprofessional (ICG, 2000c: 16). He was depicted as 'inflexible', 'stubborn', impatient, 'impervious' to advice and of possessing a 'dramatic underestimation of the sad reality' (ICG, ibid.). He was also attacked by some critics for relying on the Tanzanian facilitation team and for using the South African apartheid experience to interpret the Burundi conflict. ICG (ibid) writes, 'Mandela has not recruited a team of professional honest brokers, nor has he actually used South African expertise in solving conflicts.' The limited regional knowledge of the South African Ministry of Foreign Affairs enabled the Burundi military elite to turn the negotiations to their advantage. The South Africans made concessions to the Buyoya regime without consideration of their full consequences.

The Political Parties
Attributing equality of status in the peace talks to all groups led to a proliferation of political parties and may well have contributed to factionalism within the rebel movements. All political parties were invited to the negotiation table – those that fought the 1993 elections and even those formed after the elections. Many had no recognized constituency and had not tested their legitimacy with the disenfranchized Burundi population. Ambassador Ould Abdallah, UN Special Envoy in the region from 1993–1995 observed:

> Once allowed to create parties of their own they usually did so not to promote a distinctive platform and compete for political power but to position themselves as candidates for the presidency and to negotiate a share in any coalition government that might be formed. In some instances, they formed parties for purely mercenary reasons ... the rewards for doing so were high: each party's leader was given access to the national radio and a four-wheel-drive car. (Ould-Abdallah, 2000: 33)

---

[16] Interview with member of facilitation team, Dar es Salaam, 2005.

In all, there were 84 delegates from the political parties, the government and National Assembly.[17] Representatives of the military on the National Security Council participated as part of UPRONA or the government delegation and as consultants to one of the committees. Those rebels, Palipehutu-FNL (*Parti Pour la Libération Du Peuple Hutu /Forces National de Libération*) and CNDD-FDD (*Conseil National Pour la Défense de la Démocratie/Forces pour la Défense de la Démocratie*), who continued to fight, were not recognized by Nyerere, who refused to acknowledge leaders who 'gained power by force' (*African Confidential*, 21–2.10.1999). When CNDD-FDD broke away from CNDD, there were calls for its leader, Jean-Bosco Ndayikengurukiye, to be included in the talks. Nyerere questioned the basis on which he should be admitted, since the new movement had not declared itself to be a political party, neither had Ndayikengurukiye been constitutionally elected by the political party CNDD. Nyerere was, however, suspicious of Ndayikengurukiye for a number of reasons; he was from Bururi and his difference with CNDD leader, Leonard Nyamgoma, was personal not political; he was the brother of the internal FRODEBU leader, Augustin Nzojibwami and, allegedly, Buyoya's cousin. Nyerere also thought that his military activities had been sponsored by Buyoya.[18]

Nyerere allowed the 16, later 17 political parties,[19] to divide into two broad interest groups; G7 comprising Hutu-dominated parties and G10 made up of Tutsi-dominated parties with the addition of the Government of Burundi and the National Assembly (Table 9.1). By enabling participants to articulate a common position on key issues, these groupings may have increased the effectiveness of the debates. Nevertheless, they reinforced ethnicity as the basis of political discourse and obscured the fact that not all parties were ethnically exclusive in their membership. Buyoya was able to take advantage of the contradictions in the society that saw Hutus and Tutsis forming cross-ethnic alliances because of regional or personal differences.

The degree of ethnic allegiance varied from the integrated FRODEBU and UPRONA to the Tutsi extremist and ironically named, *Parti Socialiste et Pan-Africaniste* (INKINZO) and the purely Hutu, Palipehutu (*Parti Pour la Libération Du Peuple Hutu*). Individual parties articulated moderate to extremist ethnic ideologies. And within the broad groupings, there were considerable internal divisions. Disagreements among the leadership created breakaway groups. For example, the partnership of the Government of Burundi, National Assembly and UPRONA (G3) were often at variance with the rest of the G10. The Central Committee of UPRONA was also divided between those who were for and against the Arusha negotiations or pro-Buyoya and anti-Buyoya. Allegedly, those selected to participate in the Arusha negotiations were from the pro-Buyoya camp.[20] The

---

[17] According to ICG (2000a: 12), each participant was given a *per diem* of US $20,000 after ten sessions of about two weeks. It was alleged that many used the money to purchase '*Arusha*' houses in Bujumbura.

[18] Confidential interview with member of the facilitation team, 2001.

[19] RADDES joined the negotiations in January 2000.

[20] Interview, Brussels, 1997.

party leader, Charles Mukasi, a Hutu who first led the UPRONA delegation, was suspended from the party on 7 October 1998 for his anti-negotiations stance and his unwillingness to share power with FRODEBU *génocidaires*.

Table 9.1: Protagonists in the Burundi Conflict: Political Parties at the Arusha Peace Negotiations and Rebel Movements

Group of 10 + the Burundi Government and the national assembly	Group of 7	Rebel Movements
Gouvernment du Burundi	Front Pour la Démocratie au Burundi (FRODEBU)	Conseil National pour la Défense de la Démocratie – Forces pour la Défense de la Démocratie (CNDD – FDD)
Assemblée Nationale		Two factions led by Jean-Bosco Ndayikengurukiye and Jean-Pierre Nkurunziza
Parti de l'Unité et du Progrès National (UPRONA)	Conseil National Pour la Défense de la Démocratie (CNDD)	Parti Pour la Libération du Peuple Hutu – Forces Nationales pour la Libération (Palipehutu–FNL)
Parti pour la Réconciliation du Peuple (PRP)		Two factions led by Alain Mugarabona and Agathon Rwasa
Alliance Burundo-Africaine pour le Salut (ABASA)	Front Pour la Libération Nationale (FROLINA)	
Alliance National Pour le Droit et le Développement (ANNADE)	Parti Pour la Libération Du Peuple Hutu (Palipehutu)	
Alliance des Vaillants (AV-Intwari)	Parti Liberal (PL)	
Parti pour le Redressement National (PARENA)	Parti du Peuple (PP)	
Parti L'indépendant des Travailleurs (PIT)	Rassemblement du Peuple Burundais (RPB)	
Parti-Social Démocrate (PSD)	Parti Socialiste et Pan-Africaniste (INKINZO)	
Rassemblement Pour la Démocratie et le Développement Economique et Social (RADDES)		

Another significant point of contestation was the rivalry between Pierre Buyoya and former President Jean-Baptiste Bagaza, with the latter's party, PARENA (*Parti Pour le Redressement National*), portrayed as extremist. Bagaza became the *de facto* leader of those Tutsis opposed to Buyoya. Regional divisions, between the elite from the province of Bururi and those from central regions such as Muramyva and Mwaro and from the northern regions, particularly Ngozi and Kayanza, also led to sub-group alliances. One interesting cross-ethnic alliance took place between FRODEBU and PARENA, especially since PARENA is portrayed by the western media and by the Buyoya regime as an extremist Tutsi party (ICG, 2000b).[21] It was Ndadaye that encouraged Bagaza to return from exile, and, after his assassination, the external wing of FRODEBU – headed by Jean Minani – and PARENA joined other Tutsi parties to form *Alliance Nationale pour le Changement* (ANAC). Several Tutsi parties joined with the internal wing of FRODEBU to form the National Convergence for Peace and Reconciliation (ICG, 2000b: 19).

Regional, personality and ideological divisions surfaced among the Hutus, mainly over the issue of negotiations with the Buyoya government and on the power sharing arrangements, leading to the creation of internal and external wings of the various Hutu-dominated political parties. Radical Hutus were often critical of those with allegiance to UPRONA, and some rebels, CNDD-FDD, in particular, sought negotiations not with political parties but with the military – considered to be the real power in the regime.

Burundi's neighbouring states understood the dynamics of the warfare, and particularly the factionalism within the political elite. Yet, they, too, confined the realm of politics to political parties that were perceived as being defined largely by ethnicity, not ideology. Apart from those expressing extreme ethnic ideologies, there were very little differences between the parties. Very few had a conceptualisation of democracy that extended beyond the demand for equality between the Hutu and the Tutsi. Democracy simply amounted to equal guaranteed access to state institutions and ethnic quotas in the judiciary and army. Participating in the negotiations and signing the agreement guaranteed parties a stake in government, which they would not necessarily have achieved through democratic elections. The multiplicity of Tutsi parties has been said to reflect competing entrepreneurial cliques both among the military, political elites and 'intellectuals with political aspirations' (Bunting *et al.*, 1999; Nkurunziza & Ngaruko, 2002; Ould-Abdallah, 2000; ICG, 2000b). The formation of factions strengthened one's position in peace negotiations and guaranteed a role in any power-sharing government.

Women and Civil Society Representation
The proliferation of non-state actors in contemporary peace-making implies a greater involvement of civil society organizations. In practice,

---

[21] In December 1999 ANAC (*Alliance Nationale pour le Changement* – National Alliance for Change) was formed. It comprised of Bagaza's party, PARENA, PP, RPB, SOJEDEM, civil society representatives, and the external wing of FRODEBU headed by Jean Minani. ANAC was created in opposition to Buyoya's CNPR (*Convergence Nationale pour la Paix et la Reconciliation*), which was formed in October of that year and made up of ten Tutsi parties, UPRONA and the internal wing of FRODEBU (UN, OCHA, 1999; ICG, 2000a).

however, the frameworks remain non-transformative, denying representation and thus political agency to local civil society groups. Two arguments were put forward against their participation. First, a majority
among the Burundian negotiators were reluctant to have civil society
groups as independent members; they cited the rules of procedure agreed
in 1998, that any new group would need unanimous support in order to
be admitted. This, apparently, was to prevent Buyoya bringing in new
groups, since he was believed to have sponsored some of the Tutsi
political parties. The second argument was that Burundi's civil society
organizations, many dominated by Tutsis, were not sufficiently independent from the state and representative of 'all groups'. As stated in the
peace accord:

> Civil society in Burundi is not yet sufficiently organized to form a structure
> strong and solid enough to uphold the interests of all groups in the popu-
> lation. The notion of civil society is in fact a new one and is not well under-
> stood by the population, just as civil society itself does not understand its
> own mission. (*Arusha Peace and Reconciliation Agreement, Report of
> Committee IV, Reconstruction and Development*, Para. 2.5.6.1: 125)

This reflected the fact that Buyoya chose civil society representatives for
the National Assembly, and that the 500 civil society organizations in
Burundi are predominantly Tutsi. Civil society representatives were
requested to participate as part of the delegation of the political parties
they were affiliated to. However, their exclusion as independent participants reinforced the idea that peace making is solely the prerogative of
political parties, rebel movements and men. As a group of young
Burundians put it:

> Peace cannot be the result of only the authorities' efforts. It will result from
> the reinforcement of the civil society, whose voice has since long time
> blocked by the state power'. (sic) (Appeal from *Giheta*, Organization of
> Young Burundians, 3–9 May 1999)

The role of Burundi women in intervening in the peace process has been
lauded by numerous academics and NGOs (Burke *et al.*, 2001; Diop,
2002). However, a detailed examination of their involvement proves
instructive. *Women for Peace*, a Burundi organization was established in
1993, well before the peace negotiations began, however, the women's
campaign gained momentum when it was coordinated under an umbrella
organization, CAFOB (*Collectif des Associations et ONGs Féminines du
Burundi*), and attracted international support (Burke *et al.*, ibid.).
However, CAFOB's effectiveness depended on its cooperation with
women's organizations in the region.

In 1998, a delegation of women from Uganda, Rwanda and Tanzania
visited Presidents Buyoya and Museveni and later Nyerere, seeking
explanations for the exclusion of women's organizations from the talks.
Buyoya was reported to have said that Nyerere did not want them there.
Nyerere thought that their party affiliations prevented them from articulating alternative gender-specific visions. Nevertheless, three women

were appointed to the negotiations by the government and three by FRODEBU; the number later grew to 12. Representatives of women organizations were allowed to attend as observers at Arusha III which ran from 12–22 October and 12–19 December 1998. The status and credentials of the women were questioned; were they participating as women or as members of existing political organizations. Elite women were active members of the political class and women's organizations were affiliated to the main political parties: *Union des Femmes Burundaises* to UPRONA and *Association des Femmes Pour la Démocratie* (CAFED) to FRODEBU (ICG, 2000b). Reportedly, the women's viewpoints did not differ from that of other party delegates and some were wives of colonels. The inclusion of women, whether as tokens or articulating alternative visions of society, is beneficial, in that, as a group, women are probably the most victimised in war time and patriarchal practices might be difficult to defend in their presence.

With the support of UNIFEM and the Mwalimu Nyerere Foundation, an All-Party Burundi's Women's Peace Conference was held in Arusha from 17 to 20 July 2000, just over a month before the signing of the peace agreement. The conference aimed to be representative of Burundi women, with the 50 participants coming from all social groups, including the diaspora and refugee camps. The conference drew up proposals to engender the draft peace agreement outlining how specific gender-related clauses could be incorporated (Burke *et al.*, 2001). Virtually all of these gender-specific changes were later accepted by the parties to the agreement because, as, according to one member of the facilitation team, 'at that stage they did not matter'.

External Actors: Donors, International NGOs and Consultants
Despite the prominent role of regional leaders, the Burundi peace process was also an international peace-making exercise. The peace industry in Africa has set up an array of donors and peace consultants. Donors or governments with vested interests in the region, such as the former colonial power, Belgium, and francophone countries: France, Switzerland & Canada; major donors such as the USA, the European Union and the UK sent special envoys or supplied facilitators to play leading roles on the committees. Numerous non-governmental organizations, such as the London-based International Alert, Washington-based Search for a Common Ground and South Africa's ACCORD, became active participants in the peace process. In total, twenty-nine mediators were involved. According to UN Special Envoy Ould Abdallah, their presence was instrumental in delaying agreement among the protagonists, causing 'considerable confusion regarding the role of the international community and creat[ing] opportunities for extremists to play one intermediary off against the other' (Ould Abdallah, 2000: 131). This may be an unintentional outcome, as many westerners were concerned, at least publicly, to prevent 'another Rwanda'. As previously noted, in the USA, the Clinton government's response to the conflict was to establish the mechanism for the training of African peace-keepers in the form of the African Crisis Response Initiative (ACRI) (Chapter 7).

While there has been much written on the vested interests or biased position of regional states, little criticism has been directed at the activities of the western observers who, as representatives of donor countries and multilateral blocks, attempted to steer the negotiations to suit their interests. According to the reports (Burundi Peace Negotiations, 1998), the special envoys 'displayed a tendency to want to dominate and control the process', holding alternative 'secret' peace talks concurrently in Europe, for example at the Rome headquarters of *Comunità di Sant'Egidio*. The Rome talks and agreement of March 1997, between Pierre Buyoya and Léonard Nyamgoma's CNDD, were perceived with considerable hostility by other Hutu groups. As both Nyamgoma and Buyoya originated from Bururi province, the impression that was given to other Hutus was that a regional pact was being formed that would exclude them.

UN agencies also attempted to control the peace process; notably the UN Centre for Human Rights in Geneva and the United Nations Educational, Scientific and Cultural Organization (UNESCO). The latter used its auspices to hold peace conferences in Paris 30 June to 2 July 1997 and on 26 September 1997, which were presented as 'simply a forum for dialogue and not of negotiation'. Participants included President Buyoya, CNDD and representatives of Burundi's political parties, as well as 20 international observers, and were jointly chaired by the Malian President, Ahmadou Toumani Toure, and a high ranking UNESCO French official, Daniel Janicot (*Africanews.org*, 1997). These alternative talks conveyed international legitimacy on the Burundi president's refusal to accept Nyerere's mediation.

As well as institutions, NGOs and individual international consultants also tried to influence the process. Most provided voluminous documentation on the violence perpetrated by the military, government-backed militias and the rebels against the civilian population. Some, however, criticized consistently the Tanzanian facilitation team, accused Nyerere of being biased and were, seemingly, very supportive of the Burundi government. ICG (2000a & 2001a: iii), for example, campaigned for the international community to recruit and finance 'an international team of professional mediators [presumably westerners] to work full time on Burundi'. Others were disruptive of the talks, often failing to do the work they were assigned or insisting on placing their stamp on the outcome.

Conclusion

Realist concepts arising from contemporary geo-political situation see peace not as the absence of war, but as a reflection of the ability of a state to exercise territorial sovereignty, guaranteed by a strong military. These 'minimal conditions for peace' are the principles that inform the contemporary conflict resolution models being applied in Africa. In theory, peace negotiations should provide an ideal opportunity for transforming the state. However, this would require a broader understanding of peace, one that focuses on the endemic conditions that produce violence and instability. Conceptually, the contemporary 'liberal peace' reinforces militarism, elitism and the patriarchal logic of the state; in effect, leaving in tact the institutions of the genocidal state. A peace agreement crafted between the political elite, rebel movements and international actors that cater for their interests will, no doubt, exclude the Burundi people as active agents in the political community. In spite of the recognition given to the complex nature of the political struggles in Burundi, the negotiations bowed to the genocidal thinking of the elite by focusing on ethnicity as the basis for agreement and for post-war reconstruction, thus obscuring the multiple fault lines in Burundi society and how they affect political allegiance and outcomes.

The regional initiative marked a significant and progressive step to the ending of genocidal violence and the abuse of human rights in Africa, yet did not have the full backing of international forces for peace. As a regional commitment for peace exists, African people need to ensure that peace remains on the agenda of regional and international organizations and to be conscious of those forces that try to destabilize moments of autonomous peace-making and enforce their definition of what constitutes peace and national security. The overwhelming evidence from Burundi suggests that international organizations, regional and western governments do not necessarily share a common understanding of the complex dynamics of the violence, and often seek to champion particular individuals or groups, and even enter the process for their own vested interest.

10

Peace in a State of War | The Peace Agreement & its Implementation

Introduction

What can we learn from the Arusha peace process that would enable us to further comprehend the political dynamics that sustain genocidal violence and isolate those factors than can help in promoting an African perspective on peace in the Central African region? Examining the actualities of peace-making may help us to determine the extent to which the peace process reflected the political struggles within Burundi society; how the belligerents represented the conflict and how far the political class was prepared to share power. Here, the focus will be on the format of the talks, the committee structure, the key debates in each committee and the tenets of peace accord – the Arusha Peace and Reconciliation Agreement for Burundi. The details of the negotiations are drawn out to show that peace is an industry and how consultants, NGOs, donors and the political actors from Burundi sought to manipulate the process for their own interests. Finally, the implications for sustainable peace will be explored through an examination of the implementation of the peace agreement, in particular, the establishment of a transitional government, ceasefire negotiations, the role of violence as political leverage, demilitarization and the mechanisms for truth and reconciliation.

The Issues and Forums for Negotiations

Five broad areas of concern were identified for discussion at the first All Party Peace Talks (Arusha I), which took place on 21 June 1998; all parties except those fighting attended, including the special envoys from the EU, USA, Canada, OAU, Switzerland, *Sant'Egidio* & the UN). Five committees were established to negotiate the issues and reach an agreement on each of them (Table 10.1). At Arusha II All Party Peace Talks on 20 July 1998, each committee drew up its agenda and worked independently of the others with regular consultations with Nyerere and his team (Bunting *et al.*, 1999).

Table 10.1: Issues for Negotiation, Committees (Protocols) and their Chairs

Committee Number and Protocols	Agenda	Chair	Vice-Chair
I	Nature of the conflict in Burundi and problems of genocide and exclusion and their solutions	Armando Guebuza (FRELIMO-Mozambique)	Ruth Perry (Liberia)
II	Democracy and Good Governance; constitutional arrangements; questions of justice and the fight against impunity; judiciary, system of administration and transitional institutions	Prof. Nicholas Haysom (RSA – Mandela's legal advisor)	Prof. Thomas Fleiner (Institute of Federalism, Fribourg – Switzerland) Deputy: Julian Thomas Hottinger (Switzerland)
III	Peace and Security for all: issues of public security and defence; cessation of hostilities; permanent cease-fire arrangements;	Don/Padre Matteo Zuppi (*Sant'Egidio*)	Major-General Victor Malu (Nigeria) General Andrew Masondo (South Africa)
IV	Economic Reconstruction and Development: rehabilitation and resettlement of refugees and displaced persons; economic reconstruction and development.	Dr G Lennkh (EU – Head of Austrian Development Agency)	Madame Margaret Catley-Carlson (Canada)
V	Guarantees of implementation of the Agreement emanating from the Negotiations.	Ambassador Berhanu Dinka (Ethiopia)	

Competing interests dogged the selection of committee chairs and vice-chairs; western donors, international NGOs and the Burundi government sought to influence the appointments.[1]

Criticisms were levelled at some committee chairs and vice-chairs, who originated from outside of the continent. They were perceived as not

---

[1] For example the Nigerian, General Victor Malu, was first appointed as Chair of Committee Two, which Father Matteo Zuppi of *Sant'Egidio* challenged. The government of Burundi also objected to Malu, claiming that he was a soldier from a military regime. After considerable discussion, it was agreed that Zuppi would be appointed as Chair.

fully supportive of the peace process and of acting obstructively, often failing to perform their duties (Burundi Peace Negotiations, 1998). This is a reflection of the attempt by international actors to control the process (Chapter 9).

Four more peace talks and numerous intercessional consultations took place in Arusha before a draft agreement was submitted to all parties in March 2000. Each committee had produced a protocol outlining the agreed steps that would secure peace, even though there was not immediate or unanimous agreement on the content of each protocol. Protocol II, for example, saw seven iterations (between April 1999 and April 2000).[2] Protocol III (Peace and Security) and IV (Economic Reconstruction and Development) were the most contentious. In April, after the draft agreement was prepared, Mandela made a statement saying that the draft agreement would not be changed. However, external pressure forced him to make changes to one of the Protocols, after which, according to one observer, 'the draft agreement started to unravel' (ICG, 2000c).[3]

The first change was to Protocol 1, when Louis Michel, the Belgium prime minister and minister of foreign affairs, on a visit to Arusha in July 2000, asked Mandela for two paragraphs in the Protocol, which implicated the Belgian colonial state in the murder of Prince Rwagasore in 1961, to be removed (ICG, 2000c: 4, fn.10). The paragraphs read as follows:

> On the eve of independence, the colonizer, sensing that its power was threatened, intensified divisionist tactics and orchestrated socio-political struggles. However, the charismatic leadership of Prince Louis Rwagasore and the unity of the people made it possible for Burundi to avoid political confrontation based on ethnic considerations and enabled it to attain independence in peace and national unity. (Draft Arusha Peace and Reconciliation Agreement for Burundi, 17 July 2000, Chapter 2, Article 2, Para.6)

> Faced with failure, the colonial power planned and organized the assassination of Prince Louis Rwagasore, with the intention *inter-alia* of instigating political violence. (Draft Arusha Peace and Reconciliation Agreement for Burundi, 17 July 2000, Chapter 2, Article 2, Para.7)

The circumstances surrounding the death of Prince Rwagasore (on 13 October 1961) were one of the few points on which all the Burundi parties agreed. Mandela presented the Belgian's request to the Burundians, who refused. He then proceeded to remove the paragraphs, unilaterally, with the justification that Burundi will need aid from Belgium. Some on the negotiation team claimed that this undermined the legitimacy of the agreement and led to parties not keeping their commitments. After this, various groups were able to put pressure on the facilitator for changes to the draft document.

---

[2] Appendix I, Explanatory Commentary on Protocol III, Arusha Peace and Reconciliation Agreement for Burundi.
[3] Interview with Member of Facilitation Team, 2001.

On 3 August 2000, the UN Security Council called on all parties to end hostilities without delay and for a donor conference to help re-launch the economy. Peace talks resumed on 7 August 2000 with 19 political parties in Arusha and a simultaneous meeting in South Africa between CNDD-FDD, FNL and the Burundi government; the latter sought direct negotiations with the rebels. After a week of meeting in Arusha, no agreement was reached on the leadership of the transitional government and the 19 parties rejected the inclusion of the facilitation team in their discussions. Meanwhile, in Bujumbura, Tutsi extremists intensified their anti-Arusha street protests.

To speed up the process, Mandela set the signing ceremony for 28 August 2000 and invited President Bill Clinton of the USA. This intensified the pressure on participants and facilitators. Between April and 28 August 2000, numerous meetings were held to resolve some of the key areas of difference, notably, the kind of electoral system; leadership and composition of the transitional government; the arrangements for a ceasefire and cessation; the nature of the armed forces; the treatment of political prisoners and the granting of political immunity so that exiled leaders could return to Burundi and participate in the transitional government. In its criticisms, Luc Rukingama, spokesman for the Burundi government, said the draft agreement was not practical; it was 'replete with confusion, ambiguity and double standard' (Irinnews.org., 4 August 2000). Mandela's 'impatience' and the plethora of issues that lacked agreement gave room to key strategists to manipulate the process.

President Buyoya was able to force a result that disproportionately favoured the Tutsis and secured the continuation of his presidency during the first interim period of the transitional government, when key issues would be decided; i.e. the organization of the transitional government, the negotiation of a ceasefire, reform of the armed forces, return of refugees, disarmament of civilians and mobilization of international aid (Irinnews.org., 4 August 2000; ICG, 2000a).

On the other side, the armed Hutu groups, excluded initially from the talks, made themselves significant players in less than one year. From June 1999 to January 2000 they became a force to be reckoned with if peace was to be achieved. In June 2000, Mandela held closed door talks with the rebels and representatives of the Burundi government. CNDD-FDD had insisted that the Burundian army must be involved in negotiations and refused to accept the draft agreement, which was prepared before its involvement.

Buyoya sought to by-pass the Arusha committee by negotiating directly with Mandela in South Africa. On 7 June 2000, he and his generals went for direct talks in Johannesburg/Pretoria, where a deal was made between him and Mandela regarding the ethnic balance in the transitional government and the army. What became known as 'the Pretoria compromise' was supposed to ensure the security of the Tutsi. Buyoya emerged 'the winner on points', with assurances that Tutsis would have 50 per cent of the Senate, 60 per cent of the government and political parties with five per cent or more of the vote would gain a place in government (ICG 2000c: 6). Tutsis would also make up 50 per cent of the army. The government may have hoped to exclude, expeditiously, Hutu rebels, because as soon as the agreement was reached, the military started to recruit Hutus into the lower ranks.

The Arusha Peace and Reconciliation Agreement for Burundi was signed on 28 August 2000 amidst disagreements (Table 10.2). Articles relating to the establishment of the Senate and the composition of the armed forces were added to the draft agreement on the eve of signing, without the approval of the G7 parties, after last minute concessions were made by FRODEBU's leader, Jean Minani, in direct negotiations with Buyoya (ICG, 2000c: 3).[4] No agreement was reached on several issues: leadership of the Transitional Government, arrangements for a ceasefire, the composition of the armed forces and the treatment of political prisoners.

Table 10.2: The Main Tenets of the Agreement

- Establishment of a three-year transitional government, with the transitional period divided into two 18 months intervals; the first 18 months the president would be Tutsi from the Group of 10 and during the second 18 months Hutu from the Group of 7.
- Establishment of a Truth and Reconciliation Commission
- Request UN to set up International Judicial Commission of Inquiry on genocide, war crimes and crimes against humanity
- Request UN to set up an International Criminal Tribunal
- New constitution to be approved by senate and National Assembly
- The establishment of an independent electoral commission to organize elections Legislative power to be exercised by the National Assembly of at least 100 members and the Senate comprising of two delegates from each province (one Tutsi one Hutu)
- National army should not have more than 50 per cent of one ethnic group.
- The setting up of an implementation Monitoring Committee to monitor and guarantee the process
- The repatriation and reintegration of refugees
- The establishment of an international peace-keeping force

A scaled down version of the agreement was signed by Buyoya and by the G7. Thirteen parties signed on 28 August; six Tutsi parties did not sign, while the G10 (political parties) claimed they signed 'under extreme international pressure and with reservations'. On the 29 August, two Tutsi parties, AV-Intwari and PRP, signed and the others, RADDES, ANADDE, PSD and PIT, signed at the regional summit on 11 September in Nairobi. The rebels movements, CNDD-FDD and Palipehutu-FNL refused to sign; consequently, it was a peace agreement without a ceasefire.

The Debates and Agreements on the Causes of the Conflict

Analysis of the debates and proceedings reveal the commonalities and difference between the broad groupings; monarchists, democrats, ethnic extremists and moderates. Hutu and Tutsi parties had very few common

---

[4] Interview with Member of Facilitation Team, 2001.

areas of accord, with contrasting interpretations of history, particularly that relating to the significance of ethnicity in the violence. At the same time, there was widespread agreement among the signatories to the Agreement that the conflict was not ethnic in nature. In Protocol 1, Article 4, 'the parties recognize that the conflict is fundamentally political, with extremely important ethnic dimensions; It stems from a struggle by the political class to accede to and/or remain in power' (Arusha Peace and Reconciliation Agreement, 2000, Chapter 1, Article 4: 16, paras. a & b).

In contrast, there was universal consensus about the role of the colonial state in the institutionalization of ethnicity in Burundi politics and about the circumstances surrounding the death of Prince Rwagasore. In contrast, a major source of disagreement relates to the death of President Ndadaye in 1993 and the interpretation of the attack on the Tutsi and the military reprisals on the Hutu population. Hutus focus on the unlawful ending of the life of a democratically-elected President, while Tutsis were concerned with what they perceived as genocide perpetrated by Hutu supporters of Ndadaye. Not surprising, the Agreement called for a rewriting of the country's history. For delegates, developing a common understanding of the past was perceived as critical to achieving sustainable peace.

Inequalities along ethnic, regional or clan lines were considered to be important features in the division of wealth and power within the country, some of which go back to traditional practices in the pre-colonial period (Protocol 1, Article 1: p. 15). Consequently, the Agreement called for measures to address regional, ethnic and gender inequalities in public administration, education and the security services.

Overcoming the culture of impunity and punishing perpetrators of genocide was presented as being essential to the healing process. It was agreed in Protocol 1 (Article 6, para.10a-e) that the transitional government would request the UN to establish an 'International Judicial Commission of Inquiry on genocide, war crimes and other crimes against humanity responsible for investigating and establishing the facts relating to the period from independence to the date of the signature of the agreement', using existing international and independent reports on the matter. It was further agreed that the government of Burundi would request the UN Security Council to establish an 'international criminal tribunal to try and punish those responsible should the findings of the report point to the existence of acts of war crimes and other crimes against humanity' (Protocol 1, Article 6, para.11). It was also agreed that the transitional government would set up a National Truth and Reconciliation Commission to investigate and illuminate the truth regarding acts of violence committed since 1962 and propose measures to promote reconciliation and to clarify 'the entire history of Burundi... so that all Burundians can interpret it in the same way' (Protocol, Article 8, 1c).

The contentious issue here is which episode of genocidal violence should be investigated. The Hutu parties argued for the remit of the Commission to cover historical acts of genocide committed since independence, especially the 1972 genocide, acknowledged as such in the UN's 1985 Whitaker Report, while Tutsi parties were concerned that the

1993 acts of violence also labelled genocide in a 1996 UN's ICIB report, but on a smaller scale, were recognized (ICG, 2000a). The Commission would, however, 'not be competent to classify acts of genocide, crimes against humanity and war crimes' (Protocol 1, Article 8, 1a). Political amnesty was considered necessary to enable politicians to return and participate in the transitional government and elections. According to ICG (2000a) many politicians confused amnesty with impunity, and sought to put in measures that would result in their exclusion from prosecution (ICG, 2000c).

The Debate on Democracy and Governance

A fundamental question at the negotiations was what political arrangement would benefit Burundi since the winner-takes-all electoral democracy would, if people continue to vote largely along ethnic lines, give power to the majority Hutu population and incur, as in 1993, the wrath of the Tutsis. Burundi requires a constitution and an electoral system that recognises its socio-political plurality and an electoral solution that protects the rights of the minority.

Power sharing is viewed by conflict resolution experts as the only feasible way of promoting peace and reconciliation between warring factions, especially when lack of equity among groups is seen as a significant factor in warfare (Bangura, 1994). Spears (2000: 105) contends that power-sharing provides 'a reasonable alternative to ... high stakes winner-takes-all elections', without the abandonment of 'democratic principles and procedures', making it 'compatible with democracy while diminishing its most destabilising side effects'.

In the 1st Plenary at Arusha I (1998), Tutsi parties were vigorously against universal suffrage and sought an agreement within which they could retain key ministerial posts such as defence and foreign policy. The National Assembly's position was that 'the winner takes all model of democracy was not appropriate'; the Liberal Party (PL) wanted 'a democracy that is attuned to our interests' and claims that in Burundi 'democracy is synonymous with chaos'. In contrast, the G7 parties argued that 'power is in the hands of self-appointed leaders and their nominees' and called for 'one person one vote'. PRP sought the restoration of the monarchy (Report of the 1st Plenary, 1998). The Arusha Accords followed a standard formulae aimed at instituting a system of power-sharing between political parties and ethnic groups (rebel movements would register as parties) that would produce a consociational democracy, which ensured the presence of ethnic and gender plurality within the political structures. This is in contrast to what some commentators on Burundi have proposed, that is power sharing along federated territorial lines (Lemarchand, 1996). This would require enforced ethnic homogenization of provinces and would further inscribe ethnicity within the landscape.

It is argued that power sharing works best if the differences between the parties are minimal (Bangura, 1994). In Burundi's case, it was the balance of power between the belligerents that was critical. The Tutsis did not want to lose their control over institutions due to their monopoly of the security apparatus, a guarantor against genocidal violence and, because of the centrality of the state in wealth accumulation. Power-sharing had the potential to end direct violence only if the belligerents could be guaranteed portfolios in government. UPRONA acknowledged this at Arusha when it claimed:

> In our country the state is practically the only employer. The political game that gives access to material resources is a fact of life and death where the winner takes all and the loser loses all. For Barundi politicians the demo-cratic game has been reduced to sharing the national cake. The people only serve as a springboard for the political class. Under this system democracy loses its identity as the river in the sea. (Statement by UPRONA, Arusha III, 1998)

ICG's (2000c: 1) conclusion, that 'Burundi's political class is not prepared for fundamental political compromises on power-sharing and ultimately is not prepared to lead the country towards peace', may be correct, but does not take into account the political class' need for international acceptance and credibility, even if it is just to access aid.

Protocol II outlined the political principle in the post-transition consti-tution. Reaching an accord was difficult and the debate carried on into the morning of the signing. The final Agreement allowed for the setting up of an independent electoral commission to organise the elections; a national assembly of at least 100 members and one Senate to be composed of two delegates from each province; the President to be elected by the National Assembly and the Senate together, by two-thirds majority, and provisions were made for two vice-presidents belonging to different ethnic groups. There was no agreement on the women's recom-mendation that they receive 30 per cent of the seats in government.

The Protocol allowed for the establishment of a transitional government of three years, divided into two 18-month periods and headed by presidents of different ethnicities. Political parties were able to access seats in the Transitional Government and so could the leaders of rebel movements, who demanded guaranteed seats in the Cabinet as one of the conditions for ending the war. Power-sharing, then, was aimed at rectifying ethnic inequalities without the displacement of those already in power, since, the proposed size and membership of the National Assembly and the Senate allowed for the incorporation of past presidents and representative of most factions.

Under the Agreement, opposition parties with less than five per cent of the vote would be entitled to a seat in the Cabinet. The setting up a Senate was done as 'a counter-balance to the results of a democratic election', thus giving parity to the Tutsis and 'answering their anxieties'.[5] In the same vein, organic laws would require two-thirds majority in the National Assembly and approval by the Senate. ICG claims that:

> The changes obtained by Buyoya give the Senate the power to control all nominations to senior civil service positions and to posts in the judicial institutions and the security forces. No judge, no governor, no member of the armed forces can be nominated without their career, their alleged

---

[5] Interview with Member of the Facilitation Team, Dar es Salaam, 2005.

political relations or their competences being assessed and approved by the Senate. (ICG, 2000c: 9)

G7 (Hutu-dominated parties) opposed the composition of the Senate, which would comprise one Hutu and one Tutsi representative directly elected from each province. Despite this being a Government of Burundi proposal, some G10 parties opposed the Senate, claiming that 'unrepresentative Batutsi' would be elected rather than 'Batutsi on whom only Batutsi trust' (Arusha Peace and Reconciliation Agreement, 2000: 164). It could be argued that the proliferation of Tutsi parties was a strategy to ensure the retention of their advantage in the ruling bodies such as the Senate, as each party gets representation. The Senate, therefore, is an institution that will, to some degree, preserve the status quo.

The Government of Burundi and the National Assembly took a very partisan role in the peace negotiations siding with the Tutsi parties and frustrating what might be seen as challenges to the status quo. Agreement was reached only after the government was able to do backroom deals with Nelson Mandela, which enabled key Tutsi players to retain some leverage in the transitional government, thus restricting the extent and nature of state reforms and ensured that they gained disproportionate power in the executive and legislature.

Protocol III on Peace and Security for all
Reform of state institutions, such as the military and the gendarmerie, which are overwhelmingly Tutsi, were seen by the facilitation team as a vital step towards lasting peace. However, Tutsi-dominated parties spoke vociferously against reform, while the Hutus, especially the rebel movements, saw the 'army as the main block to peace'. FROLINA called for 'the disarmament of the militias and the de-politicization of the army and recruitment from all regions and groups'; CNDD sought 'a national army', and FRODEBU, the 'restructuring reforms and retraining of the army' (6th plenary, October 19, 1998).

The ethnic composition of the post-conflict army became one of the most contentious issues in the negotiations. Buyoya was able to win concessions from Mandela who agreed to a 50/50 percentage ethnic split. Thus, the agreement states, 'for a period to be determined by the Senate, not more than 50 per cent of the national defence force shall be drawn from any ethnic group, in view of the need to achieve ethnic balance and to prevent acts of genocide and *coup d'état'* (Article 14, Para. g/p: 64). Initially, the government's aim may have been to exclude rebel forces, because as soon as the agreement was reached, the military started to recruit Hutu into the lower ranks. The Agreement also contained stipulations for the establishment of a ceasefire commission to monitor the cessation of hostilities and a reintegration commission to facilitate the demobilization and return to civilian life of combatants. Along with other western nations, France pledged to provide financial and technical support for demobilization.[6]

---

[6] Statement made by Charles Josselin, Minister for International Cooperation and Development, at Arusha V, 21 February – 4 March 2000.

Protocol IV Reconstruction and Development

Peace negotiations involve not only a discussion of the political settlement but also the framework for the post-war reconstruction of society. Protocol IV placed the issue of the voluntary repatriation and reintegration of all Burundian refugees and displaced peoples at the centre of the reconstruction and development. It refers essentially to the then estimated 364,000 Burundian refugees residing in neighbouring countries since 1993. Article 3 outlined the mechanism for the establishment of a National Commission for the Rehabilitation of *Sinistrés* (CNRS), which would organize the 'socio-economic and administrative reintegration' of refugees. A key principle in Article 8 is the right of refugees to recover their property, especially their land or to be compensated if their land has been expropriated.' Reconstruction is defined 'as restoration of the living condition of the population to their best previous level' (Annex IV, Chapter II – 19 August 2000). It is presented as a multi-faceted process involving physical (material) and political (national reconciliation) reconstruction. Democratization is seen as a prerequisite for reconstruction and 'equity' as an essential component, with a special reference to 'the advancement of women' (Annex IV: 122).

Ideally, reconstruction should provide an opportunity to address structural violence. In the era of neo-liberalism the only formulae for a peaceful society is one modelled on western liberal democracy and a free market economy. While conflict resolution models may recognize the threat posed by weak economies and structural violence to long-term peace and stability, they are constrained by being only able to articulate economic reform of the hegemonic market liberalism. The economic proposals of the Peace Agreement emphasize a continuation of the economics of resource extraction, which, as history has shown, has been a key component of genocidal economics.

Chapter III calls for the preparation of detailed plans for reconstruction in the transition period and medium and long-term development plans. The proposals aimed at tackling poverty and its consequences (reducing infant mortality rates by at least half and increasing rural and urban household incomes), as well as addressing a whole range of development-related social issues from health, education, under-representation of women in affairs of the state, youth and the economic and social aspects of demobilization. The neo-liberal economic solutions proposed by the World Bank and the IMF emphasize macro-economic and financial stabilization through the 'initiation of structural reforms in the social sector' and the 'creation of an environment conducive to the expansion of the private sector', starting with the liberalization of the coffee sector and the promotion of coffee planters' associations.[7] Although the World Bank may claim to have an anti-poverty focus, the market liberalization strategies they propose for reconstruction will only lead to greater hardship at a time when people are attempting to rebuild household and community institutions.

---

[7] Burundi has since produced an Interim Poverty Growth and Reduction Strategy Paper in 2003. See Republic of Burundi, Interim Strategic framework for Accelerating Economic Growth and Reducing Poverty, November 2003, Burundi.

Protocol V on Guarantees
It was agreed that implementation of the Peace Accord would be monitored by an Implementation Monitoring Committee (IMC), comprising of
29 members (19 signatories to the peace accord, 6 civil society members,
1 representative each from the UN, OAU, the Great Lakes region and one
from the donor community), as stipulated in Protocol V. Again, there was
considerable debate as to who should head the IMC. Western governments pushed for the appointment of their candidate – a French man,
who was working for the UN in Burundi. After much wrangling, an
Ethiopian UN representative, Berhanu Dinka, was appointed to the Chair.
   The IMC's role would be to 'follow up, monitor, supervise, coordinate
and ensure the effective implementation of all provisions in the agreement;
ensure that the timetable is respected; ensure the accurate interpretation of
the agreement and arbitrate and rule on any dispute that may arise among
the signatories' (Article 3,1). The IMC would also give guidance to the
commissions and sub-commissions implementing the Agreement.
Security was to be guaranteed by the establishment of a UN peace-keeping
force to protect institutions and public figures and to 'provide technical
support for demobilization, aid and training and assist in the establishment of and training of an ethnically balanced special unit for the
protection of the institutions' (Protocol V, Article 8, paras. c & e: 94).

Post-Arusha Developments: Transitional Government, Ceasefire Negotiations and Democratic Elections

The incompleteness of the peace accord resulted in its slow implementation.[8] It took a year before the Transitional Government was constituted
and five years from the signing of the Agreement to the election of a
democratically-elected government. In between there were two
attempted coups – in April and July 2001. Some politicians saw the
agreement as a compromise and tried to spoil it with delaying tactics. ICG
(2000c: ii) claimed that Buyoya intended 'to take advantage of the hazy
interim period to negotiate the transition on his own terms and regain a
military advantage'.
   The slow progress also reflected the competition among Tutsi parties
for the leadership of the Transitional Government. Buyoya had already
positioned himself as leader, but faced opposition from two Tutsi coali-
tions who nominated Colonel Epitace Bayaganakandi (backed by 8
political parties) and Col. Jean-Baptiste Bagaza. Mandela, faced with
numerous petitions for and against each candidate, met with regional
Heads of State, who decided that Buyoya should be the transitional president for the first eighteen month period with Domitien Ndayizeye (G7 &
FRODEBU) as vice-president (Chhatbur, 2001). This decision was
endorsed conditionally by regional heads of state at their meeting on 23
July 2001 in Arusha. They threatened sanctions if Buyoya failed to abide

[8] ICC (2000c: 2) blames Mandela's 'methodology' as being at fault, implying that the signing
timetable was put in place hurriedly, before a new framework was agreed on to open
'constructive dialogue with the rebels and achieve a suspension of hostilities'.

by the stipulated conditions. Reports such as that Buyoya wanted to change the clause in the Constitution that prevented him from running as President and that Ndayizeye, interim President for the second 18 months of the transitional period, was put under considerable pressure by the Hutu political parties not to concede to Buyoya's request.

The Transitional Cabinet that was sworn in on 1 November 2001 had 26 portfolios, 14 to Hutus, while Tutsis retained the key ministries of defence, foreign affairs and finance. Four women party members were made ministers. The Transitional National Assembly was headed by Jean Minani (FRODEBU) and the Senate by Libere Bararunyeretse (UPRONA). Power-sharing was carefully controlled by the leaders and did not reflect any dramatic changes in the status quo. As ICG notes:

> Apart from the showy appointments to the transition political institutions, which give the appearance of power sharing for the benefit of the donors, the state's administrative, financial and security apparatus is still controlled by the same military-political oligarchy. (ICG, 2002a: 7)

Despite considerable Tutsi opposition to the regional peace-keeping force, foreign troops were considered vital to ensure the personal security of returning exiled politicians and to keep the transitional process on track. On 18 October 2001, South Africa, at the behest of Mandela, provided 701 South African troops termed the *South African Protection Support Detachment*. Over a year later, on 3 April 2003, the African Union mandated AMIB (African Union Mission to Burundi) 'to supervise, observe, monitor and verify the implementation of the [2002] Ceasefire Agreement, in order to further consolidate the peace process' (Boshoff & Francis, 2003: 1). The 2860 troops came not from neighbouring countries, but from Ethiopia and Mozambique, and included an enlarged South African contingent. In June 2004, AMIB was converted to a UN mission, ONUB (United Nations Mission in Burundi), following Security Council Resolution 1554, and increased to 5,650, incorporating troops from Ghana, Nigeria and Senegal, again countries external to the region. ONUB's presence helped to maintain a semblance of stability during the transitional and the run-up to the democratic elections, but did not stop the fighting and human rights violations by all sides in the war.

Ceasefire negotiations proceeded between the Transitional Government and the Hutu rebel movements, with the facilitation headed by Jacob Zuma, then deputy president of South Africa. The process was long and tortuous due to a) the intervention of too many mediators (holding meetings in Rome – *Sant'Egidio*, Libreville,[9] South Africa & Dar es Salaam); b) factionalism in the rebel movements (CNDD-FDD split in two factions headed by Jean-Bosco Ndayikengurukiye and Pierre Nkurunziza, so did Palipehutu-FNL headed by Alain Mugabarabona & Agathon Rwasa); c) the involvement of a host of mediators.

The smallest factions of the two rebel movements (Ndayikengurukiye's CNDD-FDD & Mugabarabona's Palipehutu-FNL) were the first to reach

---

[9] Jean-Bosco Ndayikengurukiye sought a francophone resolution by calling for Omar Bongo of Gabon to mediate.

a ceasefire agreement with the government on 7 October 2002 (Irin news.org., 2002b). A year later, on 16 November 2003, Nkurunziza's CNDD-FDD and the government agreed to the *Pretoria Protocol on Political, Defence and Security Power Sharing in Burundi*, which gave CNDD-FDD 40 per cent of the integrated general staff and the officer corps in the army. In the new army, Burundi National Defence Force, military command posts would be shared 50/50 on an ethnic basis. CNDD-FDD also signed a ceasefire agreement on 3 December 2002 in which CNDD-FDD would become a party under the new law governing parties and be allocated two ministerial posts – Nkurunziza was made Minister for Good Governance (Irinnews.org., 2002c). The largest branch of the Hutu-led Palipehutu-FNL, headed by Agathon Rwasa, requested to join peace talks in April 2005 after regional heads of state declared the FNL to be a 'terrorist organization'. On 7 September 2006, they finally reached an agreement with the Hutu-dominated government.

After a turbulent drafting phase, on 28 February 2005, a referendum on a new Constitution received overwhelming support from 91.2 per cent of registered voters. UPRONA's central Committee and three other Tutsi parties had urged a no vote and refused to sign a code of good conduct during the elections. The transitional period was extended by 6 months to 22 April 2005, due to delays in setting up the Electoral Commission and the adoption of an electoral code. The stipulation of the electoral code that parties must be multi-ethnic and the prescribed ethnic composition of the Senate forced the main political parties to recruit members from other ethnic groups.

Thirty political parties fought the communal and parliamentary elections that were finally held from June to August 2005. The former rebel movement, CNDD-FDD, was confirmed winner of municipal communal (senatorial) polls held on 3 June, with a voter turnout of 80.6 per cent of the registered voters. Of the 3,225 seats, CNDD-FDD won 1,781 (57.3 per cent of votes cast), followed by FRODEBU with 822, UPRONA came third with 260 seats and Movement for the Rehabilitation of Citizens (MRC) gained 88 seats (Irinnews.org., 16–24.6.2005). Parliamentary elections were held on 4 July 2005, with a 77.23 per cent voter turnout. CNDD-FDD won 58.55 per cent of the votes, FRODEBU 21.70, UPRONA 7 per cent, CNDD four per cent and MRC two per cent (Table 10.3).

At the end of August 2005, Pierre Nkurunziza, as the head of the largest elected party, was chosen as President by the National Assembly and Senate. Tutsis were co-opted onto the National Assembly and the Senate in order to reflect the 60/40 ethnic quota of the Peace Agreement. The composition of the Cabinet, according to Reyntjens (2005: 130), remained 'unconstitutional', having representation from parties that did not gain five per cent or more of the vote (MSP-Inkinzo and PARENA – Tutsi-dominated parties – were given one seat each, plus two ministers were without party affiliations). Both UPRONA and FRODEBU were under-represented and CNDD-FDD had proportionately more seats in cabinet than they hold in the National Assembly (Reyntjens, 2005). Women obtained 35 per cent of the Cabinet seats, achieving greater representation than envisaged in the peace agreement. And, at the local level, they

Table 10.3 Political Parties in the National Assembly Elections 2005

Party	Number of Votes	% of Votes	Number of Seats 100 (118)*
National Council for the Defense of Democracy-Forces for the Defence of Democracy (CNDD-FDD)	1,417,800	58.55%	59(64)
Front for Democracy in Burundi (FRODEBU)	525,336	21.70%	25 (30)
Union for National Progress (UPRONA)	174,575	7.21%	10 (15)
National Council for the Defense of Democracy (CNDD)	100,366	4.14%	04 (04)
Movement for the Rehabilitation of Citizens-Rurenzangemero (MRC-Rurenzangemero)	51,730	2.14%	02 (02)
Party for National Recovery (PARENA)	42,223	1.74%	– (–)
Independents & Others	109,396	4.51%	– (–)
Seats reserved for ethnic Twa members	–	–	– (03)

Note: The following parties are not represented in parliament: Party for the Restoration of Monarchy and Dialogue in Burundi (ABAHUZA); Burundi African Alliance for Salvation (ABASA); National Liberation Forces (FNL-INCANZO); National Liberation Front (Frolina); Kaze-Forces for the Defence of Democracy (Kaze-FDD); Pan-Africanist Socialist Movement-Inkinzo (MSP-Inkinzo); Party for the Integral renewal of Burundi-Intahemana (PAIBU-Intahemana); People's Party (PP); Party for Peace, Democracy, Reconciliation and Reconstruction (PPDDRR); Social-Democratic Party-Dusabikanye (PSD-Dusabikanye); Rally for the People of Burundi (RPB); Green Party-Intwari (Vert-Intwari); Burundi's Workers' Party (UBU); Party for the Liberation of the Hutu People (Palipehutu).
Source: http://africanelections.tripod.com/bi.html [Last Accessed September 2006]

gained 5.4 and 33.3 per cent of the commune presidency and vice-presidency respectively (ONUB, 2006b).

CNDD-FDD's victory was no surprise for those in the region, or for external observers. The party's growing popularity after February 2005 meant that Nkurunziza was invited to visit several western countries. As soon as the Accord was signed, CNDD-FDD presented itself as the legitimate opposition to UPRONA, challenging and even kidnapping FRODEBU members of the government. Many politicians crossed to CNDD-FDD. It is difficult to know how CNDD-FDD garnered popular support; there were reports that voters were intimidated, especially in the areas they controlled (Ligue Iteka, 2005b). Other reports pointed to admiration for their long struggle and affirming their popularity at the grassroots. Many voters may have opted for the group that was more likely to bring an end to the warfare.

Violence as a Legitimizing Force and the Challenge of Demilitarization
Violence, ranging from massacres, summary executions, scorched-earth policy, bombing and rape, was used by all factions to articulate political differences and to strengthen their negotiating arm. Prior to the signing of the peace agreement and during the period of the transitional government, Burundi witnessed an intensification of the war – both the government and rebels used the post-accord period to rearm.[10] Even FRODEBU, as late as November 2002, was reported to have established a rebel group, Ramico-Pax (Tindwa, 2002).

According to ICG (2001a: 16), 'the government's only concern [was] protecting its privilege and the impunity of the Bururi's political-military oligarchy.' Therefore, Buyoya, as leader of the first half of the transitional period, 'appear[ed] to want to sustain the conflict, rather than find a durable solution, irrespective of whether that solution is political or military'. In effect, there was considerable foot-dragging by the president and UPRONA, using the continuing war as a pretext to delay the implementation of the Peace Agreement, and the push towards ceasefire negotiations. Dometien Ndayizeye, the FRODEBU president of the second half, also found it difficult to move to transition, seeking cross-party alliances to pursue his personal ambitions. From 2000 to 2003, CNDD-FDD, the stronger of the rebel movements gained the upper hand by intensifying the war, in order to attain an agreement that benefited it. Political party members also came under attack from CNDD-FDD; an UPRONA member of parliament was assassinated in June 2003 and, in the same month, FRODEBU members of parliament were abducted to discredit the party and to enforce CNDD-FDD's case for greater representation in the transition government.[11] CNDD-FDD and Palipehutu-FNL also fought over their territory of operation; this became more frequent after the power-sharing agreement of 2003 was signed. The accession of the CNDD-FDD leader to the presidency and senior positions in government, following the 2005 elections, did little to alter the misuse of state power. Former rebels moved in to fill the posts of chief of police and chief of intelligence. Post 2004, the main political threat was seen as arising from other Hutus, in and outside the regime. The repressive tactics deployed by the new regime were already well-entrenched within the institutions of the state. Finally, Agathon Rwasa's Palipehutu-FNL faction saw violence as the means to destabilize the elected Hutu-dominated government and to access power. Militarization was not halted by the accord.

DDR: A Development Project for a Political Problem
In realist thought demilitarization defines the process by which a new national army is created through the integration of an agreed number of rebel combatants, plus the demobilization and disarmament of others and their re-integration into civilian life. International development

---

[10] In September 2002, the army massacred some 170 civilians at Iteba, Gitega Province.
[11] Irinnews.org. 3 July 2003, Burundi rebels free MP & four other hostages & HRW (2003: 15).

agencies have coined the acronym DDR (Disarmament, Demobilization and Reintegration) to describe the aid programmes linked to this process. According to the policy, DDR projects should be carried out by the transitional governments with the assistance of international peacekeepers. The national army and the UN peace-keeping agency would disarm ex-combatants, while NGOs implement programmes dealing with demobilization and reintegration.

In Central Africa, the World Bank administers donor funds allocated to the region's DDR programmes, under the Central African Multi-Country Demobilization and Re-integration Programme (MDRP), making DDR a central component of the post-conflict aid budgets. From 2002 to date, MDRP has been allocated US$ 200 million for the DRC, US$ 179.7 million for Angola, US$ 25 million for the Republic of Congo, US$ 53.3 million for Rwanda, US$ 84.4 million for Burundi and a programme is being planned for Uganda (MDRP, 2005). Although presented as locally-owned, the programmes are devised in consultation with, and supervised by, the World Bank. The stated goal of the DDR is 'to consolidate peace' through the reform of the security sector, with the long term goal of a reduction in armed personnel and, subsequently, in defence expenditure (World Bank, 2004b).

Burundi's own programme, labelled 'Demobilization, Reinsertion and Reintegration', started in December 2004 and is projected to end in 2008. It is jointly co-ordinated by the National Commission for Demobilization, Reinsertion and Reintegration and the World Bank, with NGOs as implementing agencies; for example, the National Structure for Child Soldiers and UNICEF have responsibility for ex-child soldiers. Combatants eligible for de-mobilization belonged to the national army and paramilitary groups such as the *Gardiéns de la Paix,* and the rebel movements: CNDD-FDD, Alain Mugabarabona's Palipehutu-FNL, CNDD-NY (Leonard Nyamgoma) and Frolina (Table 10.4). By May 2006, only 20, 298 of the estimated 70,000 ex-combatants had been de-mobilized. As part of the de-mobilization, the new national army, FND (*Forces Nationale Défense*), will be reduced from 46,000 to an estimated 30,000 soldiers, and the new police forces will have 20,000 officers. So far, there is very little evidence that these institutions will be engendered.

Table 10.4: Affiliation of demobilized ex-combatants as of 22 May 2006

Affiliation	Male	Female	Children	Total
FAB	7332	0	2273	9605
CNDD-FDD	5946	437	594	6977
CNDD-Nyamgoma	1321	30	51	1402
Kaze-FDD	339	1	23	363
Palipe-Agakiza	533	1	32	566
FNL-ICANZO	243	3	37	283
Frolina	528	10	5	543
FDN	559	0	0	559
Total	16801	482	3015	20298

Source: RoB, NCDRR (May 2006)

The DDR process has been slow, as some former rebel groups were reluctant to move into cantonments, and the process of identifying genuine members of paramilitary groups difficult. Demobilization payments were also not always forthcoming, causing protests from combatants and armed groups, such as the *Gardiéns de la Paix* (Irinnews.org., 24 June 2005).[12] By May 2006, some 19,944 *Gardiéns de la Paix* were demobilized, 17,335 of whom had received payments (RoB, NCDRR, 2006). Payments to the military varied according to rank, ranging from US $500 for ordinary ranks to $3000 for the generals. Payments were made in tranches and recipients were supposed to be monitored in their home areas.

The argument put forward for demobilization payments is that financial security may encourage combatants to put down their arms and, as stated by the World Bank (2004b: 22), 'empower [them] to make choices according to their own needs and priorities'. However, cash payment reinforces, at the level of the individual and the community, the notion that violence is a route to financial power. Human Rights Watch (2003) found that the prospect of demobilization with remuneration provided by the international community encouraged many young Burundian men to join the rebel movements and the army, during the implementation of the peace agreement. In 2004, Human Rights Watch (2004b: 1) refers to rebel leaders 'inflating their numbers to gain recognition and bargaining power in the peace accords and under[taking] massive child recruitment during the transition period'. Consequently, demobilization of child soldiers was often delayed to strengthen negotiating positions and to increase receipts of payment from Disarmament, Demobilization and Reintegration (DDR) projects (AI, 2004). A similar situation was being experienced in the DRC, where Save the Children Fund also notes:

> The new policy of paying incentives to military – including children ... has resulted in a relatively low number of children leaving armed groups and forces, and the evasion from transit care and re-enrollment of children who had previously left. (Save the Children, 2004: 1)

Children and men receiving direct financial assistance tended to fare better in a devastated post-war economy.

Though female ex-combatants were treated as a special target group, many encountered considerable difficulties in reinserting back into their communities. A survey for ONUB found that on their return home women who fought in or belonged to rebel movements suffered a variety of problems ranging from personal insecurity discrimination because of their rejection by families and communities (Bruchhaus, 2005). Communities had difficulty accepting women as fighters, labelling them 'savages' and 'animals'. Over 45 per cent of the women were below the age of 34, and the majority (60 per cent) came from the provinces of Bujumbura Mairie and Bubanza. Their children, often belonging to several fathers and the result of rape, faced considerable discrimination

---

[12] *Gardiéns de la Paix marching for demobilized money*, Ligue Iteka, September 2005.

and difficulty being accepted by their mothers' households. The women also suffered from abandonment by men with whom they had liaisons in the bush. To compound this situation, access to land for cultivation was often limited as their plots were either taken over by other family members or had been sold and those living alone were targeted by bandits.

A critical factor in the effectiveness of a DDR programme is the ability of demobbed combatants to reintegrate into society; many lack requisite skills and resources to establish themselves in civilian life (HRW 2004b). Public sector collapse in war torn societies has meant that opportunities for self-improvement through education have declined. Richards (1996) and Dallaire (2003) found that in Sierra Leone child soldiers wanting to return to formal education, found that is was not freely or widely available. In Burundi, the vocational training and schooling available through the DDR may have gone some way to address these gaps in state provisioning for a few, yet the wider community was only able to benefit if ex-combatants were numerous in their areas or were involved in the projects. The DDR programme placed the onus for successful reintegration on communities, yet, it was apparent, that this could only work if there were concomitant improvements in the overall material conditions of life for the community. It is worth noting that in mid-2006, donors had yet to fulfil their pledges of some US $1.032 billion for development projects and US $71.5 million for humanitarian work. Furthermore the package of economic reforms promoted by the IMF/World Bank has led to retrenchment and wage freezes in the public sector and, in the long-term, may not generate sufficient employment to absorb all those of working age.

Although no data were available for unemployment in Burundi, it is generally understood that a significant percentage of the 3 million labour force was unemployed, with the figure probably highest among the youth. The likely scenario may mirror the South African experience, where the lack of alternative employment forced many ex-combatants to retain their weaponry and turn to violent crime (Cock, 2004). In Burundi, many combatants were de-mobilized without being disarmed, adding to the increase in armed criminal activities.

In theory, disarmament should precede demobilization, but pressure to spend funds allocated for DDR often means that programmes proceed irrespective of whether there is an effective ceasefire and national debate about the nature of the military in the post-conflict society. The wise words of one Burundian woman are worth noting:

> The DDR programme completely neglects the participation of civil society and is being presently conducted under the sole (supervision) of politicians and militaries. DDR is just another form of involvement of ex-combatants and militaries. Arms proliferation among civilians is another threat to the security of the community, because weapons are used for revenge, looting and sexual violence against women and girls. (M. Goretti Ndacayisaba, DUSHIREHAMWE, Statement to the Arria Formula meeting with the Security Council, NY, 25 October 2005: Presentation of DUSHIREHAMWE on Resolution 1325)

Truth and Reconciliation

The issue of impunity was on the agenda when it affected the ability of politicians to return and participate in the elections. Buyoya was reluctant to set up the provisions allowing for the return of Hutu political exiles to participate as members of the transitional government, the parliament and the Senate, despite the request from the IMC (Irinnews.org., 7.6.2001). On 27 August 2003, a temporary immunity law was passed covering 'crimes with a political aim committed after 1 July 1962 to the date of promulgation', amidst considerable opposition from human rights groups, Tutsi opposition parties and extremist organizations (Irinnews.org., 3.9.2003).

With regard to the Truth and Reconciliation Commission, the political leaders were keen to protect themselves from any future criminal charges. On 1 September 2004, the National Assembly passed a law allowing the UN to set up a non-judicial Truth Commission, with a substantial international component and the creation of a special chamber within the Burundi justice system to tackle crimes against humanity (Irinnews.org., 29.3.2005). It is unlikely that these bodies will receive meaningful support from the government, political parties or regional leaders. As one key participant claimed 'truth and reconciliation is no longer considered to be necessary... realizing that wrong things were done in the past, but the future does not involve exclusion'.[13] This viewpoint is in sharp contrast to that presented in post-election reports by human rights organizations, citing the continuation of summary execution and torture by Burundian soldiers, intelligence agents and FNL rebels, and rape, thefts and murders by criminal elements, especially ex-paramilitary armed gangs (HRW, 2005c; Ligue Iteka, 2005a & b). Civil society organizations in Burundi have questioned the independence of a Truth Commission. Moreover, the peace settlement has reinforced the acquisition of power by many who have committed acts of genocide and crimes against humanity.

Conclusion

Although the Burundi peace negotiations signalled a major commitment by regional leaders to stop the violence and potential destabilizing effect of the war on the region, the multiple interests of the various participants limited the Agreement to the minimal conditions for peace. Ending direct violence was beyond the capacity of the negotiations as the principle focus was on ethnic inequalities as the main cause of the violence and the solution was power-sharing between ethnic elites. Thus, peace meant further encoding ethnic differences into the political institutions of the state, partly to the benefit of the Hutus (Mandela was accused of reading the Burundi situation as apartheid), more so for the Tutsis, especially representatives of smaller parties, who gained more than their performance in the democratic elections warranted.

---

[13] Interview with member of Facilitation Team, Dar es Salaam, 2005.

The commitment of the signatories of the Agreement to the ending of the war became questionable, as most intensified the war during and especially after the peace agreement. Violence, especially against civilians, was the bargaining tool used by all the belligerents. The victory of CNDD-FDD reinforces the notion that legitimate political power can be won through wreaking extreme violence on the electorate. Violence, here, seems to serve three purposes. First, to destroy or seriously impair the opposition, whether, the state or rebel movement; second, to instil fear into the local people, who, although they vote, are not treated as citizens or constituents, capable of determining access to power; and thirdly, to emphasize to external observers, the military capability of the state or rebel movement. As the military might is fundamental to concepts of power and security, its display ensures that the perpetrator is taken seriously.

Clearly, transcending this masculinist conception of peace requires a more profound articulation of the endemic conditions that produce violence and instability. Although it was right not to treat women as an essentialist category, the absence of a gendered understanding of the state and of the nature of violence has contributed to the proliferation of gender-based violence even in areas considered peaceful and 'safe'. Moreover, the narrow reading of war as fighting between the state and rebel movements has meant that Hutu and Tutsi militias, criminal gangs and others, who use the state of war to perpetuate violence, have been able to continue to wreak havoc in many communities.

Many parties signed the agreement out of political and economic opportunism. Power-sharing arrangements seem to legitimize opportunistic behaviour and reinforce the social system within which violence and inequalities are embedded. It refers, essentially, to reconciliation among the elites. The immediate financial gains were from donor funds allocated to the various post-conflict reconstruction programmes, such as DDR and the integration of refugees and displaced peoples. Judging from the neo-liberal economic packages proposed for reconstruction, there will be no significant changes in socio-economic conditions that cause impoverishment and structural violence, at least in the short term. Burundi will return to a situation of heavy reliance on international aid. The neo-liberal peace delivered in Burundi through the peace negotiations cannot produce the human welfare-oriented state-centred economic programme that is needed to rectify injustices that have deep historical and global roots. It seems, therefore, that the dominant conflict resolution model upholds a non-transformative concept of peace.

The tribal/civil war narrative that pervades contemporary peacemaking can confine warfare within the boundaries of the nation-state. This has meant that the regional dimensions of genocidal violence, though referred to in Article 9 of Protocol III, were not given much consideration at the peace negotiations; this is a serious failing, especially, as shown, in Chapter 7, the ending of warfare in Rwanda and the DRC is inextricably linked to a resolution in Burundi.

11

Conclusion   An African
Creating Spaces   Feminist Agenda
of Peace

This final chapter summarizes the key contributions of the book and seeks to suggest ways in which a feminist-historical methodology of the twenty-first century can assist in the creation of spaces of peace in Africa. The material presented throughout indicates that the theorization and the implementation of the conditions that would lead to sustainable peace are still underdeveloped with respect to Burundi and Central Africa, despite the rich literature that has emanated from scholars of the region. The discussion has shown that the mechanistic production of international peace agreements and democratic elections are unable to curb direct violence, much less address the wider issues of structural violence and social justice. Creating spaces of peace in the context of the genocidal state requires new approaches that unpack the institutional-ization of violence and the discriminatory mechanisms that reproduces the state. In effect, it requires far-reaching and inclusive debates about the nature of society and citizenship.

I want to begin by challenging the popular understanding that 'trib-alism' or 'ethnicity' is the cause of much conflict in Africa. This view-point, it is argued, is evident not just in the popular media but also in the emphasis given to identity politics among certain scholars and policy–makers. According to Myers (2001: 523), this 'tribal fixation' is also perpetuated in geography textbook representations of Africa. Not that African identities are inconsequential but, as Chachage (2003: 94) contends, the shared history of men, women and whole African peoples cannot be understood only on the basis of 'identities that emerged as a result of the arbitrary classification of African people by the colonials and neo-colonials'. What this study shows is that even in supposedly ethnically divided states ethnicity is not at the core of the problem. By considering the social, historical and political basis of ethnicity and its relationship to genocidal violence in Burundi and the region, the book argues that the attribution of violence to ethnicity is not only simplistic but serves to mask the complex web of causes that have led to protracted warfare. Genocidal violence is the consequence of a complex intersection between modernity, militarism, ethnicity, masculinity, global geo-politics, aid and refugees. There is no doubt that ethnicity is used instru-mentally by the major political groupings; thus giving much of the violence its ethnic character, yet, the origins of violent ethnicity and its increasing saliency as a factor in African politics are very much linked to the ideologies and structures associated with a modern patriarchal state and extractive economies and the support for that state in the current globalized context.

Colonialism led first to the incorporation and later displacement of the traditional elites, as the basis of accumulation shifted from tribute-paying to commodity production for the state. The intrigue which characterized intra-elite interactions in the pre-colonial era resurfaced in the post-colonial period as accumulative strategies became closely linked to state power. It is argued that although the violence has taken on an ethnic char-acter, it is rooted in a struggle for power within the political class; a struggle for which the underlying determinants are as much regional, clan and inter-personal allegiances as ethnic difference. Seeing violence in Africa primarily through the lens of ethnicity, or sometimes religion, robs African societies of their humanity and feeds into racist discourse about human development. More importantly, it affects the nature of international intervention and policymaking in relation to genocide, conflict resolution, arms transfer and peace.

Three major theoretical conclusions emerge from the study of geno-cidal violence in Burundi that have implications for a sustainable African peace. The first is distinctly geographical; that is the significance of the politics of scale in the reproduction of violence. Genocidal violence persists and is reproduced consistently because of the ordering of the African humanity within a 'nested hierarchy of spatial scales' – the product of modernity and capitalism. Dehumanization of the African has and continues to take place on a global, continental, regional, national and local scale. The militia man commits genocidal violence because of the powerlessness of his victims, the sanctioning of his behaviour by local authorities, supported by the discriminatory practices of the insti-tutions of the national state, and the prevarications and indifference of the international community. When represented at the local scale, the dehumanization of the body seems inexplicably 'primitive', as in on-the-spot accounts of bodily mutilation, yet, scaling up, its modernity is apparent in the systematization displayed by the state and the euphemistic language used by the political elite and bureaucracy.

The second theoretical conclusion is the desperate need for a concep-tualization of peace that rehumanizes the African body, physically, mate-rially and spiritually. The dismemberment, mutilation, rape, and all manner of atrocities enacted on the human body reflect wider socio-political processes that situate Africans within racial, gendered and human hierarchies. Such processes are inherently destructive. David Harvey (2000: 99) rightly points out that 'Class, racial, gender and all manner of distinctions are marked upon the human body by virtue of the different ecological processes that do their work on the body.' The discriminatory practices associated with Social Darwinism are part and parcel of the culture and ideology of the genocidal state and are repro-duced in its cultural institutions. The concept of the *évolué*, the west-ernized native, was given meaning through the Church, schools, university and military academies. Furthermore, the use of force in production for the external market reproduced these divisions.

International distancing from the violence in Africa is the consequence of the dehumanization involved in the commodification of the African body, which began with slavery, forced labour and supported by Social Darwinian pseudo-science and ending with eugenics in the biotech century; a process which has moved beyond the continent. As Depelchin (2004: 28) points out, there is a danger that 'Africanization (in the sense of being reduced to less than a human being) ...will under the present socio-economic system affect segments of humanity which might have considered themselves immune from this kind of discrimination.'

The frequent reference to tribalism, ethnicity, tradition and culture as characteristics that differentiate between lesser and more evolved human beings, implies that these socially-produced categories are 'natural' and therefore 'fixed' phenomena. Even terms such as 'civil war' and 'conflict' reduce the importance of violence, enabling, in the political discourse of national and international governments, a representation of the 'uniqueness' of the African context. Countries like Burundi are transformed by the political rhetoric of the West into 'tribal basket-cases', or 'scars on the face of the earth' that the more sane and advanced world has a moral duty to correct.

In the international arena, territorial sovereignty is used both by the state and the international community as fixed and even 'natural'. Except, of course, in relation to economic liberalization, where the neo-liberal institutions – IMF and World Bank – can dictate and impose prescriptions. We tend to forget that boundaries are rarely fixed. The movement of goods, people, refugees and arms exposes their porosity but also their subsumption in networks of regional practices and in the fluidity of people's identification with territorial space. Post-colonial Africans have known the 'terror' of territoriality and homogenous conceptualizations of the nation state. The seemingly abstract concept of sovereignty, especially in the Central African region, has been deployed to justify discriminatory state practices and used as an excuse for non-intervention in cases of genocidal violence. Theoretically, the increasing draconian treatment of refugees emanates from a discourse which sees them as separate from the body politic. I agree with Soguk's (1999) contention that in this discourse refugees falls outside the hierarchy of nation/state/citizens, so much so, that, in many respects, they are treated as sub-humans.

I argue that states, such as Burundi, have become adept at playing the politics of scale in absolving themselves from accusations of genocidal practices. At the international level, states embark on political performances that strengthen their sovereignty and credibility, and that lack legitimacy at home. These involve the ratification of numerous international human rights laws and the submission of the desired reports to various UN committees, while using concepts of genocide and ethnicity instrumentally to deflect criticism and any serious investigation of genocide and crimes against humanity within the national space.

The third conclusion relates to the dominant theme in the book, which is that violence arises from the intersection of state power, militarism and patriarchy and their dependence on destructive forms of masculinity for their reproduction, and is compounded by ethnicity. As shown, violence in Burundi and the region has been an integral component of state power from the colonial period to the present. Despite not having a monopoly on violence, the discriminatory state is able to use genocidal violence to legitimate its hold on power. Militarism is embedded in state practices; and political competition is mediated through violence, not dialogue and participatory forms of democracy. Militarism is the dominant ideology of the Burundi state. Its prevalence is the direct result of the impact of trans-formations in the global political economy on African societies and the failure of the post-colonial state to transform its discriminatory and dehumanizing socio-political and economic projects. Militarism has been strengthened by western governments' support for the 'strong-man' in African politics. The concept of the 'strong man' as leader reinforces violent masculinity as hegemonic and an acceptable mode of social practice. In a militarized state, violence is by necessity gendered, affecting both men and women in quite differentiated ways. Military men's intolerance of alternative forms of masculinity often leads to the most brutal atrocities being inflicted on men who don't fight or belong to other social and political categories. Military men feel more comfortable with circumscribed roles for women that enhance their masculinity. In a militarized culture, alternative forms of masculinities and femininities are seen as subversive and can only be corrected through violence.

The militarized culture of modernity has little time for African cultural practices, denigrating pre-existing values and norms that governed social and political interaction. This has led to the growing atomization of African collectivities varyingly into ethnicized communities, nucleated families and individualized beings. The extreme consequence of this atomization is the total breakdown of the social fabric of the society, leading to endemic genocidal and other forms of violence amidst a culture of impunity.

As exemplified by Burundi, concepts such as participatory democracy, civil society and citizenship are rendered meaningless in a militarized state. Soguk's (1999) hierarchy of citizens, though theoretically inter-esting, is less useful in the context of Africa, where, historically, the term 'citizen' rarely came with any privileges for the mass of people. In practice, the concept of the 'citizen' has been affected by the intersection of race, ethnic and gender hierarchies that are intertwined with the modern state, and have operated and gained legitimacy across different spatial scales – from the local to the global.

Throughout, the concept of the 'failed' state is an unhelpful method-ological tool to explain current conditions of life in Africa, where states have never sought to be effective in terms of caring for the reproduction of the citizenry and have been essentially agents of discrimination and violence. Perhaps in the 1980s states may have briefly 'failed', in terms of securing the conditions for the reproduction of capital, but many were immediately brought into line through structural adjustment. There is a need, therefore, to examine further the intellectual coherence of the concept of the state as it is applied to Africa.

Historically and contemporarily, the process of militarization has been dependent on the interactions across and within scale with global geo-politics playing a critical role in its intensification. The reconfiguration of global power with the ending of the Cold War has not produced a 'safer' world for Africans, it altered only the form that militarization takes, and further entrenches African people's subjection to the violent militarism of capitalism. Feminists' contention of the centrality of militarism to the modern state cannot be understood without addressing the global promotion of militarism as evident in the global sales of weaponry and more recently the rise of what De Waal (2002) terms 'commercial or opportunistic militarism' in the form of trans-national private military companies.

In Search of Spaces of Peace

Here, I return to David Harvey's vision of utopia, because like the enlightenment scholars of early modern Europe, we are at a critical juncture in history where it is incumbent upon us as ethical beings to seek ways out of the misery of the human condition that prevails on the continent.

Harvey (2000: 182) entreats us to search for a 'dialectical utopianism', which allows us to experiment with new 'possibilities of spatial form', and 'the exploration of a wide range of human potentialities (different modes of collective living, of gender relations of production-consumption styles, in relation to nature, etc.)'. This would demand a paradigmatic shift in our current thinking about political organization and human society relationships. How can we illuminate those spaces of hope that are an essential part of the human spirit and persistent struggle of impoverished people? Finding spaces of hope require actual engagement with emancipatory politics. At this historical juncture, the territorial logic of the nation-state along with the imposition of neo-liberal democracy as a means of legitimizing state relationships with the people is so hegemonic, that calls for emancipatory politics and the rehumanization of African people can be perceived, in some quarters, as heretic. Furthermore, challenging the development discourse which talks of local ownership of 'poverty reduction and growth strategy papers' is near impossible, even when it is quite clear that representatives of the 'local' are not necessarily legitimate or accountable, and the papers follow an external formulae. This manipulation of the 'local' in the developmental discourse of global institutions serves to mask top-down undemocratic policies, and demands further attention from scholars.

In the Great Lakes region of Africa, a starting point in the creation of a new paradigm, a new mode of politics, is to begin with a search for spaces of peace. To do this we have to equip ourselves with new liberation methodologies that help us to unravel the spatiality and temporality of genocidal violence. This book seeks to take seriously a feminist methodology precisely because it unveils the stark reality of the forces that oppress, and promote violence, both structural and genocidal.

Harvey's (2000: 262) route to utopia envisions a feminist proletariat 'as agent of historical transformation'. He writes, 'These women worked under insufferable conditions of oppression and continued to be lumbered with all the key responsibilities of reproduction (while being

excluded particularly under the military theocracies, from public power).'
While I also foresee the potentialities of women's transformative capacities, we need to heed the caveats that have been drawn to our attention by
feminists. Essentializing women's experience of militarism and warfare
can prevent us from observing the differentiated experience of women
according to class, ethnicity and region of origin, and especially proximity
to men with power.

The prevailing peace problematic that focuses on ethnic and gender
equity rather than the more transformative social justice is insufficiently
emancipatory and as feminists of the past found, equality meant
elevating a few women to serve their class interests in a highly unequal
system. UN Security Council Resolution 1325 represents a landmark in
the recognition of a more gendered approach to peace. Efforts to mainstream Resolution 1325 into peace processes have encountered considerable difficulties from patriarchal states, mediators and even from
scholars seeking a new dispensation in Africa. De Waal (2002) sees no
role for African women in peace-making and only a marginal one in
peace-building. As the study of the Burundi peace negotiations shows, it
is not just Burundi men who are involved in warfare and peace-making,
the peace agenda is being determined by different actors at different
scales: local politicians, regional heads of state, western governments
and international organizations, all aiming to determine what constitutes
acceptable violence, security and peace.

Feminists have rightly questioned the narrow interpretation of the
concept of demilitarization in contemporary conflict resolution models
and have exposed its inability to deal with the range of violence that gets
accentuated in wars and militarized cultures. A radical feminist reading
of the concept requires more fundamental investigations into our understanding of violence and its relationship to the state, to patriarchy and
masculinity. Without this thorough examination, policy formulation
relating to demilitarization or DDR lacks the fundamental critical perspectives that can help illuminate the basis for sustainable peace. Realist
conceptualizations of peace and demilitarization promote pragmatism as
the guiding principle, which, in the context of Central Africa, serves to
maintain the status quo, thus perpetuating cultures of impunity and genocidal violence. Campbell reinforces this view with his claim that:

> Intellectual work in the West tends to be shortsighted and guided by the
> realist paradigms that suggested that peace would involve the strongest
> forces coming together. The prevailing pre-occupation with militaristic
> solutions and the deployment of troops as a basis for peace continue to
> dominate the discussion on how to implement the peace accords.
> (Campbell 2002: 53)

Adopting a feminist agenda on demilitarization and the peace problematic
would inevitably lead to transformations of the state and the promotion of
diversity, especially the recognition of the validity of the myriad of identities which govern social and political life in African societies.

I have identified some of the key changes that would contribute to the
creation of spaces of peace. First, the transformation of the genocidal

state has to be at the core of any advancement, particularly its ethnic, racial and gendered character. This would require a concerted effort to transcend outmoded and destructive ideas of racial and ethnic superiority. Implicit in this is the revalorization of the African human through concerted actions to expunge categories that seek to denigrate its essence. This would involve the operationalization of the concept of social justice as being fundamental to any concept of development. Here, the emphasis would be on the right to life and to bodily sustenance; in sum, a focus on human wellbeing, and the abandonment of other concepts that sanction impoverishment and genocidal violence.

Second, a feminist peace agenda calls for the emplacement of a democracy that reflects and protects the human. This would mean instituting an emancipatory form of politics that would certainly not sit well with contemporary approaches to governance and accountability. In the region, the 'body politic' has been robbed of its meaning as the political community shrinks even within the framework of multipartyism and much promotion of civil society. Unfortunately, power-sharing helps to reinforce political competition of a violent kind.

Third, the privileging of alternative forms of masculinities and femininities; this should follow naturally from the institutionalization of a genuine democracy, but it may need concerted action. From the nineteenth century to the present, there have been African men who have refused to be dehumanized into committing atrocities. The promotion of non-violent forms of masculinity would help to alter the character of much of the violence. I am in agreement with Connell, who argues that the dynamic nature of masculinity and the existence of multiple masculinities show the potential for transformations in gender relations. He writes:

> The task is not to abolish gender, but to reshape it; to disconnect (for instance) courage from violence, steadfastness from prejudice, ambition from exploitation ... Making boys and men aware of the diversity of masculinities that already exist in the world, beyond the narrow models they are commonly offered. (Connell, 2002: 39)

This will involve separating political power from military might; desexualizing military activity and promoting women's full and equitable participation at all levels within the society.

Fourth, the promotion of regionality and regional citizenship as alternatives to discriminatory territorially-bound concepts of state sovereignty and identity politics are critical elements in achieving sustainable peace. Pan-Africanism has long engaged with the issue of the political unity of African people – a truly emancipatory act that has been seen as too threatening by leaders schooled in discriminatory practices and petty nationalism. Theoretically, though, at the regional level, instruments for peace and reconstruction now exist under the auspices of the African Union, which now has in its legal instruments mechanisms for the outlaw of undemocratic practices and the greater participation of African people in government. The application of these principles can start at the regional level, as there seems to be a regional impetus for peace. The inter-relatedness of the Central African conflicts makes a regional peace framework essential to the peace process. Wider interpretation of the concept of citizenship would give rights not just to those in supposedly sovereign territory but, more importantly, to the vast number of people who are dispossessed. In sum, a regional approach necessitates taking a fresh look at issues of genocidal violence, social justice, economic viability and integration, population mobility and citizenship.

And finally, we return to scale. The interconnectedness of spatial scales shows that Africans need to participate in regional and global networks for peace in order to unleash the 'potentialities' that Harvey refers to. The role of neo-liberal humanitarianism is worth considering here. The proliferation of INGOs does not necessarily spell the empowerment of Africans, particularly because of the racialized hierarchies still prevalent in many African societies. Elevation of African agency should be a critical part of any new paradigm. This would require a sustained critique of those forces that claim to speak on behalf of the people and the grassroots. The experience of Rwanda and Burundi has shown that many care neither for history nor complexity, nor even for African lives – as exemplified by their rapid departure in times of genocidal violence. Like the state, INGOs also perform a scalar form of politics, being benign and charitable at the global scale and discriminatory at the local. We need to move away from a conceptualization of humanitarian action as an essentialized good or desirability and differentiate between that which empowers and that which perpetuates marginalization. Irrespective of their position though, INGOs cannot be at the forefront of emancipatory and progressive politics in Africa.

It has been argued, and shown, in the case of Burundi, that Eurocentric and liberal concepts of peace and development cannot deliver the sort of social transformation required for the elevation of the African human. There are voices in Africa demanding more human-centred approaches as counter to the market-centred one that prevails. The culture of impunity in the Great Lakes region of Africa is embedded in the structures of global economic development and the role of the African within them. Addressing the culture of impunity requires that new relationships are forged that first and foremost recognize the intrinsic value in African lives, essentially the human in the African and the responsibilities or *ubuntu* that connects every human being.

BIBLIOGRAPHY

Abdullah, Ibrahim & Ismail Rashid (2004) 'Smallest Victims; Youngest Killers': Juvenile Combatants in Sierra Leone's Civil War', in Ibrahim Abdullah (ed.) *Between Democracy and Terror: The Sierra Leone Civil War.* Dakar: CODESRIA. pp. 238–53.

Adelman, Howard (2003) 'The Use and Abuse of Refugees in Zaire', in Stephen John Stedman & Fred Tanner (eds.), *Refugee Manipulation: War, Politics, and the Abuse of Human Suffering.* Washington: Brookings Institute, pp. 95–134.

Adelski, Elizabeth & Nancy Rosen (1991) 'Getting and Spending: Household Economy in Rural Burundi', *IDA Working Paper No.89.* pp. 1–110. Clark University: Institute of Development Anthropology.

African Business (1988) 'Burundi: Donors Ponder Tribal Massacre', October, No. 122: 37.

Africa Confidential (12 August 1994) 'Burundi on the Knife Edge', 35 (16): 1–3; (12 February 1995) 'Burundi Militant's mayhem', 36 (4): 5–6; (4 August 1995) 'Burundi: A Creeping Coup', 36 (16): 3–4; (2 August 1996) 'Burundi: Buyoya Perhaps', 37 (16): 8; (9 May 1997) 'Burundi: Buyoya Alone', 38 (10): 6–7; (6–8 March 1998) 'Burundi: Conflict Resolution', 39 (5): 5–6; (17 April 1998) 'Burundi: Secrets and Splits', 39 (8) 8; (21–22 October 1999) 'Losing a Peacemaker', 40 (21): 2. London: Africa Confidential.

Africanews.org (6 October 1997) 'Burundi: Foes Open Dialogue in Paris', http://Africanews.org.

African Rights (1994a) *Rwanda: Who is Killing; Who is Dying; What is to be Done,* London: African Rights Discussion Paper, May.

African Rights (1994b) *Humanitarianism Unbound: Current Dilemmas Facing Multi-Mandate Relief Operations in Political Emergencies.* London: African Rights Discussion Paper No. 51.

African Rights (1995) *Not so Innocent: When Women Become Killers.* London: African Rights.

Ake, Claude (1996) *Democracy and Development in Africa,* Washington DC: Brookings Institution.

Albert, Ethel M. (1971) 'Women in Burundi: A Study of Social Values', in D. Paulme (ed.) *Women in Tropical Africa,* Berkeley: University of California Press, pp. 179–215.

Amadiume, Ifi (1997) *Reinventing Africa: Matriarchy, Religion, and Culture.* London: Zed Books.

Amadiume, Ifi (2000a) *Daughters of the Goddess, Daughters of Imperialism.* London: Zed Books.

Amadiume, Ifi & Abdullahi An-Na'im (eds) (2000) *The Politics of Memory: Truth, Healing and Social Justice,* London: Zed Books.

Amin, Samir (1976) *Unequal Development: An Essay on the Social Formation of Peripheral Capitalism,* Translated by Brian Pearce. Sussex: Harvester Press.

Amnesty International (AI) (1984) *Restrictions des activitées religieuses et arrestation de members des eglises chretiennes au Burundi*; (1992) *Burundi: Sectarian Security Forces Violate Human Rights with Impunity.* 27 November; (1995a) *Burundi: Targeting Students, Teachers and Clerics in the Fight for Supremacy.* September; (1995b) *Rwanda and Burundi: A Call for Action by the International Community.* September; (1995c) *Burundi: Struggle for Survival: Immediate Action Vital to Stop Killings,* June; (1996a) *Burundi: Armed Groups Kill Without Mercy.* 12 June; (1996b) *Burundi: Refugees Forced back to Danger.* 20 November; (1998) *Mémorandum au Gouvernement Burundais sur le Projet de Loi relatif au Genocide et aux Crimes Contre L'Humanité.* 30 March; (2000) *Great Lakes Region: Refugees Denied Protection.* May; (2004a) *Tracking Lethal Weapons: Marking and Tracing Arms and Ammunition: A central piece of the arms control puzzle*; (2004b) *Burundi: Rape – The Hidden Human Rights Abuse*; (2004c) *Burundi: Urgent Need to Protect Women and Girls from Rape, Press Release.* 24 February; (2004d) *Burundi: Redress for Victims of Sexual Violence*; (2004e) *Burundi: Child Soldiers – The Challenge of Demobilization*; (2005) *Refugees at Risk: Human Rights Abuse in Returns to and from Burundi.* 27 June; London: Amnesty International http: //web.amnesty.org.
Arendt, Hannah (2004) 'On Violence', in Scheper-Hughes, Nancy & Philipe Bourgois (eds), *Violence in War and Peace.* Malden, USA & Oxford: Blackwell Publishing, pp. 236–43.
Arusha Peace Accord, *Peace Agreement between the Government of Rwanda and the Rwandese Patriotic Front,* Arusha, Tanzania, 3 August, 1993.
Arusha Peace and Reconciliation Agreement for Burundi, (2000) ARUSHA, 28 August 2000. Available online at http://www.usip.org/library/pa/burundi/pa [Last accessed 6 June 2007]
Aupens, Bernard (1973) 'L'engrenage de la violence au Burundi', *L'Ancienne Afrique Belge,* pp. 48–69.
Baines, Erin (2003) 'Body Politics and the Rwandan Crisis', *Third World Quarterly,* 24, 3: 479–93.
Bangura, Yusuf (1994) *The Search For Identity: Ethnicity, Religion and Political Violence.* Geneva: UNRISD.
Bangura, Yusuf (2004) 'The Politics and Dynamics of the Sierra Leone War' in Ibrahim Abdullah (ed.) *Between Democracy and Terror: The Sierra Leone Civil War.* Dakar: CODESRIA. pp. 13–40.
Baraka, Elias & Bahir Mfinange (1998) *France unrepentant over Economic help to Burundi.* www.Inta-Africa, 4 May 1998.
Bauman, Zygmunt (1989) *Modernity and the Holocaust.* Cambridge: Polity Press.
Bayart, Jean-Francois (1993) *The State in Africa: The Politics of the Belly.* London: Longman.
Bayart, Jean-Francois, Stephen Ellis and Béatrice Hibou (1999) *The Criminalisation of the State in Africa.* Oxford: James Currey.
BBC News. 16 January 2000. 'Mandela Slams Burundi's 'failed' leaders'.
BBC News, 11 September 2006, 'Burundi rebels to lay down arms', http: //news.bbc.co.uk/1/hi/world/africa/5332644.stm [accessed 14 September 2006].
Beaumont, Rory (2007) '*Springtime in Burundi? A tale of two visits,* Dec 06/Feb 07'
Beinart, William (1992) 'Introduction: Political Collective Violence in Southern African Historiography', *Journal of Southern African Studies,* 18, 3: 455–86.
Ben Hammouda, Hakim (1995) *Burundi: Histoire Économique et Politique d'un Conflit.*
Paris: L'Harmattan.
Bentley, Kristina A. & Roger Southall (2005) *An African Peace Process: Mandela, South Africa and Burundi.* Cape Town: HSRC Press, Nelson Mandela Foundation & Human Science Research Council.

Berdal, Mats & David Malone (eds) (2000) *Greed and Grievance: Economic Agendas in Civil Wars*, Boulder & London: Lynne Reinner.

Berger, Iris (1981) *Religion and Resistance: East African Kingdoms in the Pre-Colonial Period*, Tervuren, Belgium: Musée Royal de L'Afrique Centrale.

Betts, Tristram. F. (1984) 'Refugees and integrated rural development in Africa', *Africa Today*, 31,1: 7–24.

Bizimana, Ladislas (1999) *Conflict in the African Great Lakes Region: A Critical Analysis of Regional and International Involvement*. Bilbao: University of Duesto.

Black, Richard & Khalib Koser (eds) (1999) *The End of the Refugee Cycle? Refugee Repatriation and Reconstruction*. New York & Oxford: Berghahn Books.

Blakey, K. A. (1964) 'Economic Development of Burundi', paper presented to Specialized Course on *Manpower and Educational Planning in Economic Development*, Cairo – 18 Feb – 15 May 1964, Organized by African Institute of Economic Development and Planning and Institute of National Planning, Cairo.

Blanchard, Eric M. (2003) 'Gender, International Relations, and the Development of Feminist Security Theory', *Signs: Journal of Women in Culture and Society*, 28, 4: 1289–1312.

Boshoff, Henri & Dara Francis (2003) The AU Mission in Burundi: Technical and Operational Directions', *African Security Review*, Vol. 12, No. 3. http://www.iss.co.za/pubs/ASR/12No3/AWBoshoff.html [accessed July 2005]

Bowen, Michael, Gary Freeman & Kay Miller (1974) *Passing by: The United States and Genocide in Burundi*. Washington DC: Special Report for the Carnegie Endowment for International Peace.

Brooks, Hugh C. & Yassin El-Ayouty, (eds) (1970) *Refugees South of the Sahara: an African Dilemma*. Westport, Conn.: Negro Universities Press.

Bruchhaus, Eva-Maria, (2005) *Rapport de Mission, Revue des Aspects Genre du Programme de Demobilization, Reinsertion et Reintegration au Burundi*. Bujumbura: Executive Sercretariat of the National Commission for Demobilization, Reinsertion and Reintegration & UNIFEM.

Bunting, Ikaweba, B. Mwansasu & W. Bagoya (1999) *Overview of the Burundi Peace Process*. Dar es Salaam: Report of The Mwalimu Nyerere Foundation.

Bureau International d'Information Burundi (BIIB), (1985) *'Le Burundi Theatre de Massacres des Populations Hutu par une Minorité Raciste Tutsi*, Svendstrup, Denmark: BIIB. April.

Burke, Enid de Silva, Jennifer Klot & Ikaweba Bunting (2001) *Engendering Peace: Reflections on the Burundi Peace Process*. Nairobi: UNIFEM (United Nations Development Fund for Women).

Burundi Peace Negotiations (1998) *Report of the First Session of the Burundi Peace Negotiations*, Arusha, Tanzania, 15–21 June 1998.

Butiku, Joseph, W. (2004) 'Facilitation of the Burundi Peace Negotiations', in Mpangala, Gaudens & Bismarck U. Mwansasu (eds) 2004. *Beyond Conflict in Burundi*. Dar es Salaam: The Mwalimu Nyerere Foundation, pp. 63–118.

Buyoya, Pierre (1998) *Mission Impossible: construire une paix durable au Burundi*. Paris: L'Harmattan.

Campbell, Horace (1996) 'Humanitarian Re-colonization in Angola', *CODESRIA Bulletin*, 3: 13–16.

Campbell, Horace (2002) *The Lusaka Peace Agreement: The Responsibility of African Academics and Civil Society*. Nairobi: Nairobi Peace Initiative.

Campbell, Horace & Marc Mealy (2005), 'From the Economics of War and Planning for Exploitation to People and Reconstruction in the Democratic Republic of Congo', Mimeo.

Caplan, Richard (2007) 'From collapsing states to neo-trusteeship: the limits to solving the problem of 'precarious statehood' in the 21st century', *Third World Quarterly*. 28, 2: 231–44.

Cavalieri, Roberto (1995) 'La Guerra dell'oro', in Angelo Turco, Angelo Ferrari, Aluisi Tosolini, Roberto Cavalieri & Stefano Squarcina, *Bujumbura; Citta dell'odio*, Parma: Edizioni Alfazeta. pp. 47–66.

Centre D'Analyse et D'Action Pour le Burundi (CAAB) (1999) *Burundi: Quand le Genocide et Des Crimes Contre L' Humanité Deviennent un 'Fonds de Commerce.'* Brussels: CAAB.

Cervenska, Zdenek & Colin Legum (1994) *Can National Dialogue Break the Power of Terror in Burundi? Report on the Impact of the International Conference on National Dialogue held in Bujumbura on May 15–18, 1994*, Current African Issues 17, Uppsala: Nordiska Afrikainstituet.

Chabal, Patrick & Jean-Pascal Daloz (1999) *Africa Works: Disorder as Political Instrument*. Oxford: James Currey.

Chachage, Seithy L. (2003) 'A note on the importance of knowledge/history in the context of Susan Geiger's book and collection', in Chachage S. L. & Marjorie Mbilinyi (eds), *Against Neo-Liberalism: Gender Democracy and Development*. Dar es Salaam: Tanzania Gender Networking Programme, E & D Limited. pp. 93–6.

Chachage, Seithy L. & Marjorie Mbilinyi (eds) (2003) *Against neo-liberalism: gender, democracy and development*. Dar es Salaam: Tanzania Gender Networking Programme, E & D Limited.

Chaulia, Sreeram (2003) 'The Politics of Refugee Hosting in Tanzania: From Open Door to Unsustainability, Insecurity and Receding Receptivity', *Journal of Refugee Studies* 16, 2: 147–66.

Chaulia, Sreeram (2006) 'Angola: Empire of Humanitarianism', Journal of humanitarian Assistance', *Journal of Humanitarian Assistance*. July, http://www.jha.ac/.

Chhatbur, Sukhdev (2001) 'Mandela proposes that Buyoya leads the First phase of Interim Govt'. Internews (Arusha), *AllAfrica.com*, 11 July 2001. http://allafrica.com [accessed 16 July 2001].

Chinkin, Christine (2003) 'Gender, Human Rights, and Peace Agreements' *Ohio State Journal on Dispute Resolution* 18, 3: 867–86.

Chomé, Jules (1962) 'L'Affaire Rwagasore', *Remarques Congolaises: Hebdomadaire PanAfricain d'Information et de Documentation*, 14 December 1962, Brussels.

Chopra, Jarat (1996) 'The Space of Peace-Maintenance', *Political Geography*, 15, 3/4: 335–7.

Chrétien, Jean-Pierre (1993) *Burundi: L'Histoire Retrouvée: 25 ans de Metier d'Historien en Afrique*. Paris: Editions Karthala.

Chretien, Jean-Pierre (1996) 'Burundi: the obsession with genocide', *Current History*, May: 206–10.

Clapham, Christopher (1998) 'Rwanda: the Perils of Peacemaking', *Journal of Peace Research*, 35, 2: 193–210.

Clark, Lance (1986) 'Dependency Syndrome: Another Look', *Refugee Magazine*, May: 35–7.

Cock, Jacklyn (2004) *Rethinking Militarism in Post-Apartheid South Africa*, Development Research Centre, London School of Economics, Crisis States Programme, Working Paper Series 1.

Cockburn, Cynthia (2001) 'The Gendered Dynamics of Armed Conflict and Political Violence' in Caroline O.N. Moser & Fiona C. Clark (eds) *Victims, Perpetrators or Actors?: Gender, Armed Conflict and Political Violence*. London: Zed Books. pp. 13–29.

Cockburn, Cynthia, & Dubravka Zarkov (eds) (2002) *The Post-war Moment: Militaries, Masculinities and International Peacekeeping*. London: Lawrence and Wishart.

Collier, Paul & Anke Hoeffler (2002) On the Incidence of Civil War in Africa, *Journal of Conflict Resolution*, 46, 1, 13–28.

Collier, Paul & Anke Hoeffler (2004) Greed and Grievance in Civil War, *Oxford Economic Papers*, 56, 563–95.

Connell, Robert. W. (1995) *Masculinities*. Cambridge: Polity.

Connell, Robert. W. (2000) *The Men and the Boys*. Cambridge: Polity.

Connell, Robert. W. (2002) 'Masculinities, the Reduction of Violence and the Pursuit of Peace', in Cynthia Cockburn & Dubravka Zarkov (eds), *The Post-war Moment: Militaries, Masculinities and International Peacekeeping*. London: Lawrence and Wishart. pp. 33–40.

Crawford, James & Karen Lee (2004) 'Goetz v. Burundi', *International Convention on the Settlement of Investment Disputes Reports*, Cambridge: Cambridge University Press. pp. 3–12.

Crenshaw, Kimberle (1991) 'Mapping the Margins: Intersectionality, Identity Politics and Violence against Women of Color', *Stanford Law Review*, 43, 6: 1241–99.

Daily News (Tanzania) (17 July 1973) 'Good Neighbourly Talks with Michombero'; (23 July 1973) 'Burundi to compensate for killing'; (29 September 1978) '15,000 Rwandese apply for citizenship'; (12 July 1985) 'Refugees Misconduct won't be tolerated – Minister'; (11 April 1986) 'Refugees warned against destabilization'; (6 October 1986) 'Burundi bans catechism schools'; (29 November 1986) 'Leaders agree to disarm refugees'; (6 April 1987) 'Illegal Residents Rounded-up'; (31 November 1994) 'Hutu militias kill Rwandan Refugees in Karagwe'; (19 January 1996) 'UNHCR Chief wants aid workers in Burundi protected'; (20 March 1996) 'Mpaka appealed to the International Community'; (24 May 1996) 'Refugees Reluctant to Return Home'; (19 June 1996) 'Granted Citizenship'; (15 May 1997) 'Burundi sold most of the 1996/97 coffee despite trade embargo'; (27 July 1997) 'CNDD & Buyoya opened secret talks'. Dar es Salaam: *Daily News* newspaper.

Daily Telegraph (London) (9 June 1972) 'Atmosphere of fear in Burundi after the massacres', by Catherine Bond.

Daily Telegraph (23 June 1972) 'Burundi Massacres Ending', by David Martin.

Daily Telegraph (London) (15 May 1973) 'New Burundi massacre feared', by David Martin.

Daley, Patricia (1989) *Refugees and Underdevelopment in Africa: The Case of Burundi Refugees in Tanzania*, D.Phil. thesis, University of Oxford.

Daley, Patricia (1992) 'The politics of the refugee crisis in Tanzania', in Horace Campbell & Howard Stein (eds), *Tanzania and the IMF: the Dynamics of Liberalization*. Boulder, Colorado: Westview Press. pp. 125–46.

Daley, Patricia (1993) 'From the Kipande to the Kibali: the Incorporation of Barundi Refugees and Labour Migrants in Western Tanzania 1900–1987', in Richard Black & Vaughan Robinson (eds) *Geography and Refugees: Patterns and Processes of Change*. London: Belhaven. pp. 17–32.

Dallaire, Romeo (2003) *Shake Hands with the Devil: the Failure of Humanity in Rwanda*. London: Arrow Books.

De Heusch, Luc (1964) 'Nationalisme et Lutte des classes au Rwanda', in Willy Fröhlich (ed.) *Afrika im Wandel Seiner gesellschaftsformen: Vorträge einer Tagung de Deutschen Afrika-Gesellschaft (Bonn) im November 1962 in (Koln)*. Leiden: E. J. Brill.

Depelchin, Jacques (2004) *Silences in African History: Between the Syndromes of Discovery and Abolition*. Dar es Salaam: Mkuki Na Nyota.

De Soysa, Indra (2000) 'The Resource Curse: Are civil wars driven by rapacity or paucity', in Mats Berdal & David Malone (eds) *Greed and Grievance: Economic Agendas in Civil Wars*, Boulder & London: Lynne Reinner.

De Waal, Alexander (2000) *Who Fights? Who Cares?: War and Humanitarian Action in Africa*. Trenton, NJ: Africa World Press.

De Waal, Alexander (2002) (ed.) *Demilitarizing the Mind: African Agendas for Peace and Security*. London, Justice Africa; Trenton, NJ: Africa World Press.

De Witte, Ludo (2001) *The Assassination of Lumumba*. Translated by Ann Wright and Renee Fenby, London & New York: Verso.

D'Hertefelt, Marcel (1971) *Les clans du Rwanda and Burundi: ancient elements d'ethnographie et l'ethnohistorie*. Tervuren: Musee Royal de L'Afrique Centrale.

Diop, Bineta (2002) 'Engendering the Peace Process in Africa: Women at the Negotiating Table', *Refugee Survey Quarterly*, 21, special issue. pp. 142–54.

Diop, Cheikh Anta (1989) *The Cultural Unity of Black Africa: The Domains of Matriarchy and of Patriarchy in Classical Antiquity*. London: Karnak House.

Diop, Cheikh Anta (1991) *Civilization or Barbarism: An Authentic Anthropology*. Translated from French by Yaa-Lengi Meema Ngemi & edited by Harold Salemson & Marjolin de Jager, New York: Lawrence Hill Books.

Duffield, Mark (2001) *Global Governance and the New Wars: The Merging of Development and Security*. London: Zed Books.

East African (18–24 August 1997) 'East African Governments divided over Burundi'. Nairobi, Kenya.

East African (11 March 1998) 'Business as usual in Burundi'. Nairobi, Kenya.

Elias, Norbert (1982) *The Civilizing Process: the History of Manners and State Formation and Civilization, Vol. 2.*, translated by Edmund Jephcott, Oxford: Blackwell.

Elias, Norbert (1987) 'The state monopoly of physical violence and its infringement', in John Keane (ed.), *Civil Society and the State*. London: Verso.

Elkins, Caroline (2005) *Britain's Gulag: the Brutal End of Empire in Kenya*, London: Jonathan Cape.

Emizet, Kisangani N. F. (2000) 'The Massacre of Refugees in Congo: A case of UN peace-keeping failure and International Law', *Journal of Modern African Studies*, 38, 2: 163–202.

Enloe, Cynthia (1980) *Police, Military and Ethnicity: Foundations of State Power*. London & New Brunswick: Transaction Books.

Enloe, Cynthia (1983) *Does Khaki Become You?: the Militarization of Women's Lives*. London: Pluto.

Enloe, Cynthia (1993) *The Morning After: Sexual Politics at the End of the Cold War*. Berkeley & London: University of California Press.

Enloe, Cynthia (2000) *Maneuvers: The International Politics of Militarizing Women's Lives*. Berkeley & Los Angeles: University of California Press.

Enloe, Cynthia (2002) 'Demilitarization – or more of the same? Feminist questions to ask in the postwar moment', in Cynthia Cockburn & Dubravka Zarkov (eds), *The Post-war Moment: Militaries, Masculinities and International Peacekeeping*. London: Lawrence and Wishart. pp. 21–32.

Eriksson, Lars Gunner, Goran Melander & Peter Nobel (eds) (1981) An Analysing Account of the Conference on the African Refugee Problem, Arusha, May 1979. Scandinavian Institute of African Studies: Uppsala, Sweden.

Evanzz, Karl (1992) *The Judas Factor: The Plot to Kill Malcolm X*. New York: Thunder's Mouth Press.

Fanon, Frantz (1961) *The Wretched of the Earth*. London: Penguin.

Fanon, Frantz (1967) *Black Skin, White Masks*. London: Pluto, reprinted 1986.

Financial Times (London) (20 July 1972) 'Burundi after the massacre: Fear of economic problems', by David Martin.

Foucault, Michel (1997) *Society must be Defended*. London: Penguin. Translated by David Macey.

Gahama, Joseph (1983) *Le Burundi sous Administration Belge*. Paris: ACCT Karthala & C. R. A.

Gahama, Joseph (1995) 'Le Multipartisme: Un Facteur de Conflits Ethniques au Burundi', paper presented at the CODESRIA *Conference on Academic Freedom and Conflict Resolution in the Countries of the Great Lakes*, Arusha, Tanzania, 4–7 September.

Galtung, Johan (1969) 'Violence, Peace & Peace Research', *Journal of Peace Research*, 6, 3: 167–91.

Gewald, Jan-Bart (2004) 'Imperial Germany and the Herero of Southern Africa: genocide and the Quest for Recompense', in Adam Jones (ed.) *Genocide, Wars Crimes and the West: History and Complicity*. London: Zed Books, pp. 59–77.

Gorsz, Elizabeth (1994) *Volatile Bodies: Towards a Corporeal Feminism*. Bloomington: Indiana University Press.

Graham, Stephen (ed.) (2004) *Cities, War and Terrorism: Towards an Urban Geopolitics*, Oxford: Blackwell.

Graham, Stephen (2007) 'Everyday Infrastructure and Political Violence', in Derek Gregory & Allan Pred (eds), *Violent Geographies: Fear, Terror, and Political Violence*, New York & Abingdon: Routledge. pp. 309–28.

Greenland, Jeremy (1974), 'Les options de Bujumbura perspectives d'avenir', in René Lemarchand & Jeremy Greenland (eds) *Les Problemes de Burundi*. Bruxelles: Colloque International, pp. 53–66.

Greenland, Jeremy (1976) 'Ethnic Discrimination in Rwanda and Burundi', in Willem A. Veenhoven (ed.), *Case Studies on Human Rights and Fundamental Freedoms: A World Survey*. The Hague: Foundation for the Study of Human Rights and Fundamental Freedoms, Matinus Nijhoff: The Hague, pp. 97–133.

Greenland, Jeremy (1980) *Western Education in Burundi, 1916–1973: The Consequences of Instrumentalism*. Bruxelles: Cahiers du CEDAF 2/3, Centre D'Etude et de Documentation.

Grimshaw, Anna (ed.) (1992) *The CLR James Reader*, Oxford, Blackwell.

Guardian (London), (27 May 1972) 'Genocide' by ruling tribe in Burundi', by Stanley Meisler.

Guardian (London), (14 June 1972) 'Michombero hits back at rebels', by Jonathan Randel.

Guardian (London), (7 August 1987) 'Burundi leader pledges clean-up.'

Hanlon, Joseph (1996) *Peace without Profit: How the IMF Blocks Rebuilding Mozambique*. Portsmouth & London: Heinemann & James Currey.

Hansen, Emmanuel (ed.) (1987) *Africa Perspectives on Peace and Development*. London: The United Nations University Press & Zed Books.

Hartung, William D. & Bridget Moix (2000) *Deadly Legacy: US Arms to Africa and the Congo War*. New York: Arms Trade Resource Center.

Harrell-Bond, Barbara (1985) *Imposing Aid*. Oxford: Oxford University Press.

Harvey, David (1996) *Justice, Nature and the Geography of Difference*. Cambridge, Mass. & Oxford: Blackwell.

Harvey, David (2000) *Spaces of Hope*. Edinburgh: Edinburgh University Press.

Harvey, David (2003) *The New Imperialism*. Oxford: Oxford University Press.

Harvey, David (2005) *A Brief History of Neo-liberalism*. Oxford: Oxford University Press.

Hatungimana, Alexandre (2005) *Le Café au Burundi au XXe Siècle*. Paris: Karthala.

Hill Collins, Patricia (2000) *Black Feminist Thought: Knowledge, Consciousness and the Politics of Empowerment (Perspectives on Gender)*. New York & London: Routledge.

Hinton, Alexander Laban (2002) *Genocide: An Anthropological Reader*. Malden, USA & Oxford: Blackwell.

Hochschild, Adam (1998) *King Leopold's Ghost: A Story of Greed, Terror and Heroism in Colonial Africa*. London & Basingstoke: Macmillan.

Holborn, Louise (1975) *Refugees: A Problem of our Time: the Work of the UNHCR 1951–1972. 2 Vols*. Metuchen, New Jersey: The Scarecrow Press, Inc.

Homer-Dixon, Thomas F. (1999) *Environment, Scarcity and Violence*. New Jersey & Oxford: Princeton University Press.

Human Rights Watch (1996) *Zaire: Forced to Flee: Violence against the Tutsis in Zaire*, July; (1997a) *Burundi: Stoking the Fires: Military Assistance and Arms Trafficking to all sides in the Civil War*. 1 June; (1997b) *The Scars of Death:*

Children abducted by the Lord's Resistance Army in Uganda; (1998) *Proxy Targets: Civilians in the War in Burundi*; (1999a) *Leave None to Tell the Story: Genocide in Rwanda*; (1999b) *Tanzania: In the Name of Security, Forced Round-ups of Refugees in Tanzania*; (2000a) *Seeking Protection: Addressing Sexual and Domestic Violence in Tanzania's Refugee Camps*; (2000b) *Burundi: Neglecting Justice in Making Peace*; (2000c) *Burundi: Emptying the Hills: Regroupement in Burundi*; (2001) *Burundi: To Protect the People: the Government-sponsored "self-defense" Program in Burundi*; (2003) *Everyday Victims: Civilians in the Burundian War*; (2004a) *Burundi: Suffering in Silence: Civilians in Continuing Combat in Bujumbura Rural*; (2004b) *Child Soldier Use 2003: A briefing for the 4th UN Security Council Open Debate on Child Soldiers.* (2004c) *Burundi: The Gatumba Massacre: War crimes and Political Agendas*; (2005a) *Seeking Justice: The Prosecution of Sexual Violence in the Congo War*; (2005b) *The Curse of Gold: Democratic Republic of Congo*; (2005c) *Burundi: Missteps at a Crucial Moment*; (2006) *Une santé chèrement payee: La détention des patients sans resources dans les hôpitaux burundais;* New York, Washington, London: Human Rights Watch http://www.hrw.org.

Hunt, Nancy (1990) 'Domesticity and Colonialism in Belgian Africa: Usumbura's Foyer Social, 1946–1960', *Signs; Journal of Women in Culture and Society*, 15, 31: 447–74.

Hutchful, Eboe & Abdoulaye Bathily (1998) 'Introduction', in Hutchful E. & A. Bathily (eds) *The Military and Militarism in Africa*. Dakar: CODESRIA, pp. i-xiii.

Ijambo: les quatre vérités (9 November 1995) 'L'armée Burundaise au banc des accuses. Chatelet: ARIB.

Independent (London) (22 August 1988) '24,000 massacred' in Burundi conflict', by Richard Dowden.

Information sur Burundi (April, 1985) 'Le Burundi Theatre de massacres des populations par une minorite raciste Tutsi', Bureau International d'information sur le Burundi, Kigali, Rwanda.

International Crisis Group (ICG) (1998a) *Burundi Under Siege: Lift the Sanctions: Re-launch the Peace Process*. 28 April; (1998b) *Burundi's Peace Process: The Road from Arusha*. 20 July; (1999a) *Internal and Regional Implications of the Suspension of Sanctions*. 4 May; (1999b) *Burundi: Proposals for the Resumption of Bilateral and Multilateral Co-operation*. 4 May; (1999c) *Burundian Refugees in Tanzania: The Key Factor to the Burundi Peace Process*. 30 November; (2000a) *The Mandela Effect: Prospects for Peace in Burundi*. April 2000; (2000b) *Burundi: the Issues at Stake. Political parties., Freedom of the Press and Political Prisoners*. 12 July; (2000c) *Burundi: Neither War nor Peace*. 1 December; (2001a) *Burundi: Breaking the Deadlock*. 14 May; (2001b) *Burundi: One Hundred Days to Put the Peace Process Back on Track*. 14 August; (2002a) *Burundi After Six Months of Transition: Continuing the War or Winning the Peace*. 24 May; (2002b) *The Burundi Rebellion and the Ceasefire Negotiations*. 6 August; (2003a) *A Framework for Responsible Aid to Burundi*; (2003b) *Refugees, Internally Displaced in Burundi: The Urgent Need for a Consensus on their Repatriation and Reintegration*. 2 December; (2003c) *Rwandan Rebels in the Congo: A New Approach to Disarmament and Reintegration*; (2004) *Elections in Burundi: The Peace Wager*, 9 December; (2006) *Burundi: Democracy and Peace at Risk*, 30 November; Nairobi/Brussels: ICG, http://www.crisisgroup.org.

International Herald Tribune (6. 9.1988) 'After Burundi tribal massacre, donors rethink their aid strategy', by Blaine Harden.

International Institute of Strategic Studies (2002) *The Military Balance: sub-Saharan Africa*. Oxford: Oxford University Press.

International Monetary Fund (IMF) (1999) *IMF concludes Article IV with Burundi*, IMF Public Information Notice No.99/5. 28 January.

International Monetary Fund (IMF) (2002) *IMF Approves US$ 13 million in Emergency Post-Conflict Assistance for Burundi*, Press Release No.02/48, 9 October.

International Monetary Fund (IMF) (2005a) *Letter of Intent, Memorandum of Economic and Financial Policies and Technical Understanding*, 30 June. Washington DC: IMF.

International Monetary Fund (IMF) (2005b) *Burundi: Second Review Under the Three-Year Arrangement Under the Poverty Reduction and Growth Facility-Staff Report; Staff Statement; Press Release on the Executive Board Discussion; and Statement by the Executive Director for Burundi*. Washington DC: IMF.

Irinnews.org. (16 December 1998) *BURUNDI: Sanctions a 'blunt instrument'* – UNDP; (19 October 1999) *Burundi: Government suggests South African Mediation;* (4 August 2000) *Focus on signing the Peace Accord;* (24 May 2001) *Transition leadership talks flop;* (7 June 2001) *IMC Meeting Calls for Repeal of Law;* (6 Sept. 2002a) *Devaluation Results in Commodity Price Increases;* (8 Oct. 2002b) *Burundi: 2 factions sign ceasefire agreement, others given 30 days to comply;* (6 Dec. 2002c) *Burundi: Government, main rebel sign ceasefire deal;* (27 August 2003) *South African Forces to Remain despite funding shortfalls* ; (3 Sept. 2003) *Burundi: Approval of Temporary Immunity Law Sparks Heated Debate;* (7 March 2005a) *Burundi: Outpatients suffer as nurses begin strike to demand better terms;* (29 March 2005b) *Annan recommends dual inquiries on genocide;* (13 April 2005c) *Burundi: Senate Adopts electoral code;* (16–24 June 2005d) *BURUNDI: CNDD-FDD confirmed winner of communal polls;* (24 June 2005e) *BURUNDI: Paramilitary youth in protest over demobilisation payments;* (18 August 2005f) *Burundi: Government pleased with UN resolution on Truth Commission;* (20 September 2006) *FNL Fighters assemble but continue to tax civilians.*

Jackson, Tony (2000) *Equal Access to Education: A Peace Imperative for Burundi,* London: International Alert.

Joint Evaluation of Emergency Assistance to Rwanda (JEEAR) (1996) *The International Response to Conflict and Genocide: Lessons from the Rwandan Experience 3: Humanitarian Aid and Effects.* DANIDA.

Jones, Adam (2000) 'Gendercide and genocide', *Journal of Genocide Research,* 2 (2): 185–211.

Jones, Adam (2002) 'Gender and Genocide in Rwanda', *Journal of Genocide Research,* 4, 1: 65–94.

Jones, Adam (2004) *Genocide, Wars Crimes and the West: History and Complicity.* London: Zed Books.

Jones, Bruce D. (2001) *Peacemaking in Rwanda: the Dynamics of Failure.* Boulder & London: Lynne Reinner.

Juma, Monica Kathina & Astri Shruke (eds) (2002) *Eroding Local Capacity: International Humanitarian Action in Africa.* Uppsala: Nordiska Afrikainstitutet.

Kaldor, Mary (2001) *New and Old Wars: Organized Violence in a Global Era.* Cambridge: Polity.

Kaldor, Mary & Robin Luckham (2001) 'Global Transformations and New Conflicts', *IDS Bulletin,* 32, 2: 48–69.

Kamanga, Khoti (2001) *The (Tanzanian) Refugees Act of 1998: Some Legal and Policy Implications.* University of Dar es Salaam: Centre for the Study of Forced Migration.

Kamungi, Prisca. M., Johnstone S. Oketch & Christopher Huggins (2004) 'Land Access and Refugee Repatriation: The Case of Burundi', Africa Centre for Technology Studies *Eco-Conflicts,* 3, 2, 1–4.

Kandiyoti, Deniz (2004) 'Political Fiction Meets Gender Myth: Post-Conflict Reconstruction, "Democratization" and Women's Rights', *IDS Bulletin,* 35, 4: 134–6.

Kaplan, Robert (1994) 'The Coming Anarchy: how scarcity, crime, overpopulation and disease are rapidly destroying the social fabric of our planet', *Atlantic Monthly*, February, 44–76.

Kathina, Monica & Astri Suhrke (eds) (2002) *Eroding Local Capacity. International Humanitarian Action in Africa*. Sweden, Uppsala: Nordiska Afrikainstitutet

Kay, Reginald (1987) *Burundi since the Genocide*. London: Minority Rights Group Ltd.

Keen, David (2005) *Conflict and Collusion in Sierra Leone*, Oxford: James Currey; New York: Palgrave.

Keenan, Jeremy (2004) 'Terror in the Sahara: The Implications of US imperialism for the North and West Africa', *Review of African Political Economy*, 31, 101: 475–96.

Kelly, Sean (1993) *America's Tyrant: The CIA and Mobutu of Zaire*. Washington: The American University Press.

Keyes, Charles. F. (c1981) *Ethnic Change*. Seattle: University of Washington Press.

Laely, Thomas (1997) 'Peasants, Local Communities and Central Power in Burundi', *Journal of Modern African Studies*, 35, 4: 695–716.

Lamming, George (2004) 'An Interview with David Dabydeen', London: Queen Elizabeth Hall, November.

Leander, Anna (2003) *The Commodification of Violence, Private Military Companies and African States*. Copenhagen Peace Research Institute, Working Paper no.11.

Le Billion, Philippe (2001) 'The Political Ecology of War: Natural Resources and Armed Conflicts', *Political Geography*, 20: 561–84.

Le Billion, Philippe (2007) 'Fatal Transactions', in Derek Gregory & Allan Pred (eds), *Violent Geographies: Fear, Terror, and Political Violence*, NY, USA & Abingdon, UK: Routledge. pp. 133–52.

Lemarchand, René (1970) *Rwanda and Burundi*. London: Pall Mall Press.

Lemarchand, René (1977) 'Burundi' in René Lemarchand, (ed.) *African Kingship in Perspective: Political Change and Modernization in Monarchical Settings*. London & Oregon: Frank Cass, pp. 93–126.

Lemarchand, René (1989) 'The Report of the National Commission to Study the Question of National Unity in Burundi: A Critical Comment', *Journal of Modern African Studies*, 27, 4: 685–96.

Lemarchand, René (1994a) *Burundi: Ethnocide as Discourse and Practice*. Cambridge: Woodrow Wilson Press & Cambridge University Press.

Lemarchand, René (1994b) 'Managing Transition Anarchies: Rwanda, Burundi, and South Africa in Comparative Perspective', *Journal of Modern African Studies*, 32, 4: 605–28.

Lemarchand, René (1995) 'Rwanda: The Rationality of Genocide', *Issue: A Journal of Opinion*, 2: 8–11.

Lemarchand, René (1996) Policy Options on Local-Reconstruction, paper presented at Conference on an *Agenda for Peace in Burundi*, United States Institute for Peace, Washington DC, 10 September.

Lemarchand, René (1998) 'Genocide in the Great Lakes: Which Genocide? Whose Genocide? *African Studies Review*, 41, 1: 3–16.

Lemarchand, René & David Martin (1974) *Selective Genocide in Burundi*. Minority Rights Report 20, London: Minority Rights Group Ltd.

Ligue Iteka (2005a) *De la Logique de Guerre aux Vicissitudes d' Application des Accords, Rapport Annuel sur la Situation des Droits d l'Homme au Burundi, Edition 2004*. Bujumbura, Burundi: Ligue ITEKA, March 2005.

Ligue Iteka (2005b) *Déclaration de la Ligue ITEKA: Violence dans Certaines Localités du Burundi I*. http://www.ligue-iteka.africa-web.org/ [accessed December 2005].

Ligue Iteka (2005c) *La Ligue Iteka organise un formation sur la prise en charge des victimes des violences sexuelles*, Bujumbura, Burundi: Ligue Iteka. http://www.ligue-iteka.africa-web.org. [accessed, 10 August 2006].

Ligue Iteka (2005d) *Le viol est-il un crime de guerre?* http://www.ligue-iteka.africa-web.org/article.php3?id_article=455 [accessed 10 August 2006].

Ligue Iteka (2006a) Le Défi de lier L'acte a la parole dans le respect des droits humains. *Rapport Annuel sur la Situation des Droits d l'Homme au Burundi 2005.* Bujumbura, Burundi: Ligue ITEKA, May 2006. http://www.ligue-iteka.africa-web.org/ [accessed June 2006].

Ligue Iteka (2006b) 'A Mother is held at the Hospital of Kayanza for not having been able to pay the whole bill'. http://www.ligue-iteka.africa-web.org/article.php3?id_article=1121 [accessed August 2006].

Linden, Ian (1977) *Church and Revolution in Rwanda.* Manchester: Manchester University Press.

Luckham, Robin (1998) 'The Military, Militarization and Democratization in Africa: A Survey of Literature and Issues', in Eboe Hutchful & Abdoulaye Bathily (eds), *The Military and Militarization in Africa.* Dakar, Senegal: CODESRIA Book series. pp. 1–45.

Luckham, Robin, Ismail Ahmed, Robert Muggah and Sarah White (2001) *Conflict and Poverty in Sub-Saharan Africa: An Assessment of the Issues and Evidence.* IDS Working Paper 128, Brighton, Sussex: IDS.

Lusaka Accord (1999) *Democratic Republic of Congo, Ceasefire Agreement* and *Annex A: Modalities for the Implementation of the Ceasefire Agreement in the Democratic Republic of Congo,* Lusaka, Zambia.

Mackenzie, John (1984) *Propaganda and Empire: The Manipulation of British Public Opinion 1880–1960.* Manchester: Manchester University Press.

McClintock, Ann (1996) "No Longer in a Future Heaven": Nationalism, Gender and Race', in Geoff Eley & Ronald Grigor Suny (eds) *Becoming National: A Reader.* New York & Oxford, Oxford University Press. pp. 260–84.

Mafege, Archie (1971) 'The ideology of tribalism', *Journal of Modern African Studies,* 9, 2: 253–61.

Mafege, Archie (1995) Demographic and Ethnic Variations: A Source of Instability in Modern African States, paper presented at the CODESRIA *Conference on Academic Freedom and Conflict Resolution in the Countries of the Great Lakes,* Arusha, Tanzania, 4–7 September.

Malkki, Liisa H. (1995) *Purity and Exile: Violence, Memory, And National Cosmology Among Hutu Refugees in Tanzania.* Chicago: University of Chicago Press.

Mama, Amina (1997) 'Feminism or Femocracy? State Feminism and Democratisation', in Jibrin Ibrahim (ed.) *Expanding Democratic Space in Nigeria.* Dakar: CODESRIA. pp. 77–98.

Mamdani, Mahmood (1996) *Citizen and Subject: Contemporary Africa and the Legacy of Late Colonialism,* Princeton: Princeton University Press.

Mamdani, Mahmood (2001) *When Victims Become Killers: Colonialism, Nativism, and the Genocide in Rwanda.* Oxford: James Currey.

Maquet, Jacques (1961) *The Premise of Inequality in Rwanda,* Oxford: Oxford University Press.

Marshall, Donna (2000) *Women in War and Peace: Grassroots Peace-Building.* Washington DC: US Institute for Peace.

Maundi, Mohammed Omar (2004) 'The Internal Dynamics of the Burundi Peace Negotiations', in Gaudens Mpangala & Bismarck U. Mwansasu (eds) *Beyond Conflict in Burundi.* Dar es Salaam: The Mwalimu Nyerere Foundation. pp. 304–35.

MDRP (Multi-Country Demobilization and Reintegration Program) (2005) Progress Report and work Plan, July-September 2005. www.mdrp.org/PDFs/progreport_2005_q3.pdf [Last accessed 8 August 2006].

Melady, Thomas, P. (1972) *Burundi – The Tragic Years.* New York: Orbis.

Melvern, Linda, R. (2000) *A People Betrayed: The Role of the West in Rwanda's Genocide.* London: Zed Books.

Melvern, Linda & Paul Williams (2004) 'Britannia waived the rules: the major government and the 1994 genocide', *African Affairs.* 103, 1–22.

Metcalfe, George L. (1970) 'The effect of refugees on the national state', in Brooks, Hugh. C. & Yassin El-Ayouty (eds), *Refugees South of the Sahara: an African Dilemma.* Westport Connecticut: Negro Universities Press, pp. 73–85.

Mianda, Gertrude (2002) 'Colonialism, Education, and Gender relations in the Belgian Congo: the *évolué* case', in Jean Allman, Susan Geiger & Nakanyike Musisi (eds), *Women in African Colonial Histories.* Bloomington: Indiana University Press. pp. 144–63.

Milliken, Jennifer & Keith Krause (2002) 'State Failure, State Collapse and State Reconstruction: Concepts, Lessons and Strategies', in *Development and Change*, 33, 5: 753–74.

Le Monde (1 June 1972) 'Burundi: L'extermination d'une ethnie'; (19 July 1973) 'Le Président Nyerere dénonce les massacres au Burundi' (20 October 1985) 'L'Expulsion de dix missionaries étrangers'; (20 October 1988) Burundi government stop Médecins sans Frontiers from working in the North; (21 October 1988) 'Le Président Buyoya nomme un gouvernement à majorité hutue'; Paris: *Le Monde* Newspaper.

Mkandawire, Thandika (2002) 'The Terrible Toll of Post-Colonial Rebel Movements in Africa: Towards an Explanation of the Violence Against the Peasantry', *Journal of Modern African Studies*, 40, 2: 181–215.

Moyroud, Celine & John Katunga (2002) "Coltan Exploration in Eastern Democratic Republic of the Congo (DRC)', in Jeremy Lind & Kathryn Sturman (eds), *Scarcity and Surfeit: The Ecology of Africa's Conflicts.* Pretoria: Institute of Strategic Studies, Nairobi: African Centre for Technology Studies. pp. 159–85.

Mpangala, Gaudens & Bismarck U. Mwansasu (eds) (2004) *Beyond Conflict in Burundi.* Dar es Salaam: The Mwalimu Nyerere Foundation.

Mthembu-Salter, Gregory (1998) *A Policy Passed its "Sell-by" Date: an Assessment of Sanctions against Burundi.* London: Action Aid, December.

Musah, Abdel-Fatau (2002) 'Privatization of Security, Arms Proliferation and the Process of State Collapse in Africa', *Development and Change,* 33, 5: 911–33.

Museveni, Yoweri (1986) 'Address to the twenty second ordinary session of Assembly of   Heads of state and Government of the OAU', Addis Ababa, Ethiopia, 29 July.

Mustapha, Abdul Raufu (1999) 'Back to the Future? Multi-ethnicity and the African state', in Lidija R. Basta & Jibrin Ibrahim (eds) *Federalism and Decentralisation in Africa: The Multiethnic Challenge.* Switzerland: Institut du Fédéralisme Fribourg, pp. 101–31.

Mustapha, Abdul Raufu (2002) *States, Predation and Violence: Reconceptualizing Political Action and Political Community in Africa.* Paper presented at the Annual General Assembly of CODESRIA, Kampala, Uganda.

Mworoha, Emile (1977) *Peuples et Rois de l'Afrique des Lacs*, Dakar, Senegal: Les Nouvelles Editions Africaines.

Myers, Garth Andrew (2001) 'Introductory Human Geography Textbook Representations of Africa', *Professional Geographer*, 53, 4: 522–32.

Ndarishikanye, Barnabé & Jean-François Dupaquier (1995) *Burundi, Le venin de la haine: Etude sur les médias extrémistes*, Paris, France: Reporters sans Frontières.

Ndarubayige, Léonce (1995) *Burundi: The Origins of Hutu-Tutsi Conflict.* Nairobi: ARIB.

Ndikumana, Léonce (1998) 'Institutional Failure and Ethnic Conflicts in Burundi', *African Studies Review*, 41, 1: 29–47.

Ndikumana, Léonce (2000) 'Towards a Solution to Violence in Burundi: A Case for Political and Economic Liberalization', *The Journal of Modern African Studies*, 28, 3: 431–59.

Ndimira, Pascal-Firmin (1995) 'Le Systeme Educatif et le Processus Démocratique', in Guichaoua, André, (ed.) (1995) *Les Crises Politiques au Burundi et au Rwanda (1993–1994)*. Lille: Université des Sciences et Technologies de Lille.

Newbury, Catherine (1988) *The Cohesion of Oppression: Clientship and Ethnicity in Rwanda, 1860–1960*, New York: Columbia University Press.

Newbury, David (1998) 'Understanding Genocide', *African Studies Review*, 41, 1: 73–97.

Ngaruko, Floribert & Janvier D. Nkurunziza (2000) 'An Economic Interpretation of Conflict in Burundi', *Journal of African Economies*, 9 (3): 370–409.

Nindorera, Agnes (c. 2000) '*Ubushingantahe* as a base for political transformation', http://www.womenwagingpeace.net/content/conflict_areas/ubushingantahe.pdf.

Niyonzima, Herménégilde (2004) *Burundi: Terre Des Héros Non Chantés du Crime et de L'impunité*. Geneva, Switzerland: Editions Remesha.

Nkurunziza, Janvier D. & F. Ngaruko (2002) *Explaining Growth in Burundi: 1960–2000*, Draft Paper, University of Oxford: Centre for African Economies.

Nnoli, Okwudiba (ed.) (1998) *Ethnic Conflicts in Africa*. Dakar: CODESRIA.

Nordstrom, Carolyn (2004) *Shadows of War: Violence, Power and International Profiteering in the Twenty-First Century*. Berkeley, Los Angeles: University of California Press.

Ntampaka, Charles (1999) 'Reconciling the Sources of Law in the Burundi Code of Persons and the Family', International Society of Family Law, *International Survey of Family Law 1999*. The Hague: Kluwer Law International, pp. 65–77.

Ntibantunganya, Sylvestre (1999) *Une Democratie Pour Tous les Burundais: La Guerre "ethno-civile" s'installe (1993–1996)*. Paris: L'Harmattan.

Ntibazonkiza, Raphael (1993) *Burundi: Au Royaume Des Seigneurs de la Lance: Tome 2 – De L'indépendance a nos Jours (1962–1992)*. Brussels: L'Association sans but lucratif – Bruxelles – Droits de l'Homme.

Nyamitwe, Alain Aimé (2006) *J'ai échappé au Massacre de L'université du Burundi*. Paris: L'Harmattan.

Nyerere, Julius, Kamabagraye (1979) Opening address at the Pan-African Conference on *The Situation of Refugees in Africa*. Arusha, Tanzania, 7–17 May 1979, in UNHCR, report on the conference, HCR/120/14/80, Geneva, annex 1. pp. 1–7.

Nzongola-Ntalaja, Georges (2002) *The Congo: from Leopold to Kabila: A People's History*. London: Zed Press.

Observer (London) (1 July 1962) 'Bloodbath fears after Burundi execution', report from Andrew Wilson.

Observer (London) (28 August 1988) 'Tribal bloodbath', by Catherine Wilson.

OCHA – see United Nations Office for the Coordination of Humanitarian Affairs.

Oketch, Johnstone Summit (2004) *Socio-Political Context of Land Access, Refugee Repatriation and Resettlement of IDPs in Burundi*. A Briefing Paper for ACTS, Nairobi: African Centre for Technology Studies.

Oketch, Johnstone Summit & Tara Polzer (2002) 'Conflict and Coffee in Burundi', in Jeremy Lind & Kathryn Sturman (eds), *Scarcity and Surfeit: The Ecology of Africa's Conflicts*. Pretoria: Institute of Strategic Studies, Nairobi: African Centre for Technology Studies. pp. 85–156.

Omach, Paul (2000) 'The African Crisis Response Initiative: Domestic Politics and Convergence of National Interests', *African Affairs*, 99: 73–95.

ONUB – see United Nations Operations in Burundi.

Organization of African Unity (OAU) (2000) *International Panel of Eminent Personalities to Investigate the 1994 Genocide in Rwanda and the Surrounding Events, Special Report*, OAU, 7 July.

Ould-Abdallah, Ahmedou (2000) *Burundi on the Brink 1993–1995: A UN Special Envoy reflects on Preventative Diplomacy*. Washington DC: US Institute for Peace Press.

Oxfam (GB) (2002a) *Burundi Refugee Protection Assessment*. Jan–Feb 2002.

Oxfam (GB) (2002b) *An Economic Analysis of Crisis in the Coffee Sector in Burundi*. Burundi: Oxfam GB.

Oyewumi, Oyeronke (c. 1997) *The Invention of Women: Making Sense of Western Gender Discourses*. Minneapolis & London: University of Minneapolis Press.

Oyewumi, Oyeronke, (ed.) (2003) *African Women and Feminism: Reflecting on the Politics of Sisterhood*. Trenton, New Jersey: Africa World Press.

Pax Christi Netherlands (2005) *World Map of Failing States 2004*. Utrecht: Pax Christi Netherlands.

Pendergast John & David Smock (1999) *Postgenocidal Reconstruction: Building Peace in Rwanda and Burundi*. Africa In-Depth Special Report, US Institute of Peace, Washington.

Peterson, V. Spike (1992) 'Security and Sovereign States: What is at Stake in Taking Feminism Seriously?' in V. Spike Peterson (ed.) *Gendered States: Feminist (Re) Visions of International Relations Theory*. Boulder: Lynne Rienner. pp. 31–64.

Pieterse, Jan Neederven (1992) *White on Black: Images of Africa in Western Popular Culture*. New Haven & London: Yale University Press.

Prunier, Gérard (1994) *Burundi: A Manageable Crisis?* WRITENET UK, http://www.grandslacs.net/doc/2505.pdf [accessed 1 April 2006].

Prunier, Gérard (1995) *The Rwandan Crisis: History of a Genocide*. London: Hurst & Co.

Prunier, Gérard (2004) 'Rebel Movements and Proxy Warfare: Uganda, Sudan and the Congo (1986–1999)', *African Affairs*, 103 (412): 359–83.

Puechguirbal, Nadine (2003) 'Women and War in the Democratic Republic of Congo', *Signs: Journal of Women in Culture and Society*, 28, 4: 1271–81.

Pye, Lucian W. (1959) *Armies in the Process of Political Modernization*. Cambridge MA: MIT, Center for International Studies.

Radio Burundi, 4 July 1996, *BBC Summary of World Broadcasts*. London: BBC.

Ranger, Terence, O. (1983) 'The Invention of Tradition in Africa', in E. J. Hobsbawm & T. O. Ranger (eds), *The Invention of Tradition*. Cambridge: CUP. pp. 113–43.

Ranger, Terence, O. (1993) 'The Invention of Tradition Revisited: The Case of Colonial Africa', in T. Ranger and O. Vaughan (eds), *Legitimacy and the State in Twentieth Century Africa*. London: Macmillan. pp. 62–111.

Ranger, Terence, O. (1996) 'Postscript: Colonial and Post-colonial Identities' in Richard Werbner & Terence Ranger (eds), *Post-Colonial Identities in Africa*. London: Zed Books. pp. 271–81.

Refugees International (2004) *Burundian Refugees in Tanzania: Mounting Pressure to Return*. http://www.refugeesinternational.or/cgi-bin/ri/ bulletin?bc=00760.

Reliefweb (16 June 2001) *Burundi Minister in Tanzania to Discuss Border Security*, Agence France-Presse, Dar es Salaam. http://www.reliefweb.int [accessed 19 June 2001].

Reno, William (2000) 'Clandestine Economies, Violence & States in Africa', *Journal of International Affairs*, 53, 2: 433–60.

Reno, William (2002) 'The Politics of Insurgency in Collapsing States', *Development and Change*, 33, 5: 837–58.

Reporters sans Frontières see Ndarishikanye & Dupaquier (1995)

Republic of Burundi (RoB). 19 September 2002. *Letter of Intent, Memorandum of Economic and Financial Policies, and Technical Memorandum of Understanding*. http://www.imf.org/External/NP/LOI/2002/bdi/01/index.htm.

Republic of Burundi (RoB) (2003) *Interim Strategic Framework for Accelerating Economic Growth and Reducing Poverty (Interim PRSP)*, Burundi.

Republic of Burundi (RoB) (2004) *Manuel de Formation pour la prise charge des victimes de violences sexuelles à l'attention du personnel de santé*. Bujumbura: Ministry of Public Health.

Republic of Burundi National Commission for Demobilization, Reinsertion and Reintegration (RoB NCDRR) (2006) *Summary Weekly Report*, 22 May.

Republic of Tanzania (RoT) (1995) *The Tanzania Refugee Policy, Implementations Record and the Tanzania Position on the Rwanda and Burundi Refugee-Related Problems*. Dar es Salaam: Tanzania Ministry of Foreign Affairs.

Republic of Tanzania (RoT) (1998) *The Refugees Act, 1998*. Dar es Salaam: Government Printer.

Reyntjens, Filip (1993) 'The Proof of the Pudding is in the Eating: The June 1993 Elections in Burundi', *The Journal of Modern African Studies*, 31, 4: 563–83.

Reyntjens, Filip (1994) *L'Afrique des Grand Lacs en Crise: Rwanda, Burundi: 1988–1994*. Paris: Éditions Karthala.

Reyntjens, Filip (2005) 'Briefing: Burundi: A Peaceful Transition After a Decade of War?', *African Affairs*, 105/418, 117–35.

Reyntjens, Filip (2006) 'Post-1994 Politics in Rwanda: Problematising 'liberation' and 'Democratisation'', *Third World Quarterly*. 27, 6: 1103–17.

Richards, Paul (1996) *Fighting for the Rainforest: War, Youth and Resources in Sierra Leone*. Oxford: James Currey & Bloomington: Indiana University Press.

Richards, Paul (2005) New War: An Ethnographic Approach. In Richards, Paul (ed.), *No Peace No War: An Anthropology of Contemporary Armed Conflicts*, Oxford: James Currey, Ohio University Press.

Rist, Gilbert (1997) *The History of Development: From Western Origins to Global Faith*. London: Zed Books.

Roberts, Dorothy (1996) *Killing the Black Body: Race, Reproduction, and the Meaning of Liberty*, New York: Vintage Books.

Rodney, Walter (1972) *How Europe Underdeveloped Africa*. London: Bogle L'Ouverture.

Rutake, Paul and Gahama, Joseph. (1998) Ethnic Conflict in Burundi, in Nnoli, O. (ed.), *Ethnic Conflicts in Africa*. Dakar: CODESRIA. pp. 79–104.

Rutinwa, Bonaventure (1999) *The End of Asylum? The Changing Nature of Refugee Policies in Africa*, New Issues in Refugee Research, Working Paper No. 5, UNHCR http: //www.unhcr.ch/refworld/pubs/pubon.htm.

Rutinwa, Bonaventure (2005) *Identifying Gaps in Protection Capacity Tanzania*. Dar es Salaam, UNHCR Strengthening Capacity Project.

Rwegayura, Anaclet (2000) 'Ugandan Connection to the Trouble in Burundi', *Pan-African News Agency*, 16 November 2000.

Sanders, Edith. R. (1969) 'The Hamitic Hypothesis: Its Origins and Functions in Time Perspective', *Journal of African History*. 10, 4: 521–32.

Save the Children Fund (SCF) UK, DRC (2004) *Multi-country Demobilization Program (MDRP) Special Project Report Grant (TF052337): Support to the Demobilization and Community Reintegration of Child Soldiers*, Quarterly Report, January–March.

Scheper-Hughes, Nancy & Philippe Bourgois (2004) 'Introduction: Making Sense of Violence', in Scheper-Hughes, Nancy & Philippe Bourgois (eds), *Violence in War and Peace*. Malden, USA & Oxford: Blackwell, pp. 1–32.

Sénat de Belgique (2002) Session Ordinaire 2000–2003, *Commission d'enquête parlementaire (Grands Lacs)*, Auditions Vendredi 6 décembre 2002, Compte Rendu, Audition de M. Alain Goetz, Tony Goetz and Zonen.

Slim, Hugo (2003) 'Humanitarianism with Borders?: NGOs, Belligerent Military Forced and Humanitarian Action', paper for the *ICVA Conference on NGOs in a Changing World Order: Dilemmas and Challenges*, Geneva, 14 March.

Reproduced in the *Journal of Humanitarian Assistance*, http://www.Jha.ac/articles/a118.htm [accessed 12 Dec. 2005].

Soguk, Nevzat (1999) *States and Strangers: Refugees and Displacements of Statecraft*. Borderlines II, Minneapolis & London: University of Minnesota Press.

Spears, Ian (2000) 'Understanding Inclusive Peace Agreements in Africa: The Problems of Sharing Power' *Third World Quarterly*, 21, 1: 105–18.

Spears, Ian (2002) 'Africa: The Limits of Power-Sharing', *Journal of Democracy*, 13, 3: 123–36.

Steans, Jill (1998) *Gender and International Relations: An Introduction*. New Brunswick, New Jersey: Rutgers University Press.

Stein, Barry. N. (1987) 'ICARA II: burden-sharing and durable solutions', in John R. Rogge, (ed.) *Refugees: A Third World Dilemma*. New Jersey: Rowman & Littlefield, pp. 47–59.

Stockholm International Peace Research Institute (SIPRI) (2007) *SIPRI military expenditure database*. www.sipri.org/contents/milap/milex/mex_database1.html [last accessed April 2007].

Sunday Times (London) (29.9.1961) 'Huts Blaze as Terror Wave Sweeps Ruanda', by Richard Cox.

Sunday Times (4.6.1972) 'Burundi's green hills are drenched in tribal blood again', by Philip Short.

Taylor, Ian (2003) 'Conflict in Central Africa: Clandestine Networks & Regional/Global Configurations', *Review of African Political Economy*, 95: 45–55.

Terry, Fiona (2002) *Condemned to Repeat? The Paradox of Humanitarian Action*. Ithaca & London: Cornell University Press.

Thompson, Carol B. (1999) 'Beyond civil society: child soldiers as citizens in Mozambique', *Review of African Political Economy*, 80, 26: 191–206.

Times Newspaper (London) (13 November 1959) 'Ruanda state of Emergency'; (7 December 1959) 'Mission criticisms of Ruanda authorities: Lack of impartiality alleged'; (24 September 1961) Huts Blaze as Terror sweeps Ruanda, by Richard Cox; (1 February 1965) 'Burundi breaks with Peking', by Clyde Sanger; (18 December 1969) 'Burundi sentences 26 plotters to death'; (30 April 1972) 'King killed in attempted Burundi coup'; (9 June 1972) 'Growing evidence that Burundi killings are deliberate policy', by Philip Short; (14 August 1998) 'Kabila regime calls for Slaughter of the Tutsis', by Sam Riley, p.13; (23 December 2004) 'Sex scandal in Congo threatens to engulf UN's peacekeepers', by Jonathan Clayton & James Bone, London: News International.

Tindwa, Peter 'Burundi's FRODEBU forms military wing', *The Tanzanian Guardian*, Monday, June 3, 2002, Dar es Salaam, Tanzania.

Trouwborst, Albert (1965) 'Kinship and geographical mobility in Burundi, East Central Africa', *International Journal of Comparative Sociology* 6, 1, 166–82.

Tull, Dennis M. & Andreas Mehler (2005) 'The Hidden Cost of Power-Sharing: Reproducing Insurgent Violence in Africa', *African Affairs*, 104 (416): 375–98.

Turner, Simon (2004) 'New Opportunities: Angry Young Men in Tanzanian Refugee camp', in Philomena Essed, Georg Frerks & Joke Schrivjers (eds), *Refugees and the Transformation of Societies: Agency, Policies, Ethics & Politics*. New York & Oxford: Berghahn Books. pp. 94–105.

Turshen, Meredith (2001) 'The Political Economy of Rape: An analysis of systematic rape and sexual abuse of women during armed conflict in Africa', in Caroline O. N. Moser & Fiona C. Clark (eds), *Victims, Perpetrators or Actors?: Gender, Armed Conflict and Political Violence*. London: Zed Books, pp. 55–69.

Turshen, Meredith (1998) 'Women's War Stories', in Meredith Turshen & Clotilde Twagiramariya (eds), *What Women Do in Wartime: Gender and Conflict in Africa*. London: Zed Books, pp. 1–26.

Twagiramariya, Clotilde & Meredith Turshen (1998) 'Favours to Give and Consenting Victims: The Sexual Politics of Survival in Rwanda', in Meredith Turshen & Clotilde Twagiramariya (eds), *What Women Do in Wartime: Gender and Conflict in Africa*, London: Zed Books, pp. 101–17.

Umutesi, Beatrice (2000) *Surviving the Slaughter: The Ordeal of a Rwandan Refugee in Zaire*, Madison, Wisconsin: University of Wisconsin Press.

United Nations AIDS/WHO (2005) AIDS epidemic Update: December 2005 Sub-Saharan Africa. http://www.unaids.org/epi/2005/doc/report_pdf.asp [accessed 1 April 2006]

United Nations Committee on the Elimination of Discrimination against Women (CEDAW) (2000) *Initial report by Burundi submitted to the Committee on the Elimination of Discrimination against Women, (CEDAW/C/BDI/1)*, 3 July 2000.

United Nations Committee on the Elimination of Discrimination against Women (CEDAW), 24th session, 15 January–2 February 2001, *Concluding Observations of the Committee on the Elimination of Discrimination against Women: Burundi. 02/02/2001*. A/56/38, para. 32–67.

United Nations Committee on the Rights of the Child (UNCRC), (19 March 1998), *Initial reports of State Parties due in 1992: Addendum Burundi. 31/07/98. CRC/C/3/Add.58. (State Party Report)* UN Human Rights Website – Treaty Bodies database –State party reports.

United Nations Conference on Trade & Development (UNCTAD) (2005) *Economic Development in Africa: Rethinking the Role of Foreign Direct Investment*, UN.

United Nations Development Programme (UNDP) (2001) *Human Development Report*, see http://hdr.undp.org/statistics/data/cty/cty_f_BDI.html [accessed 2003].

United Nations Development Programme (UNDP) (2003) *Human Development Report*. Oxford: OUP, and at http: hdr.undp.org/statistics/countries [accessed July 2005].

United Nations Development Programme (UNDP) (2005) *Human Development Report*. Oxford: OUP, and at http: hdr.undp.org/statistics/countries [accessed July 2005].

United Nations Economic Commission for Africa (UNECA) *et al.* (1968) *Conference on the Legal, Economic and Social Aspects of African Refugee Problems*, 9–18 October 1967, Final Report.

United Nations Economic and Social Council (UNESC) (1985) Commission on Human Rights, Sub-Commission on Prevention of Discrimination and Protection of Minorities. *Revised and updated report on the question of the prevention and punishment of the crime of genocide (Whitaker Report)*, Thirty-eighth session, Item 4 of the provisional agenda, (E/CN.4/Sub.2/1985/6). 2 July.

United Nations Economic and Social Council (UNESC) (1994) Commission on Human Rights, Fifty-First Session, Report of the Representative of the Secretary General, Mr Francis M. Deng, submitted pursuant to Commission on Human Rights Resolution 1993/5, Addendum, *Profiles of Displacement: Burundi* (E/CN/1995/50/Add.2). 28 November 1994.

United Nations Economic and Social Council (UNESC) (1995a) *Report of Special Rapporteur on Extrajudicial, Summary, or arbitrary executions, Mr Brace Waly Ndiaye, submitted pursuant to Commission resolution 1995/73. Addendum, Report of the Special Rapporteur on his Mission to Burundi from 19 to 29 April 1995*, 24 July, E/CN.4/1996/4/Add.1.

United Nations Economic and Social Council (UNESC) (1995b) *Initial Report on the Human rights Situation in Burundi submitted by the Special Rapporteur, Mr Paulo Sergio Pinheiro, in accordance with Commission resolution*, 14 November *(1995/90. E/CN.4/1996/16)*.

United Nations Economic and Social Council (UNESC) (2000) *Report of the Representative of the Secretary General, Mr Francis M. Deng, submitted pursuant to Commission on Human Rights Resolution 2000/53, Addendum,*

Profiles of Displacement: Forced relocation in Burundi, Commission on Human Rights, Fifty-seventh session, (E/CN/1995/50/Add.2). 6 March.

United Nations Economic and Social Council (UNESC) (2005), Commission on Human Rights, Sixtieth Session, *Rights of the Child, Report of the Special Rapporteur on the Sale of Children, Child prostitution and child pornography, Juan Miguel Petit.* (E/CN.4/2005/78/Add.3). 8 March. Burundi, para.19–20.

United Nations High Commissioner for Refugees (December 2002) *Refugee Situation Update,* Dar es Salaam, Tanzania: UNHCR.

United Nations High Commissioner for Refugees (UNHCR) (2004) *Return and Reintegration of Burundian Refugees, Supplementary Appeal, July 2004–December 2005.* http://www.unhcr.org/cgi-bin/texis/vtx/home?id=search [accessed June 2005].

United Nations High Commissioner for Refugees (UNHCR) (2005) Funding: Burundi repatriation/reintegration operation as Risk, 28 October 2005/UNHCR Briefing Notes. http://www.unhcr.org. [accessed June 2006].

United Nations International Covenant on Civil and Political Rights (UN ICPPR) (1996) *Summary of the 1350th meeting: Burundi,* 2 August 1996 (CCPR/C/SR.1350).

United Nations International Human Rights Instruments, (1999) *Core Document Forming the Initial Part of the State Party Reports: Burundi (16/06/99),* 16 June.

United Nations Office for the Co-ordination of Humanitarian Affairs (OCHA) (1999) *Affected Population in the Great Lakes Region (displaced-refugees) 24 December 1999.* Nairobi: OCHA.

United Nations Operations in Burundi (ONUB) (2006a) *April Monthly Report of Allegations of Human Rights Violations and Breaches of Common Rights,* Bujumbura, Burundi, April.

United Nations Operation in Burundi (ONUB) (2006b) *Position des femmes elues aux communales,* Gender Unit, June 2006. Bujumbura: ONUB.

United Nations Protocol against the Illicit Manufacturing of and Trafficking in Firearms, their Parts and Components and Ammunition, A/Res/55/255, 31 May 2001 and Nairobi Protocol for the Prevention, Control and Reduction of Small Arms and Light Weapons in the Great Lakes Region and the Horn of Africa, 21 April 2004.

United Nations Security Council (UNSC) (1996) *International Commission of Inquiry For Burundi, Final Report.* United Nations Security Council, S/1996/682

United Nations Security Council (UNSC) (2000) *Resolution 1325 on Women and Peace and Security: Adopted by the Security Council at its 4213th meeting, on* 31 October 2000. (S/Res/1325 (2000)), http://www.un.org/Docs/scres/2000/sc2000.htm [accessed 14 June 2006].

United Nations Security Council (UNSC) (2001a) *Report of the Panel of Experts on the Illegal Exploitation of Natural Resources and Other Forms of Wealth of the DR Congo,* 12 April, (S/2001/357).

United Nations Security Council (UNSC) (2001b) *Addendum to the report of the Panel of Experts on the Illegal Exploitation of Natural Resources and Other Forms of Wealth of the Democratic Republic of Congo,* 13 November, (S/2001/1072).

United Nations Security Council (UNSC) (2003) *Final Report of the Panel of Experts on the Illegal Exploitation of Natural Resources and other forms of wealth of DR Congo,* 23 October, S/2003/1027.

United Nations Security Council (UNSC) (2004) Letter dated 15 October 2004 from the Secretary-General addressed to the President of the Security Council – Report regarding the events that occurred at Gatumba on 13 August 2004. UNSC S/2004/821.

United States of America, Department of State (1998) *Burundi Country Report on Human Rights Practices for 1997*. Released by the Bureau of Democracy, Human Rights, and Labor, January 30.

United States Committee for Refugees (USCR) (1993) *Transition in Burundi: The Context for a Homecoming*. Washington. DC: USCR.

United States Committee for Refugees (USCR) (1998) 'Burundi: A Patchwork of Displacement', in Roberta Cohen & Frances Deng (eds), *The Forsaken People: Case Studies of the Internally Displaced*. Washington DC: Brookings Institution Press. pp. 14–56.

United States of America, National Security Council (10 October 1972) Memorandum from Fernando E. Rondon of the National Security Council to Henry Kissinger, The Secretary of State. http: www.state.gov/r/pa/ho/frus/nixon/e5/54745.htm.

Uvin, Peter (1998) *Aiding Violence: the Development Enterprise in Rwanda*. West Hartford: Kumarian Press.

Uvin, Peter (2001) 'Difficult choices in the new post-conflict agenda: the international community in Rwanda after the genocide', *Third World Quarterly*. 22, 2: 177–89.

Vail, Leroy (ed.) (1989) 'Introduction: Ethnicity in Southern African History', in L. Vail, (ed.) *The Creation of Tribalism in Southern Africa*, London & California: James Currey, pp. 1–19.

Van Acker, Frank & Koen Vlassenroot (2000) 'Youth and Conflict in Kivu: 'Komona Clair', *Journal of Humanitarian Assistance*, July 2000.

Vansina, Jan (2004) *Antecedents to Modern Rwanda: The Nyiginga Kingdom*. Oxford: James Currey.

Verme, Paolo (1994) *Constructing and Deconstructing Human Capital: Ethnicity and Education in Burundi (1800–1988)* IDS, Sussex, M.Phil. Dissertation.

Volman, Daniel (2003) 'US Military Programs in sub-Saharan Africa, 2001–2003', Washington DC: African Security Research Project.

von Clausewitz, Carl (1918) *On War*. London:Kegan Paul. Translated by J. J. Graham.

Waldron, Sydney R. (1987) 'Blaming the refugees', *Refugee Issues*, 3, 3: 1–15.

Wamba dia Wamba, Ernest (1997) *Protracted Political Crisis, Wars and Militarism in the Regions of Central Africa and the Great Lakes*. RCD/Kisangani: Dar es Salaam.

Wamba dia Wamba, Ernest (2000) *Project for the New Congo: The RCD/K Political Programme*. RCD/Kisangani: Dar es Salaam.

Wamba dia Wamba, Ernest (2004) *Conversations with History*. UC Berkeley: Institute of International Studies.

Wandia, Mary (2004) 'Trail blazers: The Comoros, Libya and Rwanda lead the way on Ratification', in Ndirangi Gichinga & Shereen Karmal (eds) *The African Union Protocol on the Rights of Women: Not Yet a Force for Freedom*, Equality Now, FEMNET, CREDO, Oxfam GB & Fahamu.

Waters, Tony (2001) *Bureaucratizing the Good Samaritan: The Limitations of Humanitarian Relief Operations*. Boulder, Colorado: Westview Press.

Webster, John B. (1966) *The Political Development of Rwanda and Burundi*, Syracuse University: Social Science, Maxwell School.

Weinstein, Warren (1972) 'Conflict and Confrontation in Central Africa: The Revolt in Burundi – 1972', *Africa Today*, 4: 17–37.

Weinstein, Warren (1974) Burundi 1972/73: A Case Study of Ethnic Conflict and Peasant Repression, *Pan-African Journal*, 7 (3): 217–34.

Weinstein, Warren with Robert Schrire (1976) *Political Conflict and Ethnic Strategies: A Case of Burundi*, Foreign and Comparative Studies/Eastern Africa XXIII, Maxwell School of Citizenship and Public Affairs, Syracuse University.

Whitaker, Beth Elise (2002) *Changing Priorities in Refugee Protection: The Rwandan Repatriation from Tanzania*. UNHCR: New Issues in Refugee Research, Working Paper No.53,

Williams, Garland H. (2005) *Engineering Peace: The Military's role in Post-Conflict Reconstruction.* Washington, DC: US Institute of Peace Press.
Winter, Roger (1993) *Transition in Burundi: The Context for a Homecoming.* Washington, DC: US Committee for Refugees.
World Bank (2004a) *World Development Report 2004: Making Services Work for Poor People,* Oxford: Oxford University Press.
World Bank (2004b) *Technical Annex for a Proposed Grant of SDR 22.2 Million (US$ 33 Million Equivalent) to Republic of Burundi For an Emergency Demobilization, Reinsertion and Reintegration Program, Report No. T7616-BU,* Burundi: World Bank.
World Bank (2006) *World Development Report 2006: Equity and Development.* Oxford: Oxford University Press.
Wynants, Maurits (1997) *Des Ducs de Brabant aux Villages Congolese: Tervuren a l'exposition Coloniale – 1897.* Belgium: Musée Royal d'Afrique Centrale, Tervuren.
Young, Iris Marion (1990) *Justice and the Politics of Difference,* Princeton: Princeton University Press.

International Legal Documents

Organization of African Unity/African Union

OAU Convention Governing the Specific Aspects of Refugee Problems in Africa 1969 AHSG,CAB/LEG/24.3.
Protocol to the African Charter on Human and People's Rights relating to the Rights of Women of Africa (Adopted September 2003, entered into force 25 November 2005)
Protocol relating to the Establishment of the Peace and Security Council of the African Union (adopted 9 July 2002, Durban) [www.africa-union.org/root/au/organs/psc/Protocol_peace%20and%20security.pdf]

United Nations

Convention on the Elimination of all Forms of Discrimination against Women (CEDAW) (Adopted in 1979, entered into force September 1981)/ Optional Protocol (December 2000)
Convention on the Prevention and Punishment of the Crime of Genocide (The Genocide Convention) (adopted by UN, 9 December 1948)
Convention (IV) Relative to the Protection of Civilian Persons in Time of War (1949 Geneva Convention) (12 August 1949, Geneva)
Convention Relating to the Status of Refugees (429 (V) (Adopted 28 July 1951, entered into force: 22 April 1954))
Convention on the Rights of the Child (Adopted by General Assembly Resolution 44/25 of 28 November 1989 (entered into force 2 September 1990 (CRC))
International Covenant on Civil and Political Rights (A/6316 (1966) (entered into force March 1976))
International Covenant on Economic, Social, and Cultural Rights (2200A (XXI) (adopted 16 December 1966, Entered into force 3 January 1976))
Optional Protocol to the Convention on the Rights of the Child on the Involvement of Children in Armed Conflicts (A/RES/54/263 of 25 May 2000)
Security Council Resolution 1325 on Women, Peace and Security (31 October 2000 Resolution (S/RES/1325)
World Declaration on the Survival, Protection and Development of Children (30 September 1990)

INDEX